A World Full of Women

Fourth Edition

Martha Ward
University of New Orleans

Monica Edelstein
University of New Orleans

PEARSON

A and B

Boston • New York • San Francisco
Mexico City • Montreal • Toronto • London
Madrid • Munich • Paris • Hong Kong • Singapore
Tokyo • Cape Town • Sydney

Series Editor: Jennifer Jacobson
Series Editorial Assistant: Elizabeth DiMenno
Production Editor: Beth Houston
Editorial Production Service: Publishers' Design and Production Services, Inc.
Compositor: Publishers' Design and Production Services, Inc.
Composition and Prepress Buyer: Linda Cox
Manufacturing Buyer: Megan Cochran
Cover Coordinator: Kristina Mose-Libon
Marketing Manager: Laura Lee Manley

For related titles and support materials, visit our online catalog at www.ablongman.com.

Library of Congress Cataloging-in-Publication Data
Ward, Martha Coonfield.
    A world full of women / Martha C. Ward and Monica Edelstein—4th ed.
      p. cm.
    ISBN 0-205-45442-9
    1. Women's studies. 2. Women—Cross-cultural studies. 3. Feminist anthropology.
I. Edelstein, Monica. II. Title.

HQ1180.W37 2006
305.42—dc22   2005047670

Printed in the United States of America

10 9 8 7 6 5 4 3 2 1   10 09 08 07 06 05

Photo credits appear on page 292, which constitutes a continuation of the copyright page.

Dedication

To:
  Jo, Meg, Beth, and Amy
  Marlowe, Moselle, Tommie Louise, and Nellie
  Heidi, Meg, Emalene, Elizabeth
  Ann, Orissa, Kay, Katy, Corinne, Gayle, Alvina, Toni, Natashe, Nicole Grace

M.W.

  Kenneth and Molly

M.E.

Contents

Supplements

An author-written Instructor's Manual with Test Bank is available for adopters as a downloadable item from Allyn & Bacon's online Instructor Resource Center (www.ablongman .com/irc). Register for access at this website or contact your local publisher's representative.

In addition, the authors have selected readings from Pearson Education's *Reading Women's Lives* database to supplement the text. This selection is available in an Author's Choice reader. Contact your publisher's representative for more information on packaging this reader along with the text for your students.

REVIEWER ACKNOWLEDGMENTS

We would like to thank the following reviewers of this edition for reading the manuscript and responding so eloquently: Nancy Johnson Black, Metropolitan State University; Barbara Bonnekessen, University of Missouri, Kansas City; Leigh Clemons, Louisiana State University; Tracy Bachrach Ehlers, University of Denver; and Anne Marie Goodfellow, Western Washington University. We would also like to thank the reviewers of the previous three editions: Barbara Bonnekessen, University of Missouri, Kansas City; Suzanne Cherrin, University of Delaware; Diana J. Fox, Bridgewater State College; Mary Jill Brody, Louisiana State University; Craig Janes, University of Colorado at Denver; Dolores Koenig, American University; Sue Ellen Jacobs, University of Washington; Christine Loveland, Shippensburg University; Paul Bohannan and Candice Bradley, Lawrence University; Dona Davis, University of South Dakota; Ellen Gruenbaum, California State University of San Bernardino; Penn Handwerker, University of Connecticut; Homes Hogue, Mississippi State University; Jane Lancaster, University of New Mexico; Nancy McKee, Washington State University; Claire Renzetti, St. Joseph's University; Mary Jo Schneider, University of Arkansas; Ann Weber, University of North Carolina at Ashville; and Karen Wedge, Colorado State University.

Introduction

elcome to a world full of women. This book has two goals: to explore and validate woman-centered experiences, and to illuminate the common grounds of being female on Planet Earth.

You will find many voices for or about women. These include examples from ethnography, autobiography, biography, journalism, research, or other sources that explore the varieties of female experience. You will meet anthropologists and other scholars who do fieldwork and critical research. We will highlight women's lives, including some secret parts, and underscore strategies, negotiations, and maneuvering rather than static social structures. This book does not exclude men; it simply puts women in the foreground.

The foundations of the book are firmly woman-centered and gently humanistic. I hope to speak to people who are not anthropologists or whose fascination with the field has only started. I treat women as code-switching creatures who live in at least two different worlds. As a result, women may be strategists or actors in our own lives on a stage we did not invent. Sometimes we cooperate with each other in resistance, and sometimes we participate in systems of domination.

Many theories and positions come into play. I have long-standing friendships with Charles Darwin, Karl Marx, Margaret Mead, many theorists, some postmodernists, and a few modernists, as well as structuralists, functionalists, materialists, and those who think best in symbols and myths. As with other friends, I have spent many hours in their company and appreciate the insights they give me about the world. However, I have no intention of eloping or setting up housekeeping with any of them. You will, of course, find their fingerprints throughout the book. There are many theoretical debates in anthropology about gender, gender ideologies or feminism, and many ways to look at women and our lives around the world. Please feel free to add your own interpretations, friendships, experiences, and intellectual commitments, and to use the books and articles cited to follow your own direction.

Much of the book is ethnographic. Ethnography literally means "a portrait of a people," that is, research on groups of people, generally ordinary people in cultures different or distant from one's own. The discipline of anthropology started as a small science, a group of researchers who assumed responsibility for studying small-scale, preliterate, or preindustrial societies. In those days, everyone called such groups "primitive." Their lives were thought to be less complicated than people who lived in "civilizations." This social science coincided with the rise of colonial empires throughout the world and what everyone perceived as an enormous rate of social and cultural change. The subject matter of anthropology seemed to be disappearing rapidly. Anthropologists tended, therefore, to take an odd view of time and space; we spoke of before contact with the West and after contact with the West.

Anthropology grew out of the European and specifically the Victorian worldview, in which women were "naturally" subordinate, inferior, and taken for granted. It had a clear masculine bias. With a few dramatic exceptions, much of the research tended to ignore, misinterpret, or trivialize the lives of women: When people believed that "women's place was in the home," they could not see much else. So women were invisible. And the best strategies of survival probably did not involve drawing themselves to anyone's attention. So much of women's lives in our own and in other cultures has been hidden.

Many traditional anthropologists only saw women in the role they were believed to be playing right here at home: supporting and nurturing men, dutifully following orders, working at home raising children, gossiping, preparing food, and so forth. They did not even see women in other roles: women whose deepest emotional relationships were with each other; middle-aged women who came into their power so easily that no one noticed they were in charge; married women who supported husbands and children but who could not claim the tributes of that labor; women who cooked or cured but were never addressed as chef or doctor; women who both mothered and fathered, and who, denied formal access, found radical, resistive, and restorative private routes to sensuality, spirituality, artistry, or professionalism.

Old Words and New Realities

The names for various cultures and social divisions in the world are a problem. We can no longer refer to the First World (Europe, the United States, and other Western democracies), the Second World (Communist-bloc countries), and the Third World (countries mostly in the southern hemisphere who invented this term for themselves to avoid the labels of "developing" or "underdeveloped"). At the same time, we speak of the Fourth World, or the growing consciousness of First Nations and tribal peoples who may share more with each other than with the dominant political systems. Concepts like "the West" or the "Free World" may exclude "the Other," people who are somehow different, exotic, pagan, female, or poor.

Caught up of necessity in our habits, our languages, and our outlooks, we sometimes cannot see beyond our own cultural patterns. So I want to reach out to your sense of being a citizen of the planet, connected or tied to women regardless of our cultural differences. At the same time, I want to honor those cultural differences.

A number of terms or words are used for women's condition in the world: *sexism, patriarchy, sex* or *gender stratification, sexual asymmetry, male dominance, female subordination, gender segregation, paternalism* or *paternalistic dominance,* and *women's oppression.* The meanings are clear. They indicate a form of social inequality based on gender; we know these conditions vary in intensity from place to place and time to time in complex ways. I am not using these terms in any technical or cleverly theoretical sense. I'm not even going to argue that these phenomena really exist. They just do.

We also have a set of terms to describe our goals and hopes for changing these conditions. We speak of feminism, feminist consciousness, women's rights, women's movements, women's emancipation, consciousness-raising, and women's liberation. A great many books and articles, some of which I included in the bibliography, throw light on these concepts. However we use these terms, we are speaking out about awareness, our sense of working together, and our shared commitment to alternative visions of the future.

These themes will cross and crisscross in many complex ways. I have found it impossible to find words, labels, or terms that will please everyone in every context. The glossary includes terms used in the text, with some interpretations.

Where We're Coming From

In the international women's movement, women tell each other that "the personal is political." We have learned from each other that our stories count for more than our feelings, our opinions, or our observance of the rules. We know that no writer or researcher can claim complete objectivity or can be honest if we separate ourselves from what we say. This is no longer the age of disembodied experts who speak authoritatively from high places. So you should know something about the people who are speaking with you on these pages.

Martha says of herself: I have taught anthropology at the University of New Orleans (UNO) since 1969. I wrote up and taught the first official women's studies course in the state of Louisiana. At that time, such a seditious act was possible only because I was "chairman" of my department. In the mid-1980s, a group of faculty women at UNO started a Women's Studies Minor Program and a Women's Center; their dedication and collegiality inspired this book.

I grew up in a wonderful, loving family in a fundamentalist Christian community in small-town Oklahoma. Fleeing that quiet life at the first opportunity, I escaped into the institution of marriage, the study of anthropology, and the city of New Orleans. In the early 1970s, my husband and I spent almost two years doing research in medical ethnography in Pacific Micronesia, on a tropical island named Pohnpei. I fulfilled my dream of doing fieldwork in a faraway place. It was simultaneously scary, boring, sweaty, confusing, exhilarating, and addictive. And I got pregnant.

Becoming a mother changed me. My life in the early 1970s became a series of what *Ms.* magazine calls "clicks," that moment when something shifts forever inside us. A vice-chancellor at UNO said, "Women don't look feminine when they carry briefcases." Click. My university health insurance refused to pay for my daughter's birth because they claimed that I neither had nor was a faculty wife. The hospital refused to admit me because my husband was a graduate student and their blanks could not be stretched to include me as head of household. Click. I could not get credit in my own name, and under the head and master laws in Louisiana could not own property under any name or vote in my "maiden" name. Click. My husband said, "I like the dessert my sister served us. Get the recipe for it." My brothers said, "While you're up, get me the mayonnaise." Click. I realized I would protect my daughter with my life; that meant I had to take care of myself first. Click. A well-loved relative revealed the sexual abuse her father had hoped to conceal. CLICK. A pregnant friend was beaten by her husband and the baby died. CLICK. Friends, relatives, and students were raped, stalked, beaten, and battered. CLICK. CLICK.

Yes, of course, I am a feminist. I am also happily divorced, a proud mother, a loving daughter, a good sister, a passionate anthropologist, a voter, a homeowner, and I can claim many wonderful people as friends. And I teach anthropology.

The third edition of *A World Full of Women* fell in the middle of a new project I wanted to do. I had begun to immerse myself in the lives of the women who founded and led the interracial ritual and benevolent societies of Voodoo in New Orleans. Through my research and fieldwork in the community, I met its most famous practitioners, a mother and daughter of the same name. I published one book about them—*Voodoo Queen: The Spirited Lives of Marie Laveau*—and started several more about New Orleans Voodoo. Then only weeks after I signed a contract for this fourth edition, my mother fell and broke her hip, precipitating a cascade of effects for which, like so many women in my generation, I had primary responsibility. Suddenly I needed help to write. By good fortune or perfect design, I met Dr. Monica Edelstein at a wedding. I was a friend of the bride, she of the groom, both of them anthropology graduate students. She agreed to be the co-author for this and forthcoming editions. So this is where she is coming from.

Monica says of herself: I have been teaching courses in cultural anthropology and gender in New Orleans for the past six years. How I got here is another question entirely. I grew up in a privileged, upper-middle class neighborhood in New Jersey. It was also a majority Jewish neighborhood. My Jewish identity has certainly informed my perspectives of privilege and oppression. My grandparents fled Nazi persecution and landed on Ellis Island. They were lucky. But not nearly as lucky as I have been. Lucky to have been born white in a world where white is privileged. Lucky to have grown up in reasonably good health with economic security. Lucky to have had access to education and resources. The sort of privilege I have experienced is rare in history and in the world.

In the late 1980s, I attended Vassar College. By that time, feminism was a household word (not always in a positive sense), and AIDS had begun to dominate the social and personal consciousnesses around campus. I studied anthropology and astronomy vigorously, spent a year at the University of Sydney, and returned to enroll in my first Women's Studies course. We—women (and a few men) of different ethnicities, religions, economic classes, sexual orientations, and ages—sat in a circle and discussed our own experiences, Simone DeBeauvoir, and Rigoberta Menchú. Glimpsing other women's worlds changed our lives. We were moved to sympathize with each other and with women we'd never met. Many of us took these feelings further, into action through various protests and volunteer projects. It prodded me further toward the work I would eventually do in a low-income community organizing and fighting for reproductive rights.

(Excuse me while I tend to the baby.)

I spent my early twenties working as an activist for ACORN, a national organization aimed at empowering low-income communities. I volunteered with ACT-UP, working on AIDS education projects. In my early thirties, I completed my

Ph.D. in cultural anthropology at Tulane University. I spent over a year in Israel living with Ethiopian immigrants and inquiring into their practices of *zār* spirit possession. Now in my mid-thirties, I am happily married and, after some fertility struggles of my own, am fortunate to be parenting a healthy one-year-old girl. (You may have been able to tell from the interruptions to this narrative.) Motherhood opened my eyes to the world in an entirely new way. Suddenly, things I had been studying made sense—my dissertation, child language acquisition, birth and menstrual rituals, miscarriage and pregnancy, responsibility and spirituality, being a being in this world.

(Excuse me while I tend to the baby.)

I now teach cultural anthropology part-time at the University of New Orleans and raise my daughter with my wonderful husband. My experiences are not universal. They are personal. They are political. I hope that my intellectual pursuits and personal friendships with men and women of different ethnicities and cultures, income and education levels, ages and sexual orientations have enabled me to think and write beyond my own experiences and to consider our positions in this world full of women.

Where to Begin and What Follows

Finding a starting point for discussing women's lives can be problematic. I do not want to essentialize or reduce women to biology by beginning with physical experiences: menstruation, fertility struggles, childbirth. Biology is too often used as the reasoning behind subordination. Yet, these experiences are real and cannot be totally ignored. Neither do I want women's real-life experiences to be subsumed by theoretical principles. Theory is important. It helps us make good arguments. My aim, however, is to keep these theories grounded in actual ethnographic examples. I present women as actors (or rather actresses) in their own lives, not as passive subjects. Finally, I wanted to begin with concepts and experiences that would be readily accessible to students, and then proceed to examples and ideas that are more challenging to those with **Western** cultural biases. Throughout, you will find a dynamic interplay between familiar and unfamiliar cases, as well as ethnographic, political, and theoretical orientations.

We will begin with gender. The idea that what it means to be a woman is largely culturally determined is an important one. Women are active participants in constructing genders, as well as living them out. Women have **agency**. Gender also helps explain the separations that exist between the cultures of women and men. Gendered language helps us recognize such separations in our own daily experiences, as well as those in distant lands. Chapter 1 brings us from gender and language into the sphere of work. The many ways that women work in the world have often been ignored, overlooked, or undervalued. Chapter 1 seeks to remedy this by looking beyond industrial and postindustrial societies and including ways of working that do not neatly fall under the rubrics of production and wage labor. Here again, we are stressing women as active.

After grounding ourselves in the concrete realities of work, Chapter 2 addresses the beginnings of the relationship between anthropologists and gender studies. The lives, works, and relationships of Margaret Mead and Ruth Benedict set the groundwork for many of the theories that have since directed gender and women's studies. Where did they find the gumption to act against the gender roles assigned them? How did their pursuits lead them to other cultures? Their research profoundly questioned the naturalistic gender dichotomies of their time.

Chapter 3 returns us to an essential question: What do we do with these bodies? Biological markers identify us as women and are the platform upon which we erect gender ideologies. While women cannot be reduced to biological entities, we do live through our physical bodies. Chapter 3 discusses this experience of being in the flesh and some of the ways we interpret and express this culturally. Chapter 4 further challenges assumptions of what is natural. We turn to our closest genetic relatives: primates. Among primate groups we see examples of sexual activity, family structure, child rearing, and nurturing that help us to define which parts of our experiences might be biologically given versus culturally learned. Human patterns of partnering are the subjects of Chapter 5. In this chapter, we present several examples of households composed of various combinations of adults and children. Heterosexual monogamy emerges as only one partnering option among many found throughout the world.

Chapters 6 and 7 bring us deeper into the concept of gender as cultural construction. In Chapter 6, we look at ethnographic examples in which the worlds of women and men are sharply divided. Chapter 7 questions the dual model of gender classification. Several cultures lend themselves to more than two genders. What then does it mean to be a woman in societies where man and woman are not the only clearly defined choices?

Chapters 8, 9, and 10 address issues of suffering, violence, exploitation, power, and resistance. Chapter 8 focuses on women's experiences of suffering and healing. Around the world women suffer from ailments that are not recognized by biomedical systems. What makes these forms of suffering unique to women and why do they pattern as physical symptoms? We will see that these afflictions occur at the junction of medicine and religion, oppression and resistance. Chapter 9 addresses violence against women. This violence, though varied, is systemic in a number of cultures. In the face of battering, rape, daughter "disappearances," and genital surgery, it is necessary to overcome the extremes of cultural relativism and look to the voices of world women for answers. Chapter 10 brings us back to work. Whereas Chapter 1 introduced us to work from a local perspective, Chapter 10 approaches work from a global angle. Here, multinational corporations and the global factory are discussed, as well as some of the internationally instituted health crises facing women around the globe. Chapter 10 concludes with women as warriors—fighting and struggling for rights, welfare, and survival against military and economic powers.

A World Full of Women, Fourth Edition opens our eyes to experiences and strategies of women worldwide. We are encouraged to move beyond Western notions of womanhood, and even feminism, into a respectful recognition of difference at home and abroad. We learn from women in other cultures that there are more ways to be and act as a woman than we thought possible.

Speaking of Women

In 1992, the Nobel Peace Prize was awarded to a Quiché-Mayan woman from Guatemala. Her name is Rigoberta Menchú Tum. Rigoberta grew up in a mountainous, agricultural region of Guatemala. She survived a period of increasingly violent dictatorship, genocide, and insurrection, which decimated the region in the late 1970s and early 1980s. It is estimated that over one hundred thousand people were killed. Hundreds of Mayan villages were destroyed. More than one million people became refugees. Members of Rigoberta's family, friends, and neighbors were horrifically raped, tortured, and murdered.

Contrary to her culture's expectations, Rigoberta did not marry and have children. Instead, she decided to dedicate herself to the fight for indigenous rights. Fearing for her life, Rigoberta eventually fled to Mexico. When she was 23 years old, she recorded a **testimonial** of her life experiences. It was published and eventually translated into English as *I, Rigoberta Menchú*. Toward the end of her testimonial, she comments on women in Guatemala. This is what she has to say:

> *I still haven't approached the subject—and it's perhaps a very long subject—of women in Guatemala. We have to put them into categories, anyway: working-class women, peasant women, poor ladino women, and bourgeois women. There is something important about women in Guatemala, especially Indian women, and that something is her relationship with the earth—between the earth and the mother. The earth gives food and the woman gives life. Because of this closeness the woman must keep this respect for the earth as a secret of her own. The relationship between the mother and the earth is like the relationship between husband and wife. There is a constant dialogue between the earth and the woman. This feeling is born in women because of the responsibilities they have, which men do not have.*
>
> *That is how I've been able to analyze my specific task in the organisation. I realize that many* compañeros, *who are revolutionaries and good* compañeros, *never lose the feeling that their views are better than those of any women in charge of them. Of course, we mustn't dismiss the great value of those* compañeros, *but we can't let them do just whatever they like. I have a responsibility, I am in charge, and they must accept me for what I am. (Menchú 1984:220)*

Rigoberta Menchú Tum's story will bring you to tears. In her life, she has been both powerful and powerless, challenged and challenger. At times, her identity and desires as a woman conflicted with her drive to fight. In other ways, being a woman fueled her response. A woman who has achieved an atypical measure of international influence, she nevertheless represents the struggles and strengths of many women the world over. Her words hit home.

Tender Trap or Super Woman?

In the last quarter-century of research and writing about women's lives, anthropologists have often concentrated on status and power. Who has it, who doesn't, and why? But the fine-grained analyses many anthropologists have produced confound any easy conclusions, and anthropologists still face some major theoretical dilemmas. As best I can determine, there is a theoretical continuum, a standing argument, a scholarly debate over women that runs from crude biological determinism to crude cultural determinism. Between these ends, however, are an amazing variety of very nuanced, sophisticated, and fascinating theories.

In the model of biological determinism, women have babies. Babies are helpless; therefore, the little women stay at home and tend the kids. This brings in female hormonal changes, pregnancy, lactation, women's preoccupation with children, and consequent limited participation in public affairs, particularly war, politics, or anything that makes lots of money. In this view (at its most unsophisticated), male dominance is more or less inevitable. Female "nature" is more or less predictable. In the basically biology viewpoint, the rights and duties assigned to each gender will "naturally" follow. Therefore, the rights and duties *should* stay "essentially" the same. Women are *essentially* born this way. "Essential nature" cannot be changed. The reality of dominance and subordination can't be questioned either. According to this theory, the deviations from the baseline roles women were assigned in hunting cultures or in the 1950s, or whenever it was that women did their job properly, have already damaged us psychologically, even undermined the stability of civilization.

The other end is crude cultural determinism—bodies don't matter. Human lives are really assorted identities, representations, and cultural artifacts. We are the way we were raised to be and that varies dramatically between families, cultures, and ethnic origins. What we do and how we do it can be credited only to cultural and subcultural differences. Women can be hunters and men can be mothers with equal facility. Everything is relative (and presumably right) within a given culture's expectations and norms. In this view, we're forced to swallow such customs as breaking and binding little girls' feet in traditional Chinese history or husbands who batter their wives to death. After all, their culture made them do it—or at least allowed it.

So how can we make women's lives visible without falling into essentialist or relativizing traps? How can we safely explore the dangerous topic of the differences we hold in common? At this point, I am often accused of being what one friend called a promiscuous heretic. The sexual revolution (for good or bad) taught me that there are many ways to have sex or to make love, more than one position to do it in, and much to desire. The history of wars taught me that merely to think about certain ideas is not a reason to die for them or because of them. So I want as much freedom and flexibility in thinking about the anthropology of women as I can get.

At points along the theoretical spectrum are those who hold the view that the bodies, personalities, and social lives of men and women are—for an animal species—extremely plastic. Let's also assume there are some biological and psychological differences between women and men. Not only do individuals have a wide range of physical and emotional characteristics, but so do the human cultures we know about. In this approach, people see not the similarities, but the large-scale differences in how we sculpt our plasticity. When women began to counter the essentialist or "just doing what comes naturally" position, we were at great pains to point out women as achievers in "nontraditional" fields: women as warriors, women carrying bricks, women making businesses. We would say that in some societies the healers were women, in others they were men, and in many other groups healers were anyone with a recognized gift for the work.

Now many scholars say that the idea of gender itself is a broad continuum of possibilities, that categories such as "having sex" or "motherhood" are susceptible to serious shape-shifting. Not all women are biological mothers, not all biological mothers are social mothers; anyway, women don't have babies through the entire life cycle.

Human beings transcend sex or biology with gender. We assign social roles and determine how people defined as females will act, dress, speak, get married, or be friends with others; the same is true for males. These are basic **gender roles**. Then human beings assign symbols and spell out the social meanings of being male or female. These are called **gender ideologies**; they include the prescriptions and sanctions for what is considered appropriate female or male behaviors, and cultural rationalizations or religious explanations for the social and political relationships that are believed to exist between the genders.

The basic point is that gender is a **construct**. Through time and in adaptation to their environment, groups of people construct, build, forge, or fabricate what they think women are really like and what they believe men are really like. Looking across human cultures, it is clear that what is "naturally" feminine, either in roles or in personalities, is a matter of local conventions. It would be very difficult to put the blame or the credit on biology or on culture exclusively. Our behaviors and belief systems are the complex interaction of many factors: social, organic, random, historical, chance, or mischance. Anthropologists now speak of gender not only as constructed, but also as *performed*. All the world's a stage; all of us are taking the elements of plot, character, and costume and turning gender into performances of possibilities.

Code Switching

There is no culture in the world in which people don't notice gendered people and things. Being male and female are not fixed categories, biological givens, but a part of how people position themselves and each other. Gender, sexuality, and reproduction are culturally and historically specific notions invested with meaning in specific situations. Wherever humans get together, they create social lives with each other, their babies learn a language, and then they are hard-wired for these capacities. The specific language, the specific codes—like women's political status—are just software, possible programs.

In keeping with the idea of constructing and performing genders, let's go a step further. Being a human female is quite different from being a *woman*. The latter is a cultural category. Women are not just biological organisms with physical traits different from males of the same species; women are embedded in complex social, cultural, and personal histories. We have feelings, attitudes, role expectations, and identities that we have been assigned to, acquired along the way of growing up or taken up deliberately.

It is often helpful to think of human societies as divided into more than one culture or cultural code. One or more of these may belong exclusively to women. This means women learn a culture that men rarely enter and few know about. Here is a definition of **women's culture:**

> *The term has also been used in its anthropological sense to encompass the familial and friendship networks of women, their affective ties, their rituals. It is important to understand that woman's culture is never a subculture. It would hardly be appropriate to define the culture of half of humanity as a subculture. Women live their social existence within the general culture. Whenever they are confined by patriarchal restraint or segregation into separateness (which always has subordination as its purpose), they transform this restraint into complementarity and redefine it. Thus, women live a duality—as members of the general culture and as partakers of woman's culture. (Lerner 1986:242)*

The concept of women's culture is useful, but it does not mean that all women are automatically sisters or that the political agendas of one group of women are the same as the agendas of a different group. In fact, most of us live in more than two cultures or cultural subsets. Many of us are fluent in more than one cultural code. Where these cultures and codes begin and end is a complicated issue. As we grow up, we learn to switch cultural codes depending on situation and context. This is similar to a bilingual speaker learning to switch languages. When applied to language, linguists call this process **code switching**. We can apply a similar model to women's culture. For example, women may alter their behaviors, mannerisms, speech, role expectations, affect, and ways of relating to others depending on whether they are in a group of women raising children, at work in a male-dominated field, dancing in a gay bar, or protesting at a political action. Women may switch cultural codes depending on whether they are among blood relatives or in-laws, friends or complete strangers, or according to perceptions of race and ethnicity.

Some women fear—and rightly so—that talking about differences between men and women is still about women being different from the norm, the standard, the construction of the world called "mankind." At the same time, men think they hear criticism of the status quo or of them personally. They have trouble hearing anthropologists when we say that, for example, different styles of communicating between men and women or among different cultures are *equally valid*. They want to deny differences and make everyone the same. But assuming we are all the same invalidates our personal experiences as well as our experiences of being a member of a social group. Here is a sample of some research that opens up these questions about the differences between men and women.

Talking Troubles and Carrying Conversations

Some riveting research about the differences between a male world and a female world comes from anthropologist Deborah Tannen. Her book, *You Just Don't Understand: Women and Men in Conversation* (1990), was on the best-seller lists for many years. This book touched a sensitive nerve in women and men of good-will, people who genuinely want to communicate with their partners, co-workers, and friends, who talk together in mutual respect, and still misunderstand each other.

Here's one of her classic examples. A wife comes home from work and mentions some problems to her husband. "Honey, I had a bad day at the office" [or words to that effect]. He thinks she is asking for advice. "You should quit that job—tell off your boss" [or words to that effect]. She wants sympathy. She thinks she has asked for symmetry and closeness. He tells her what to do. She hears asymmetry and distance. He offers problem-solving skills; she wants to share her feelings. With all the love in the world, they are still not communicating. She may talk to friends, women who acknowledge her troubles, "Honey, I know just what you mean." She may tell a marriage counselor, "He just doesn't listen." She is speaking about *rapport;* he thinks she is making a *report.*

Tannen calls this conversation a ritual of "trouble talk." It is sharply diagnostic of the different conversational styles that separate the sexes. Her major point is this: male–female communication is cross-cultural communication. There are gendered cultures of speaking, *genderlects* or dialects specific to the sexes. Here are some words Tannen uses to describe genderlects:

Women's Talk	Men's Talk
rapport	reporting
community	contesting
affiliation	competition
interdependence	independence
accommodation	conflict
flow of support	verbal sparring

For most women, communication is about establishing rapport, making connections, and negotiating relationships. Rapport talk is sharing experiences and speaking of similarities. For most men, talking is about their independence, their competence, or their status in a hierarchical social world. They hold center stage with story-telling, jokes, or offering information. They are reporting. Or as one male friend told me, "I don't discuss feelings; I have opinions." If this is true, then we understand why a wife complains that her husband's silence is not golden but leaden. We understand husbands who swear that they can't get in a word edgewise.

Each group "hears" and "speaks" from the vantage point of its own ways. The problem, however, is that these styles are not symmetrical. Men's styles are the norm. In public settings, they hold sway, and women adjust in ways men do not have to. In public settings, when she uses the male style of speaking, guess what happens: She may be accused of talking just like a woman, or someone will say she is just trying to act like a man. In a society in which equality and equity are agreed-upon if not always honored goals, women are in a double bind out in public. In private settings, women swear that he never talks, that he just doesn't understand.

I became aware of these patterns when the husbands of several friends remarked, "I don't like the way you and my wife talk to each other when you're together." Sometimes I noticed that groups of women altered our conversational styles when a man entered the room. We stopped talking at the same time in excited voices; we ended what Tanner calls "cooperative overlapping." We switched topics and changed postures. I notice that my teaching style varies with the gender composition of the class. When I use women's conversational styles in large public lectures, the reactions of men and women are both predictable and dramatic—but very different. In women's groups, you can count on a woman who stops the flow of conversation and assists a person who has said little to speak. She is using the floor to give away the floor.

So what can we conclude? Between these separate cultures—the ways that women and men approach the world—is sometimes frustration and bewilderment. Men go home and use report talk. Women bring rapport talk to their jobs. Tannen suggests that these are culture clashes and a reasonable source for our mutual dilemma, "You just don't understand."

Loss and Lamentation

Will Deborah Tannen's findings of gendered cultures of speaking hold up when we apply them to other cultures? Do men and women have different speech styles in other places, or is this just about the United States? A very convincing case of difference by gender comes from folklorists who have studied women's laments (Sherzer 1987). Laments are spontaneous, oral poems delivered in ritual settings and in ritual ways to express grief over the loss of loved ones. As we shall see in other chapters, loss looms large in women's culture. All over the world, women characteristically perform laments—and perform them in the company of other women. Men certainly have the verbal abilities to lament publicly; their losses are just as great. But "tuneful weeping" for death, woundings, and other deprivations is inevitably the work of women, even in vastly different cultures. Throughout the world, women bond in pain, and then talk and sing about it. Men and women do this together on occasion. But men do this with each other only rarely. Laments are the most extreme form of "troubles talk" and provide a solid distinction between men's culture and women's culture.

Anthropologist Joel Kuipers (1986) has written about laments in eastern Indonesia, where men and women are said to have complementary and subdued, certainly not antagonistic, relationships with each other. They participate on a relatively equal basis in the familial, social and political, and economic tasks of life. But when trouble strikes, each responds in his or her own speech style, each richly metaphoric and poetic. In the verbal and ritual contexts of misfortune and vulnerability, men and women show striking gender differences. Men speak of their patrilineal ancestors; they strive to produce repeatable narrative histories. They speak and reason with the sacred spirits of their patrilineal clans. They get paid, but they are fined for a mistake. Women's laments are designed for evoking immediate emotions and moving the audience. They are doing it well when fellow sufferers spontaneously grieve with them. In doing so, they systematically violate the norms of using couplets or repetitions. But they are not judged by their mistakes. Kuipers summarizes the differences between men's and women's speech this way.

Women's Speech	Men's Speech
nonnarrative	narrative
direct	indirect
expressive	historical

This research on speaking about troubles or carrying conversations, from everyday domestic interactions to the most public and dramatic forms, such as laments, provides an example of both biology and culture at work—what anthropologists often call the biocultural feedback model. We could think of this as a kind of mind–body connection for human social life. It also gives us a practical way to think about women's culture. Gender is not a body or body parts; it is more than a role, a status, or an identity. It is also a set of experiences formed and performed in the interactions with many people. The differences anthropologists like Tannen reveal are not intrinsically about better or worse, higher or lower. She is talking about a division of labor. The next chapter discusses division of labor as it is more traditionally applied to work. In this context, the labor of men and women are often assigned asymmetrical values. The examples of Rigoberta Menchú, lamentations, and gendered speech place us on a path to hearing women's voices. In Chapter 1, we will begin to see women's work.

Some Books That Changed Our Lives

At the end of each chapter, there are some suggestions for additional readings. Early in the decade of the 1970s, a number of books came out that heralded an explosion of knowledge, debate, and revelations for and about women. Since then, we have seen an exponential growth in visibility and understanding about women's lives. That generation of research centered on three basic questions: (1) How is gender built, assembled, forged, or constructed in a myriad of cultural settings? (2) When and where and how, if ever, did women have status and power? (3) What do the voices of women sound like when we emerge from our silences?

Michelle Rosaldo and Louise Lamphere's collection of articles, *Women, Culture and Society,* (1974), is probably the classic statement for the generation of how we can view women in human society. It set out the theoretical range and many of the definitions for women's studies and for anthropology. Rayna Reiter's 1975 book, *Toward an Anthropology of Women,* is a still-valuable collection of articles. It remains one of the most-cited and most influential series of statements about women in anthropology we ever had. In terms of language and gender, Robin Lakoff's volume, *Language and Woman's Place* (1975, 2004) is another classic.

I, Rigoberta Menchú (1984) gives voice to an experience of oppression, suffering, and struggle that resonates with the experiences of many women throughout history and the world. As such, it, too, has become a classic in women's studies and anthropology. In 1999, Rigoberta Menchú Tum and her book became embroiled in an international controversy. David Stoll, an American anthropologist, published a book questioning the veracity and presentation of Rigoberta's account. The international media quickly jumped into the fray. Academics and political activists followed suit. Rigoberta had challenged a world governed in part by rules of literacy and science painstakingly established by men of European descent. *The Rigoberta Menchú Controversy* (2001) edited by Arturo Arias provides a comprehensive collection of media articles and academic essays concerning the 1999 controversy, as well as a response by David Stoll.

Chapter One

"What's for Dinner Honey?"

Work and Gender

n the tiny coastal village of Grey Rock Harbour in Newfoundland, where residents earn their living in the precarious, cold, hard work of ocean fishing, one woman asks another, "How are you today?" Her neighbor replies, "My nerves is some bad." Another woman stirs her boiled caribou stew and concentrates on her husband fishing from a small boat in rough seas. "It grates on my nerves, I worries some awful when he's out and the weather turns." A friend compliments her. "After the life you've led, my dear, you can't expect much more from your nerves."

Some Newfoundlanders say that men don't have nerves, that men can't feel much. Others say they have heard about men who had nerves. But chiefly, as everyone knows, women have nerves. One woman summarizes: "I worries about the worst happening. That's what nerves is."

Ethnographer Dona Lee Davis conducted this research on nerves in icy Newfoundland. She notes, "It is the women, who carry the burden of worry, who deserve nerves. Her lot in life is harder than the male's. Nerves belong in the emotional, affective realm, the domain of women" (Davis 1989:74).

By taking on the burden of worrying over their menfolk at sea, women in Grey Rock Harbour are valued in their community for easing the dangers and deprivations of maritime life and freeing the men to fish. In Newfoundland, under the harsh conditions of earning a living there, wives, sisters, and mothers have become women the worriers. Fulfilling this role involves an expenditure of time and energy that suggests worrying is actually a form of work. This work is part of the work of being married, of husbanding resources, of being a housewife.

Chapter 1 centers on work and gender in ways that everyone has experienced. It introduces some ideas, theories, and controversies that swirl around the problems of defining work, valuing work, or rewarding work. When we talk about women and men, work and survival, what matters most: biology or culture? Should we point up some differences between men and women or deny that any exist? Is there such a thing as just being "natural," some irreducible minimum, some universal or essential floor under us? Or are patterns of work and gender the products, the constructions, of the cultures we live in? Perhaps, you say, all this is completely up to individuals.

Work: The First Fact of Life

Women, like men, work for a living. In every human society that anthropologists ever studied, people divide the work they have to do between women and men. This is called the **sexual division of labor**, the assignment of the survival tasks of the society according to gender. Men get some of the jobs and women get some of the jobs. A few jobs may be done by both sexes. Generally, people feel strongly that their way of dividing up work is the best way or the "natural" way. Generally, some other group does it differently. That this division of work may be neither equal nor equally rewarding is quite beside the point.

Some jobs are "women's work" and others are defined as "men's work." The catch is that these tasks are not the same from group to group. For example, in cultures along the Sepik River in New Guinea, people eat flour made from sago palms. Someone must cut, haul, and process the trunk of the palm tree for the soggy flour it reluctantly yields. In some groups along the dramatic river, only men do this work. There people say, "Of course, it is naturally men's work." Down-river or upriver, women gather to strain the flour out as people in that group remark, "Naturally this is women's work." Then, just as they think they have it sorted out forever, something changes—the environment, the world economy, or historical forces beyond their control. Their division of labor by gender changes as well, predictably and irrevocably.

This book begins with work and gender for two reasons. First, scholars who disagree with each other on everything else are, in the main, agreed that human beings divide up the work of survival and put meaning in their lives by assigning tasks based on gender and age. Anthropologists, notoriously independent thinkers, still think that the sexual division of labor is true across time and space. Conservative male sociobiologists and radical Marxist feminists all admit that the sexual division of labor is fundamental to being human. Work divided by gender is somehow a true statement about the human condition. This will be the last time for such easy agreement in this book. Such people do not, however, agree on *why* the sexual division of labor is true. Some say God, religion, nature, science, or mothers make us live this way. And no one concurs on *how* to translate this agreement over the sexual division of labor into decent and life-affirming social policies. In fact, there is no widespread agreement that human beings even need such policies.

But the second and even more important reason to start this book by discussing work and gender is the pain, denial, defensiveness, and heated arguments that currently surround this topic. Who takes out the trash, feeds the children, brings home the bacon, fries it up, remembers to buy and wrap presents are not abstractions. They are the topics of tense political discussions about "family values" and marital arguments about who does the household's work. One of the most difficult ideas women's studies faculty have had is getting our students and ourselves beyond the culture-bound notion that some women work and some don't. Some of us think that women have perfectly obvious choices between "staying at home" or "going out to work" or that our personal worth or mothering abilities are tied irrevocably to these categories. Some people think that work is defined as nuclear suburban families do it or that work equals collecting a paycheck and that work done without a paycheck or title is not really work.

So work is at the heart of the theoretical arguments swirling around gender relations. The goal of this chapter is to make women and women's work visible in ways you may not have considered. Here we're taking a rather domestic and familiar viewpoint. In sharp contrast, the last chapter talks about women and work from the point of view of international development and economics. These are very different ways to bracket the lives of women.

We are used to looking at work from a perspective of production or earning a wage. Though emphasized in industrial and postindustrial societies, this is only one type of work. The basic point to understand is that all women work, even if they are not being paid, recognized, or otherwise rewarded. Women work as mothers or wives. We work as healers and caregivers. We work to keep our communities together. These jobs may be easy or life-threatening. The rest of this chapter offers a number of approaches to making these and other forms of women's work visible.

The **work** that human beings do falls into four categories: production, reproduction, status enhancement, and morale building. Although both men and women do all of these kinds of work, we do them to a very different drum beat. We are rewarded and recognized in separate ways. Women's work in these spheres often looks and feels quite distinct from men's work.

The first kind, *work as production,* generates goods, money, wages, or income of some kind. Generally this kind of work is associated with men. People tend to call this "real work" or "going to work." The work of women in production is often seen as only an extension of household work. An example is a woman selling her handmade, homemade, or homegrown products in local markets. These economic activities in the **informal sector** are usually not listed in statistics about productivity or regulated by national laws. Jobs in the **formal sector** or the official part of the economy are thought of as genuine productive work.

Then there is the *work of reproduction.* This is having babies and raising them. Overwhelmingly associated with women, these tasks are often more undervalued and underpaid than the work of production. Moreover, the work of reproduction is routinely broadened to include extensions of "housework," such as home gardens; subsistence farming; food preparation, preservation, and storage; as well as caring for those who are like babies—sick people, old people, or helpless people.

The third kind of work is what we might call the *work of status enhancement.* These activities promote prestige and social worth—however they are defined. This kind of work includes leisure-time activities and volunteer work, which not only integrate, but also enhance the status of a husband or family. Conspicuous consumption, effective consumerism, and social climbing are still work and are often highly valued. Among the upper classes all over the world, wives of prominent (rich) men organize large-scale events like charity balls. A wife is a public acknowledgment of a husband's ability to afford a "nonworking" wife. She may arrange other status-enhancing activities, such as dinner parties, rounds of seasonal festivities, or the debutante seasons. The latter are training grounds for daughters as status enhancers, as future wives, and as fodder for parental ambitions. Sometimes women in these social circles are widowed, divorced, abandoned, or bankrupted. They may have to "go to work" and find paying jobs using the same abilities they developed as wives. Although the activities of status enhancement are often valued as entertainment or special events, their importance as work—skilled, necessary, and time-consuming—is largely invisible.

The last major type is *work as morale, caring, repairing, and integration.* These tasks are overwhelmingly assigned to women in human cultures. Inevitably, they include feelings, emotional responsibilities, and social obligations, which start with parents, husbands, and babies and flow directly into public life. This kind of work includes arrangements for crucial and regular rituals and religious observances and the care of elderly and disabled people or other nonworkers, as well as children. Women visit, write notes, call others, and plan weddings, family reunions, or holiday celebrations. Women often create community, build bonds that hold groups of people together, and provide crucial services to others in times of trouble. This is the work of integration. While men frequently have titles, positions of authority, and salaries attached to this kind of work, women usually work through their networks without pay, simply because the work is there to be done.

The following are some specific examples of work women do. Some fall neatly into one of the four categories of production; reproduction; status enhancement; and morale, caring, repairing, and integration. Others combine several aspects of these types of work.

"What's for Dinner?": Gender and Practical Economics

All of us eat; we know that food is basic to survival and that food carries as much symbolic and practical significance as any activity humans do. Anthropologists categorize human cultures now and in the past by how people get the foods they eat. We talk about hunting and gathering, horticultural, and agricultural societies or working for wages to purchase food. Archaeologists classify and analyze cultures by the kinds of tools people make and use to survive. Tools mean actual material objects (emphasized in this chapter) as well as social tools such as marriage, kinship reckoning, and political organization (coming later).

Subsistence technologies, whatever they are, have critical consequences for the way work is divided and rewarded within genders and ages, and the quality and quantity of relationships between men and women. The continuum of cultural experiences in earning a living runs from our human ancestors, all of whom were gatherers and/or hunters, through cultivators, farmers, and pastoralists who care for animals to those of us who live now in complex, multicultural, urban, post-industrial nation-states. The rest of this section offers examples of this key proposition and the continuum of subsistence. Drawn largely from archaeology, they center on food, fibers, fabrics, and other practical technologies. The goal is to illuminate women's work in ways you may not have seen before.

Hunting, Gathering, and Being Human

The hunting–gathering or **foraging** way of life is extremely significant for anthropologists. All *Homo sapiens* lived this way before the beginnings of agriculture, the invention of plant and animal domestication about 10,000 years ago. A fraction of the world's peoples still earn a living this way in geographical regions where agriculture and industrialization have not reached. Foraging peoples collect wild plants; small creatures like rabbits, birds, or fish; wild fruits and berries; eggs; roots; tubers; insects; and many other delicious, healthy foods in their environment. They may also hunt large land animals like buffalo, bear, and deer or large sea mammals like whales or seals. They may fish with elaborate traps.

What foragers catch or collect to eat varies with their environment. What does not vary is their inevitable, extensive, intense, and intimate knowledge and experience with their local environments. What does not vary is the inevitable, skilled tool-making and reciprocal sharing of work and food. The significant question for us is how much latitude for independent action a woman has in her household, in her body (sexual–reproductive life), and in her pocketbook (economic matters). It is generally agreed that the sexual division of labor in foraging groups was relatively **equalitarian** or **egalitarian**.

Thanks to several generations of scholarship, we are no longer prey to popular culture's stereotypes of "man the hunter," "man the tool-maker," or the ever-popular "caveman." In this silly sexual division of labor, men brought home the bacon and women cooked it. In some accounts, women apparently hung around the campfire cooking meat, grateful for every morsel, available for sex and bearing little hunters of the future. Popular depictions show them wearing tanned animal skins and carrying tools, food, and children. Note all the work implied in this picture.

Our hunting–gathering ancestors had a small number of children and low population density. The basic social divisions they knew were age, which shifts through an individual's life, and gender, which generally doesn't shift. Men and women control some of the resources and services required by the other. Food-getting is work. It requires many tools, sharing and other social skills, wide variability in diets, and extensive knowledge of local environments. The facts of human survival offer no argument for idleness by either men or women.

Typically the group structure comes close to being equalitarian. A senior man or woman acts as a focus for collective decisions. Their taking on of serious responsibility must not be confused with power or authority. Elders and their networks of kinspeople are mobile most of the year, following the movements of game and the availability of gathered foods. As a result, foragers have no more possessions than they can comfortably carry in skin and net bags. Women carry babies or small children. For all foraging groups, there are predictable problem points: bad weather and changing seasons, vanished game, dangerous predators, sickness, childbirth, correct relationships with in-laws, and effectively bringing young people into the full knowledge and experience they will need to survive. Over time, they develop significant "religious" and "medical" experience to deal with all of these problems. Foraging cultures classically acquire knowledge and information through altered states of consciousness, dreams, trances, or other visits with the spirit world with the help of shamans who may be male or female.

The Pot-Luck Principle

Sharing, gathering, and carrying in foraging societies are complexes that shaped human life as we now know it. The pot-luck principle is one key to human survival. People contributed what they had and fed themselves and several others better than they could do it alone. In foraging cultures, a woman gathered foods from a source she knew about; then she exchanged some for a foodstuff she had not found. One day she gave foodstuffs to relatives who couldn't go out foraging that day; on another day she prepared a soft, easy-to-chew dish for an old person or an easily digestible dish for a sick person or a child. Salads, soups, and stews, for example, contain a number of ingredients put together rather flexibly. Mixing food together enhances the nutritional value for everyone. But no one person could gather and prepare his or her own bowl of salad each day. Imagine preparing a rich vegetable soup or stew from scratch for one person each day. Now imagine helping someone make a soup and sharing from a large pot. In most animal groups, individuals must find their own food each day. In sharp contrast, all known contemporary foraging groups divide subsistence tasks by gender and age. Increased sociability, sharing of resources, structured giving, and ordered social relationships would have contributed to growth and survival. Shared food is good for everybody. In some fashion or another, the metaphors of shared food around a fire are at the heart of many religions.

Sophisticated new research and analysis of contemporary foraging groups over the last 40 years reveals the complexity and contributions of gathering. Our ancestors used plants for making medicines, drinks, clothes, equipment, and tools. At the same time, females carried and nursed an infant almost continually for three to four years, did a lioness's share of food-gathering, and 90 percent of child care. A woman often walked miles carrying an equivalent of 75 percent of her body weight in baby, firewood, gathered foodstuffs, or other raw materials. Women contributed dietary proteins, clubbed turtles, and collected eggs and insects. Women made systematic observations about the availability of game or tracks and reported back to the men. Anthropologists know that women hunted as well and gathered small game and fish. Mothers often, as they still do, left small children in the care of kinfolk, sister-like cooperatives, brothers, or other adult males. Males also gathered, for themselves and in groups.

Honey, Meat, and Babies

As part of a research team, anthropologist Marjorie Shostak did fieldwork in the Kalahari desert of southern Africa (Botswana). There she listened to and recorded the life story of Nisa, a woman who was born into one of the last gathering–hunting cultures, the !Kung Bushmen. Here Nisa discusses food and her memories of childhood. The fathers brought animals home for everyone to eat. Nisa loved to eat meat dripping with fat.

> *We lived, eating the animals and foods of the bush. We collected food, ground it in a mortar, and ate it. We also ate sweet nin berries and tsin beans. When I was growing up, there were no cows or goats. . . . Whenever my father killed an animal and I saw him coming home with meat draped over a stick, balanced on one shoulder—that's what made me happy. I'd cry out, "Mommy! Daddy's coming and he's bringing meat!" My heart would be happy when I greeted him, "Ho, ho, Daddy! We're going to eat meat!" Or honey. Sometimes he'd go out and come home with honey. . . . Sometimes my mother would be the one to see the honey. The two of us would be walking around gathering food and she'd find a beehive deep inside a termite mound or in a tree. (Shostak 1981:87)*

Honey and animal fat are two foods deeply prized and symbolic in hunting and gathering cultures. Folklorist Megan Biesele has also worked in the Kalahari desert on the foraging ideologies of a related group called Ju/'hoan. She found that even symbolic and expressive domains are divided between genders. This means that art, music, poetry, mythology, and other expressive parts of the Ju/'hoan culture are codes that contain knowledge—information that helps them survive as a group. The verbal traditions are imaginative legacies strongly imprinted with ideas about work, social life, and the supernatural, which have adaptive value.

> Hunting as a male activity is typically valued and ritually elaborated over either gathering or fishing, despite the relative economic importance of the latter activities in specific instances. Men's hunting is often symbolically opposed not to the complementary female activity of gathering but rather to women's reproductive capacity. (Biesele 1993:41)

In other words, producing babies is the equivalent of producing meat in terms of making the most significant contribution to group survival. "Men have trance-curing and hunting. Women have childbirth and plant food gathering. All are indispensable ingredients of traditional Bushman subsistence and social life" (Biesele 1993:98). Men cannot produce babies. Women produce babies—itself a potentially dangerous enterprise—and make the intensive investments of raising them. They are not likely to be hunters as well. But babies were a gift to their cultures, hard as this is to imagine in a world full of billions of people.

Tools with a Feminine Twist

It's often difficult to find ordinary women in the archaeological record. A great irony of studying gender and work is how transitory and perishable women's productions are. Objects made of stone survive better than tools or objects made of wood, skin, bone, horn, fibers, or other perishable organic materials. Songs, stories, recipes, babies, fibers, clothes, fabrics, comfort care, or social skills may be crucial to survival but still vanish easily. This is one reason why some scientists in the past emphasized stone and saw tools only as weapons and only men as tool-makers or users. Despite the immense toil in producing clothing or children, for example, little or no evidence survives.

More and more anthropologists, however, see women in the role of tool inventors. The absolute best example is the simple act of carrying things. For starters, females carry babies in all nonhuman primate groups and in all human cultures. Slings for carrying infants are found in most human societies, so this is probably one of the earliest and most profound applications of tool use. Contemporary foragers use skin bags, fiber nets, or woven baskets for carrying food, wood, and other objects for long distances. Never mind that people in many places speak of a pregnancy as "carrying a baby." Today humans make thousands of kinds of containers. We buy them, give them as gifts, and rely on them for a thousand tasks: purses, pocketbooks, pockets, knapsacks, backpacks, shoulder bags, handbags, tin cans, paper bags, plastic sacks, boxes, baskets, briefcases, cosmetic cases, and brown paper packages wrapped up in string. These are major inventions. Frankly, I think women should boldly claim credit for inventing containers for carrying and celebrate the incredible developments that followed.

Here is a powerful example of finding women's work in the scholarly record. Elizabeth Barber is an archaeologist who has done the authoritative study of the development of cloth in the ancient and early modern worlds. She uses linguistics, anthropology, and history to reveal women's industry over the last 20,000 years. She herself spins and weaves and often recreates the fabrics found in archaeological sites to learn more about them. In most parts of the world, until the Industrial Revolution, fiber arts were an extraordinary practical force belonging primarily to women.

Our foraging ancestors gathered more than eatable wild plants. They collected plant fibers such as flax, hemp, nettle, ramie, jute, sisal, esparto, maguey, yucca, elm, linden, willow, and many others. These fibers were then processed for baskets, cordage, nets and traps for catching fish or other animals, mats for floors, roofs, beds, and fences—and thousands of other useful, necessary, everyday objects that made life safe, comfortable, and even possible. Some hunted animals like wild mountain goats for their fleece, which could be spun into warm yarns, or collected the hair other animals shed in the spring. In the great temple cave of Lascaux used 24,000 years ago, archaeologists found the remains of the string that led people into its darkness for stunning artwork and probably profound rituals and ceremonies. Should women give serious attention to something as humble and mundane as string? Barber says yes.

> We don't know how early to date this great discovery—of making string as long and as strong as needed by twisting short filaments together. But whenever it happened, it opened the door to an enormous array of new ways to save labor and improve the odds of survival, much as the harnessing of steam did for the Industrial Revolution. Soft, flexible thread of this sort is a necessary prerequisite to making woven cloth. On a far more basic level, string can be used simply to tie things up—to catch, to hold, to carry. From these notions come snares and fishlines, tethers and leashes, carrying nets, handles, and packages, not to mention a way of binding objects together to form more complex tools. . . . So powerful, in fact, is simple string in taming the world to human will and ingenuity that I suspect it to be the unseen weapon that allowed the human race to conquer the earth, that enabled us to move out into every econiche on the globe during the Upper Paleolithic. We could call it the String Revolution. (Barber 1994:45)

String was invented and used everywhere in the world humans went. But the women of 24,000 years ago did much more than catch fish, carry food, or lead others into caves with their practical invention. They made skirts—swinging cords fastened from a twisted hip band, some with long beaded fringes. By any standards, their skirts could not have been modest or warm. But skimpy string skirts keep appearing in the archaeological records, and always on women. From archaeological sites dating to 1300 B.C., we can see actual skirts preserved in burials of young girls. The miniskirts scandalized some European archaeologists. Well into the twentieth century, one could still find descendants of string skirts in elaborate belts and aprons in some peasant cultures of Eastern Europe.

Barber asks: What could have been so important about such impractical, eye-catching miniskirts that the style lasts for thousands of years? Her best guess is that the skirts signified something about childbearing abilities, readiness for marriage, or both. There were many times and places in our human past when how a young women dressed signaled her marriage status, even a sense of honor and specialness, and linked her with the ability to create new life—often a valuable gift to her society. A number of the so-called Venus figurines are wearing string skirts. The divine Hera in the epic poem of Homer wears a "Girdle of a hundred tassels." Her skirts are too short to do much good—except for social signaling. This may be a subtle example of a woman's language.

Planting and Harvesting: The Next Revolution

So what have anthropologists learned? The most equalitarian groups we know about are probably hunting and gathering groups. Do women and men do exactly equal work and get treated the same way? No. They do not have equality, just relatively equalitarian traditions and a sexual division of labor. No known groups allow one gender to be idle or excused from the basic work of survival. The foraging lifestyle required an amazing amount of practical intelligence; in fact, anthropologists know that horticulture and agriculture grew out of the increasingly skilled carrying, sharing, and gathering complexes of our early ancestors.

About 10,000 years ago, groups of people in various parts of the world learned how to cultivate and harvest plants and care for domestic animals as sources of food and fibers. This striking new relationship to the environment is called the **Neolithic Revolution**. But—and here is the key insight of anthropology—when people changed their patterns of earning a living and their eating habits, everything else shifted too. Eventually this key transition in food-getting would have extraordinary implications for women's work and daily lives.

Digging Sticks

The revolution didn't happen overnight. Gradually some groups adopted **horticulture**, the hand-cultivation system of growing food with the highly efficient but simple tools of hoes and digging sticks. Women played the major role as food producers of grain, cereal, and vegetable crops. Men did fishing and hunting to supplement diets. Horticulture is still the basic source of subsistence for many of the rural descendants of cultivators who were neither driven off their land by colonialism nor became dependent on commercial crops and agricultural wage labor. Once our ancestors began to cultivate their food, the potential for new kinds of gender relationships exploded. These kinds of cultures have amazing variety, so it's very difficult to generalize.

Only a few things apply uniformly. In all horticultural societies, men clear the land for planting. It's heavy, dangerous work. But depending on how fast things grow, it doesn't have to be done often. Beyond that fact, there is no consistent adaptive advantage to whether females or males plant and harvest their crops. Horticulture is quite compatible with child-tending. In some places, men clear and both genders cultivate—sometimes their work is separated into "women's crops" and "men's crops." In other places, such as highland New Guinea or the island of Pohnpei, where I did fieldwork, men raise the ceremonial and prestige crops; women raise staple crops for domestic use. The common pattern in which men clear and women cultivate—like the Iroquois of Native North America—is generally associated with economic control and high status for women. In West Africa, both men and women cultivate staple crops for use value and prestige crops for exchange value. Reciprocity is still important, but trading in market arenas increases. In the advanced horticulture societies of West Africa with well-developed market systems, women handle a large share of the trading. Women rarely become wealthy or powerful, but trading the products they grow and make does give them more autonomy in their personal lives and power in their marital relationships (Clark 1994).

Horticultural societies (with some notable exceptions) do not seem to promote very amicable relationships between women and men. I can't find a convincing argument why this is true, but my theory is that men and women are freed from the mutually shared dangers of the foraging lifestyle; competition can flourish without the imperatives for cooperation. There may be within-group female solidarity as well as male group linkages. But between men and women as groups or as couples, distance, disruption, hostility, and accusations mark their common lives. The key seems to be their relationship with local environments.

In simple horticultural societies, production is largely for use value. Exchange is usually within kin groups and based on reciprocity. Such groups are not yet oriented to markets and trade outside the village. In environments with plentiful, relatively uncontested resources and abundant arable land, groups are frequently matrilineal and still relatively equalitarian. Women work and live in localized groups with their kinfolk. Matrilineal descent makes sense under these circumstances. The status and safety of women is appreciably high in matrilineal horticultural societies in which the local community is organized around related women. When the societies practice **matrilineal descent** [tracing kinship through a female line], have high degrees of female solidarity and female economic control, and when males are absent in war or trade, women have reasonably high status. When kin groups are nearby, women are more rarely abused or beaten.

However, in circumstances in which (for whatever reason) production is increased or there is competition or environmental pressures, men tend to live in local groups and eventually move to **patrilineal descent** systems. In these systems, a husband and his immediate kin group are the beneficiaries of a woman's labor. Men may also take more than one wife—all the better to increase production of crops and children. When patrilineal descent systems, male solidarity, male economic control, population pressures, the need for local defense, and warfare complexes occur, women become second-class people.

Plows

Horticulture, with its extensive varieties, is not intrinsically predictable in its effects on women's work and lives. But the same cannot be said for **agriculture.** Women's lives overall are heavily impacted in agriculture, and it would be difficult to argue that these new systems are improvements. Agriculture is complex cultivation using a plow, domesticated draft animals, or farm machinery. Farming may involve irrigation, livestock breeding, and cash crops or farm products that have no use value and are grown for sale. This extensive means of earning a living includes all plantations, agricultural industries that produce such commodities as heroin, cocaine, tobacco, rubber, sugar, cotton, spices, and coffee. Agriculture, agribusiness, plantations, and animal husbandry are the subsistence bases for all contemporary industrial societies.

At various times and in many places in the world, people in horticultural societies needed—for whatever reason—to increase their productivity. They began to use more intensive and advanced cultivation techniques. They revitalized the soils with fertilizer; they harnessed animal power for harvesting and planting, and diverted water into fields under cultivation. These particular and increasingly widespread activities required male labor; the work was hard, long, dangerous, and strikingly incompatible with women's work styles and the demands of child care. The most spectacular new tool in intensive agriculture was plows. Plows are the tool most heavily blamed among some archaeologists for altering the balance of men's and women's lives. In gathering and horticulture societies, women use hoes and digging sticks; women produce food directly, often working together in processing and distribution. But men with plows and draft animals replaced women as primary producers. Women cooked and processed food; they worked very hard at many tasks. But they did not produce food. Men increasingly did, and they did so in the company of other men. The effects on women were so dramatic that we are still living with them thousands of years later.

The realization that animals could be domesticated and used for wool, milk, and muscle power was truly a revolution. People settled down on farms and in villages; in many parts of the world, cities developed. Instead of mobility, human lives were characterized by settled village life. As you can imagine, things accumulated. Like children. The number of births per family increased. Children were very useful in subsistence tasks. There was lots of homestead work to be done: herds of sheep, goats, or cattle to shepherd, milk, and tend; barnyard animals to tend; family clothes to make; food to process to last the winter; goods to produce for trade—thousands of specialized tasks, dawn-to-darkness labor, lots of children to bear and raise. Farm life requires the most broadly skilled and hardest working women and men I've encountered on the planet. It also means concentrating intensively only on a few aspects of the environment.

Distaffs

Once again I note: It's easier than ever to lose sight of women in these male-heavy agrarian societies. So I want to add one splendid example of making women's work visible. Remember string. In settled horticultural villages and agricultural societies across the planet, from Greece and Egypt to China and Peru, women took simple string, their spun fibers, and taught each other to weave them. They invented looms and woven cloth, fabric for high-fashion clothes, home furnishings, rugs, blankets, belts, baby dresses, and the sails of ships. Once woven, cloth wrapped the dead and the newborn; it often served as currency, bedding, bandages, and the mark of social status and sacred spaces. In most nomadic cultures, women still weave the floors, the walls, and the roofs of their portable tent homes; they are architects. They spun wool from their practical sheep and beautiful flax fibers for linen. They fed exotic worms and wove their cocoons into silk—the ultimate luxury fabric and for its weight as strong as steel. In other places they grew cotton or hemp (useful for rope as well as medicines).

The folk saying claims, "Clothes make the man." But Elizabeth Barber says, "women make the clothes." She found a cloth-crazy world in the archaeological records of the Middle East and Europe. Innumerable temple walls, pottery, and paintings show women and men planting and harvesting fiber plants or tending flocks of sheep. Women are continuously shown combing, carding, spinning, dyeing, weaving, wearing, giving, trading, and selling fabrics, miles and miles of the flowing stuff, caravans of cloth. However, nowhere in the world was textile manufacture simply women's economic and household labor. Textiles became symbols of creation and fertility in some places, freedom in others. Barber says that patterned cloth is like a language. Like clothing, it speaks of many human events or feelings.

> *What did ancient people try to accomplish when they deliberately made cloth bear meaning? A good look at folk customs and costumes recently in use reveals three main purposes. For one thing, it can be used to mark or announce information. It can also be used as a mnemonic device to record events and other data. Third, it can be used to invoke "magic"— to protect, to secure fertility and riches, to divine the future, perhaps even to curse. (Barber 1994:149)*

Cloth was women's work and women's status, even women's language par excellence. It marked statuses such as married and dead. Social rank was coded through fabrics, designs, colors, and embellishments. Cloth marked ceremonial or ritual states and told the stories, myths, and histories of peoples. Cloth encoded women's magical, wish-fulfilling, and fantasy lives. Everywhere Barber looked women coded their common objectives into cloth: fertility, prosperity, and protection. Slave women and queens alike put their fingers to this work. Sometimes women acted as business owners; sometimes they were part of family businesses. In some places and at some times, there were free, middle-class, independent-minded women who created textiles, both beautiful and in volume, for the busy commercial markets and trade routes, working with their menfolk. There were innovations in dyes and efficiency of looms. Sometimes I think of all the hard work of cloth production and I'm glad to be spared. At other times, I glimpse something about autonomy, creativity, deep personal privacy, even a meditative healing that comes from producing fabric from scratch. It is also clear from the archaeological and anthropological record, in which women worked together or even for each other, that they had more control over their lives, more autonomy.

The history of "civilization" is woven in these extraordinary crafts. Men helped; they participated in a thousand ways. But the fiber and fabric production industries centered on and were the inspiration of women. I am impressed that in every culture in which women spin fibers into thread and yarns, spinning is associated with female economic, sexual, and spiritual freedom. Distaffs—the tool that holds the unspun fibers for spinning—are the symbol for women's work around the world. People who can spin a good yarn are valuable.

Peasants

In agriculture, women's roles changed rather dramatically from those of foraging or horticulture societies. This period, often hailed as the "dawn of civilization," undisputedly brought a loss of status and power for women relative to men of their social class, and for the majority of the growing populations relative to a tiny ruling elite. A significant result of this new adaptation was the production of surpluses. People had exchangeable wealth: stored food, domesticated animals, or other products they produced, such as cloth, butter, wine, salt, and many others. They lived in permanent, larger, and denser populations. In these societies, there was still a division of labor by gender, but people had more options and statuses, more shifting by class or age or task. Plows, draft animals, fertilizing, and irrigating increased both productivity and the complexity of social organizations. But the work was strenuous, demanding, dangerous, and time-consuming. Gatherers, hunters, and horticulturalists are rightly appalled at the sheer unending physical labor of farming.

Agriculture transforms the bulk of people into *peasants*. Peasants have the highest birth rates of any group of humans on the planet. But land is always finite, and landless peasants must migrate into cities, find other occupations, or form armies. The consequences of agriculture as a way of life include social phenomena such as class oppression, slavery, caste systems, and exploited or expendable classes of people such as beggars, criminals, or the chronically unemployed. Don't forget to add in war, famine, and plague. There are always merchant or business classes, growing bureaucracies or retainer classes, and priestly classes. The world religions (Islam, Judaism, Christianity, Hinduism, and Buddhism) all spread and became institutionalized within agrarian societies. Complex trade, transportation, and communication systems as well as powerful central governments are developed. Standing armies and warfare become chronic. In short, marked social inequality and exploitation are built into the economies and social organizations of all the great agrarian civilizations.

In this bleak picture, where are women? If you have a family business and inherited wealth, then kinship is important. In other places, such as Europe and North America, people moved into the constellation of monogamous marriages and nuclear families. Economic productivity of wives declines, as do collective female work groups. Wives have typically left their parents' households and are living in their husbands' natal homes. Females are like cattle—the property of males and intensive breeders for the labor supply. Peasants try to produce big crops and many sons. Women in agricultural societies have the largest number of children, and their births are more closely spaced than in any other group. The hunters of the Plains of North America marveled at European farm families with eight to

A Folktale
What's for Dinner Honey?

Once upon a time, a couple lived on a farm. They quarrelled constantly about the work they had to do on their homestead. Each claimed that her or his labor was the most difficult and that the other one was not properly appreciative. Finally, when there seemed no other way to settle the issue, the husband and wife agreed to trade tasks for an entire day.

Early the following morning, the wife arose and went out to plow the fields and make hay. When she returned that evening, her muscles were sore and her hands had new blisters. But she had enjoyed her quiet, simple day outside in the fields. She was fiercely hungry; the leftovers from breakfast and the small lunch her husband packed for her had not been enough. As she stepped through the carved wooden door of their cottage, she called out, "What's for dinner honey?"

But instead of dinner, she faced a disaster! Feathers coated in honey clung to the rafters. The cat, who should have been in the barn catching rats, crawled from the overturned butter churn, licking her paws with glee. Chickens cackled as they laid eggs on the mantel; they cackled as the eggs rolled off and broke on the floor. Ducks left their droppings and droolings as they marched across her handmade white quilt. From somewhere, the mooing of an unmilked and unhappy cow filled the air. The bread dough had not risen and the beer she was brewing had spilled. Flax fibers, soaking as the first stage in making linen cloth, were strewn damply about the dirty floor. Her garden was not weeded and something had happened to the fruits and vegetables she was preparing for winter. But worse, her husband, tied by his foot, hung upside down in the chimney, his face covered by her best apron and his head only inches away from a pot of uncooked soup teetering above the dead fire in the hearth.

"Don't ask," he moaned. "I've had a very bad day." Before she released him, she satisfied herself that he had a new appreciation for her work and her work skills. Then she began to clean up enough to fix dinner for them. They lived and worked together for a very long time after that.

twelve children. "Like dogs," they whispered. Men need the labor of their wives, and women are required to have husbands—it's their work. But this is *unequal interdependence,* because males control the primary productive processes and females are relegated to secondary tasks. They are working harder than ever but are still disposable and isolated.

You will not be surprised to hear how agriculturalists value virginity for their daughters and chastity for their wives, how women are used as pawns in vast male political alliances. Women are a key reserve labor supply for intense periods like harvest or planting. The rest of the time they are available for childbearing, child-rearing, extensive fiber and fabric production (spinning, weaving, sewing), and food processing. To these major activities are added jobs like small animal husbandry, nursing, and running complex households while men are away at war. On top of all of this, agrarian societies develop elaborate religious, moral, and legal justifications for their sexual stratification systems. Hammurabi's Code was the first set of laws written down and provided the basis for legal systems in the Middle East, ancient Israel, and cultures of this important region. Of the 270 laws engraved on an upright stone pillar, approximately 100 of them dealt with the problems of keeping women in line, assigning ownership and responsibility for them, and defining the boundaries of their sexuality. In the ideologies of agriculturalists, women are subordinate, unclean, and not bright enough to be trusted out alone. Women are viewed as suited only for inside and domestic tasks; they are incapable of public political and economic roles. Family units shrink. They become self-sufficient. A man's home is his castle. Women have to rely on husbands for their livelihood—in short, institutionalized dependency, subordination, and political immaturity. If some of this sounds familiar to you, that's because European-American culture and society grew from its peasant agricultural roots. Summer vacation, for example, is time off from school to help with the harvest. "Naturally," women are at home fixing their meals.

Peasant cultures do not paint a very pretty picture of women's lives. Sometimes women resist in subtle ways. They gossip or tell stories that make their work visible. In the box is a folktale about the sexual division of labor, collected from storytellers in the peasant societies of northern Europe. I think it's shamelessly a woman's story because she believes his job is simple and hers is complex and that he doesn't see or value her contributions. But you are free to interpret or rewrite it as you like.

Off to Work We Go

Over the last 500 years, many largely peasant societies have become industrialized and "developed." Some have created immense colonial empires and heavy war machinery. In the Industrial Revolution, factories became the work place. People worked in an assembly line, mass producing goods they couldn't sell or use at home. Only their time at work had value. Although people still need to eat, it takes only a very few to produce their food. What did the first factories of the industrialization and its capitalistic methods produce? Thread and cloth. What is the name we give to our current age? The Age of Information. Computers come from looms, based on the same binary principle: yes-no, over-under, in-out. Huge looms for

Jacquard woven fabric used the first computer cards. The image of this brave new age is a web the size of the world. Were there massive changes in women's lives in each of these "revolutions"? Did marriage, family life, and economic prospects change with each new age? Of course. These are the revolutions we're currently experiencing. The forms of women's work discussed in the following sections illustrate some of these transformations.

Home-Work

The following description of the sexual division of labor in Grey Rock Harbour will feel familiar to most readers. This describes the traditional relationship of work and gender in peasant farming and fishing cultures until quite recently.

> *Despite the physical separation of the sexes, the family remained important. Nuclear and extended family networks were extensive and defined local social organization. Kinfolk could be counted on for support when times were hard. Marriage was universal and was considered essential for entry into full adult status. There was no divorce. Couples married in their midteens, started their families early, and looked forward to a life of fishing or work at the fish plant. Flexible hiring patterns at the local fish plant make it easy for women (and men) to schedule wage labor around family obligations. (Davis 1993:461)*

The equalitarian ethic in Grey Rock Harbour was "we'll help each other out, but we all come up together or we don't come up at all." Most men fished; most women ran households. Men and women equally worked at the fish-processing plant. Every person was expected to be a hard worker. Other tasks filled their extra time; women knitted and men built or repaired their equipment. Figure 1.1

Figure 1.1
An Old-Fashioned Model of
Work and Gender

illustrates this old division of labor, one similar to many traditional peasant, fishing, and farming societies around the world. Note that women do 100 percent of women's work, men do 100 percent of men's work, and only some overlap is shared.

Marriage as Work

If we follow the sexual division of labor to its logical conclusion, then marriage is a form of work. If a man is a "breadwinner" and his wife "keeps house," then they have a sexual division of labor. They have an agreement or contract about sharing work. Advice books for women emphasize that being married is hard work. "You have to really work at it," they say. My friends say, "We're taking some time off to work on our relationship." At a cocktail party, a man may ask of a woman, "What kind of work do you do?" She replies, "I'm just a housewife." Either or both may think, this is not really work. But it is. Unpaid or unrecognized, it's still work.

The contemporary view of marriage and women's work in the West centers on assumptions of equality and an equalitarian division of labor. Figure 1.2 illustrates this model of how work is supposed to be distributed in modern families. Men do their share of the work (for example, 50 percent), and women do their share (the other 50 percent). Unlike women's and men's work in traditional societies, the tasks are interchangeable in modern settings. Both genders are supposed to do the same jobs, whether in the work place or at home. However, this idea of equivalency or equality does not offer cross-cultural comparisons. They only recently evolved in the middle class of America.

Figure 1.2
A Modern Model of Work and Gender

You have heard this before, but it bears repeating: Women who are married and have children already have a full-time job. If they work for wages or salary somewhere else, then they have still another job.

Mother-Work

In all human cultures, regardless of political pressures or social fashions, being a mother is a different kind of work than is being a father. In many cultures, there is simply no word for being a "parent." A gender-neutral relationship to a child, as in the current concept of "parenting," is an alien, even absurd idea. The chronic devaluation of mothers in our own culture can best be seen by looking at women as mothers in other cultures in which reproductive roles are held in high esteem. Being a mother is vastly more than biology. Women can be mothers through social forms such as adoptions, and the metaphors of mothering, birth, and rebirth redound throughout human religions. Many women in the world start what we call "families" with having a baby, not with finding a husband. Their passage into adulthood and the meaning of their lives center on their child, their children.

Anthropologist Ellen Lewin interviewed a group of lesbian mothers in the San Francisco Bay area. These women talked about rhythms of mothering, the daily rounds of cooking, cleaning, shopping, laundry, and child care arrangements. Each of them had to devise complex strategies for day care, transportation, babysitting, play groups, supervision, emergencies, after-school, summer vacations, or the times when their kids were sick. The practical challenges of raising a child shaped their lives. They defined "motherhood" not only as affective, that is, a source of love and delight, but also as concrete restraints and challenges that demanded innovative solutions. Being a mother dramatically eclipsed and overshadowed their lives as lesbians.

> *If anything is a consistent theme in the lives of both lesbian mothers and heterosexual single mothers, it is the persistence of economic pressures, the nearly constant fear that they may not be able to manage. The mere fact of their survival becomes a mark of honor for some mothers; for others, the reality of an unpredictable financial situation is a source of ongoing anxiety. . . . In instances, of course, financial strain can be traced directly to nonpayment of child support, so mothers must weigh the benefits of leveling with their children against the possible harm of attacking a fragile link to their fathers. (Lewin 1997:197)*

These lesbian mothers describe women who have no children as "single." But they don't describe themselves as "single mothers." That's someone else's construction. The women in this study talked about the sheer quantity of obligations having a child brought to their lives. All other relationships or identities in their lives, however definitive, revolved around being a mother. They had not expected or anticipated the degree of involvement and the changes in their lives that stemmed from taking on the work of mothering. Making a living and taking care of their children became the center of their women's existence. Peggy speaks:

> *Being a mother is so big. I have much more in common with all mothers*
> *than I have in common with all lesbians. It's so big. It starts out as a*
> *twenty-four-hour-a-day job, and it just goes on and on and on. (Lewin*
> *1997:198)*

These women testify that raising children is the source of considerable difficulties and hardships. They also affirm that the intimacy, the kinship links, the paradox of deepest joy and strength that comes from having them is worth it. Christine is a successful professional artist. She says that her son "brings out feelings in me I have never experienced before, both love and anger. He's the first thing in my life that means more to me than I do." Before her child was born, Inez took some hard knocks and overcame problems with drugs and alcohol; she says,

> *being responsible for somebody—like having a stake in the future—like*
> *wanting the world to be a better place. . . . But when I started to see her*
> *mirror me, it made me want to change, and be a better person. (Lewin*
> *1997:206)*

These voices are relevant because they separate women's sexual lives from their reproduction and economic lives.

Anthropologists think that the number of children, the spacing of children, and the customs of raising children are everywhere adjusted to the kinds of work women customarily do. Bearing and raising children will depend on how the energies of adult women are used in subsistence and other economic or social tasks. So the phrase "working mother" is a contradiction in terms. The main task of being a mother anywhere in the world is to organize resources for their children. Having a husband, being married, has been a very common way to find resources. Having kinfolk, people already related to your baby, is another way of organizing resources on behalf of children. Getting welfare, Aid to Families with Dependent Children, is like having the government as a job or a husband.

Women in societies that depend on hunting and gathering or foraging space the time between pregnancies and organize child care around the work they have to do. The spacing of births in hunting–gathering cultures is not an accident; it is one of the clearest examples we have of how women manage work. In classic gathering–hunting societies, for example, births are rarely closer than three to four years apart. Babies nurse for long periods. A female cannot easily carry a pregnancy, a nursing baby, and a toddler or any two of these and still carry out her work in gathering. Do not think that her job is unimportant or that she will automatically be excused because child care comes first. Her first job is gathering. Arrangements around raising children will adjust to her work.

One thing we have learned from other cultures is that mothering is shared. Women may do the tasks of mothering whether or not they are biological mothers. Women as mothers in such societies are not the exclusive caretakers of small children. In fact, this labor is generally shared between a number of women in ways structured by kinship and networks of friendships. There are many ways for men to assist. Job or no job, being a mother is only one stage of life.

The subject of mothers presents some core dilemmas both in the women's movement and in anthropology. How can we make mothering important and visible without condemning women without children to be less than real women—without defining women, whether mothers or not, only or primarily on the basis of reproductive potentials? Life is much more than motherhood and yet being a mother really is one of the planet's major roles.

Kin-Work

In Turkey, where ethnographer Jenny White conducted her research, women may spend up to fifty hours per week producing goods for export. When women and their families moved from the rural areas to the city to find jobs, they started doing piecework, hand work, or finishing work on products destined for the world market. One such woman, Hayriye, skillfully embroiders nightgowns, blouses, head scarves, and doilies for neighbors and friends and night clothes for trousseaus. Occasionally she knits sweaters for a merchant. He pays her by the piece. She speaks:

> At holidays work piles up so I do the urgent ones first. I am a housewife and how much I can stitch depends on the time I have left over from housework and my other duties. (White 1994:111)

Hayriye and her peers insist on making a distinction between labor and work. They do the labor and give the products out. But this is not a job or employment. "I am busy," they say. Busy means doing housework, tending children, or helping kinfolks and neighbors. Among themselves they maintain the fiction that they are not working; they are merely staying busy.

> This allows them to avoid the onus of being considered a woman who has economic dealings with strangers, a woman who has to "work," demonstrating that her husband is not able to support his family financially. This latter dishonors the family as a whole, including the women. . . . This allows them to contribute financially, while remaining reconciled with the moral standards of the traditional family. This conflation of labor with a woman's traditional identity is one of the factors that keep production costs low and profits high for distributors, intermediaries, merchants, and exporters. (White 1994:130)

In their view, women who work among strangers outside their homes cannot be good wives or moral Muslims. But economic circumstances are difficult in the cities; family survival may depend on more than a man's salary. So men work at more than one job. Women and children bring in extra income through piecework.

At the same time, women affirm and cement their membership in community life through sharing and exchanging labor. They do not keep track of the time spent or calculate hourly wages and piece rates. They put the work down and pick it up again as the day unfolds; they may finish up another woman's piece during some spare time. Within these networks, women pool money with each other rather than in pensions, health insurance, or social security. The crocheting, knitting, embroidery, and stitching are also investments in the financial and emotional support a mother can expect from her grown children. They call this "milk debt." So a woman's son may be a more important man in her life than is her husband; it may also mean that she has internalized a kind of gender ideology others call the patriarchy.

These Turkish women would say that they do *kin-work*, not piecework. To them, piecework or sewing in workshops is not work, but an expression of group identity, solidarity, and redistribution that sustains their families in tough economic times. The fact that men and women alike devalue women's work creates a pool of cheap labor for the world market and provides consumers in the West with what we think of as bargains in handmade table cloths, hand-stitched clothing, or boutique sandals and purses (among many similar items). But women still work, even when work operates on the logic of kinship rather than on the logic of capitalism.

Sex-Work

Other models for looking at women's work are the prostitutes' rights organizations around the world. Women "in the life" or "in the trade," that is, women selling sex, maintain that prostitution is not always forced servitude or sexual slavery. They say that prostitution or sex-work is not a crime, a sin, or a vice. It may be a career choice as well as a legitimate and necessary social service. These women assert that sex workers have a right to work in conditions they themselves control. For them, the power in prostitution is the chance to choose, to set the terms of sexuality, and to demand substantial payment for their time and skills.

> *Prostitution, by definition, is the exchange of sexual services for money. Some prostitution is forced, and forced prostitution is clearly rape combined with kidnapping and perhaps brainwashing. At the other end of the spectrum, there are women who make a clear decision to work as prostitutes, a few because they enjoy sex and have no qualms about enjoying sex as work. Most women who work as prostitutes, I think, do so out of economic motives—the hourly pay is better than that paid for most of the work women are allowed to do. Some get to like the work as they become skilled at it. Other women hate it from beginning to the end. And still others like some aspects of the job while hating parts of it. (Delacoste and Alexander 1987:15)*

This example is not about whether prostitution should exist or not; nor does it concern moral judgments about people who sell sex. It is only about how some groups of women define the marketing and sale of sexual services as work.

Sex workers have formed unions, guilds, or professional organizations with imaginative names. The first was called COYOTE—Call Off Your Old Tired Ethics. Others followed: CAT—California Advocates for Trollops; SPARROW— Seattle Prostitutes Against Rigid Rules Over Women; and, in Britain, PLAN— Prostitution Laws Are Nonsense. Sex workers in nonwestern countries are working to organize, demonstrating against the injustices they face, and demanding human, civil, political, and social rights for the work they do. They have sponsored international conferences like the World Whores Congresses and the Network of Sex Work Projects. They have tied their working conditions to public health issues like the spread of HIV and AIDS. They parade, demonstrate, and put up posters. They form groups with women in the same situation: Sex Workers! Encourage, Empower, Trust, and Love Yourselves! SWEETLY of the Dominican Republic; and SWEAT of South Africa–Sex Worker Education and Advocacy Taskforce.

Work and a Revolution

Early in the twentieth century, after the socialist revolution in Russia, Lenin, the ideological father, decreed that women must work for wages if they wanted to be equal to men. As he noted in a newspaper interview,

> Housework is the most unproductive, savage and most arduous work a woman can do. . . . Women must participate in common productive labor. . . . We are setting up model institutions, dining rooms and nurseries, that will emancipate women from housework. And the work of organizing all these institutions will fall mainly to women. (Pravda No. 213: Sept. 25, 1919)

Under Lenin's new socialism, Russian women would be paid as wage laborers for the same work they did for no pay before the revolution. But his socialist ideals never materialized. The state did not provide day care, laundry, or food preparation. Wives continued to do that work in addition to working for wages. The same thing is true now that Communism is dead and the Soviet Union disbanded.

As of this writing, no country or economic system in the world has solved the problem of valuing women's domestic work. The capitalist solution pays only lip service to motherhood—phrases that include "family values," "stay at home and take care of the kids," or "women in the labor force." No socialist country has been able to organize large-scale socialized domestic services. There has been no liberation from what Lenin called "household bondage and petty individual house-keeping." None of these systems provide adequately for the economic problems of divorce or widowhood. Worse, they assume that all women find satisfaction in domestic work, do it "naturally," and are always available to do it. And even worse, women who have made this a life career and are truly geniuses at their work find themselves fired in divorce, trivialized in feminism, and ignored the rest of the time.

The current American middle-class solution to this age-old dilemma is to affirm the belief that women and men are equally responsible for child care and domestic work. By contrast, people in many countries are shocked at the demand for day care in capitalist countries; staying at home with their children would be an unimaginable luxury. In fact, in traditional societies or in socialist societies, there was never a category of women's work Americans call "staying at home."

Value, Valued, and Valuable

Many women naively believe that if women's work and labor is so vital to human survival and comfort, then we should be treated accordingly. Our work is valuable and the reward should correspond to the importance of our contributions, we protest. Alas, women's work is not always valued. In fact, there is often no system for placing a value on female labor. For example, look at the concept called **use value**. This means that products made and services rendered within families are not sold and do not have a monetary value. They have a "value" only in private domestic settings. This contrasts sharply with **exchange value work,** which is the production of commodities or services for sale in the marketplace. When goods or services are exchanged for money or other financial considerations, then people say they have value.

The underlying economic principle is this: The ability to distribute, exchange, and control valuable goods and services to people who are not in our own domestic unit buys whatever we treasure: status, time, privacy, power, prestige, income, or goodies. This is true in each and every human group. Just working hard within our domestic units is only that: just working hard within our domestic units. This work, however hard, exciting, or crucial to survival it may be, does not automatically translate into power, control, status, money, or whatever. If women produce wonderful services or objects and cannot market them or keep the proceeds, then there is little or no exchange value or power. This principle applies to the products of women's bodies, too. After all, the term "labor" refers to birthing an infant. This is also why sex workers sometimes claim that offering sex in return for marriage is much the same as selling it in a free market.

But the control or power any woman has over the process and the product of her labor varies greatly between cultures. In most societies, men seem to have greater rights than women to distribute goods outside their domestic networks. So the best question is not about how hard women are working; ask instead if women control access to the resources they need. Resources typically include education, employment, child care, legal standing, land ownership, the freedom to marry and divorce, and access to the tools of survival or the **means of production,** as Karl Marx called them.

A related example of the sexual division of labor and the gendering of work is the **family wage ideology.** Family wage laws and practices are still a fundamental part of gender ideologies in the Western world. They developed in nineteenth-century industrializing, capitalist societies. The premise is that a male worker (as head of a household) is hired and paid enough to support his wife and their children. Females (for example, young single women) who work the same jobs are not paid the same as males. Presumably they do not have to support families. Married women are assumed to have access to their husband's income; they are said to be working at home for him. If wives take wage-labor jobs, it is seen as supplementing their husbands' income. This cultural formulation of the sexual division of labor has been enormously instrumental, even seductive, in western European and North American societies. You may recognize the impact of this gender ideology on your own salaries and lives.

Women don't just work; we are often overworked and invisible. Sociologist Arlie Hochschild interviewed two-career couples about their own sexual division of labor; she also visited these modern working partnerships to see how they divided up their "home-work." Then she reviewed a large number of studies on who did what in contemporary households. No matter how she approached the topic, she came back to the same conclusion: the revolution is stalled. Despite the hopes and rhetoric of a generation of women, working mothers still carry the major burdens of childrearing, household maintenance, and whatever emotional work needs to be done. She averaged estimates from major studies on time use done from the 1960s on and discovered that women worked roughly fifteen hours longer each week than men do. Over a year, women worked an extra month of twenty-four days a year, and over a dozen years, they worked an extra year. Mirroring the wage gap between men and women in the workplace, there was a "leisure gap" between them at home.

> As masses of women have moved into the economy, families have been hit by a "speed-up" in work and family life. There is no more time in the day than there was when wives stayed home, but there is twice as much to get done. It is mainly women who absorb this "speed-up". . . . Even when couples share more equitably in the work at home, women do two-thirds of the **daily** jobs at home, like cooking and cleaning up—jobs that fix them into a rigid routine. . . . Beyond doing more at home, women also devote **proportionately more** of their time at home to housework and proportionately less of it to childcare. Of all the time men spend working at home, more of it goes to childcare. That is, working wives spend relatively more time "mothering the house"; husbands spend more time "mothering" the children. Since most parents prefer to tend to their children than clean house, men do more of what they'd rather do. (Hochschild 1990:8)

Hochschild calls what happens at the end of the day in American two-career families the **second shift**. Writers about international economics usually call this the **double day**. In the double day, women do child care, household and domestic duties in addition to agricultural work, and full-time or part-time wage-labor jobs. Figure 1.3 is a way of diagramming these work loads. The professional career women Hochschild interviewed are supposed to "have it all." But she found that in only 20 percent of dual-career families do men share housework equally with their wives. Over and over women revealed that they accepted this inequity to keep peace and continue the connections. They also reported chronic exhaustion, low sex drive, and more frequent illnesses. They felt intense feelings of time

Figure 1.3
The Double Day or the
Second Shift

pressure, guilt, and anxiety. "Emotionally drained" was a constant refrain. Their deepest fantasies started with getting some sleep. Low wages, lack of support services, feeling tired all the time, and the double day or the second shift compose probably the most characteristic pattern for women's work on the planet.

Interpreting Food, Work, and the Facts of Life

Today, in Grey Rock Harbour, Newfoundland, women no longer worry about their men at work fishing. That way of life ended in the late 1970s when the fishing industry collapsed. Men are now land-bound. A combination of policies from the Canadian government and a changing ecology has resulted in chronic unemployment, the loss of a work ethic, and what the women call "ruined men." There is conflict and hostility between men and women. One man says, "You want to know about women in Grey Rock Harbour? They've changed, let me tell you. Newfoundland women now are possessive, jealous, and everything you do is wrong, wrong, wrong." A woman responds,

> *The young unmarried men you'll find at the club all the time now.*
> *They're of an age for it but I think they will never grow out of it. . . .*
> *Most of these guys will remain single because no woman will marry a*
> *drunk. These days you're better off alone. (Davis 1993:470)*

Men now stay at home; they have invaded the domains of women. They spend dreary daytime hours at local bars and some turn to confrontational bravado. Women don't need the romantic and idealized job of worrying any longer; they don't have to be helpmates to earn a living. They are advantaged competitors for the few jobs available, which they can do as well as the men. Divorce, extramarital activities, single mothering, and expensive TV dinners, unheard of in traditional times, are now common. Women are now "unhusbanding" their resources because marriage has few survival advantages for them. The sexual division of labor changed as the means of earning a living changed.

Arlie Hochschild, who spoke so eloquently about the second shift, has discovered a "third shift" in the rapid changes in women's work in the last half-century. Both men and women are experiencing a new twist to their lives that she calls the "time bind," or the third shift. This is when work becomes like home, and home becomes work. The third shift is the emotional dirty work of making children adjust to their industrialized home, where *time*—not food, clothes, silks, jewels, perfumes, or money—is the most precious commodity in the household economy. This work is another form of repairing or making up emotionally for never having "family time," quantity time, enough time.

> *As the first shift (at the workplace) takes more time, the second shift (at home) becomes more hurried and rationalized. The longer the workday at the office or plant, the more we feel pressed at home to hurry, to delegate, to delay, to forgo, to segment, to hyperorganize the precious remains of family time. Both the time deficit and what seem like solutions to it. . . force parents to engage in a third shift—noticing, understanding, and coping with the emotional consequences of the compressed second shift. (Hochschild 1997:215)*

Her point is that work now feels like home—it's where everybody wants to be—and home feels like work. Homes have somehow become more "masculine" in that they need to be managed efficiently. At the same time, workplaces are correspondingly "feminized" through management philosophies that stress trust, team building, and courtesies to customers. This is one reason why many say that Euro-American countries have post-industrial and **post-modern** societies. One meaning we can draw from this is: as our economies constantly change, our work changes. Parents are still adjusting childraising to the work they have to do to earn a living. Mothers and fathers handle the wealth of technology and the poverties of time, but they do it in different ways.

Furthermore, nothing in anthropology or the archaeological record comes close to concepts such as "happiness," "self-esteem," or "fairness." We cannot, however tempting, write onto the past or onto different groups our contemporary arguments about who does household work and who doesn't. But what if you don't happen to like the way your culture does it and you don't want to live that way? What happens if a person just doesn't fit into the group goals or if women's lives are so overdetermined and controlled that they can barely move socially or psychologically? Is there no room for serious differences or for ignoring gender? The next chapter is a special story about two "fore-mothers" who struggled heroically to find their answers to the questions about individuality, culture, personhood, and who fits the stereotypes of "feminine" or "masculine."

A Few of the Many Books You May Want to Read

Scholars Louise Lamphere, Helena Ragoné, and Patricia Zavella have brought together a lively assortment of unusually readable ethnographic accounts and first-person narratives, *Situated Lives: Gender and Culture in Everyday Life* (1997). *Women Writing Culture* (1995) is an unusual perspective on visibility. The editors, Ruth Behar and Deborah Gordon, organized the book as a response to two crises. The first was the challenge to feminist anthropologists who were left out of an influential theory book in the field; the second stemmed from critiques of white middle-class feminism from lesbians and women of color.

Seeing women's work in prehistory and women studying prehistory are both fairly recent happenings. Archaeologists are writing innovative and much-needed works that make women visible. The following volumes are particularly helpful. Sarah Milledge Nelson takes on the formidable task of providing the first comprehensive feminist, theoretical synthesis of the flood of new archaeological work on gender in her *Gender in Archaeology: Analyzing Power and Prestige* (1997). The very special collection edited by Annette Weiner and Jan Schneider, *Cloth and the Human Experience* (1989), honors women's work around cloth, clothing, and the production of fabrics, and the reproduction of people, society, and ideologies in material goods. The emotional, spiritual, anthropological, and historic associations of fabrics, women, and weaving are one of the golden threads you will be able to pick up throughout this book.

The Power of Women's Informal Networks: Lessons in Social Change from South Asia and West Africa (2004) edited by Bandana Purkayastha and Mangala Subramaniam looks at poor women's agency through their informal networks. The essays in this collection cover topics ranging from contraceptive use to political participation to weaving. Examining informal networks reveals some of the ways women have always worked as well as newer forms of agency, organization, and production wrapped up in globalization.

Chapter Two

Love and the Work of Culture

n the autumn of 1922, two women met in a classroom at Columbia University in New York. The instructor, Ruth Fulton Benedict, was a shy, awkward person with a tendency to stutter, a tentative speaker whose hearing problems were not apparent. Ruth was registered as an older, or what we now call nontraditional or reentry student, and she was working as a teaching assistant for Dr. Franz Boas, who had founded the first department of anthropology in the United States. She often wore the same dress to work on successive days because men were allowed to wear the same suit without comment.

In her class was a self-confident and energetic undergraduate named Margaret Mead, a psychology major trying out her first anthropology class. Gradually, Ruth opened up the ideas of anthropology to Margaret; she said, we have nothing to offer but an opportunity to do work that really matters.

> *Ruth, on her side, was warmed by Margaret's admiration and saw her, fifteen years younger, at least at first, as somewhat of a daughter to be helped with problems and career choices. Often deeply depressed, she appreciated Margaret's outgoingness, her sunny personality, her energy, her intensity toward living. Though they were attracted to each other by differences, both were fanatically tolerant freethinkers with a radical bent of thought and both were of superior intelligence and attracted to intelligence in others. Both thought ideas important and valued creative, original thinking. Both felt a need to be useful, to make a difference in the world. (Caffrey 1989:187)*

More Than Personal Lives

This chapter centers on some core concepts in anthropology and the methods of fieldwork and ethnography. Here we will talk about culture, culture relativism, male and female, feminine and masculine, and normal and deviant, as cultural categories. The personal lives and professional careers of Margaret Mead and Ruth Benedict form the scaffolding that supports these topics.

At the heart of this chapter are stories about women and men who live in dramatic cultures on the Sepik River in New Guinea. They are the players in Margaret Mead's most debated and yet most enduring contribution to studying women, a book called *Sex and Temperament in Three Primitive Societies*. Many of us who teach about gender turn to this book. It informs, provokes, and illuminates. Mead went into the field to study what she called the social personalities of the two sexes. Today scholars tend to use the term "gender." But she found that her fieldwork and data shed even more light on differences in the temperaments or personalities of individuals.

Margaret Mead's and Ruth Benedict's basic questions live on. How can we reconcile the obvious biological differences between the sexes on the one hand and ourselves as individuals with temperaments or personalities on the other hand? Everyone has a sex, or what we now call gender, which we share with others in the same category. But each one of us also has a temperament—what we now call personality—in which we may look like, feel like, or act like people in another

gender are said to be. Mead felt that "temperament" or personality ranks higher than biological sex in influencing or affecting who and what we are as adults. People can be typically gentle, assertive, aggressive, or nurturing. The culture and subculture we are born into will, however, reward or discount these traits unevenly.

One of the primary organizing principles in human societies is gender. So people within one group say, "This is just the way women are." Yet people in another area will say exactly the opposite, "That is just how women are." Sex roles or gender codes can differ in amazing ways. Yet we know that biology is everywhere the same.

Does this mean there is some absolute bottom line or a universal set of rules about gender? How "should" males act? How "should" females act? How do girls grow up to be what we define as women, as "feminine"? How do boys grow up to be what we call men, to act "masculine"? What if people in our own culture don't act the way our cultural definitions say they should? What if people in other cultures don't behave the way we in this culture think women and men should "naturally" act? Where do the misfits, the abnormal, and the deviates fit in? Who makes up these categories?

Both Mead and Benedict wrote for ordinary people, in a readable and popular style. Some anthropologists have criticized them heavily for this defection. But the major themes of their work remain, particularly when we study women. Human beings are more than just a collection of our ideas or thoughts. We are also our autobiographies or our biographies. It may be particularly important for women to study how other women live, whether we are lovers, professionals, wives, mothers, or making sago flour on the Sepik River.

The Personal Is Professional

Ruth Fulton had attended Vassar College and thrived in its all-female atmosphere. After several years of teaching and social work, she married an engineer named Stanley Benedict. As one of her biographers notes:

> *After three years of emotional turmoil, of internal struggles over conforming or not conforming to society's expectations of her as a woman, of hesitancy over what to do in the world, and the frustrations of what she was allowed to do, she surrendered. She fell head-over-heels in love and the whole world changed. (Caffrey 1989:74)*

Ruth hoped, as have many women, that love, a husband, and a baby or two would grant a measure of calm and the answers to her tormenting questions. But no babies came, and her suburban marriage soon proved to be a suffocating trap. Her idea of wedlock was a meeting of two equals, sharing thoughts and feelings. But Stanley Benedict wanted a wife to play homemaker, to take care of his house, and to put him first in her thoughts and actions. Ruth felt betrayed, and observed privately that she had to work hard to avoid the unconscious moments where she might carelessly end her life. She was often depressed; she called her mood swings the "blue devils."

In anthropology, however, Ruth Benedict found an intellectual community who tolerated differences and offered alternatives to the restrictions of American culture. More to the point, Ruth Benedict found women who had created a place for themselves in this new discipline. She was ready in her own gentle way to throw off her religious background, Victorian morality, husband, and other social conventions, in order to embrace this source of understanding and meaning.

As an undergraduate, Margaret Mead was in a group of lively students called the Ash Can Cats; they planned activities that felt sophisticated, daring, even radical or liberated. At the same time, she had been engaged for years to a man studying for the Episcopalian ministry. Margaret Mead had grown up in a liberal, academic family in which her paternal grandmother, Martha Mead, was her granddaughter's conscience and the only person whose opinion about Margaret's proposed career in anthropology mattered.

At some point, Ruth Benedict and Margaret Mead moved from being mentor and student to colleagues and friends, and then to lovers. Remember that both of these women grew up with traditions of passionate and romantic love between women. Women in those days wrote each other letters full of love poetry, hugs, kisses, embraces, and news of the latest baby, husband's health, or church socials. Deep emotional involvements and erotic attachments between women seemed innocent and nonthreatening. But in the years after World War I, the idea of same-sex romances changed. Deep love required making love or having sex. Romantic friendships between women sounded like lesbianism, and this frightened the establishment.

In the poetry Benedict and Mead wrote, and in their personal and professional lives, separately and together, they explored the meanings of alternative standards. Both worked with and respected men who voiced strong judgments about "unnatural acts" and "personal sex problems." So they talked about being deviate or being a misfit within one's own culture. For example, they decided that

> *women who loved women, dubbed Lesbians by society, were healthy when they accepted their love as an alternative standard to that of the mainstream. Women-loving women became unhealthy when they internalized society's condemnation of them and the sinfulness of their love. (Caffrey 1989:198)*

Benedict wrote that there were no universally valid definitions about what was abnormal; so-called deviates were only people for whom their culture had no appropriate categories, rewards, or names. Today what they said seems obvious to contemporary women working out the questions of "our sexual identities." It was

Margaret Mead in the Admiralty Islands in 1954

not so obvious at that time. These themes remain one of their enduring legacies to anthropology and to an understanding of how individuals live within the culture assigned at birth.

Husbands, Lovers, and Fieldwork

In 1923 Margaret married her fiance, Luther Cressman, in the Episcopal chapel where at the age of eleven she had defied her agnostic parents to be baptized. Mead kept her own name and her lifelong affiliation with the church. The couple settled into a student marriage. They had a plan: no children until they both finished school, then a large parsonage, a frugal lifestyle, and six children. Luther and Margaret would serve a parish, a country rectory—he as minister, she as minister's wife. He liked her friends and the new discipline of anthropology she was learning.

But, in fact, Luther was drifting out of church work and Margaret was writing poems with suggestive imagery: "denied the power to bloom," and "throttled by sullen weeds I die." So in 1925 they agreed to do separate things with their marriage and their respective careers. She wanted passionately to do fieldwork, to test herself in the rigors and dramas of exotic places amidst people unlike herself. She also needed to finish and publish her dissertation.

In order to do fieldwork, Mead had to negotiate with her husband, her father, and her advisor, Franz Boas. She also had to teach herself many practical skills and raise money to finance her trip. As usual, Ruth assisted her. Boas thought Mead was too high-strung and emotional; no women had traveled so far away alone. But he also knew she was absolutely determined to go, and so he urged her to study how teenage girls grow up and pass through adolescence in another culture. He wondered if there were predictable stages when teenage girls were passive, submissive, bashful, strongly rebellious, sullen, or capricious. He enjoined her to look at the crushes and extremes of romantic love among adolescent girls. He set up the primary research questions and told her to stick to observing individuals and patterns.

Boas and Mead agreed that she could go to Samoa, a legendary and beautiful island chain in the South Pacific. So she made preparations, packed clothes, cameras, notebooks, and lamps, endured inoculations, and developed the psychological tests she wanted to administer. In her grant application, she noted a need for anthropological investigation in a virgin field, as it were. No one had ever studied "feminine reactions and participation in the culture of the group." She craved to see how individuals and individual psychology responded to the general patterns within a culture.

On the long journey to Samoa, Margaret Mead stopped off in the Southwest to visit Ruth Benedict, who was doing her own groundbreaking field research there. They visited the Grand Canyon together and there apparently began an affair, or continued one already begun.

Mead's Samoan fieldwork was a success. She established a rapport with the girls and a degree of empathy that male fieldworkers could not hope for and which even today tells a kind of truth about their lives. She was, however, very lonely. A fellow passenger on the long return boat trip was a fascinating psychologist from New Zealand. Reo Fortune was going to England after having completed fieldwork among a group of dour sorcerers called the Dobu on islands off the coast of New Guinea. Hungry for intellectual challenges and the English language, Margaret Mead and Reo Fortune talked nonstop through the many weeks of slow boat travel. With anguish, Margaret realized that she was falling in love with a genuinely unsuitable person, "unlike anyone I had ever known." He was younger than she, fiercely ambitious, possessively jealous, and quite inexperienced with women or the wider world.

Margaret's life at this point reads like a novel or a soap opera. This was her first trip to Europe and, as she records in her autobiography, she was pulled between two men, the intensity of fieldwork, the shipboard conversations, and her own feelings. Her husband, Luther, met her as the boat docked. At the same moment, she parted from Reo in confusion. Then she and Ruth met for another glorious holiday week—this time in Rome. Margaret commented on how beautiful Ruth looked to her; Ruth, shy and modest, was always embarrassed when Mead or others remarked on her beauty. Meanwhile, both women were married, and Margaret was trying to decide whether to continue with Luther, her husband, or Reo, a fascinating lover in her mind.

Once back in the United States, Ruth and Margaret wrote poetry to each other. Margaret was Ruth's teaching assistant. They were also lovers, collaborating on projects, and supporting each other through books, career development, and marital maneuverings. Mead took a job as assistant curator at the American Museum of Natural History in New York. She wrote a technical monograph on Samoan kinship, a few papers, and a little book she entitled *Coming of Age in Samoa*. Mead reported in her autobiography (which is often unrevealing, even misleading, but always riveting) that a doctor told her that she could never have children. So she reassessed her life plans and decided to marry Reo, a man whom she believed would be radically unsuited for fatherhood but an exciting partner for field research. She and Luther parted amicably and with respect.

More Love, Husbands, and Fieldwork

So in 1928, at the age of 27, Margaret Mead departed with her second husband for her second field trip, this time to the island of Manus off the coast of New Guinea. She had wanted a man with whom to do joint research. Throughout most of New Guinea, culturally based antagonisms between males and females were so strong that no single field worker could possibly hope to understand the other gender and as a result would miss half of the culture. In Manus Mead studied childhood; she created new techniques for studying children, invented new fieldwork methods, and laid the groundwork for a lifetime of commitment to telling the story of how this particular group changes before our very eyes.

When Mead returned to her museum job, she discovered that the little book on Samoa had become a best-seller and she a famous author! She had answered Boas's questions: The teenage girls of Samoa did not experience the same pressures and struggles Americans take for granted. She wrote that the transition through adolescence for Samoan girls

represented no period of crisis or stress, but was instead an orderly devel-
opment of a set of slowly maturing interests and activities. The girls'
minds were perplexed by no conflicts, troubled by no philosophical
queries, beset by no remote ambitions. To live as a girl with many lovers
as long as possible and then to marry in one's own village, near one's
own relatives and to have many children, these were uniform and satisfy-
ing ambitions. (Mead 1973:87)

She was particularly impressed that Samoan teenagers lacked the craziness of romantic or obsessive love, or the notion that one boyfriend or one husband will fulfill a woman and make her whole. Margaret was pleased to find an alternative approach to the problems bound up with ideas of monogamy, exclusiveness, jealousy, and undeviating fidelity.

Her field trip and research in Samoa have been dissected by many scholars; they remain a major legend in anthropology. But the book was not just about teenage girls on a tropical island. In a simple and profound way, this book offered an antidote to notions of racism and fascism growing in Europe, forces of hatred that would culminate in World War II. Mead said that culture shapes our lives more than biology does. Human cultures have the capacity to change and to allow for many different expressions of personalities. The book said that human beings are not assigned to a place or a position by biology, which can never be changed and for which we may be judged or killed (as in the Holocaust that followed). We are not just the sum of our genes, but the products of belief systems, collective experiences interpreted over time and filtered through value systems that she and her colleagues later called *ethos*.

Margaret and Reo rented a small apartment and spent the next two years working, writing up their respective fieldwork into new books, finishing a field stint among the Omaha Indians, and making preparations for both of them to return to New Guinea. In her autobiography, she talks about the nature of their domestic life living in New York just as the stock market crashed and the great depression hit. Reo was British, and she attributed disagreements in their marriage largely to their differences in nationality or cultural background.

Reo did not like to see me doing the housework, which he did not intend
to help me with; yet he felt it was a reproach to him that I had to do it at
all. As a result, I became expert at tidying up on Sunday morning while
appearing to give complete attention to what he was saying. I would wait
for a pause in the conversation to slip out and spread one sheet or wash
one cup and then appear again. In this way I managed to get the neces-
sary things done so unobtrusively that later, when Gregory Bateson vis-
ited our camp on the Sepik, he remarked that he had never seen me
perform a domestic task. (Mead 1972:207)

Today Reo's attitude might be attributed to his being a man trained and socialized in male attitudes and privileges. Contemporary women might give Margaret advice on getting him to help in the house or taking equal responsibility. At any rate, the Mead–Fortune household had its own sexual division of labor and gender roles of the kind Mead was so eager to study in others.

Sex and Temperament

From 1931 to 1933, Margaret Mead and Reo Fortune mounted an anthropological expedition to the Sepik River region of New Guinea. The map (Figure 2.1) shows Mead's fieldwork sites in the southwest Pacific and a closeup of the Sepik River cultures. What happened during this trip is an incredible story about four cultures, three anthropologists, two genders, and one river. This story is enormously significant to what anthropologists know about women, men, and culture. In fact, the story has achieved its own mythic status in the history of science.

The Sepik River is a land of mosquitos, crocodiles, cannibals, and floating corpses, Mead would write. People ate tasteless flour laboriously processed from sago palms, yams, bananas, and other produce from their garden plots and fish from the Sepik and its tributaries. Until the Australian government imposed a colonial peace a few years earlier, the peoples of the river region had been cannibals and headhunters. But memories and the social organizations that supported these activities remained potent. People constructed narrow dugout canoes with carved prows, villages raised on stilts over flooded river plains, and men's houses

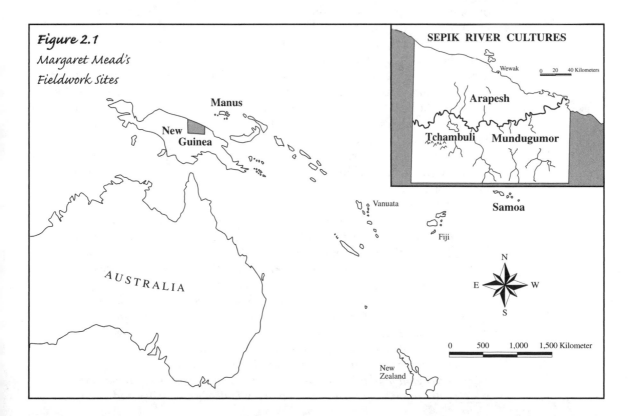

Figure 2.1
Margaret Mead's Fieldwork Sites

with painted gables filled with exquisite art. Sepik peoples' striking and dramatic "primitive art" complements their ceremonies and rituals, which appeared to worship, subvert, or invert the differences between females and males. In common with much of New Guinea, these small, intact cultures seemed to play with elaborate permutations of being male or female.

In the first group Mead studied, the Arapesh, both men and women acted in a mild, parental, and responsible manner—like the stereotypes about females at various times in human history. In the second group, the Mundugumor, both men and women were fierce, sexually charged, assertive, and loud—a view some people hold about males from time to time. And in the third, the Tchambuli, men gossiped about each other and worried about their hairstyles, pretty costumes, or whether any women would marry them. The women in this region of beautiful dark lakes were competent and no-nonsense business managers. These three groups showed Mead that a culture may impose personalities and patterns on one gender or both genders that are only a subset of the whole spectrum of possibilities available to human beings.

The Arapesh

When they first arrived in New Guinea, Margaret and Reo were not certain where to go or which group to study. They hired carriers from the interior to help them up the slippery trails and across the rivers; these workers even had to carry Margaret because her ankle was broken. The decision was made for them when their carriers simply stranded them, with six-months' supplies, in a mountain village.

In the steep hills above the flood plain of the Sepik, level land is scarce. Collecting enough firewood and food is difficult. The women carry loads of sixty to seventy pounds suspended from their foreheads, often with a nursing baby in a bark sling or bag. Precious pigs die easily and yams grow poorly in shallow tropical soils. Mead described the sexual division of labor as a necessity for survival. Men were freer to assume authority, a necessary but evil responsibility. Men worked desperately hard to keep the dangerous secrets of the men's houses; women were excluded from ceremonies to protect them and unborn children from malignant spirits.

> *When the Arapesh are questioned as to the division of labour, they answer: Cooking everyday food, bringing firewood and water, weeding and carrying—these are women's work; cooking ceremonial food, carrying pigs and heavy logs, house-building, sewing thatch, clearing and fencing, carving, hunting, and growing yams—these are men's work; making ornaments and the care of children—these are the work of both men and women. If the wife's task is the more urgent—if there are no greens for the evening meal, or a haunch of meat must be carried to a neighbour in the next village—the husband stays at home and takes care of the baby. He is as pleased with and as uncritical of his child as is his wife. . . . And in recognition of this care, as well as in recognition of the father's initial contribution, if one comments upon a middle-aged man as good-looking,*

the people answer: "Good looking? Ye-e-s? But you should have seen him before he bore all those children." (Mead 1963:39)

Mead called the Arapesh cooperative, oriented to the needs of the next generation, gentle, responsive, carefully parental, and willing to subordinate themselves in caring for those who were younger and weaker. She noted that the Arapesh would probably find the Western notion of parenting and paternity repulsive. They said that a man and a woman cannot make a baby from a moment of passion or a simple act of intercourse. Rather, sex is the strong purposeful work of feeding and shaping a baby during the early weeks in its mother's womb. Since the child is the product of both father's semen and mother's blood, combined in equal parts in the beginning weeks, both parents must work diligently to make the child both desire. This arduous labor begins when menstruation ceases. When this hard work is done, intercourse is strictly forbidden and a wide array of taboos are placed on the mother to protect the unborn child and ensure a safe delivery.

Mead's descriptions of mothers nursing their babies are one of the most authentic and enduring images from *Sex and Temperament*. The emotional content of the culture for her came through in these ordinary moments. Always a skillful observer, she related how mother and infant nursed together to how men and women have sex later in life. She tells how Arapesh mothers, like mothers everywhere, have to go back to work at some point. By the time her child is walking, it may be too heavy for a mother to carry on long trips to her garden. So she may leave it with its father or her sister or mother. When she first leaves the baby, it cries. When she returns, however, she spends an equal time in playing with and nursing the child.

This is an experience that the mother enjoys as much as the child. From the time the little child is old enough to play with her breasts, the mother takes an active part in the suckling process. She holds her breast in her hand and gently vibrates the nipple inside the child's lips. She blows in the child's ear, or tickles its ears, or playfully slaps its genitals, or tickles its toes. The child in turn plays little tattoos on its mother's body and its own, plays with one breast with its hands, plays with its own genitals, laughs and coos and makes a long, easy game of the suckling. Thus the whole matter of nourishment is made into an occasion of high affectivity and becomes a means by which the child develops and maintains a sensitivity to caresses in every part of its body. It is no question of a completely clothed infant being given a cool hard bottle and firmly persuaded to drink its milk and get to sleep at once so that the mother's aching arms can stop holding the bottle. Instead, nursing is, for mother and child, one long delightful and highly charged game, in which the easy warm affectivity of a lifetime is set up. (Mead 1963:42)

But what about Arapesh individuals who do not conform to these cultural patterns she described? Mead was deeply concerned about people who did not "fit in" their culture; the term she used was "deviant." If the Arapesh insisted that everyone was gentle, maternal, and not sexually aggressive, then they would have trouble with others who did not fit these patterns. In fact, Mead said that egocentric, possessive, or jealous women suffered most from their deviation from the norms of Arapesh society. They were likely to act out violently because there were no boundaries or acceptance for them as part of the continuum of human culture.

But Margaret Mead left the Arapesh disappointed. She had not found temperamental differences between women and men. So how could she examine the differences between the sexes if both had roughly the same temperament or social personality?

Moreover, Margaret and Reo had other frustrations. Her bad ankle kept her confined to the unstimulating Arapesh while her restless and volatile husband went off on trips. It is clear from her autobiography that she found Arapesh values of nurturing over aggression compatible with her own personality, while her husband found them particularly shapeless and offensive. She attributed their marital troubles to differences in their respective temperaments. Reo, it seems, was equally disgruntled with both the Arapesh and his wife.

The Mundugumor

Their second field site was equally arbitrary. Margaret and Reo looked on a map and selected the nearest group accessible by water, patrolled by the government but not visited by missionaries. The river-dwelling Mundugumor were in sharp contrast to the Arapesh. Both males and females acted like stereotypes of men we would probably like to avoid. In fact, until the early 1930s, the Mundugumor had been cannibals and headhunters.

Mead called both men and women of the Mundugumor virile, actively masculine, positively sexed, jealous, violent, hard, and arrogant. She witnessed many episodes of angry defiance, mutual hostility, and ruthless individualism. She said they could be charming but hypocritical.

The Mundugumor lived on high, fertile land between swift and treacherous tributaries of the Sepik River. Their neighbors and trading partners spoke of them as ferocious and reckless, and avoided crossing their lands. Rich by Sepik standards, the Mundugumor waterways were filled with fish, and with little effort, their gardens produced plenty of sago palms, coconut trees, and yams. The Mundugumor did not have to cooperate with each other to live well.

> Upon the basis of women's work, the men can be as active or as lazy, as quarrelsome or as peaceful, as they like. And the rhythm of the men's life is in fact an alternation between periods of supreme individualism, in which each man stays at home with his wives and engages in a little desultory labour, even an occasional hunting-excursion with his bow and arrows, and the periods when there is some big enterprise on foot. The competitiveness and hostility of one Mundugumor for another are very slightly expressed in economic terms. They quarrel principally over women. (Mead 1963:186)

The rules of Mundugumor kinship and marriage were elaborate and harsh. In fact, they appeared made to be broken at the earliest opportunity. In their best-possible kinship system, every man was supposed to acquire a wife by giving his sister in return for some other man's sister. But this principle never worked well. First of all, men wanted more than one wife; they also wanted to marry younger women who should have been properly married to a man in their sons' generation. So men competed with their sons for women because these young men wanted to use their sisters to make their own marriage alliances. Fathers used their daughters to make matches for themselves.

But Mundugumor women as sisters or daughters were never docile or cooperative in the marital schemes of their fathers or brothers. Furthermore, mothers plotted for themselves and against their daughters! A good Mundugumor mother wanted to see her daughter out of the way, replaced by a daughter-in-law living under her control. The best strategy of these two women was to become allies against their respective husbands. For obvious reasons, a Mundugumor woman preferred to have sons; a man preferred to have daughters.

The same atmosphere of jealousy and hostility prevailed after marriage. A man whose wife announced her pregnancy was a marked and unhappy man. He had to observe many public taboos while his peers taunted and teased him. He resented his wife and cursed the contraceptive magic which had so clearly failed him. A pregnant woman was deprived of sex and worried that her husband would desert her or take another wife altogether.

Mead wondered how any infant survived Mundugumor babyhood. Her discussion of nursing as the crucible for adult personality makes her points very forcefully.

> *Mundugumor women suckle their children standing up, supporting the child with one hand in a position that strains the mother's arm and pinions the arms of the child. There is none of the mother's dallying, sensuous pleasure in feeding her child that occurs among the Arapesh. Nor is the child permitted to prolong his meal by any playful fondling of his own or his mother's body. He is kept firmly to his major task of absorbing enough food so that he will stop crying and consent to be put back in his basket. The minute he stops suckling for a moment he is returned to his prison. Children therefore develop a very definite purposive fighting attitude, holding on firmly to the nipple and sucking milk as rapidly and vigorously as possible. They frequently choke from swallowing too fast; the choking angers the mother and infuriates the child, thus further turning the sucking situation into one characterized by anger and struggle rather than by affection and reassurance. (Mead 1963:196)*

Poor Mundugumor babies. They were not comforted with their mother's breasts; they were put in scratchy, harsh baskets until they learned to kick their way out of them. Once out of their baskets, they had to cling strongly to their mother's hair and make lots of noise to gain even the minimal attention necessary for survival. Mothers resented their smallest illness, accident, or weakness. Blows and cross words marked their weaning. They were surrounded by rules, a series of prohibitions: Don't go in the houses of your father's other wives and ask for food; don't cry or demand attention; don't wander out of sight, and so on.

It is not surprising that sex for Mundugumor adults potently mirrored their childhood experiences. Children who fought for every drop of milk and every ounce of nurturing would be unlikely candidates for romance, docility, or cooperation with parents' plans for arranged marriages. So girls put on their best jewelry or grass skirts and boys watched for the slightest sign of opportunity. The following quote is an obvious complement to her discussions about breastfeeding.

> *The love affairs of the young unmarried people are sudden and highly charged, characterized by passion rather than by tenderness or romance. A few hastily whispered words, a tryst muttered as they pass on a trail, are often the only interchange between them after they have chosen each other and before that choice is expressed in intercourse. The element of time and discovery is always present, goading them towards the swiftest possible cut-and-run relationship. . . . Foreplay in these quick encounters takes the form of a violent scratching and biting match, calculated to produce the maximum amount of excitement in the minimum amount of time. To break the arrows or the basket of the beloved is one standard way of demonstrating consuming passion; so also is tearing off ornaments, and smashing them if possible. (Mead 1963:215)*

What would happen, Mead asked, to a Mundugumor couple who somehow invented long, languorous lovemaking, to a Mundugumor man who rejoiced in his children's growth, or to a Mundugumor woman who cuddled and comforted her crying child? Too bad. They would be defined as deviates in Mundugumor society. While such individuals did not cause trouble in their communities, they were outsiders nonetheless. Who would marry a man who wished to be loyal or parental, or a woman who suckled a foster child?

The Mundugumor called some individuals "really bad men." They had more than their share of wives; some they stole or bought from neighboring groups; some they cheated their sons out of or traded their daughters for. These men garnered allegiance from younger, less established men who jockeyed for power. At the same time, the bad men conspired secretly to betray these opportunistic alliances. The Mundugumor men worked together only when headhunting and eating their enemies at the victory feasts. But such men were not deviates; they were only exaggerations of the expected.

The three months among the Mundugumor were troubled and discouraging for Mead. For starters, the group did not throw any light on her central theme of showing the contrast between female and male temperament since both sexes were so aggressive and assertive. As in the Arapesh, there were no behavioral styles that seemed to separate women and men. She hated the way they treated children and used them in conflicts between the parents. The village flooded regularly and the mosquitos were even more hostile and aggressive than the Mundugumor.

Judging from her autobiography and their letters from the field, it is also clear that Margaret and Reo were getting on each other's nerves. She notes: "Reo was both repelled and fascinated by the Mundugumor. They struck some note in him that was thoroughly alien to me, and working with them emphasized aspects of his personality with which I could not empathize" (1972:206). When she was ill with malaria, her husband offered no sympathy or assistance. When he was sick, he raged, fought the sickness, and climbed mountains.

The couple had an odd division of labor, which strained their marriage and seriously affected the results of their research. Reo assigned Margaret to study mothers, children, and language, topics that were not important to him. Everything else was his. So she would "do gender" and he would do the official ethnography.

When Margaret and Reo decided to leave this troubled field site, the government patrol boat took them upstream in time for Christmas. With the kind of luck, good and bad, that had so marked this trip, the boat deposited them on the doorstep of an English anthropologist named Gregory Bateson, who had been working in a dramatic culture called the Iatmul. This group set their tensions between the sexes into elaborate dances and ceremonials, using cross-dressing with costumes and makeup, and mock and ritual homosexuality.

The Tchambuli

"You must be tired," Gregory said to Margaret tenderly as he pulled out a soft chair for her. She melted. Everything about this new anthropologist and the village was a relief for the aching ethnographer.

So Mead and Fortune decided to stay and finish their fieldwork with a group called the Tchambuli. They were neighbors to the Iatmul and had many similar practices. Both groups had splendid artistic traditions and complex cultures. Both lived in settled villages and traded fish with bush dwellers who made sago flour, the other staple of their diet. For both groups, women fished for a living and retained sole control of the disposition and marketing of their catches. Women manufactured large, woven, mosquito-proof sleeping bags traded throughout the Sepik.

The Tchambuli lived on a blue-black lake. Small, sharp hills rose beyond the indistinct shores of the lake. In Mead's time a road wound near the lake margins. Men's houses, thirty to forty feet long, with painted, carved gables and figures of bird-men at the ends, lined the road. Paths ran from the ceremonial houses up the rocky hillsides to the women's houses. These were built to last three or four lifetimes and house three or four families.

For Mead, the Tchambuli dwelling house revealed the solidarity and solidity of women. Women, competent, collegial, and certain of themselves, occupied the center of the house. Men sat at the edges near the doors, uneasy, wary, ready to bolt back into their ceremonial houses. There they gathered their own firewood and cooked their own bachelor meals. While the women fished and wove, the men practiced dances, prepared extravagant costumes of feathers, fibers, and shells, or arranged each other's curls.

To men, the thing that mattered most in life was art. Every man knew at least one art: carving, weaving, painting, dancing, music, costume-making, drama productions, and the creation of a graceful pattern of social relations that allowed the unadorned women to draw sustenance and return to their work or trading activities. The women tolerated and even appreciated the games, dances, and theatricals the men staged. But the dance was valuable, not the dancer.

The relationships of Tchambuli men to each other were delicate. By contrast, men related to women as the most solid and predictable element in their lives.

> *As a small child, he was held lightly in the arms of a laughing casual mother, a mother who nursed him generously but nonchalantly, while her fingers were busy plaiting reeds into sleeping-baskets or rain-capes. When he tumbled down, his mother picked him up and tucked him under her arm as she went on with her conversation. He was never left alone; there were always some eight or ten women about, working, laughing, attending to his needs, willingly enough, but unobsessively. (Mead 1963:248)*

Tchambuli women weaned their children in the same careless, casual manner as they nursed them, stuffing their mouths with sweet delicacies to stop their crying.

Mead concluded that Tchambuli women had what she called dominance. She pointed out that the group practiced both patrilineal descent and polygyny (having two or more wives). These customs would seem to be oppressive or degrading to women. Yet these women had real power. While men bickered and reconciled, the women quietly carried on with their work. Mead spoke of women as impersonal, vigorous, and efficient.

The Tchambuli view of sex and sexually active females was firmly illustrated in the problem of what to do with young widows.

> *A young widow is a tremendous liability to a community. No one expects her to remain quiet until her remarriage has been arranged. Has she not a vulva? they ask. This is the comment that is continually made in Tchambuli: Are women passive sexless creatures who can be expected to wait upon the dilly-dallying of formal considerations of bride-price? Men, not so urgently sexed, may be expected to submit themselves to the discipline of a due order and precedence. (Mead 1963:258)*

Women, it is clear from her description, exercised their own choices for a mate despite patrilineal clans, polygyny, and a shallow mystique of arranged marriages.

Do not, however, be misled. Assuming that Mead presented a proper perspective on what she witnessed, women's freedom to ignore the rules of patriliny and arranged marriages still produced jealousy, conflicts, and soap opera dramas. For boys, there was a deeper discontinuity; a young man had no real training for his future role. By contrast, girls were thoroughly and practically trained in handicrafts, fishing, and the responsible, practical lives of women. The young men Mead saw in this society were confused; she says they were more maladjusted than any other group she had known. The patrilineal system justified a young man's wish or need to dominate, to initiate marriage choices, and to dictate economic decisions. But for reasons that are clear only in a later historic context, a man could not do these things. So some young men grew angry, violent, and neurotic. This was the primary example of deviancy she noted for the group.

Situations on the Sepik

Meanwhile, the anthropologists were having a crazy time. During part of this period, the three of them worked together in a tiny eight-foot by eight-foot mosquito room. Relentlessly, they analyzed themselves, each other, and their respective cultures. Then they added the four Sepik cultures they studied and others they had known. The three of them talked continually about their work, their theories, and the implications of their findings for studying a topic such as marriage. Bateson lacked the methodological sophistication of the American researchers, but Margaret and Reo lacked his theoretical elegance. From all existing accounts, the events and feelings of this time changed their lives profoundly and probably the discipline of anthropology as well.

All were experiencing some depression in the field. Margaret and Gregory were beginning to build a deep communication that Reo could never share. Margaret was at the apex of a triangle; two men courted her, competed for her, and even coerced her on occasion. No wonder she wrote of the confused Tchambuli men living in a charged atmosphere of courtship and of energetic and competent women who chose at leisure.

> *The intensity of our discussion was heightened by the triangular situation. Gregory and I were falling in love, but this was kept firmly under control while all three of us tried to translate the intensity of our feelings into better and more perceptive field work. As we dealt with the cultural differences between Arapesh, Mundugumor, Tchambuli, and Iatmul, we talked also about the differences in temperamental emphasis in the three English-speaking cultures—American, New Zealand, and English—that we represented and about the academic ethos that Gregory and I shared. No part of this was irrelevant to our struggle to arrive at a new formulation of the relationships between sex, temperament, and culturally expected behavior. (Mead 1972:217)*

None of them, as they saw it, fit the classic gender roles for their respective cultures. At various times in their writings and in conversations with each other, Mead, Benedict, and Bateson identified themselves as "cultural misfits." Mead certainly did not fit the stereotype of the American wife and mother nor the image of a career women with no children. Bateson was brilliant but uncertain what to do with his intelligence. In her writings, Benedict often expressed a sense of herself as a person living so far from the cultural norms or expectations that only anguish and unhappiness would result. She wished she had lived in a time more in tune with her personal characteristics.

So the people of the Sepik were not the only ones testing the possible configurations of gender. Benedict's best-seller, *Patterns of Culture*, argued forcefully for accepting the many ways humans learn to love each other. Margaret Mead brought her own temperament and sex into the field with her. Bateson's work on the transvestite or cross-dressing ceremonics of the Iatmul people who live in the same area would become a classic and lead to some formative work on schizophrenia, cognition, and the boundaries of human thought. For Mead and Bateson, this was the beginning of an extraordinary collaboration, a personal and professional journey that had enormous impact in anthropology and beyond. As Margaret's third and last husband remarked to their daughter,

> *It is not accidental that when Margaret was on the Sepik, struggling with the question of diversity in herself and in her ways of loving, she was formulating the contrasts between three New Guinea peoples who dealt very differently with maleness and femaleness, with assertion and creativity. (M.C. Bateson 1984:160)*

Daughters of Sex and Temperament

In the years that followed the publication of *Sex and Temperament*, many readers had trouble believing that within a 100-mile area of a remote river region Mead conveniently found three societies that perfectly illustrated her points. During her lifetime, she was criticized forcefully for this book; she called it "my most misunderstood book." Mead always insisted that the sites selected for their three phases of fieldwork were only good luck. Ultimately, each was a theoretical bonus. As we shall see a little later, later ethnographers tend to back her up on these points.

In addition to this influential book on gender and personality, Mead published five volumes on the Arapesh. Few anthropologists have left such a record, and this one remains unsurpassed and unchallenged. Bateson's work on the Iatmul also complements and validates her work. And, fortunately, we have the fieldwork of contemporary anthropologists, Nancy McDowell in the contemporary Mundugumor (now called the Biwat) and Deborah Gewertz among the Tchambuli (now called the Chambri). So we can ask these anthropologists and the host of excellent ethnographers who do fieldwork in this area: Was Margaret Mead losing it on the Sepik? Did she know what she was doing? Can we trust her conclusions? What can we really learn from studying sex and temperament in such settings?

Anthropologist Deborah Gewertz went to the Sepik River to do fieldwork in the early 1970s with the Chambri (Tchambuli). Although she was primarily concerned with trade and exchange networks, Deborah knew that she would be working in a group that had become an icon in women's studies. After all, Margaret Mead had labeled the women of Tchambuli "dominant."

Deborah concludes that Mead was essentially correct in what she saw, but she didn't stay long enough or have the viewpoint at that time to see the Chambri embedded in a long history of which 1933 was only a piece. Mead studied the Tchambuli as the group had just returned to the shores of the beautiful lake after a 20-year exile in the hills above. While Mead was there, competition between males decreased temporarily while they rebuilt their base, the men's houses, the male rituals, and the symbolic equipment: slit drums, costumes, art, and musical instruments. It is no wonder the men seemed strained and watchful, worried about marital prospects, or that they appeared preoccupied with artistic productivity and building activity. The women had already rebuilt their barter market system, trading fish for sago in the complementarity that ensured their food supply. So the women appeared "dominant."

According to Deborah Gewertz, Mead did not take complex regional histories into account nor push her own brilliant methodology to its fullest conclusions: She should have noted that women can move throughout a hierarchy without changing into men. Women can move through time taking on different attitudes and practices without losing basic functions. Sex roles (or gender roles) have enough flexibility to use in adjusting to changing circumstances. We cannot just label a group of women as dominant or submissive. Instead, we may find an underlying pattern of relationships that persists through time and provides us a range of negotiations for a complex variety of social situations.

With the blessings of Mead, anthropologist Nancy McDowell reworked the field notes from Margaret and Reo's sojourn among the Mundugumor in 1932 and compared them to her fieldwork with the group (now called the Biwat) in the early 1970s. Nancy concludes that "Mead's ethnographic skills, as well as her powers of observation and perception, were exceptional and clearly superseded the theory she espoused" (McDowell 1991:77). Unlike Mead, however, Reo Fortune never wrote up his notes from this trip. Margaret did some of them for him (as many academic wives have done for husbands), but the rest in his handwriting are useless.

> There are indications that they were not fully sharing data with each other. Fortune's notes are fragmented, disorganized, and practically unreadable. The theoretical paradigms within which they worked led them to ask only certain kinds of questions and neglect others. Mead's American cultural anthropological approach led her to assume that human culture was far more simple than it really was, that it could be encapsulated by particular themes or as "personality writ large," and she fell victim to oversimplification. (McDowell 1991:290)

Margaret Mead and ethnographers who followed her put a great deal of emphasis on women's economic powers. Bateson did not even notice the economic roles and autonomous activities of the women; he saw them only in complementary relationships with men, their fathers and husbands. Gregory Bateson recognized that women and men do not always follow the rules or conform to anyone's stereotypes.

> For the most part, the [Iatmul] women exhibit a system of emotional attitudes which contrasts sharply with that of the men. While the latter behave almost consistently as though life were a splendid theatrical performance—almost a melodrama—with themselves in the centre of the stage, the women behave most of the time as though life were a cheerful cooperative routine in which the occupations of food-getting and child-rearing are enlivened by the dramatic and exciting activities of the men. But this jolly, cooperative attitude is not consistently adopted in all con-

texts, and we have seen that women occasionally adopt something approaching the male ethos and that they are admired for so doing. (Bateson 1958:148)

He found that women occasionally took assertive roles in warfare, in the dancing grounds, and with husbands who could not or would not compete with other men.

What do we learn from these researchers? We see that gender roles are not fixed, rigid, or defined for all time. Sex roles are not divinely assigned nor inherent in something we call "nature." They are flexible; they can be used as problem-solving devices. For example, the Arapesh believed that women should avoid the yam gardens because the yams did not grow well around females; both women and gardens were believed to be protected by this belief. By contrast, Mundugumor couples took advantage of a similar mindset and deliberately copulated in other people's gardens just to ruin them.

What Mead called sex roles are only a script, not a prescription. She quoted Ruth Benedict, who said culture is "personality writ large." In Benedict's view, writes Mead,

It is possible to see each culture, no matter how small and primitive or how large and complex, as having selected from the great arc of human potentialities certain characteristics and then having elaborated them with greater strength and intensity than any single individual could ever do in one lifetime. (Mead 1959b:v)

Their view of culture as a pattern or configuration of homogenous and integrated elements, often linked with a unified theme, lacks the dimensions of contemporary theories. Now anthropologists think that culture is never simple, uniform, or well integrated. It is a messy, complicated, and often contradictory set of differences or oppositions that may exist side by side within the same group claiming the same territory, history, or worldview. This is why, today, we can talk of a female culture and a male culture within complex and contradictory ethnic, national, and world cultures.

Mead published *Sex and Temperament* in 1935; in the same year, Gregory Bateson completed *Naven*, his still-stimulating study of Iatmul culture. And in 1935 they married and went to the island of Bali in Indonesia to begin their first, last, and most extraordinary collaboration.

Beyond the Sepik

The Mead–Bateson collaborative research in Bali was probably far ahead of its time, involving systematic observations and an innovative use of photography. But for purposes of our story, the key event was Margaret's unanticipated pregnancy. There she was, 38 years old. Her English husband had been called up for the war just beginning. In a forthright and organized way, she took charge of her pregnancy and delivery. She taught a young pediatrician, Dr. Benjamin Spock, about comparative styles in childrearing and the importance of breastfeeding. She showed a film on births in New Guinea to those attending her birth.

Gregory and Margaret were delighted with their newborn daughter, Mary Catherine, called Cathy. In the mellowness of breastfeeding the baby she had never expected to have, Margaret was full of empathy for young mothers and grateful for the advantages she had.

> *I had nothing to do except keep my milk up and feed and hold the baby.*
> *I did not have to go anywhere, I had no housework to do, no uneasy*
> *husband to placate, no worries about money—in fact, I faced none of the*
> *problems that can make the first baby so difficult for an inexperienced*
> *young mother. But I was trying to do something, consciously and in a*
> *new way, that combined our best knowledge and my own observations of*
> *mothers and babies in many cultures. (Mead 1972:306)*

She acknowledged the desperation of many young mothers, isolated and afraid, lacking experience, support, or confidence, even sinking into depression.

One has the feeling reading her autobiography that Mead was constructing her life as she went along. She was building it out of pieces of people she studied and admired, bringing other people, friends, and husbands into her life, enriching theirs at the same time. Her daughter comments:

> *In* Blackberry Winter, *Margaret again and again uses metaphors that*
> *suggest her sense of herself as directing a play, as a producer, assembling*
> *and placing a particular constellation of people. (Bateson 1984:111)*

The households she constructed after Catherine's birth are a major case in point. Although Margaret was always sensitive to the lives of wives and mothers in American nuclear families, she herself did not wish to create such an arrangement. Mead thought that nuclear families were too isolated or limiting. As she grew older, she did not want to own or clean an apartment or house or do any domestic tasks beyond salad making; she always lived with close friends in assorted households and hired assistants in the museum where she worked.

Catherine had a nanny, the nanny had a child. Catherine's father was away most of the time. So Catherine grew up in the households of loving and responsible people, in the families of others. Margaret created extended households, although not an extended family in the genetic sense. As she notes in her autobiography, mothering was not a full-time occupation for her. In fact, it would appear from her autobiography that she and Gregory spent little time alone with their child. It is also clear that each parent had close ties with Catherine throughout their lives. In fact, their only child did not grow up "weird," disturbed, or neurotic. Catherine had a number of mothers in this arrangement; she knew her biological mother was loving but different from the American norm. This is an important example for any who perceive American culture as monolithic or one-dimensional or who think only one family style will work.

Intimacy and the World Stage

Margaret Mead continued to puzzle out the meanings of gender and to speak out about women and children throughout the rest of her long career. She taught at Columbia University and worked for the American Museum of Natural History. She was finally promoted to curator in 1964. Although neither institution gave Mead the status or the salary she probably deserved, they offered her flexibility and the much-valued freedom to work as anthropologist-at-large.

Most of her advances and royalties went into the Institute for Intercultural Studies, which gave grants to young anthropologists and supported research, public service, and the discipline of anthropology in numerous ways. Margaret Mead was mentor to dozens and dozens of young anthropologists at key turning points in their careers. She called for a woman's viewpoint in anthropology long before we knew it had a male-centered bias. As feminism and a female-centered viewpoint became established, she reminded us to remember the men. She brought large numbers of women into the calling of anthropology and refused to listen to protests about discrimination. She would say, "Don't complain about women's status or problems. Just get to work."

All of Margaret Mead's husbands were anthropologists. Each was involved with the questions of how to relate their personal lives to their work as anthropologists. Mead met and liked the women her ex-husbands married and helped the three men at many stages in their careers. As one of her friends remarked, "Margaret was always a gentleman." Margaret sustained an intimate life throughout her adult years with a man and with a woman. While this double pattern satisfied her, it required a certain secrecy and thus a certain isolation. As her daughter, Catherine, notes in her own autobiography,

> *Margaret worked hard and incessantly to sustain relationships, caring most about those in which different kinds of intimacy supported and enriched each other, the sharing of a fine meal, the wrestling of intense intellectual collaboration, the delights of lovemaking. . . . The intimacy to which Margaret and Ruth progressed after Margaret's completing of her degree became the model for one axis of her life while the other was defined in relation to the men she loved or married. (Bateson 1984:117)*

But Ruth Benedict died in 1948 and Margaret's marriage to Gregory Bateson was gradually dissolving in the same period. Gregory, more than anyone else, resented Margaret's management of his life and eventually left her, moving far away. That was not part of her life plan, and she grieved the loss for a long time. They remained friends, colleagues, and co-parents. For Margaret, intense conversations and collegial involvement were linked to lovemaking; this theme appears again and again in her writing.

In 1975 Margaret Mead wrote an article for her regular column in *Redbook* magazine and talked about bisexuality. She defined it and defended it without identifying herself publicly. The time has come, she says, to view this as normal. That a person is capable of loving members of both sexes should not be such a taboo subject nor such a strange phenomenon. She talks about cultures in which boys or girls go through a stage of relating almost exclusively with each other. They fall in love and have deep physical attractions. She spoke of times in history when people experimented with a great variety of personal relations in politics, art, music, drama, and intellectual projects, crossing barriers of race, sex, and age.

> *Changing traditional attitudes toward homosexuality is in itself a mind-expanding experience for most people. But we shall not really succeed in discarding the strait jacket of our cultural beliefs about sexual choice if we fail to come to terms with the well-documented, normal human capacity to love members of both sexes. . . . What is new is not bisexuality, but rather the widening of our awareness and acceptance of human capacities for sexual love. (Mead 1975:30)*

When Margaret married Reo (a jealous and straitlaced type) and went into the field for two years, her physical relationship with Ruth ended. But the separation of marriage and travel did not alter their intellectual intimacy. Theirs was a spiritually permanent relationship. Margaret, however, cared about the consequences of living openly with a women and desired to protect her public image and professional position. She might see herself as marginal or a misfit, but she never intended to become a social outcast.

For Ruth, however, her relationship to Margaret was the touchstone of her life. From the start of their deepest friendship until the end of her life, Benedict was what she called "a woman-loving woman." In the early 1930s, Ruth Benedict separated from her husband and found the first of two women who lived with her and shared her life and spiritual sensitivities until her death in 1948. Benedict's writings from that time on talked about redefining the categories of abnormal and normal; she spoke out strongly about the absurdities of treating homosexuality as an illness. She pointed out cultures that treated homosexuals as healers or leaders, or allowed alternative gender roles. She wrote about the Native American customs in which men wore women's clothes and did women's work. "Normal," in her view, was relative to the culture in which a person lived.

Her masterwork, *Patterns of Culture,* was an instant success. Some have called it "a paradigm shift," which means its radically new perspective forever changed the collective worldview. It replaced the absolute standards of morality and harsh value judgments of the nineteenth century with the enduring concept of **cultural relativism.** If cultural standards are relative to place, time, and people, then all of us can reevaluate the relationships between men and women in our own society. She made a very clear statement about biology: If women are weak, this is because we have learned to be or are expected to be, not because our biology has predetermined our weakness. She used her own field experiences in the American Southwest and those of her colleagues from around the world (including Reo Fortune's work on Dobu) to show how matrilineal cultures differ from the patrilineal model of Euro-American societies. The book and its radical message moved beyond anthropology and other intellectual circles into popular consciousness. At its core was a profound feminist vision that has become, in effect, the coin of the realm. Ordinary people, not just anthropologists, now talk about particular cultures and the patterns that give their lives meaning.

Her book caused serious arguments among anthropologists. Some felt that it threatened the status of the discipline as a science. Some said it was too humanistic, too fuzzy, too literary, too subjective, too simplistic. The book was, of course, one of the inspirations for Mead's *Sex and Temperament* and other studies that talked about the "approved personalities of each sex." Out of these two books came an entire school of anthropology, the study of culture and personality, as well as reaction against this kind of theory and research. But these are stories for another day.

Conclusion: Their Last Great Work

World War II and Margaret's child care responsibilities prevented more fieldwork after 1940. So Mead and Benedict gathered a host of dynamic colleagues to work on a project they called Research in Contemporary Cultures or "the study of culture at a distance." They formed a research team of scholars and citizens from many places in the world and did ethnography without the fieldwork. Well funded, they believed that their work had national significance and would be their contributions to winning the war and establishing the peace to follow. They developed innovative and interdisciplinary methods with an emphasis on complex modern civilizations grounded in cultural relativism and the culture and personality approach.

The project probably did not change the course of American anthropology nor did it enter popular awareness as their earlier works had done. Nonetheless, there are reasons to look at this venture today. Their project addresses questions that women in contemporary social movements regularly ask. If women organized and controlled the institutions that seem to control us, would the world be a different place? A better place? Do women structure people and activities differently than men do?

Mead and Benedict would answer yes. In their project there were no hierarchies, no pyramids of status, no ladders of success. There were only co-equal circles. Conveners took responsibility for getting groups together. The only titles they used marked types of responsibility, not types of prestige. Volunteer or paid, beginners or professionals, part-time or full-time, everyone worked together and gave away power to get results. They did not even have a central office. Ruth Benedict thought of this as a synergy in which the framework and goals of the group complemented and enhanced individuals and their contributions. They treated interpersonal relations, not formal structure, as the foundation of productivity. This meant that raising a family, being a parent, spouse, or lover, were rewarded; these activities were considered relevant to the project and accorded prestige! They talked about fostering diversity, accepting dissonance or diversification, and the creative use of chaos.

This project, as was everything Ruth Benedict touched in the last period of her life, was gently but firmly feminist. As president of the American Anthropological Association, she said that insight and intuition are as important to the nation as are the findings of science. She also believed that societies that honored maternal principles had greater peace and balance. In her publications she emphasized women's values and a woman's perspectives.

Both Mead and Benedict practiced warm ties of interdependence cemented with rituals, shared meals, all-night conversations, and physical intimacies. They contrasted these activities with war. War, they said, is not an innate or biological response of human beings. It does not result from some instinct, some gene, or some drive. It is not "natural for mankind." Instead war, for all its terrors or triumphs, is purely cultural. It is only another, albeit murderous, social institution. If this is true, they said, then human beings can change; we can choose to "study war no more." We could teach each other and raise our children to adopt other cultural and psychological means to avoid conflict and destruction. Naive by our standards, yes, but influential throughout the world and beyond their lives.

In the next chapter, we continue these themes as we look at how women in human cultures have marked our passages through biology and the life cycle.

So Many Books: Where Can I Start?

Start with autobiographies and biographies. The best ones on Ruth Benedict are by Margaret Caffrey, *Ruth Benedict: Stranger in This Land* (1989) and Judith Modell, *Ruth Benedict: Patterns of a Life* (1983). Margaret Mead wrote two biographies herself, *An Anthropologist at Work: The Writings of Ruth Benedict* (1959) and *Ruth Benedict* (1974). Margaret Mead's own autobiography is fascinating: *Blackberry Winter: My Earlier Years* (1972). So is her daughter's autobiography, which is combined with biographies of her famous parents: Mary Catherine Bateson, *With a Daughter's Eye: A Memoir of Margaret Mead and Gregory Bateson* (1984).

Esther Newton has tied together the themes in this chapter in her intellectual autobiography *Margaret Mead Made Me Gay: Personal Essays, Public Ideas* (2000). A cultural anthropologist, Newton's account moves from early feminism in the 1970s to queer theory in the 1990s, always centered in the sexual and erotic dimensions of fieldwork.

Chapter Three

Blood and Milk

Biocultural Markers in the Lives of Women

he Navajo People of the American Southwest tell of a spirit named Changing Woman. She is enigmatic; young at one time, old at another, and then young again. She is the mystery of reproduction and birth; sometimes she is the earth's mother. Changing Woman decrees fertility and sterility and has elaborate mythic ties to Sun, Moon, the Holy People and to the power of rainmaking.

The ceremony for Changing Woman at her first menstrual period was the first ever performed and the model for all to follow. The great epic tale about the creation of the world instructs the Navajo how to honor menstruating girls in a four-day ritual called Kinaaldá (Frisbie 1967). The Navajo, the largest group of Native Americans in the United States, practice matrilineal kinship, tracing descent through the female line. This may be one reason why they honor the biological beginnings of womanhood with a celebration.

Where Biology and Culture Meet in the Bodies of Women

In this chapter, we will discuss the intersections of biology, our life cycle as females, and the cultural constructions of these processes. The juxtaposition of biological processes with social imperatives, or **biocultural markers,** are the core of women's existence on the planet. It is probably here that woman's lives differ most substantially from men's lives. This is the arena where authorities (of whatever kind) place their most substantial controls on women. These transitions in women's lives are also rich, deep sources for strong feelings and spirituality. These passages link women across political boundaries and cultural differences.

We will start with first menstruation, or **menarche,** and the social constructions called **maidenhood.** Then we will go on to the end of menstruation and reproduction, **menopause,** and the social constructions of middle age. We will discuss the *life stream,* the potentials for conceptions, pregnancies, and births, and ways and reasons to understand, alter, or control this stream. The "life stream" concept helps us understand that arbitrary breaks and definitions for women's reproductive lives are cultural artifacts.

In most human societies, pregnancy and childbirth, if not menstruation and menopause, are treated as major life passages. They may be transformative experiences or a source of status or recognition. These moments represent a kind of growth or initiation that only women experience. Menarche as biological experience is universal, but social recognition takes many forms. Some are public; some are private. Some are controlling and others feel liberating. All human cultures recognize the biological meaning of menstruation. But not all human cultures honor the coming of age of young girls as do the Navajo.

Moonstruck Maidenhood: Taboo and Meaning

In recent years, many scholars (including a large number of women) have looked at menstruation, menstrual symbolism, and the diversity in cultural approaches to menstruation. New contributions of human reproductive biology have led us to question the received wisdom of the past or the Western medical–scientific belief systems. Cross-cultural studies demonstrate the enormous ranges of meanings attributed to this phenomenon.

In many times and places, menstrual blood has been considered dangerous and defiling; it could somehow contaminate or harm men, babies, plants, food, or the group as a whole. Menstruating females pollute others. So precautions, rules, and customs, or **menstrual taboos,** regulate contacts with such women.

Here are a few examples of events menstrual blood is said to cause: It stops fermentation in winemaking and cheesemaking; poisons men in intercourse; frightens away deer or other prey; attracts bears and other predators; cures medical conditions such as epilepsy, eye problems, open sores, intestinal parasites, rabies, or liver problems; or sours milk and causes rising bread to fall. In some cultures, it is believed that the possibility of menstrual blood on the ground makes it dangerous for men to walk on streets or paths, and certainly under balconies where women may be walking overhead.

> *Many menstrual taboos, rather than protecting society from a universally ascribed feminine evil, explicitly protect the perceived creative spirituality of menstruous women from the influence of others in a more neutral state, as well as protecting the latter in turn from the potent, positive spiritual force ascribed to such women. In other cultures menstrual customs, rather than subordinating women to men fearful of them, provide women with means of ensuring their own autonomy, influence, and social control. (Buckley and Gottlieb 1988:7)*

Positive myths and metaphors of life force, generativity, and fertility use menstrual blood as a symbol. Menstrual blood is said to be used in witchcraft or in the manufacture of various kinds of love charms and potions. Sometimes there is protection from evil in the uses of menstrual blood. What this shows most profoundly is that menstrual taboos are arbitrary, symbolic, and "culturally constructed." They make sense only in context. There is no cross-cultural evidence that menstruation is everywhere considered unclean, that women uniformly feel shame or pain, or that menstrual blood repulses men.

One popular interpretation of menstrual taboos is that they oppress women, and that the isolation of a woman during her period is evidence of her low status. The problem with such theories is that they rarely come from menstruating women themselves. It is men who have by and large defined menstruation as polluting. Ethnographers typically report what men have said about menstrual periods.

Anthropologists have been fascinated with a widespread type of taboo, the seclusion of women in "menstrual huts." Imagine how these customs would sound today if an early generation of anthropologists, missionaries, or travelers had labeled them "menstrual sanctuaries." Unfortunately, we have no detailed studies of the lived experiences of women themselves in these places, and the customs have largely disappeared. In 1931 anthropologist Ruth Underhill recorded the experiences of a Papago woman named Chona. Chona's story of her menstrual hut is told in the box on page 73.

Was the little house solitary confinement or rest and recreation? Some accounts suggest resentment, but others hint that women enjoyed a communal break from men and work. Most women can imagine taking out five or six socially sanctioned days a month to nap, meditate, talk, weave, or just mope around. In some times and places, women systematically used rules of seclusion for spiritual or economic enhancement, even for nonmarital love affairs. Sometimes there were ritual powers associated with female seclusion practices. Menstrual customs do not simply discriminate against or suppress women.

The time between the beginning of menstruation and actual adulthood (however defined) is important to the social lives of females. It is customary in anthropology to call this period *maidenhood*, or the culturally constructed period between menarche and marriage, motherhood, or other socially constructed adult statuses. Not one human society ignores this period. People in all human groups worry about and try to regulate female sexuality or the consequences of it during this time. Every single human society has cultural rules and customary strategies for controlling young girls at this time. At least they try.

Anthropologist Victoria Burbank went to Australia to see how adolescent girls in a community called Mangrove made this transition through maidenhood. This is one of the first ethnographic studies on teenagers since Margaret Mead went to Samoa.

> *At one time it appears that the Aborigines of Mangrove attempted to regulate female sexuality, as least as far as adolescent females were concerned, by marrying them off before they were sexually mature. Thus ideally, by the time a female was likely to be interested in sexual activity and could reproduce, she had been placed with a male that her community deemed an appropriate sexual partner and father of her children. (Burbank 1988:7)*

Today, the Australian government, supported by missionaries and social workers, have banned early marriages and infant betrothals. Now the teenage girls of Mangrove want to choose their own husbands. They often manage to exert personal choices by having sex with boyfriends and getting pregnant. The elders are predictably upset that young women no longer observe traditional laws about marriage.

In all societies, however, maidenhood is the time to learn and practice the social skills of adulthood. The length of maidenhood and the amount of restraints vary. If girls are engaged before birth and married before menarche, as in traditional Aboriginal Australia, they never have a maidenhood. In complex Western societies, girls may enter puberty at 12 or 13 and not marry until their late twenties (if ever). Others have babies before they finish high school. A teen's viewpoint of the regulation of sex and reproduction looks very different than a traditionalist's does. There is often amazing incongruity between teenagers' strategies for maximizing maidenhood and what adults want them to do. This is particularly true in complex societies such as ours.

Social controls are heaviest for females in maidenhood, regardless of how long this phase lasts, how much young girls conform or struggle, or which society we

Chona's Little House

When I was nearly as tall as my mother, that thing happened to me which happens to all our women though I do not know if it does to the whites; I never saw any signs. It is called menses. Girls are very dangerous at that time. If they touch a man's bow, or even look at it, that bow will not shoot any more. If they drink out of a man's bowl, it will make him sick. If they touch the man himself, he might fall down dead. . . . Our mothers watch us, and so mine knew when it came to me. We always had the Little House ready, over behind our own house. It was made of some branches stuck in the ground and tied together at the top, with greasewood thrown over them to make it shady.

Chona could crawl in her little house but she could not stand up. Her mother brought her food without meat or salt; her father gave her a sharpened stick to scratch her head with.

It was a hard time for us girls, such as the men have when they are being purified. Only they give us more to eat, because we are women. And they do not let us sit and wait for dreams. That is because we are women, too. Women must work.

So she walked far up the mountain to bring water and firewood back before daylight. The old woman who was supervising the work of ritual seclusion told her to work hard in order to find a good man to marry. Her mother came before dawn of the fourth day and made her bathe in icy cold water. Then her mother washed Chona's hair with soapweed fibers so it would never turn gray and cut it. In the month that followed, until the moon completed its rounds, the people in the village danced and sang and honored the girl who had been to the Little House for the first time.

Source: Ruth Underhill, *Papago Women* (1979), 57. Data collected from 1931 to 1933.

are talking about. Males, on the other hand, have no events that correspond to menarche and may experience a great deal of freedom after childhood.

Prime Time or Dirty Old Ladies

At a point in the middle of the females' lives, menstrual cycles end. Generally *middle age* is that phase defined by the universal physiological changes of *menopause*. So women are no longer bearing children or living with that potential. In some cultures, women in this stage are known as crones, matrons, or wise women. The changes that happen to women do not parallel or have counterparts in men; if they do, no one can discern them.

Research on women getting older is often fueled by pro-male and pro-youth biases. Ethnographers tend to ignore or take for granted the presence and activities of midlife females. But comparative research offers a better picture of this stage.

> *First and foremost, this is the time in which a woman enjoys her greatest power, status, and autonomy. In some cultures this increase in power and status is gradual; in others, there is a sharp break with earlier requirements for women's seclusion and deferential behavior. Second, both in societies that sharply oppress young women and those that have egalitarian gender ideologies, the freedom, prestige, and authority of women increases at middle age and comes closer to that of men than it did in earlier years. So, whether it is seen in relation to a woman's own life or in relation to the lives of men of her culture and generation, middle age is a woman's prime. (Sacks 1992:2)*

In many cultures, the restrictions that encumber younger women fall away. Typically, a woman no longer has to defer to a husband, a mother-in-law, or other senior relatives. She can travel, talk back, and be bawdy, outrageous, or independent. In some cases, she can safely take a lover; in other cases, she is relieved never to have sex again. She can drink too much, use forbidden language, or dress in a way that pleases her. The whole complex of obligations or taboos surrounding fertility (menstrual management, birth control, or the possibility of pregnancy) drops away. The displays of respect are now her dues as once she paid them.

Moreover, middle-aged women gain control over other people and have social or economic authority. Often women do administrative work, organizing and delegating to others. Good examples are the societies in which middle-aged women have serious power over food production, processing, preparation, preserving, and ultimately, over food distribution. Observers may overlook her authority and see only the work of young women, daughters-in-law, nieces, or daughters. In societies with strong rules of separation for males and females, middle-aged women pick brides for kinsmen and act as go-betweens for marriage arrangements. These tasks carry power and traditionally belong to menopausal females.

In some societies, the high status and subtle power of being a mother-in-law are the reward for middle-aged women. What a woman lacked in influence over her husband she can have over her grown son. In societies in which young girls are betrothed to older men, an aging woman may come into her personal and structural power at the time her tired husband is losing his. The best examples of structural autonomy for middle-aged women come from patriarchal groups, particularly those that have fairly strict separation for the sexes. Traditional China, India, and the Islamic Middle East are prime examples. Maidenhood and the early years of marriage are times when controls are the heaviest in such societies; these fall away as women age.

Better still, middle-aged women often aspire to leadership or achievement in politics, religion, or medicine. They often become midwives, healers, or holy women of many kinds. When a woman is pregnant, nursing, or managing husband and children, she predictably does not have either time or energy for ritual roles. So one of the virtues of middle-age is that female fertility is separated from female sexuality; this is the opposite of adolescence. New forms of sensuality or spirituality may emerge. This is why aging females are widely linked to occult or psychic powers.

Middle age is also a time of striking individuality. Women often develop novel personalities and find unpredicted paths. Some say midlife women become androgynous, sexually bimodal, or that women become men or like men—they say this time is "the Big Bang," the eruptive energies released when women no longer work as full-time parents and wives. Margaret Mead called it "menopausal zest."

Not all women, however, encounter this time as positive growth. The potential for and general increase in power may be destructive as well as sacred; for some it may be accompanied by severe depression. Women without the support of male kin, husbands, sons, or alternative forms of economic security predictably suffer.

Anthropologist Judith Brown asks, "Why don't we seem to experience positive changes for middle-aged women in the United States?" Although there are many entrepreneurial and energetic midlife women on the one hand, we know of many depressed or struggling women on the other. Her answer is that American life-passage for women is very different from that of other societies. We have few restrictions on ourselves in our early years, so there is less to look forward to. Adult children may live far away and our lives are no longer linked to each other for growth and survival. Other social institutions and specialists (mostly men) do the food growing, processing, or medical care and healing; it is difficult to develop a career in these fields at midlife. It is clear that the managerial roles open to midlife women in other societies are not available in most Western societies. Some observers suggest that the admiration of and quest for perpetual youth in American culture further reduce middle-aged women's options. As Judith Brown says, "The crosscultural evidence suggests that our society may be wasting the potential of its middle-aged women" (Kerns and Brown 1992:27).

New research on industrialized societies like Canada, Japan, the United States, or other places defies any conventional wisdom of middle-aged women as passive, predictable, sick, or empty-nesters. The cross-cultural data indicate enormous diversity, creative responses, and resistance to medical models or other social scripts. Many women refuse to accept the limitations of cultural codes, husbands, or biology.

The only universal experience of menopause is the end of periods. Feelings, emotions, bodily states, and specific symptoms like hot flashes are not universal. They are constructed from authority figures, other women, and assigned cultural meanings. Researcher Yewoubdar Beyene (1989) compared the experience of menopause for rural Mayan Indians of Yucatan Mexico and rural Greek women. The only symptom Mayan women reported was the end of periods; they did not report anything that resembled the "power surges" North American women emphasize. Indeed, they looked forward to a symptomless menopause they associated with youth and freedom. On the other hand, the Mayan women were poorly nourished, had poor overall health, and had spent their reproductive years in early and repeated pregnancies.

By contrast, the Greek women she studied married later, used birth control, and had fewer children and better health. They experienced some of the conditions we are told about—hot flashes, cold sweats, irritability, depression—but considered them normal. Anthropologist Margaret Lock (1993) compared middle age in Japan and North America. Japanese women are very sensitive to their body states, but they did not have the range of symptoms American women report. Lock notes that Japanese women are adopting the negative and biomedical views of menopausal pathologies imported from the West. In both cultures, the overriding issue appears to be contested viewpoints about what kind of people aging women are.

Desire and Control

Between menarche and menopause are about three decades of potential reproduction for women. So this section is about the ways women across human cultures modify or control the reproductive life stream. When we talk about women constructing our lives, one of the major plots or subplots in the drama is managing our fertility—whatever that may mean to an individual woman at a specific time.

Why do people want control over their bodies, the products of sex, and the life stream of reproduction? What are the major motivations? Ethnographic and historic literature as well as our personal experiences reveal the following reasons: Women want to get pregnant. Women don't want to get pregnant. Women want child spacing. Women and men want temporary or permanent sterility. Women want to stop a pregnancy from proceeding. Women want to relieve barrenness. Women and men want to enhance lovemaking or to cure impotence. Women and men want babies when they want them and no babies when they don't want them.

So how do humans achieve control over their bodies, the products of sex, and the life stream of reproduction? The ethnographic and historic sources are clear: Humans beings have widespread and ancient ways of contraception, abortion, and infanticide. These methods are universal. So the reigning principle or fact of life is: People want control over the life stream and they will do *anything* they have to to get it. Call this the Do Anything principle.

Techniques and Methods

I used to believe that birth control somehow started with the Pill and that my generation was the first to really know about contraception and good sex. I assumed that people in the past just had babies without thinking about it, perhaps acted unconsciously or unscientifically or just followed the rules. But now I know that contraception

> *is a social practice of much greater historical antiquity, greater cultural and geographical universality than commonly supposed even by medical and social historians. . . . Men and women have always longed for both fertility and sterility, each at its appointed time and in its chosen circumstances. (Himes 1970:xii)*

The first written accounts in human history mention methods of birth control. These include the earliest scriptures of the great religions, and the first law codes or medical texts. In ancient times, groups of men debated intensely about motivations and methods for controlling fertility. The anthropological literature is filled with references to these practices from all over the globe. In all of my fieldwork experiences, from islands in the Pacific to urban teenagers in the United States, and in all of my personal friendships or anthropology classes, I hear stories about what women do.

Women who have periods, pregnancies, miscarriages, and stillbirths, as well as the burdens of childlessness or too many children, talk to each other. We share information, stories, and trial-and-error methods, in secret if necessary. It is clear that so-called primitive peoples knew about and used contraceptive techniques. It is clear from all the ethnographic and historic accounts we have that human desire for controlling the life stream is universal; it transcends place or time. As historian John Riddle remarks of women and the desires for control in antiquity,

> *I suggest that their knowledge was primarily transmitted by a network of women working within the culture of their gender and that only occasionally was some of it learned by medical writers, almost all of whom were men. (Riddle 1992:16)*

Basic birth control methods involve modifying or avoiding vaginal intercourse by technique or timing, taking something by mouth, or using some means of blocking the "eye" of the cervix—or all of the above. These methods demonstrate a working, practical knowledge of reproductive physiology. That none of these techniques works perfectly or predictably is quite beside the point. They will work some of the time. All of them imply practical intelligence and the desire for control. There is also an abundance of what we think of as magical reasoning and unproven remedies. These cannot be dismissed as superstitious or unscientific; they indicate a search for and organization of knowledge and useful actions. Furthermore, many of the so-called old-wives remedies are effective; they are often only older versions of what any one can buy in a drugstore or pharmacy.

Recipes and Recommendations

Consider the numerous ways in which human beings have modified or avoided vaginal intercourse. One of the most consistently reported is "pulling out," withdrawal before ejaculation, or in its Latin form, **coitus interruptus.** One ancient rabbi recommended, "During the twenty-four months after the birth of a baby, the husband must thresh inside and winnow outside." Some teenagers in New Orleans whom I have interviewed think that they have invented this new, sophisticated, and safe technique of birth control.

Sexual variations such as oral and anal intercourse avoid completed vaginal intercourse. Times of tabooed intercourse are commonly reported after the birth of a baby or during sacred or ritual times. **Post-partum sex taboos,** the rules against having intercourse while nursing a child, might last two to five years. Abstinence, or sexual practices without vaginal intercourse, are highly effective contraceptives.

Knowing how to time intercourse to avoid the fertile period is also an ancient practice. All the historical, anthropological, and old-wives' literatures contain references to periodicity, that is, safe periods based on the moon and women's menstrual cycles. People sometimes have the timing wrong; in fact, the knowledge of ovulation and the "safe period" has been known for less than fifty years in American society. Many contemporary parents, for example, cannot tell their own kids when that period is. Many so-called primitive groups calculated it accurately.

Contraceptive recipes widely reported from cultures around the world involve ingredients found in most ordinary households. A common recipe recommends this: Cut a lemon in half, squeeze it, and insert it as a cervical cap. Lemon juice or citric acid is probably a more effective spermicide than lactic acid, the basis for our contemporary contraceptive jellies.

Similar recipes over the last seven thousand years recommend a wide variety of oily, astringent, acidic, gummy, or fibrous substances, alone or in combination. The bark and nuts of many kinds of trees provide tannic acid, an astringent vegetable compound that is a remarkably effective spermicide. Vinegar or acetic acid, yogurt, honey, salt, butter, and buttermilk are also reported from China, India, or the Middle East. The housewives of history made tampons or contraceptive suppositories out of lint, cotton, wool, silk, seaweed, or other common household fibers and absorbent substances. Any household spermicide could be used with a tampon or as a douche for washing out the vagina. These were relatively effective and easily available.

Sponges as a birth control device are noted regularly in historic accounts over the last six thousand years. Any housewife might have natural sponges in her possession. She simply soaked the sponge in an ordinary household spermicide and placed it against the eye of the cervix, where it absorbed semen, killed sperm, and prevented impregnation. In Europe, women acquired sponges as gifts at marriage from experienced older women or from lovers. In some periods, it was against the law to use them or even to own them. A sponge moistened with lemon juice is one of the most effective and ancient contraceptive measures in the entire range of indigenous or folk medicines.

Old recipes consistently mention alum (colorless, odorless, water-soluble crystals that have astringent or drying properties). Alum has dozens of domestic uses, such as pickling fruits and vegetables or dying cloth and tanning leather. Alum was a common household chemical for thousands of years and is often cited as useful in contraceptive sponges or applications to the vagina to cause the eye of the cervix to close before intercourse.

Counterparts of contemporary cervical caps or diaphragms abound in the literature. Women in northern Europe using softened beeswax pressed in a cap against the cervix. In the Corn Belt of the United States, where hogs are raised, lard was used the same way. Prostitutes in Japan placed a disk of oiled tissue paper made from bamboo against the eye of the cervix. There are many suggestive accounts of devices like buttons, stones, or gems placed in a woman's uterus; such items acted as IUDs, or intrauterine devices.

Through the ages, both women and men were advised to avoid simultaneous orgasms. Or women were counseled to jump up after intercourse, sneeze, or shake themselves assertively. It seems obvious to us that many techniques were based on magical reasoning, such as being very still during intercourse, holding one's breath, or avoiding orgasm. Expelling the semen by violent bodily movements such as jumping up and down, sneezing, and coughing are regularly reported; I have also heard these methods extolled among American teenagers.

There are literally thousands of accounts of women drinking teas or taking something by mouth to control fertility. These come from every continent and from all types of observers, travelers, missionaries, colonial health officials, ethnographers, and many others. The oral methods used throughout antiquity and in many places today operate as both **abortifacient** and **emmenagogue.** These terms refer to anything that establishes regular menstrual cycles. Oral methods work to "make the blood come down," as some women in Louisiana say. Women knew ways to prevent implantation or bring on a period late in coming. These may also end a pregnancy in its early stages. Under these circumstances, the line between birth control and abortion is blurry. What one drinks or eats achieves the desired result, that is, regular menstrual periods. Other teas or potions were chosen for their sterilizing properties or to help a woman conceive when she wanted to.

These data are confusing to those who perceive abrupt boundaries between preventing a pregnancy and ending a pregnancy, between wanting and not wanting a child. But historic and ethnographic accounts make no sharp distinctions between contraception and abortion.

In German folk medicine, teas of marjoram, parsley, or lavender are recommended for regular periods. Cherokee women desiring to remain sterile permanently were told to chew and swallow the roots of spotted cowbane for four consecutive days. Ancient Jewish rabbinic teachings speak of drinking a "cup of roots" to induce sterility. Arabic literature, some of the most extensive existing records, cited teas of sweet basil, weeping-willow leaves, pulp of pomegranates and alum, myrrh, rue, hellebore, or tampons impregnated with peppermint juice, pennyroyal, leek seeds, pepper, bindweed, and others.

Women in the Appalachian mountains of the United States and the Rajasthan state in India rely on the seeds of Queen Anne's lace, or the wild carrot plant, to keep from getting pregnant (Figure 3.1). Hippocrates, another Greek physician, swore by these seeds, which, taken orally, establish a regular menstrual cycle. Pennyroyal is another plant widely cited as an abortifacient among women in the United States. Pomegranate, myrrh, and the plant, Artemisia, named after Artemis, goddess and protector of childbirth, are also antifertility potions. Rue prepared as a tea is a traditional abortifacient and emmenagogue in many places in Latin America (Browner and Ortiz de Montellano 1986; Newman 1985; Riddle 1992).

All of the literature contains reasons or motivations people have for controlling fertility. The grounds include a woman's poor health, repeated miscarriages or stillbirths, or her physical inability to care for a baby. Girls of tender years, women of advanced years, or those whose marriages are not on firm emotional or financial grounds are candidates for contraception. See the box on page 81 for anthropologist Hortense Powdermaker's discussion of the island of Lesu.

Many treatments mentioned are used with affirmations, prayers, and chants. They are often related to love potions or involve rituals of cleansing. Frequently, the same means are used to attract and keep a lover as to attract and keep a baby.

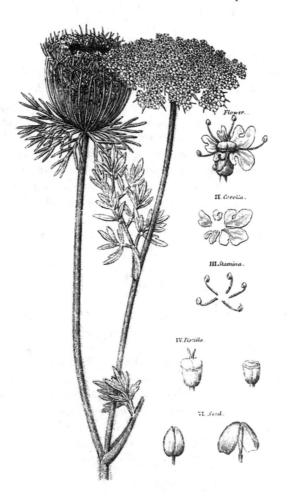

Figure 3.1
At many times and in many places, women chewed up or brewed the seeds of Queen Anne's Lace, the wild carrot plant, to prevent or end their pregnancies.

Some of the techniques may have been more available to privileged women than to poorer women. Nonetheless, even the simplest kitchens or workrooms had the basic ingredients.

These methods for controlling the life stream are not magic, superstition, or folklore. To the contrary, they argue for advanced knowledge of the properties of plants, for clever herbal gardens, and for practical gathering in marshes, forests, and fields. These methods speak of experimentation and knowledge transmitted verbally from generation to generation, as easily lost as painfully gained. Even so-called folk beliefs or old-wives' tales illustrate knowledge and a desire for understanding and autonomy. It is entirely possible that in many places and many periods in the past, women knew more than they are credited with or than we know today.

If you think some of these recipes sound uncomfortable, tricky, or dangerous, then concentrate on this principle: "Women will do *anything*." Think about using so-called modern techniques. Or think about the alternatives.

We must carefully note that all the techniques had counterparts for those who had not conceived. The literature on control is just as much about wanting babies as it is for not wanting babies.

Women of Lesu, Melanesia

Fear of pain at birth is one reason for not wanting a child, and one woman who had had one child told me that she then ate the sterility leaves because she did not want to go through the birth pains again. Several other women told me they did not want children because it interfered with their dancing, which forms so large a part of ritual life, and which they so thoroughly enjoy. Still another reason advanced was that it interfered with their having sexual relations. No woman would ever admit this as her own reason, but some of them gave it to me as the motive for other women not wishing children. These were the only three reasons for not desiring children that I was able to secure, and it must be remembered that these women were in the minority. The larger number of women said that they had never eaten sterility or abortive leaves, and had no desire to. As has already been said, when a child is born nothing could exceed the affectionate care bestowed on an infant by his mother and the whole family. There are thus the two contradictory sentiments, desire for and rejection of motherhood existing side by side in the same society.

Source: Hortense Powdermaker, *Life in Lesu* (1933), 243. Collected in field trips, 1929–1930.

Some women in every human culture know about being barren. If the only route to adulthood, social status, physical safety, or personal worth is by having children, these are truly women who will try anything. Couples without children subjected themselves to tests, trials, or divinations to find the source of their infertility and thus a cure. The variety of ways to create a much-desired pregnancy involves the same use of plants, fruits, concoctions, potions, and rituals as preventing a pregnancy does.

Pilgrims for Pregnancy

On her first fieldwork trip to Egypt, anthropologist Marcia Inhorn was neither married nor a mother. Only gradually did she begin to hear and understand that having no babies was a cultural calamity for a woman. Ironically, when she returned to learn more about infertility, she was both married and concerned about her own ability to conceive and bear children.

Inhorn makes a powerful case that biological parenthood is paramount for the Egyptian women she talked with for a host of practical, personal, religious, political, and marital reasons.

> *In a society where the patriarchal fertility mandate is emphatic, the social and psychological consequences of "missing motherhood"—of being a woman unable to deliver a child for her husband, family, affines, community, faity, nation, and not inconsequentially, herself—are nothing if not profound. (Inhorn 1996:1)*

She will be called "Mother of the Missing One." She will be stigmatized on three fronts: poor, female, and barren.

Forget adoption, child substitutes, or reframing the issue. For poor husbands, women's work outside their homes is viewed as dangerous and degrading, shaming a hard-working husband. Without children, depression, loneliness, isolation, and despair mark women's lives. Infertile women face threats of divorce, becoming a co-wife in a polygynous marriage, and community ostracism. Senior women in her husband's family, her mother-in-law and sister-in-law, may make her life miserable. Islamic emphasis on motherhood as women's only social role poses a powerful threat to childless women. But doctors in the colonial, Western-biomedicine hospitals concentrate obsessively on overpopulation, family planning, and birth control. They have no real interest in solving infertility.

The women Inhorn met truly fit our definition of "try everything"—from colonially imposed Western biomedicine to practitioners of indigenous medicine. Often they do both simultaneously. They become pilgrims, making the "do anything" journeys for fertility. There are

> *many sojourners, women searching for a solution to their unacceptable childlessness in a world filled with fertile others. Whether or not they solve their problem (and, in this book, few do), many of these women manifest a heroic quality in their refusal to give up on their costly, time-*

*consuming, often tortuous quests for conception; in their resilience fol-
lowing sickening therapeutic regiments; in their sacrificing of meaningful
possessions, bodily integrity, and emotional well-being in their determination to be cured; and in their bravery in confronting and learning to cope
with the problematic social world of discontented husbands, adversarial
in-laws, suspicious neighbors, fraudulent healers, and supercilious
physcians. That they survive multiple encounters of an overtly taxing
nature is a testament not only to their suffering, but to their courage and
to their unceasing hope. (Inhorn 1994:29)*

For these poor Egyptian women, children are their careers. One is only a full
person when one is a parent. Even more profoundly, one cannot hope for immortal life. Women say, "Husbands are just for the night; children are for the
days." Childlessness is compared to food without any salt or pepper, empty tast-
ing. Children are the taste, sound, smell, and light—the senses—of a life worth living. But most of these pilgrims will never find them on their painful journeys.

Abortion

Many people are surprised to learn how universal abortion has been through
human history. The sense I have from studying the historic and anthropological literature is that "they" (society, religion, husband, or family) usually want some kind
of control. At the same time, "she" (a pregnant female) also wants control.
Sometimes these motivations and desires coincide. Sometimes they do not. The alternatives and strategies at this point are the material of high drama. "They" could
lock her up, marry her off at gunpoint, kill her or the baby, give the baby away, or
threaten her with exile, stigma, or eternal damnation. "She" could commit suicide,
do something in secret, lie, run away, conform, get married, or give the baby away.

On the island of Pohnpei in Micronesia, where I once did fieldwork, a pregnant
woman may decide to have an abortion. She may feel that she is too young, having too much fun, and not yet ready to be a mother. Her friends and relatives
might say, you should give the baby to us. Adoption on this island, as in much of
the Pacific, is common and carries no stigma for women. Indeed, it is regarded as
a positive contribution to others who do not have the babies they desire. In the
past, women used abdominal massage to end a pregnancy. The procedure is effective although painful. Such decisions were accepted with regret; they were
probably rare.

Anthropologist George Devereaux examined ethnographies for 400 preindustrial societies (1976). Each of the 400 groups knew about or practiced abortion in
some form. There were many techniques for abortion reported: hard work, lifting
or carrying heavy objects, climbing, jumping, starving, shaking a woman, or placing hot things on her abdomen or somehow causing bleeding. Massage or pressure
through the abdominal wall is reliably reported from a number of groups, and
from all evidence is safe although uncomfortable. This may include leaning on
hard objects, rolling around, constricting or squeezing the abdomen, or being
pulled through a forked tree. The types of instruments that can be introduced into

the vagina are limited only by imagination. Knitting needles or coat hangers have their sharp equivalents in many if not most human cultures.

Here again is the consistent blurring of categories or interventions along the life stream. In some societies, it is said that hard, repetitive work and lifting or carrying heavy burdens can bring on a miscarriage, a spontaneous abortion. Yet doing such work is normal for millions of women. What is planned? What is unavoidable but welcomed? It is often difficult to tell the difference between a miscarriage and an abortion. Women may believe an abortion attempt has ended a pregnancy never established.

There are literally thousands of reports of effective teas or potions from all over the world (Newman 1985; Himes 1970). Herbal remedies and a broad pharmacopeia are too commonly mentioned to be discounted. They are forerunners of birth control pills, RU 486, and the morning-after pills. Sometimes these pharmaceuticals "make the blood come down"; sometimes they prevent pregnancy in other ways; and sometimes they temporarily or permanently prevent pregnancy. Rates of miscarriages (or spontaneous abortions) are high at various times, at various places, and for certain women. Because of this, we may give more credit or place more hope in these methods than they deserve. Nonetheless, oral abortifacients and contraceptives are probably the oldest and most widespread of all the techniques for desire and control.

Earlier descriptive studies on traditional societies documented the extensive knowledge of fertility regulation in women's lives across cultures. Studies, such as those collected by anthropologist Barbara Rylko-Bauer (1996), offer more complex analyses and place such knowledge and decision making about abortion into broader sociocultural contexts and woman-centered viewpoints. She shows how both pregnancy prevention and abortion fit into the ethnomedical system of beliefs and practices, for example, the regular flow of bodily substances. Delayed menses may be a pregnancy or a blockage. Women can and do use many multipurpose substances to regulate their menstral flows. This is a degree of both control over the life stream and health-seeking behavior in situations of diminished autonomy. The same ambiguities may exist between ideologies and practices. A woman may be well aware of the dangers or the legal and social consequences of having an abortion. She may believe it is immoral or unethical. But the social and economic realities of daily life, her obligations to kin, family, and children already born, call out a justification for abortion that fits these unalterable conditions.

Above all, options for women anywhere in the world are shaped by large-scale economic and political forces beyond her control. Governments, states, religions, and other powers define ideologies about "family," gender, sexuality, and reproduction, and determine the availability of contraception, family planning, or other educational–medical services surrounding reproduction.

Infanticide and Social Birth

This is a hard topic. Most of us condemn the killing of infants and children as morally wrong or as acts done by people not like us. But scholars know that human infanticide is widely practiced, in many places, in many periods of time, by many people for many reasons. Infanticide seems to occur primarily when it aids one parent, both parents, or other children to survive better, or where the infant itself has little chance of survival.

Look at the legends about Oedipus Rex, Moses, and Romulus and Remus; they were male babies abandoned to die. Greeks in classical times, as have other human societies, did away with weak, deformed, or unwanted children. People in other societies killed one or both twins, babies born too close to another sibling, or one born in some unusual manner, for example, under the wrong zodiac sign. Margaret Mead says the Arapesh sometimes resorted to infanticide if food were scarce, if there were several children, or if the father had died.

In China, Japan, India, and other places, girls were killed, "thinned out" like rice fields. In Europe, in various periods and places, dead newborns were a common sight floating down rivers or left in parks. Orphanages were founded to take in these children. Newborn babies, alive or dead, are found abandoned in cities all over the world; newspapers regularly print such stories.

Parents in hunting–gathering societies used infanticide to space children and to adjust a woman's workloads. We know that overpopulation, famine, or other disasters, and power politics may require the sacrifice of selected children. Infanticide appears to be more common when the mother is very young or when, like the old woman in the shoe, "she had so many children she didn't know what to do." This does not mean it is casual or painless.

Anthropologists regard infanticide as a way to alter the reproductive stream at a point before the infant or child has the status of a real person, however that is locally defined.

> In most societies, including Christian societies, personhood is conferred on infants via birth ceremonies. Human infants do not become legal entities or social beings until some adult or group of adults (e.g., parents, godparents, kinsmen, religious practitioners) have named, purified and/or blessed them in a rite that says "This child belongs to us." By this ceremony adults admit infants into their group and assume the responsibility of supporting and raising the babies they claim as their own. (Minturn 1989:93)

So **social birth** is the event, ceremony, ritual, or marked point in time when an infant child takes on or is given a cultural identity. This is always different from biological birth. The deaths of weak, illegitimate, excess, deformed, and unwanted infants are not defined as murder when the infants have not yet been born into a social world.

Once again, the boundaries are not as we in the West have defined them. The point at which life begins has many cultural definitions. Some people in the world believe that birth is the beginning of regular life. Others say that conception is the marker; yet others refer to some point in the pregnancy. In some cultures, life begins only when the infant is formally named or ritually incorporated. In some places, life is said to begin only after the first day, the first week, the first month, or the first year—depending on the culture. Before the child is accepted as a full member of the society, infanticide is possible. After a commitment, it is not. Seen in this light, it is safe to say that people in some cultures regard infanticide as an abortion late in the reproductive stream. The social statuses of fetuses, newborns, and young children are always and everywhere locked to broad social contexts.

> *This observation is not new: a burgeoning literature illuminates the links between abortion, childrearing, women's status, social stratification, child welfare, ethnic and gender discrimination, and changing relations between the sexes. The process through which young human lives come to be valued is derived in part from these factors, but personhood is also a function of cultural divisions in the life cycle, attitudes toward death, the social organization of descent and inheritance, and social systems of authority and achievement. (Morgan 1989:97)*

Who makes the decision? Birth attendants may decide in cases of physical or mental defects in the infant or when something is drastically wrong with the mother. Very often the family decides; but in the majority of cases, the father or the mother of the infant decides.

It is more common to throw away girl babies. Perhaps their families believe it is too expensive to raise them and give them a dowry or wedding. Perhaps the investment in nursing and feeding them would be better spent on older children or sons that might follow. Doing away with daughters may be done in such a covert fashion that the patterns show up only in statistics from the entire population. In many countries of the world, there is an excess of female infant mortality over male; that means that noticeably more females die in infancy and childhood than do males.

Anthropologists have also studied infanticide resulting from aggressive neglect, abuse, or circumstances in which women have inadequate support from partners, family, or other sources. In many cases, parents favor some children over others. Where resources are inadequate, one child may be neglected or parents may fail to invest time, attention, medical care, or other resources in a child. Some children just "fail to thrive" or "lack the will to fight." Their parents say, "She is not for this world," or "He's just another angel baby gone to heaven." This lack of investment in children is common. Although outright infanticide is outlawed in most of the world, scholars tell us that neglect and abuse are abundant. As anthropologist Susan Scrimshaw notes:

> *Perhaps the greatest tragedy of all in today's world is that modern contraceptives and even induced abortion have not sufficiently replaced infanticide as a means of fertility control. Further, infanticide has been superseded in many societies by abandonment, neglect, and differential care rather than methods of fertility control less costly in terms of lives and resources. . . . Ironically, the decline of infanticide may result in more suffering for older infants and children, and even adults, than when an infant's fate, be it life or death, was determined swiftly, early and irrevocably. (Scrimshaw 1984:462)*

Some families are unable or unwilling to offer biological support and emotional support to children. Sometimes this kills as effectively, although more slowly, as exposure of infants to wild animals or numbing cold.

The beginnings and the ends of the life stream, the physical sensations and the emotions women experience are culturally rather than biologically defined. This is important. People in human cultures may reckon the beginning of pregnancy from ovulation, which provides the egg; from intercourse, which provides the sperm; from conception, which unites them; or from implantation, which gives the united parts a habitat. Women in many cultures reckon the beginning of pregnancy from a missed period, from the first felt movement, or from the moment they become aware of a spirit or ghost entering their bodies.

Comparative Childbirth

Childbirth, too, is far more than a physiological or biological event, far more than just a rite of passage for a woman or a day for a child to celebrate. Cultural values become awesomely visible at each human birth. Giving birth, however, is not just reproduction; it is *social production*. That means that each act of giving birth reproduces the society, the belief systems, and all the unspoken but powerful connections within that culture. Each birth carries the message: "This event shows how we do things in this culture and what we really believe about life and about each other."

Women throughout all human history and prehistory typically gave birth to babies in their own domestic surroundings and with the help of their friends, relatives, or other women with special experience and knowledge. This is a very important fact of life, but easy to forget. Most of us have not participated in such a birth and tend to project contemporary technologies, hospitals, and personal issues onto other cultures.

The first anthropologist to describe human births in cross-cultural perspective was Brigitte Jordan. The following summary of births she witnessed in Mayan families living in Yucatan, Mexico, comes from her pioneering fieldwork on childbirth in four cultures. The midwife in this example is named Doña Juana; she is about sixty years old and the widowed head of an extended matrifocal household. The woman she aids in delivery is characteristic of the women Jordan and her colleague observed. The key point of this account is to see it as a social event, not a medical event.

Midwife and Mother

A pregnant woman in Yucatan sees her **midwife** several times during the pregnancy. They talk at length about her reproductive history, attitudes about birth, and who shall attend and assist. The midwife assesses her patient. What will be her attitude toward pain? Would she like traditional practices like prayers or burning rosemary to ward off evil spirits? The midwife gives the pregnant woman soothing massages, comforting touches, and helpful advice in the form of case histories and stories. Together they determine the approximate date of delivery.

Massage is the central event of the prenatal visit. As the midwife spreads oil on the woman's abdomen and massages her back, they chat and gossip. The midwife probes to feel the position of the baby's head; she explains why she is doing deep massage. Doña Juana, like many midwives around the world, believes that pregnancy is a normal state of things; she does not treat the mother-to-be as sick or her condition as a pathology.

Like many midwives around the world, Doña Juana does not do vaginal examinations; she believes that midwives should keep hands and everything else out of the birth canal. She is, however, an expert at shifting a baby that is not lying head-down. Sometimes a baby rests in a bottoms-down position (breech) or on its side (transverse). In a method called external cephalic inversion, a midwife can turn the baby with strong even pressure on the mother's abdomen. Then the infant's head points down. This procedure averts a Caesarean section, a hospital birth, a protracted labor, or a dead baby, all undesirable outcomes for Mayan families.

A Mayan woman's first birth is at her mother's compound; the rest are in her own home. An area in the sleeping part of the compound is screened off and the other household activities go on about the birth scene. When someone comes to tell Doña Juana that a labor is underway, she grabs her equipment. Doña Juana greets the family and checks the mother, her contractions, feelings, and special needs. She gives her a massage; this feels good to the laboring woman and yields important information for the midwife about the position of the baby.

The midwife shows the laboring mother how to use a birthing chair, how to hold on to a rope, how to twine her arms around a husband's neck, and how to push hard when the time comes. Doña Juana says that every woman must find her own style. The midwife's function is only to help. In the later stages of labor, the woman stretches crosswise on the hammock. At the end, she decides her position.

Women in labor are entitled to the support of their husbands, their mothers, and often other women summoned to the birth, such as sisters, sisters-in-law, mothers-in-law, good friends, or godmothers. The women run errands, cheer on, scold, and offer physical as well as emotional support to the about-to-be-delivered woman. In Yucatan a husband is said to experience both the birth and his wife's pain rather than merely witnessing it. This is believed to lead him to *cuidar,* to care for, his wife after the birth. The verb is also a local euphemism for spacing the arrival of babies by abstinence or withdrawal.

A trusted person supports the woman's body and helps her push at the high point of contractions. Another person may rub her abdomen, legs, or back. If the labor slows down, the midwife may give the woman a raw egg to swallow; the vomiting that results usually enhances contractions. Someone may blow on her head to give strength through long contractions or help hold her nose and mouth shut for greater pressure during the pushes. Those in attendance chant with rhythm and words that rise and fall in time to the contractions. This is called "birth talk."

Having a baby is clearly regarded as work. The mother is always expected to do her part, though she may become discouraged, even some- what panicked. Although the expectation is of a quick, fairly easy birth, at least some pain is recognized as a normal part of bearing a child. It figures in the birth stories that have been told all along, preparing the mother for what is to come. Consequently, she receives little sympathy if she complains. (Jordan 1993:38)

A laboring woman may be reminded that the baby is at the center of the pain and that pushing hard is simply her job at that time. When the baby is "at the door" (its head begins to emerge), the midwife grasps it firmly. When the body emerges, she places the baby on the mother's lap. She announces its gender and watches until the umbilical cord is emptied of blood. Generally, she waits until the placenta is delivered completely before cutting the cord. The women sponge off the mother and help her rest comfortably back lengthwise in her hammock.

The midwife and birth attendants cauterize the stump of the umbilical cord with a candle flame. They bathe, dress, diaper, and swaddle the baby tightly. They say swaddling makes its legs straight and offers security like its home in the womb. Doña Juana will pierce the ears of a newborn girl for earrings. Because the mother is resting safely and the baby looks fine, the mood of the household is light. Their talk turns to practical matters, and those who are hungry will eat.

The period immediately after a birth is regarded in every human culture as lim- inal, suspended, or potentially dangerous. It is certainly not an ordinary time. As a result, humans customarily do things that honor the event and avert the dangers, however these are defined. In Yucatan, spirits from the bush may bring harm to the mother and infant so they remain inside and take various precautions to keep the spirits at bay. The midwife checks every day or so; she sponges off the baby with warm water or oil and examines its navel, puts more alcohol on it to prevent the infant's illness or the death that can result from improper care of the stump.

Although she does not need to examine the mother, the midwife gives advice about nursing, especially to a first-time mother. Mayan mothers begin nursing minutes after their babies' births and nurse whenever the babies fret. Babies are held most of the time, first by their mothers and then by other family members. Bottle-feeding has increased in Yucatan, as in most places in the world, but is gen- erally a supplement rather than a replacement for the breast. On the twentieth day, the midwife gives the mother another massage and finishes it by binding her abdomen tightly with a long cotton cloth. The new mother can return to work.

More Facts of Life-Giving

The birth just described is a far more generic human and female experience than are technologically assisted hospital births in the United States. It testifies more to the norm or to modal events than anything most of us know or that doctors are taught in medical schools. So what can we conclude?

Fact of life: Birth practices are rigidly shaped. People have strong opinions about what should go on and what that means. We believe that certain practices are absolutely right; furthermore, the mother and baby are in danger if they are not done in the prescribed manner.

> *It is therefore difficult to separate, within any given cultural setting, what is physiological necessity and what is social production. Doña Juana, for example, considers breaking the membranes dangerous and unnatural, while American obstetricians find this practice useful and routinely advisable in light of their conceptions of the physiology of the birth process. (Jordan 1993:45)*

Women who help others in birth are another fact of life. In all human cultures, we find birth attendants and support systems. The cross-cultural record is very clear; we cannot overestimate the benefits of caring human companionship during labor. There are specialists, like midwives or physicians, and nonspecialists, such as the laboring woman's family or friends. Sometimes helpers are called **doulas**, a Greek word meaning "a woman who serves women." A doula typically provides emotional support and expert guidance from mid-pregnancy through delivery and the adjustments afterward. The empathy, collaboration, active coparticipation, or colaboring of other women is believed in most human cultures to contribute to the safety and the special qualities of giving birth. A woman who has helped to birth a baby may be more willing to care for that child if something happens to its mother. Attending a woman through this sacred, liminal, scary, and suspended time probably helps her develop skills as a mother and contributes to her survival.

Another fact of life: Most of the humans who ever lived on this planet were born in a place we would call "at home." Where a birth takes place determines whether the woman can walk around during labor, can choose her own positions, can select the people present, can be with her infant at will, or whether professionals will make these decisions for her. The technology of birth for our species has involved only ordinary items found in any household. A sharp instrument to cut the umbilical cord has been the most important article of a midwife's kit throughout human history. Soft cloth or absorbent fibers are useful for cleaning. I point these facts out at some length because most readers of this book tend to think that hospital births are the normal thing, the safest thing, the best thing, the status thing, or the progressive thing to do.

So we could ask: What is the prevailing attitude about labor in any given culture? Is it "wait and see" or "Let's get this show on the road"? Does labor ebb and flow like the tides? If so, one does not hurry it. Or does labor progress in a mechanical momentum? If so, then failure to progress on a schedule is grounds for intervention. Who offers information, when, and what kind? How is pain defined? What do people really mean when they say "natural"? Is pain in childbirth decreed by some ancestral god; is it women's lot in life? Is pain avoidable? For example, American women seem to feel quite strongly about pain: in repeated studies, they opt for reducing pain to the point of not feeling it at all while remaining as conscious as medication permits (Jordan 1993:80).

Who owns a birth? Who has the power to make key decisions? Who is delivering the baby: the laboring mother or the medical specialist? The issue of birth position is probably the best example of how these questions get answered. For assorted reasons, the standard practice in American childbirth is the **lithotomy position:** The woman lies on her back with her legs in the air. Now that anthropologists have looked seriously at birthing practices around the world, we know that this particular position, almost an article of religious faith, is known only in the United States and in a few countries to which we have exported our medical standards. Laboring women do not seem to choose this position spontaneously. Combinations of lying down and squatting, sitting–lying down on one side or the other, or semi-sitting with support of a helper or chair, are far more common. Some studies show that walking around and sitting up, changing postures frequently, and moving from one side to the other, eases and shortens labor and the passage of the baby through the birth canal. But the problems and disadvantages of the lithotomy position have not altered its prevalence. This peculiar cultural interpretation of how women give birth works against gravity, makes pushing much harder, and thus may result in irregular, weaker, less frequent contractions. The lithotomy position is most advantageous for the professional birth attendants and their machinery.

In the United States, a typical birth is in a hospital attended by a physician and other paid professionals whom the mother may or may not have met. The orientation is professional rather than personal, and involves increasing amounts of disputed and rather mysterious technology. The woman is a patient who signs over most of the decision-making power to hospital personnel. The physician in charge is concerned, among other things, about administering drugs for pain relief or for other conditions and the hospital policies that relate to deliveries. There is a sharp tendency to think of the patient as "being delivered" rather than as her doing the work of giving birth, and another tendency to think of pregnancy and birth as an illness, to make it a curable pathology. Anthropologists call this the **medicalization of childbirth.**

This is not to say that Mayan practices are automatically better, somehow more "natural," or should be imitated by others. It is to say, however, that they express the values of social production within that culture. Furthermore, they provide a sharp contrast to technologically assisted hospital births in other cultures.

Many anthropologists believe that being a midwife is the world's oldest job, craft, or professional specialization. We are not surprised that metaphors about birth and rebirth are profoundly part of mythology, spiritualism, and religious or healing practices everywhere in the world.

Motherhood and Fetal Subjects

In the time since the Supreme Court's decision on women's privacy rights in abortion, *Roe v. Wade,* there has been increasing public interest in the fetus, partly as a result of anti-abortion organizing and partly as a result of developments in medicine and technology. We see images, real or manipulated, on roadside billboards and on videotapes circulated among a pregnant woman's family and friends. Over the past several decades, there has been an explosion of interest in genetics and genetic inheritance within both the research community and the mass media. The science of genetics now forecasts great advances in alleviating disease and prolonging human life, but each new development challenges the definitions of family and kinship. Some technologies are part of an emerging reproductive service industry in which traditional, heterosexual reproductive activities have become both professionalized and commercialized. In vitro fertilization, transnational adoption, surrogacy, assisted conception, prenatal screening, visualization and imaging technologies, and frozen embryos offer new ways to be pregnant, to be a mother, and to be a parent. At the same time, complex technologies make it possible to see and image, or imagine, the fetus growing in a woman's body. Hence, fetuses have begun to have *social personhood*. We can know their gender, name them, test them for diseases, treat them for some, and make life-altering decisions about their identities and place within the larger social world.

High-profile controversies rage about such topics as cloning, orphaned embryos, the human genome project, artificial life forms, and organisms with the genes of different species, to name only a few. It is increasingly difficult in North America to argue that reproductive acts are private, domestic, or "merely biological" phenomena that have little to do with politics, national elections, science, health policies, or the law. Biotechnologies have unseated many deeply rooted assumptions about what is "natural," how kinship works, and how much control women have. Public debates challenge the notion of "natural" and offer many "motherhoods." The convergence of conception management and the intensification of interventions in the life stream challenge traditional definitions of family, disability, parenting, kin connections, and inheritance, as well as philosophical views of nature, humanity, morality, the future, and even life itself. It forces women and men to confront questions of child custody, fosterage, adoption, nationality, property, patrimony, gay parenting, and parenting rights.

I am suggesting that reproduction is increasingly subject to a wide range of professional and technological interventions, all of which arouse intense public interest, confront women with the "do anything" principle, and elevate fetuses to the status of persons. The emergence of the *fetal subject* offers increasing moral significance to fetuses in the middle of the dialogue about the agency or control women ought or ought not to have over their pregnancies, bodies, and reproduction. Sometimes, the social organization of reproduction in the United States seems to erase women from the picture. Fetuses become "natural" beings with more social identities than their mothers who are merely "maternal environments." This has consequences. A society that attributes special person qualities to fetuses is more inclined to hold women responsible for protecting them. On the other hand, women's chronically devalued social position may bar them from complying with ever-expanding maternal duties.

> *Fetuses are special, innocent, possessed of personable qualities, and thus need maternal protection. Yet women contravene the canons of good, responsible sexual/reproductive behavior and the truths of biology, and so can't be trusted to exhibit the sort of individual responsibility requisite to harmonious fetal life. Hence, fetuses need to be protected from the women upon whom they depend. (Morgan and Michaels 1999:4)*

In the *prenatal paradox,* the fetus is socially constructed more and more as a consumer commodity but equally as a person. A pregnancy is a tentative or negotiable condition, yet technologies like ultrasound allow, even encourage, unconditional "bonding" of parents with baby. "Advances" in reproductive technology may create a new triangle: women, fetuses, and the health care workers who manage the new technologies. Sometimes women as mothers may "disappear" in these new technologies as the social life of fetuses becomes the center of reproductive politics.

The **medicalization of reproduction** and emergence of new reproductive technologies bring up old questions: When is a fetus a social person? How much control do women have over their bodies? How much should they have? In the United States in particular, the abortion debate partly centers on the relationship of the morality of abortion to the status of the fetus.

To Test or Not to Test? A Case Study

In 1983, anthropologist Rayna Rapp underwent amniocentesis during her first pregnancy. In this procedure, which is often recommended for older, first-time mothers or women in some "at risk" category, a doctor withdraws some amniotic fluid and laboratory technicians test it for a series of specific genetic or congenital problems. Genetic counselors explain the procedure to the woman and discuss the options the woman has: She can refuse to take the test. She can have an abortion if the test is "positive," that is, if the fetus will, in all probability, be born with a physical or intellectual disability that will affect not only his or her life chances, but also the character of family life and/or the mother's future. In Rapp's case, the positive results showed that the baby had Down syndrome. She and her husband decided to seek an abortion.

In the face of such a painful decision about a much-desired, planned-for baby, Rapp began to interview pregnant women and their supporters who used or refused the test: genetic counselors, geneticists, laboratory diagnosticians, and others involved in the provision of the related health care services; parents of children with some of the same disabilities that can now be diagnosed prenatally; and professionals who work with those children. She followed a diverse group of New York women through counseling and their decisions to use or refuse amniocentesis. Then Rapp visited the homes of women who had the test during the waiting period before the test results were finished. She spoke with the women about their fears and aspirations, what they felt would constitute a "healthy baby," and what specific diagnoses would mean to their families and to them. She described to them the highly skilled techno-scientific laboratory procedures to produce a "positive" diagnosis, the term used to confirm that a fetus had Down syndrome or some other hereditary or genetic condition. She then talked with women who had decided to end their pregnancies, as well as to those who decided to carry the pregnancy to term and integrate a child with a noticeable and stigmatized difference into their social networks. Although most of her research was conducted in hospitals, laboratories, and prenatal clinics, she also worked with two programs for children with developmental delays. Women, at once constrained and empowered by the new technologies, had given great thought to their options. They spoke wholeheartedly to an anthropologist who had also crossed the same moral minefield.

Rapp called women who participated in the new reproductive technologies and hoped to reap its biomedical benefits *moral pioneers*. These women had been drafted into techno-scientific practices of quality control and normalization; they had unwittingly become explorers of new ethical territory, moral philosophers of the private. No one made the decision to undergo amniocentesis lightly. Genetic counseling was a sobering experience for each woman. The counseling process is full of language about "risks." It is shadowed by fears, fantasies, and phobias that pregnant women and their supporters have about childhood disabilities. Overriding the testing and consultations is the possibility of ending a pregnancy to which they may have made a serious commitment.

> *As I have tried to show throughout, the decision to use (or refuse) prenatal diagnosis engages deeply held values concerning the acceptable limits of maternity or parenthood, the importance of biomedical control over "nature," and the justification of abortion. While many upper-middle class, professional women and/or couples may take it for granted that they will undergo amniocentesis in a pregnancy if it is deemed "medically appropriate," and working-class and working-poor women and their supporters may express only polite silence to obstetricians and genetic counselors when the test is explained to them, all hold firm and complex opinions concerning these topics when interviewed outside of an overtly medical framework. (Rapp 1999:307)*

Women facing amniocentesis articulated the limits of "normality" and the differences a differently abled child would make in their lives and in the lives of their intimates. They were participants in an unscripted and large-scale social experiment. Whatever intensely private decisions they made, they were shaping a national reproductive map. Although the women often spoke eloquently of their own families, religious backgrounds, and spiritual values, none of them wanted to limit the choices of other women in the same situation. None gave voice to a universalist ethic; they never said that all women should do the same thing they did, that only one way was the right way.

One surprise finding: All of the women who entered genetic counseling emerged changed. They acquired a raised consciousness about disability. In the new intersection between techno-science or biomedicine and the medical, legal, educational, and social terrain of disability consciousness, women who confronted amniocentesis were forced to think carefully and long about raising a child with the kind of problems the test could diagnose. For a brief moment, they became part of a broad, underground community of families with hard-earned experience and children for whom life-care and social integration are special challenges.

Health care professionals have a biomedical notion of "risk" that never fits women in the process of deciding whether to take the test or not and, if they do, how to incorporate its findings into their pregnancies. The counselors spoke in the language of risk analysis—specific statistics and genetic probabilities—and about the dangers of any pregnancy given a woman's age and medical history. The idea of risk reduction may make sense to a 36-year-old professional woman undergoing her first pregnancy. But for a less privileged woman who has experienced more partners, more pregnancies or pregnancy losses, or whose child has died, an unfelt break in an invisible chromosome doesn't feel all that risky. Joblessness, racism, domestic violence, poverty, and environmental hazards feel more dangerous. The reduction of fetal risk involves far more than chromosome or DNA testing. It resides in the highly stratified and discriminatory social environments in which many women live. Not everyone uses the language of scientific and mathematical literacy that biomedical practitioners favor, nor does everyone share the same assumptions of what a problem pregnancy might look like. The women had developed a nuanced ethic of reproduction:

> *Under circumstances of extreme misfortune, they reasoned that the burdens of motherhood tipped against the present, diagnosed fetus in favor of their commitments to other children, adults, and themselves. Selective abortion after the diagnosis of what they considered to be a serious condition was thus justified. Latina women were most likely to describe their reasoning in terms of the prevention of a child's future suffering; recent immigrants saw a disabled child as an impediment to survival in a new homeland; and white women of all classes worried about selfishness even as they protected themselves and other dependents from the imagined life-transforming obligations entailed in raising a child with congenital disabilities. Yet all enunciated a 'philosophy of the limit.' (Rapp 1999:308)*

Rapp began to concentrate on these limits. Motherhood is over-determined. Prenatal testing takes on a huge role for pregnant women because the weight and the burdens of caring for a healthy child, much less an intellectually or physically disabled one, are not widely or fairly distributed. Women with "positive" diagnoses about their pregnancies knew that there was potentially no limit to their liabilities, no end to their responsibilities for the quality of life an impaired child would have. Some women with broad and accepting networks felt that they could handle a Down syndrome baby with cognitive and intellectual problems, but not a child with impairments of mobility as found with spinal bifida. But for each pregnant women who sat in a counselor's office, the need to imagine a justifiable limit to maternity under her own ethical standards was clear.

Testing of fetuses presents a fundamental contradiction about women's lives: That is, the knowledge of heritable disorders brings a worldview that is firmly scientific, modernist, and rationalist. Reproductive technology occupies a privileged place in scientific literacy, cultural goals, and health aspirations for the nation's children. It is connected to the desire for "perfect" babies, the threat of litigation, and intense educational competition in middle-class life. Yet many women live in communities that share the worldview that miracles are possible, many different types of babies are routinely welcomed, and social support for young mothers is stressed.

Rapp began to see the diversity of desires, aspirations, and experiences that travel along with this new biomedical technology in contemporary America. She learned two lessons. First, there is no uniform "women's way"; there are only individual women in vastly different social matrices doing the best they can to play the hand they were dealt. Second, she learned that these new decisions and new technologies lead to a profound consciousness of the consequences of the life stream and human worth.

Social Women in Biological Bodies: Some Conclusions

Reproduction always means two things: (1) Women give birth to babies, but, (2) at the same time, they also "reproduce," redefine, and represent their cultures in how they raise those babies. Social theorists as well as ordinary people often reduce reproduction to something merely "natural"—biological facts separated from social facts, a domestic activity associated with femininity, maternity, and women. Because it was traditionally a "woman's subject," reproduction was on the margins of anthropology. Anthropologists took for granted their assumptions about the sexual division of labor, gender differences, and an essentialist view of family life. Putting reproduction at the center of social analysis is a relatively recent project for anthropologists. In the early 1980s, feminist scholars challenged the false dichotomy of culture and nature through which reproduction was reduced to "mere biology" while culture was defined as everything else. This new paradigm is paralleled by an extraordinary rise of medical technologies that are mediated through culture and all of which flow through the bodies of women.

The ideas in this chapter challenge the notion of "natural." There seems to be nothing in the life cycles of women that cultural forces do not influence, mediate, or transform. Indeed, the notion of "natural" often functions as a putdown of women in other cultures—it is a synonym for "primitive" or without a proper culture. Most women feel guilty when we cannot or do not conform. Moreover, women are often drafted or conscripted into motherhood, wifedom, and high fertility. We do not "naturally" fall into these categories. Many women love nursing their babies. Others do it in a perfunctory manner. Yet others want to nurse but cannot for reasons that range from physiological to economic. Most women on the planet choose to bottle-feed. Most of us will do anything to control our fertility—to have babies when we want them, no babies when we don't, and even the kind of babies we desire. The technologies of blood and milk are always and everywhere part of women's reproductive lives. All human cultures we know about put constraints on the individual reproductive relations of women and exercise various forms of social control over them. Sexuality and maternity live at the intersection of private and public morality, which is subject to public scrutiny. Reproduction has inevitably been a concern of population policies, global health initiatives, and international development, all of the powerful arenas of public and political conflict and private resistance.

The next chapter concerns females in primate societies, human and nonhuman. We will use weaning, sex, matrifocal families, and friendship to open more questions about "nature versus nurture" in the lives of women.

Some Very Important Books to Read

Women's bodies are a controversial and contested site upon which human cultures want to write their own agendas. Ideologies of class, nation, health, gender, nature, and kinship all have reproductive models at their core. Each of the following books offers strategies of resistance and creative accommodation that women have fashioned around these issues of motherhood. Helena Ragoné and France Winddance Twine examine the lives of white mothers of black children, homeless mothers, lesbian co-parents, mothers who adopt, and those mothers who are infertile, have miscarried, or have borne children with disabilities in *Ideologies and Technologies of Motherhood: Race, Class, Sexuality, Nationalism* (2000). Sarah Franklin and Helena Ragoné highlight the social and cultural aspects of reproduction that social theorists have neglected in favor of the biological givens of human reproduction in *Reproducing Reproduction: Kinship, Power, and Technological Innovation* (1998). Editors Lynn Morgan and Meredith Michaels present a collection of articles that focuses on public debates and private decisions in *Fetal Subjects, Feminist Positions* (1999).

Comparative, biocultural, female-centered approaches to childbirth, as well as critiques of the medicalization of childbirth, are best seen in Robbie Davis-Floyd and Carolyn Sargent's benchmark book, *Childbirth and Authoritative Knowledge: Cross-Cultural Perspectives* (1997); and in Robbie Davis-Floyd and Joseph Dumit's *Cyborg Babies: From Techno-Sex to Techno-Tots* (1997). With the increasing significance of fetuses as persons and technologies as decision makers, how much agency does a woman have to make private reproductive decisions? I recommend two books: In *Experiencing the New Genetics: Family and Kinship on the Medical Frontier* (2000), Kaja Finkler shows how the new genetics can turn a healthy person into a perpetual patient, redefine family life in American society, and lead to a diminished social responsibility for the unhealthy environmental conditions that afflict women. Historian John Riddle wrote *Eve's Herbs: A History of Contraception in the West* (1997) to illuminate European–American women's experiences with birth control, probably the oldest technology to regulate the life stream.

Chapter Four

Primate Connections

How Natural Is Nature Anyway?

hen I began this book, I wanted to include a society in which females controlled their sexual and economic lives; where they negotiated friendships with both males and other females; lived with or near a network of kinfolks; and raised their offspring in cooperative, multi-generational settings. I was looking for interesting, independent women and flexible social arrangements. What I found was non-human primates like chimpanzees and baboons, and the women who did the research that brought their lives to light. As a result, there are two central motifs in this chapter.

First: A revolution in evolutionary biology and physical anthropology started in the 1960s when women began to study groups of apes and monkeys, societies of nonhuman primates. What did women as researchers do that was different from what men had done? What can we learn from their research?

Second: As a result of this new scientific consciousness, females in primate societies became the lively subjects of investigation, not just fixed objects in a male world. What can monkeys and apes teach us about being female on the planet or about being animals in complex and gendered environments?

To answer these questions, we will look at a generation of female scholars who did extensive long-term or longitudinal research on primates living in free-ranging groups. They developed sophisticated and innovative techniques of research and applied them to issues in evolution and contemporary life. Most important, this research has made females in primate societies visible. Past research tended to cast females in supporting roles, while males performed at center stage.

> *In part because nonhuman primates cannot be interviewed, it took years of patient observation to recognize that in most primate societies males come and go, playing only cameo roles, whereas females remain to carry the plot. (Fedigan and Fedigan 1989:42)*

Before the 1960s and a generation of female scholars, one of the most popular portraits of primate societies showed males in rigid hierarchies competing with each other for sex. Females dedicated themselves to the care of infants and the sexual needs of dominant males. Sex was the glue that held the groups together. Males needed it; females had it. Everything else followed.

Females were passive or squabbled among themselves. But for rigid and competitive male hierarchies, things would simply fall apart. Females were sexual receptacles or the primate equivalent of a stay-at-home helpmate for he-man the hunter. If primates were like this, it was thought, so were humans. Political domination was the "natural" way for males to act. Domestic passivity was the "natural" way for females to act.

Phenomena situated in "nature" or "in the wild" are good. Like certain breakfast cereals, they are healthy for you. If you resist or differ, you are "unnatural," probably sick in some way. You can locate many other models and myths in American culture as examples of this kind of "natural" reasoning. These views, quite frankly, looked like projections from television shows from the 1950s in the United States, Judeo-Christian myths of creation, or King Kong and Tarzan narratives. It took years of patient observation to understand the hard work and social skills primate mothers exercise to raise their offspring or the friendship and cooperation males and females display.

Primatologists now say that members of most primate societies are biologically and socially related to each other through females of the group. They form *matrifocal units* or groups that center on mothers. These genealogies last through subsequent generations and form the stable core of group life. Of course, there is competition (the degree and significance varies according to whom we read). There is also intelligence, thinking, manipulation, strategies and feelings we are tempted to call love, jealousy, trust, affection, and grief.

The grand theory on which most of this research rested was, of course, Charles Darwin's. He wrote about the principles of natural selection, or the adaptation of animals to their environment; he wrote that the only ultimate survival was in producing offspring and raising them to adulthood so they could do the same thing. To him, the most telling features of evolution were males competing with each other for the sexual favors of females, and females choosing which male to favor. In the years since Darwin proposed this theory, the key element of females choosing mates somehow got lost. But a contemporary generation of scholars studying the lives of chimpanzees, baboons, and other primate species has restored female agency or action.

Today scientists in the field of evolutionary biology or physical anthropology use the theories of Charles Darwin to answer questions about human origins and the evolution of species. But applying theories of evolutionary biology to the meaning of gender generates controversies and sexual or biopolitics. In popular consciousness, we are often tempted to turn to "nature" to explain or justify human behavior. Women are particularly susceptible to this kind of interpretation.

So the goal of this chapter is to give you a solid framework buttressed by some fascinating examples about the words "natural" or "naturally." You will never again see "nature" in the same old way. Meanwhile, look for some central themes in the following examples drawn from chimpanzee and baboon societies: mothers and matrifocal units; sex and reproduction; friendships and social skills; and males and females at work, together and apart.

Studying Chimpanzees

Why start with chimpanzees? First, genetic analysis reveals the close kinship in evolution between chimps and humans. Second, chimpanzee social activities and behaviors may resemble those of our early ancestors. Third, and most important, watching animals is one of the best ways of confronting and getting beyond cultural biases. But fourth, the behavioral scientist with the most name-recognition in the world today is Jane Goodall.

Jane Goodall has been observing chimpanzee groups in Tanzania since July of 1960. No researcher has ever worked this long or presented an animal species as individuals with feelings and complex social behaviors. She was one of the first Western scientists to observe primates in what many call "the wild" or "natural" settings. Women who followed often worked under tough, arduous, even dangerous field conditions. Their long-term or longitudinal research provided insights that short field stays or studies of captive animals did not provide. Scholars like Goodall, who write for ordinary people, are often criticized in the profession. In fact, the *National Geographic Society* articles and documentaries about Jane were both popular and popularized. But her research was the first of its kind and the model for much more that was to follow.

Chimpanzees are great apes (not monkeys). They are omnivorous, which means they eat a wide variety of plant and animal foods. Chimps have tools. That is, they modify and use materials—such as leaves for sponges, twigs as probes to obtain termites, rocks and sticks as hammers to crack nuts. They eat meat when they can catch smaller animals. Individuals in small groups range over many square miles each day in search of food. They do not share food with each other in the way our early ancestors probably did with salads, potlucks, buffets, or picnics.

Chimpanzees have a flexible social organization called fission–fusion. This means that the composition of groups will vary from day to day.

> *Fusion and fission in chimpanzee society are carried to the limits of flexibility; individuals of either sex have almost complete freedom to come and go as they wish. The membership of temporary parties is constantly changing. Adults and adolescents can and do forage, travel, and sleep on their own, sometimes for days at a time. This unique organization means, for one thing, that day-to-day social experiences of a chimpanzee are far more variable than those of almost any other primate. (Goodall 1986:147)*

Individuals relate to each other in shifting and complex patterns of kinship and friendship. Chimps communicate with postures, gestures, facial expressions, and vocalizations in ways human observers are not even close to interpreting. These skills allow them to negotiate unique or complicated social situations.

Chimps, like other primates, concentrate their social life in the mothers and children and among siblings. These bonds endure for life. Female chimpanzees spend most of their lives either pregnant or lactating. They invest more time and energy in rearing offspring than males do.

Chimpanzees, like humans, practice **grooming.** Grooming is the intensely social activity of cleaning and handling each other's hair and skin; this keeps primates clean and gives pleasure. The groomer removes dirt, parasites, scabs, and other debris. This smooths thick, coarse hair and keeps wounds clean. The contribution of grooming to health is obvious. All primates, including humans, groom each other, their mates, and their offspring. Should anyone doubt the importance of grooming among *Homo sapiens,* they are advised to remember haircuts, manicures, squeezing their beloved's pimples, oils or sunscreens applied to each other's backs, or the mothers who straighten their collars and push a lock of hair from their eyes.

Jane Goodall

Jane Goodall was waiting tables in England and saving money to travel. She found a job in Kenya, East Africa, and contacted Louis B. Leakey, the famous paleontologist. He suggested that she study chimpanzees and arranged preliminary funding for her. He believed that women, even untrained ones, would bring much-needed sensitivities to field research.

So Jane and her mother went to Tanzania and set up camp in the Gombe Stream Reserve. For two years, she worked day after day with only occasional sightings of chimpanzees. But she persisted quietly until the chimpanzees became accustomed or habituated to her presence. Within four years she had acquired a chimp mentor named David Greybeard, started to accumulate systematic data, and built the Gombe Stream Research Centre. Students began to come to the center to study chimpanzees and other animal species. Meanwhile, Jane had to finish a graduate degree and work to establish scholarly credibility in a tightly controlled and masculine academic world.

In those days, animals were not supposed to have feelings. Neither were scientists. Feelings were something only emotional women had. Jane argued with her advisers. She insisted that the chimps she observed did feel sad, happy, or afraid. Jane claimed that chimps set goals, made plans, and worked cleverly around the obstacles or opportunities presented to them. In her writings, she referred to animals by name and by the personal pronouns, "she" or "he." A chimpanzee was never "it."

Flo

Primatologists assign personal names to animals they observe. This practice allows them to follow individuals and their genealogies. Figure 4.1 shows the genealogy or family chart for a chimpanzee female named Flo. Chimpanzee and other primate genealogies are always traced matrilineally, that is, through the mother's line. This kind of kinship in human or nonhuman primates is also called **matrifocal**. The reasons for these terms will be apparent when we come to Flo's sex life.

Flo was an animal Jane describes as bulbous-nosed, ragged-eared, and ugly by any human standards.

> *Even in those days Flo looked very old. She appeared frail, with but little flesh on her bones, and thinning hair that was brown rather than black. When she yawned we saw that her teeth were worn right down to the gums. We soon found out that her character by no means matched her appearance: she was aggressive, tough as nails, and easily the most dominant of all the females at that time. (Goodall 1971:92)*

When Jane Goodall first met Flo, the chimp mother had two sons, Faben and Figan, and a daughter, Fifi. Flo had begun to wean Fifi from nursing at her breasts. Chimpanzee mothers start to wean their infants when they are about four years old. Weaning is a major trial, a turning point for both mothers and infants in chimp society. A mother tries to prevent her child both from suckling and from riding on her back. She distracts her offspring with tickling or heavy play, but the little one often responds with temper tantrums. This stage of chimp growth is stressful, particularly to inexperienced mothers.

Figure 4.1

Flo's Chart: A Chimpanzee Matrifocal Genealogy

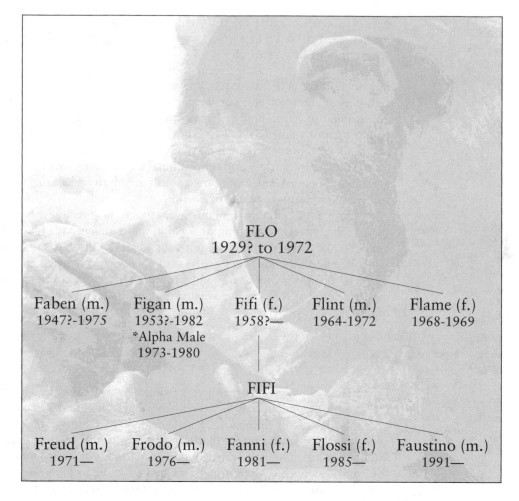

FLO
1929? to 1972

Faben (m.) 1947?-1975	Figan (m.) 1953?-1982 *Alpha Male 1973-1980	Fifi (f.) 1958?—	Flint (m.) 1964-1972	Flame (f.) 1968-1969

FIFI

Freud (m.) 1971—	Frodo (m.) 1976—	Fanni (f.) 1981—	Flossi (f.) 1985—	Faustino (m.) 1991—

But Fifi had learned many skills from her mother and was ready for some independence. As chimp children do, Fifi wandered farther from her mother's protection as she played with other youngsters most of the day. Fifi started to eat a grownup diet, the kinds of food she watched her mother pick each day. Fifi no longer needed to ride on her mother's back as they traveled the mountain trails in search of food. She still jumped in her mother's lap when startled. They groomed each other daily.

When Flo was no longer nursing Fifi, she stopped lactating and came into heat, or **estrus**. This means that she was ovulating and, all other things being equal, could get pregnant at this point in her **estrous cycle**. Chimpanzee females have estrous cycles and menarche just like humans do. The difference, however, is that chimpanzee females have sex, indeed want to have sex, only during the period they are ovulating. This period of sexual desires and activity is fairly dramatic. The hidden agenda is that they can conceive at this time.

The skin of Flo's genital area swelled and turned a bright shade of pink. This sent out a signal to males: Flo was "in the pink." Ardent suitors knew that courting and mating could begin. Males saw the swelling; they often put out a finger to touch and then sniffed their finger. Adolescents and other low-ranking males followed Flo around, but in unrequited passion. Flo could pick and choose. She was extremely popular with the senior adult males, who vied with each other for her favors. Though intercourse itself lasts only ten or fifteen seconds, the public dramas of sex lasted for days. Jane Goodall once counted fifty copulations for Flo in a twenty-four-hour period. Despite her looks, Flo was a chimpanzee sex pot.

Chimpanzee females are generally "in the pink," pregnant, or lactating through much of their adult lives. Unless they are in the pink, however, they have no interest in sex. The literature on primates calls this attitude **sexually proceptive**. The term recognizes the active part females play in selecting, enticing, or rejecting certain males. Females conceive at the peak of the estrous cycle. So there is an evolutionary purpose for this dynamic combination of simultaneous sexual swelling, interest in sex, and ability to conceive. Together they enhance the chances for pregnancy. Completed pregnancies and effective childrearing, that is, rearing offspring who themselves grow up to reproduce, are the heart of what Darwin defined as successful adaptation and evolution.

The infant Flo conceived in this round of sexual adventures was named Flint; he is one of the best-described and observed babies in all the scientific literature. Neither scientists nor mother, however, will ever know the identity of his biological father.

Flo was an excellent mother. Her older sons romped nearby in the rough-and-tumble play of juvenile chimps. Fifi watched intently, ready to touch, groom, or hold the infant. Flint treated his mother's body as a playground. At Flint's first whoop of distress, Flo gathered him up and kissed him in the open-mouthed smooching chimps favor. She slept at night with him in a nest she built in a tree, and carried him against her chest during her travels, supporting him with one hand when he needed it.

When Flint was not quite five years of age, Flo came into estrus again. She was pink for only four or five days and Flint was not allowed to suckle. In the sixth month of her pregnancy, her milk dried up. During these periods as well as during her earlier attempts to wean him, Flint had acted like "a spoiled brat." He threw temper tantrums; he clung, he whimpered, he bullied her for attention. Flo tried to comfort and reassure Flint even as she encouraged him to give up his dependency. Flint appeared to accept the birth of a younger sister, Flame. But within a few months, he reverted to the clingy, irritated, and irritating brat he had been. When baby Flame was six months old, a flu-like illness swept the Gombe. Flo became ill and Flame died. Flint was once again the baby. Even at the age of six in chimp years, Flint clung, climbed on his mother, needed constant grooming, and slept with her at night. Flint had become what Jane called "a very abnormal juvenile."

The Dating Game

We cannot judge chimpanzee sex life by the standards of human society, particularly the dating customs of our own culture. It does, however, make sense in terms of evolutionary biology. Let us assume that females have different strategies than do males when it comes to sex and reproduction; call these **differential reproductive strategies** and **differential sexual strategies**. The basic idea, which comes from the work of Charles Darwin, notes that each gender experiences results or consequences from having sex and makes an investment in being a parent. But the consequences or the investments are not the same for males as for females. Please note that Darwin and those who follow in his footsteps are talking about groups of animals, or species. They are not providing interpretations of individual behavior. This can get confusing.

Let's use Goodall's chimpanzees to illustrate these points about differential strategies.

What's a fellow to do? A male chimpanzee does not initiate sex. He must wait until the "pink ladies" are ready. Then he needs some techniques or a history of cooperation with a female. Sexual swellings are, for male chimpanzees, a time of tension. They may tear down and wave tree branches. They may pick fights with each other for no apparent reason.

Sometimes a male chimpanzee manages to take a pink lady off into the woods for a few days together. They then are a **consort pair,** a temporary but exclusive mating relationship. This is sometimes called a **pair-bond** or a consortship. Only in this way can a male keep an estrous female away from rival males. At the peak of her swelling, she is most likely to conceive. Exclusive access to her increases the likelihood that he is the father. If chimpanzees reasoned this out (and there is absolutely no evidence they do), then his strategy for getting her off alone is not only about sex. It is about reproduction from the male point of view. It is the kind of survival Darwin talked about.

Goodall and the researchers at Gombe report that all of the male chimps squired females on sexual getaways at some point in their lives. Often a male had to work very hard to take and keep a female on a consortship; others simply had good manners and better techniques. Some males were notably more successful than others. Some used aggressive and bullying tactics until they wore a female out. But once the pair left the group and mated, the male became docile or conciliatory. In customary behavior, chimps follow aggression or hostility with gestures of reconciliation. They make amends and restore social harmony. So perhaps consortships are a chimp equivalent of a honeymoon; perhaps they are also conducive to conception. That's what **courtship** is for.

Mothers and Daughters

An enduring result of primate research is the striking differences between mothering styles in individuals and the contribution that good mothering makes to succeeding generations. The closest relationship at Gombe is between a mother and her grown daughter. Until she is about ten years of age, a female will be separated from her mother only a few hours at a time. Her mother protects and supports her. In return, however, her mother may dominate and smother her.

Goodall says that most chimp females are relatively efficient at being mothers; this is similar to the concept of "good enough" or adequate that childrearing experts talk about in the United States. She compares Flo's mothering style with another female, called Passion.

> *In the wild almost all mothers look after their infants relatively efficiently. But even so there are clear-cut differences in the child-raising techniques of different individuals. It would be hard to find two females whose mothers had treated them more differently during their early years, than Flo's daughter Fifi and Passion's daughter Pom. In fact, Flo and Passion are at opposite ends of a scale: most mothers fall somewhere between these two extremes. (Goodall 1990:33)*

The two daughters, Fifi and Pom, came into sexual maturity about the same time. After weaning, the beginning of estrus is the next major transition in the life of a female. Fifi and Pom were both sexually attractive and active for about ten days each month for two years, but neither got pregnant.

Fifi flourished in the bloom of adolescence; she learned how to be self-reliant without depending on the high status of her mother. She rejoined her mother for companionship between episodes of sexual availability and enjoyed grooming six-year-old Flint, playing with baby Flame, and gaining valuable maternal experience. Fifi was charmed by her new power.

> *Sometimes, when a male was, quite obviously, uninterested in what she had to offer, she would recline close by and, ever hopeful, stare at him. Or rather, stare at a certain portion of his anatomy that was, so far as she was concerned, disappointingly flabby. Once she went so far as to tweak the limp appendage—with highly satisfactory results! It soon became clear that the males regarded Fifi as a most desirable sexual partner. She did not have quite the sex appeal that Flo had once radiated—but in those days she was, after all, younger and less experienced. (Goodall 1990:35)*

Pom, by contrast, was a troubled teenager. Tense and anxious with males, she often leapt away screaming after intercourse. She seemed to lack the social skills which would endear her to sexual partners; thus she remained less popular than Fifi. Pom seldom went off alone with a male during her estrus. In fact, she and her mother, Passion, fought off and defeated such attempts by senior males.

So what was Passion's problem? Was she a bad mother? Cold and brusque with Pom, she had seldom played with her infant. Passion had pushed Pom onto her back long before the infant was ready for riding in that style. Passion had no close female companions; she herself was tense and edgy around males. Pom and Passion had a close bond and supported each other in community quarrels. The two of them backed each other up when either picked a confrontation with another chimp, male or female.

In May 1971 Fifi gave birth to Freud—named in honor of his mother's sexual exuberance during her adolescent years. Fifi was as relaxed and competent as her mother. Indeed, she lifted baby Freud with one foot and tickled him just as mother

Flo had done. When at age thirteen Pom gave birth to infant Pan, she treated him better than she herself had been treated as an infant. Although Pom was more attentive and tolerant than mother Passion had been, she never developed the maternal proficiency or loving vigilance that marked Fifi's care of her infant.

In chimpanzee society, individuals may take on mothering roles even when they have not given birth. One daughter helped her mother, who had just borne twins. Another chimp, Gigi, was a large sterile female who cycled vainly into estrus every thirty days or so. She radiated sex appeal and basked in popularity. Her consorts performed valiantly, but she never conceived. After a time, she made friends with and acted as an older sister for Patti, whose mothering skills began to improve only after her third child was born. "Aunt" Gigi, in effect, adopted Patti's offspring, rescued them from their mother's intermittent neglect, and modeled vigilant, caring parenting for the hapless Patti.

Such fostering or **fictive kinship** appears common in chimp society, and its value for survival and adaptation is quite obvious. The research from Gombe contains many examples of older brothers or sisters looking out for younger ones after the death of their mother. It also points out once again the fact that being a mother is not a matter of instinct or "natural" impulses. Mothering is a learned and practiced set of behaviors. Some individuals who give birth are better at it than others. People other than biological mothers can and do perform these tasks.

Sons, Lovers, and Others

The advantage of years of fieldwork is tracking individuals through complex and shifting relationships or friendships. Jane Goodall's observations of chimpanzee social life make it clear that males and females have different life courses or cycles, that they are distinct individuals, and that they negotiate and interact in complex ways. Females, in estrus or out of it, prefer the company of some males to others. They will actively avoid other individuals. Both males and females have ongoing, active friendships with each other. The links between siblings are obvious throughout their adulthood. They often form close alliances after the death of their mother, for example. Two brothers may support each other in a bid for moving up the hierarchy. Brothers and sisters may groom each other or spend time in each other's company more frequently than they do with any other individuals.

But male chimps must break early from their mothers. Although a male may draw status from his mother and strength and insight from positive early social experiences, he still has to learn the skills of an adult male from other males. He must work his way around the loose dominance hierarchy, an ever-shifting matrix, dominating the females first and then his peers and age-mates before he can tackle the older males.

The highest ranking male in a primate troop is called an **alpha male**. Such powerful or dominant males often act to suppress community conflicts. Alpha males will terminate otherwise destructive quarreling and promote strategies of social accord. Some males, however, seem to have no desire for being at the top. They may serve the alpha males in return for protection and a degree of tolerance when food and sex are available. Flo's son Figan, for example, was intelligent, well

brought-up, and determined to make it to the top of the status hierarchy in his band. He worked on his charging display: He made his hair stand on end, shook heavy branches, slapped the ground, and stomped loudly. The threatening gestures and facial expressions are designed to impress rivals without resort to actual physical conflict. Audacity and persistence count for more than size or strength. Figan enlisted the support of his older brother, Faben, who seemed to be happy in his role as brother of an alpha. Thus Flo left a legacy of leadership through her sons—Figan, alpha male, and Faben, loyal supporter.

By contrast, a female in chimp society remains with her mother, her siblings, and the network of associations she was born into. She will learn by observing and participating how to care for an infant and what the sexual swellings mean. However traumatic weaning, a new sibling, or alpha rivalries are, the ultimate broken bond is a mother's death. When Flo died, Jane Goodall recorded the event and mourned a friend.

> As I kept my vigil in the bright moonlight, I thought about Flo's life. For nigh on fifty years she must have roamed the Gombe hills. And even if I had not arrived to record her history, to invade the privacy of that rugged terrain, Flo's life would have been, in and of itself, significant and worthwhile, filled with purpose, vigour, and love of life. (Goodall 1990:31)

Flo is the only nonhuman ever to have an obituary in the *London Times*. When she died, Flint was eight-and-a-half years old. Under different circumstances, he would have been able to care for himself. But he was desolate. He visited the last nest they had shared and returned to the place where he had last seen her. Sick and refusing to eat, he curled up and died.

Jane Goodall saw in these individuals and their life stories what we think of as the "human" qualities of chimpanzees. Sometimes they show compassion, ambition, love, self-sacrifice, and sharing. However, it is dangerous to romanticize or sentimentalize chimpanzee life or to compare ourselves naively to other animal species. On occasion, and under conditions scientists are just starting to understand, chimpanzees hurt and kill each other. Females and males kill infants; adult males kill each other and adult females.

Studying Baboons

Baboons are monkeys and the most widely studied nonhuman primates in the world. In no danger of extinction, it is said that baboons outnumber human beings in Africa. They provide a primary model of how our ancestors lived on the savannahs of that continent. For decades, baboons in their rich varieties have been the major portrait of primate life for introductory anthropology classes.

Based on research done in the 1950s and 1960s, professors like me used to teach that baboons lived in male-dominated societies and had a clear-cut sexual division of labor. Like humans, some species even had harems. Aggressive, competitive males were the building blocks and cement, the structure and the stability, of their groups. But a generation of female primatologists in the 1960s and 1970s challenged the scientific validity of these notions. Here are three illustrative examples from the works of these women.

Maternal Care and Friendships

Jeanne Altmann was married to a baboon researcher and spent years watching baboons. Even before she earned her doctorate, she proposed observational methodologies and unbiased sampling techniques that are now standards in the field. She said that statistics, however sophisticated, are useless without a conceptualization of the problem. Her book on baboon mothers and infants emphasized the enduring conflict between females' productive and reproductive lives. Their work was a constant trade-off between maternal care or childrearing and the time and energy needed to forage for food. For example, youngsters wanted their mothers to carry, nurse, or amuse them endlessly; but mothers had to work. Once again we learn, if we needed this lesson, that females are involved first in tasks of subsistence or earning a living; then they arrange nursing, mating, or quality time with their kids.

Prior researchers, focused on topics such as food and sex, had missed a whole arena of possibilities, namely friendships, social skills, and emotional qualities. Primatologist Barbara Smuts studied female–male friendships in baboon groups living in Kenya. She learned that *relationships between males and females transcend the narrow context of the sexual act. Flirtation, courtship, possessiveness, and jealousy are apparent in interactions between the sexes throughout all phases of the female reproductive cycle. Baboons are strongly attracted to members of the opposite sex independent of their immediate motivations to copulate. (Smuts 1985:231)*

If a woman is going to say that animals like baboons have an awareness of self and others, and live in complex systems of affiliation, then she better have convincing scientific methods. So Smuts developed rigorous procedures to measure friendship and sort relationships into categories she called Relatives, Friends, and Non-Friends. We know who Relatives are. What are Friends for? Friends groom each other and spend time in each other's company. This can be measured in terms of the frequency of mutual grooming and calculations of physical proximity to each other. Baboon Friends don't just have sex. They sleep together and spend time with each other. So sex and friendship are intimately twined.

What are the benefits of having a Friend? A male Friend protects a female and her vulnerable offspring. In doing so, he establishes a long-term alliance with the infants as they grow up.

What made Friends special was, most of all, the unusual quality of their interactions. Female baboons, in general, are wary of males. This is understandable: Males sometimes use their larger size and formidable canines to intimidate and bully smaller troop members. Females, however, were apparently drawn to their male Friends, and they seemed surprisingly relaxed around these hulking companions. The males, too, seemed to undergo a subtle transformation when interacting with female Friends. They appeared less tense, more affectionate, and more sensitive to the behavior of their partners. (Smuts 1985:61)

A female favors her Friend as a mate when she is again in estrus. At other times she will spend long hours grooming her Friend. Becoming a Friend to an established female integrates a male in the social life of the group.

Primate Kinfolk

Shirley Strum went to Kenya to observe olive baboons, one group of which she called the Pumphouse Gang. But the baboons refused to cooperate. They seemed not to have heard about the scientific model for their lives. High-ranking males did not routinely monopolize sexy females. In fact, females often chose the losers in male contests to groom and befriend. Males often participated in caretaking friendships with youngsters; they acted like older brothers or "uncles." Females handled most disputes within their own hierarchies and family groupings. Both females and males had power. Confused and confounded, Shirley Strum spent months, then years, observing the baboons.

Strum puzzled about gender and personalities in the same way Margaret Mead, Ruth Benedict, Jane Goodall, and others have. Yes, baboon societies have certain styles of childrearing, just as human or chimpanzee cultures do. But individuals within the same troop or family are very different from each other.

Take Peggy, for example. Peggy had outstanding social skills; she was calm, solid, and assertive but not pushy. She was a forceful yet loving mother to her adult daughter Thea, adolescent son Paul, juvenile Patrick, and infant Pebbles. By contrast, Thea had a troubled temperament. She relied on her mother to intervene for her in awkward social situations she herself had created. As Shirley Strum remarks, "Thea was, in fact, a bitch."

> Thea was always poking her nose into other people's business. Whenever females or juveniles were involved in a tiff, Thea would be there in seconds, adding her weight sometimes to one side, sometimes to the other, frequently almost schizophrenically switching sides unpredictably. She often managed to prevent the quarreling individuals from settling the argument. . . . I badly wanted to understand Thea's ambivalence toward her mother. What was she thinking and feeling? What was driving her? What made her so different from Peggy in her interaction with the other females? (Strum 1987:40)

Thea's three daughters preferred grandmother Peggy's company. She groomed them and spent so much time in their company that an inexperienced person might believe they were Peggy's own. Peggy's high status and strong character was an umbrella of protection for all the members of her matriline. Anyone who messed with members of her family would have to deal with Peggy herself. Although every adult male was larger and stronger, Peggy could get what she

Baboon societies have certain styles of child rearing, just as human or chimpanzee cultures do.

wanted—a shady spot, a bit of food, or grooming—by moving in and waiting. When Peggy sponsored a male, he was in with the group.

The core units of the Pumphouse Gang and other baboon groups were females and their kinfolk. These matrifocal units have stable rankings. Peggy's unit or matriline happened to outrank all the other matrilines. In fact, every member of Peggy's matriline, male or female, infant or adult, enjoyed the fruits of this female's high status. That a mother's status somehow covers her offspring and is passed on is one of the most important insights we have from primate studies. But primatologists are not sure why this is true or how it works.

More about Friendships

The research by Strum and others showed that females had long-lasting friendships with each other, an easy mutuality of sitting together, resting, sleeping, or grooming. When they disagreed with each other, they worked things out. Female baboons like Peggy also had friendships or "special relationships" with males. Strum witnessed many friendships between females and males but none between adult males.

The major fact of life for males in the Pumphouse Gang was mobility. For various reasons, they moved back and forth, in and out of other troops. Each time they moved they had to work their way up. Newcomers used the only tactic at their disposal, aggression. Males who lived with the troop for a short time developed social ties, so they fared better. But males who had lived with the troop the longest had to develop serious social strategies. Males who used finesse rather than force and subtlety rather than strength achieved much more in the long run. Males who moved into a new troop fared best when they made friends with a female. Then she championed his cause with others.

> The more I understood males, the clearer it seemed that they had a hard life. Where did their size, strength and physical power get them? . . . They had to reconstruct whole new lives for themselves after leaving behind all that was friendly, secure and familiar. Once in their new troop, they had to recapture all they had lost: the social closeness, allies, friends, experience and knowledge that ultimately constituted baboon wisdom. Despite great effort and enduring patience, they ended up with less than a female who had never left home could command simply with a look, gesture or grunt. I felt sorry for males. (Strum 1987:126)

Shirley Strum did not see what the theory predicted she would. Individual baboons had distinct personalities. There was no clear-cut male dominance. Aggression happened but rarely achieved anything. Rank among females seemed stable. Yet females were not in control, there was no primate matriarchy. Strum settled for the idea of **complementary equality**. Females and males did separate things, had different jobs, and exchanged favors with each other. Both male and female baboons were involved in politics, peacekeeping, and caretaking. They practiced elaborate social reciprocity and complicated exchanges of favors and friendships.

Females were not powerless or passive no matter how busy they were in maternal care; in fact, their work as mothers conferred status. Wisdom, knowledge, and social skills were as important as strength or size. Allies, friends, and relatives were any individual's greatest asset.

In Darwinian terms, all these good habits contribute to reproductive success and survival. But baboons do not reason that way. Instead, they act as though friendships were central to a meaningful social life. They act with intelligence and reciprocity and they reap the rewards of their emotional investments.

Research such as this challenges notions like "the law of the jungle" and "dog-eat-dog" world. Aggressive competition and male domination are not the "natural" order of social life for primates. Instead we see the centrality of the mother–child unit, the capacity for friendships across age and gender lines, the need for social skills, and the two-bodied, bicultural worlds of females and males.

Studying the Human Nature of Women and Men

Many ideas flow from the decades of research only briefly presented here. I want to cover two.

The first one is that the sexual and reproductive lives of females and males are radically different. We are not mirror images; we are not equal. On the contrary, women and men have different agendas; each has separate interests and strategies.

The second point I want to make is that interpreting these differences and applying them in the cultural contexts we live in is fiendishly difficult. Let's examine the differences first.

What is the human nature of being female? Here is an explanation from evolutionary biology. Human females make eggs, one per month from menarche to menopause. If one month's egg is not fertilized, we have a period. If that month's egg is fertilized, we are pregnant, and may carry the fetus through a gestation period of ten lunar months and give birth to a tiny and very helpless infant. The baby develops slowly and requires feeding and extensive training in life-survival skills for approximately two decades. (This includes college!)

Females require access to necessary resources in the environment to rear these offspring to full adulthood, when they will begin the cycle for themselves. They organize such aid from mates, kinfolks, friends, or cooperative nonrelatives. This is a form of work called female **parental investment** and may last through a meaningful segment of their life cycle. Females of the human species require lots of assistance in raising their young. Sometimes the trade-off in human cultures has been sexual access and assurance of paternity for males in exchange for protection and economic resources for females. Females may compete, not over the best-looking male, but over access to resources to sustain themselves and their offspring. This proposition provokes many thoughtful questions. It may help us to understand contemporary patterns and predict how they will change.

What are males like? What is their human nature as seen from evolutionary biology? Men typically produce billions of tiny sperm from early adolescence to the end of their lives. They never get pregnant, give birth, or have a period, not even once. A male may go from female to female contributing sperm and thus may have a great many offspring, some of whom he may not know about or who are in various stages of gestation and growth simultaneously. A male must theoretically be worried about the competition, about the availability of females, and about how much mating will cost him. This is called mating effort.

For a male there is no physical connection between fertilization and childbirth. Under many circumstances, however, there are deep economic, psychological, or social bonds between men and their offspring. So a male parental investment centers on the contributions a man makes to the growth or fitness of his offspring. Males are also affected by the degree of confidence they have in their own paternity. Unlike females, they can never really be certain. On the other hand, males may assist in rearing children who are not biologically theirs.

Given these two styles of reproduction, we can see strikingly different tactics that females and males use in what we can call reproductive and sexual careers. For example, females may be very careful in choosing a mate; they will ask the question, Is he a good provider? I have heard women say, "So he's not a perfect husband, at least he's good to the kids."

Men of the human species, however, may well emphasize physical qualities in women that highlight sexuality and maternity. This includes breasts, fat storage on buttocks, and youthfulness. This theory explains men who are old, ugly, and smelly but rich or powerful, who can compete successfully with other males for young females. By the same token, the theory explains how and why women promote or acquiesce to alliances with such men.

The theories about differential strategies are sometimes used to explain marriage systems that emphasize brides' virginity, dowries, chaperones, modesty, chastity, or punishments for women who commit adultery. A woman has access to a resource base and childrearing assistance in exchange for a guarantee that all the children she bears belong genetically to her husband. All kinds of customs can be explained in this framework. This theory also makes sense in understanding soap operas!

Poor dead Charles Darwin. He and his theories of evolution have been dragged out for almost 150 years to justify whatever is politically current in fashions for the treatment of women. It is clear that complicated genetic, biological, or hormonal processes are in operation in our animal lives. But it is not at all clear why or how. It seems clear there are evolutionary advantages for survival of species. But scholars don't agree about the mechanisms. These theories do not provide us with models for marriage, monogamy, sexual adventures, or other social practices humans engage in. We are different from chimpanzees or baboons.

Human courtship customs are complex and full of emotions. They cannot be summarized easily. In fact, we can and regularly do have sex when we could not possibly conceive or when our motivations and feelings have little or nothing to do with "a sex drive." Human females conceal their ovulations; it is unclear if they are fertile, infertile, or even interested in trying. They place value judgments on copulation; they call it making love, promiscuity, adultery, safe sex, marital hygiene, screwing, rape, or many other terms. Humans, generally speaking, don't have intercourse in public. But they have sex without intercourse and with a variety of people; we have intercourse without pregnancy. We make connections between intercourse, pregnancy, birth, and **social paternity**. We think of males as husbands and fathers. We attribute immense moral and social characteristics to having and feeding an infant. We call this "motherhood."

One place in which evolutionary biology has been seriously confused with contemporary gender politics is what we should call the "cultural construction of motherhood." Examples are rife. Yes, some women have babies. Does that mean that all women's place is "naturally" in "the Kitchen, the Church, and the Nursery" as one German proverb states? Some women don't want to have children. Some who have them are not great mothers. Some women feel sensual pleasures in activities like nursing. Others have babies without sex. These women are not "unnatural."

The Cultures of Breastfeeding

Parenting styles not only vary within primate groups, but also among human societies. How babies are conceived, where and when to put the baby to sleep, how to feed, dress, toilet train, talk to, and discipline children are some of the areas where there is a great deal of variety cross-culturally. Both women and men, as well as other adults and older children, play varying roles in the care of children in different societies. Child rearing, while taken as natural, is actually highly culturally determined.

Breastfeeding is one aspect of mothering that has long been identified as "natural." True, humans have evolved to nourish our young through the secretions of mammary glands. The mammalian order is named after this aspect. Despite its association with human biology, when, how, and if to breastfeed a child is culturally determined. Breastfeeding, outside of pregnancy, represents the largest physical commitment a mother has toward her offspring. It requires an even higher caloric intake on the part of the mother than pregnancy. Even so, the amount of energy and time a mother should focus on caring for her child in this respect varies from culture to culture.

All cultures seem to agree that babies need some sort of milk. Breastmilk is the only option unless other mammals (like cows, sheep, or goats) are raised for their milk. Even so, the baby's biological mother is not always the sole source of breastmilk. In other times and places, nursing at the breast of a woman other than one's mother has been commonplace. **Wet-nursing** began in Europe in the eleventh and twelfth centuries and was a common practice through the eighteenth century. In many other societies, letting another woman nurse the baby allows the mother to engage in other physically demanding activities, or provides a good alternative when the mother is sick or otherwise unable to nurse.

Today's **formula**, introduced in the United States in the 1930s, is still derived from cow's milk (except for the more recent formulas based on soy and other vegetable fats for those who are lactose intolerant or allergic). Following the introduction of formula, from 1940 to 1970 only 25 percent of mothers in the United States nursed their babies (Yalom 2002:358). The use of formula, however, poses health risks in many parts of the world where water supplies used to prepare formula might be unsanitary, or when poor women try to stretch powdered formula by diluting it. While today's formulas come closer than ever to mimicking the proteins, sugars, and carbohydrates of breastmilk, they lack the immunological protection conferred by the real thing: Breastmilk fights its own bacterial battles and does not need to be sterilized, and babies absorb their mother's antibodies through the milk.

Breastfeeding is one theme that runs throughout the essays in *A World of Babies,* edited by anthropologists Judy DeLoache and Alma Gottlieb. DeLoache and Gottlieb collected essays based on child-rearing practices in seven different societies. In putting this volume together, DeLoache and Gottlieb questioned the expectation that child rearing is uniform and universal. People the world over are concerned with keeping their babies alive and healthy and face similar challenges when it comes to raising their young. Yet, the essays in this volume illustrate the variety of approaches to raising children.

From the essays in *A World of Babies,* as well as other ethnographic accounts, it is apparent that breastfeeding carries different meanings throughout the world. These are as important as its nutritional aspects. In Turkey, for example, children nursed by the same woman share a special bond and are considered "milk siblings." Among the Fulani of West Africa, an infant is expected to acquire his personality traits from the woman who nurses him. If a baby is not nursed for at least two years, the Fulani believe the child will not be sufficiently attached to his mother. Nursing is also said to assist in birth spacing. The Puritans believed that women had a religious obligation to nurse their infants. In the United States, the Academy of Pediatrics currently recommends breastfeeding because of the nutritional, immunological, and psychological benefits to both baby and mother. At the same time, new mothers are given messages about how often and when to feed their infants that carry latent messages about independence and time management. Meanwhile, the American public largely views breastfeeding as an indecent pursuit. The female breast has become such an object of sexual desire that it is difficult to comfortably bare it in public.

There is an entire industry surrounding nursing in the United States and Europe. Lactation specialists are common staff members at hospitals. Breast pumps for the working mom are big business, as are nursing bras, nursing pads, nursing ointments, compresses, nipple shields, feeding tubes, nursing pillows, and instruction and support manuals. In the United States, where breastfeeding is still considered a private affair to be kept for the most part out of public spaces, women receive very little informal education and exposure to breastfeeding techniques. More and more, hospitals offer breastfeeding classes. Breastfeeding instructors teach that it is not natural to know how to suckle an infant. There are techniques to get the baby to latch on properly. Four holding positions are typically recommended: cradle, cross-over, side-lying, or, yes, the "football" hold. In Bali, these positions are frowned upon because they all result in the baby lying supine. In Bali, babies are considered gods. Their heads should be elevated. Moms should hold them upright, in a sort of sitting position, to nurse them.

There are also varying approaches to when to nurse your baby—on a schedule or on demand. In the United States, some experts abide by the on-demand method, whereas others favor a scheduled approach. Both argue that their method improves the milk supply. In many cultures around the world, the baby should be fed on demand, day and night, as soon as she starts to cry. Of course, in these other societies, mothers and babies usually **co-sleep**, that is sleep next to each other, with husbands and other children and relatives not too far off. The idea of a baby sleeping by herself is shocking to many other cultures, but ideal for most Western families and pediatricians. Pediatricians and lactation specialists also recommend extended feeding periods in order to get to the fatty "hind" milk. In other places, shorter, more frequent suckling sessions are the norm.

In the United States, women are advised to begin nursing immediately after the birth, or the baby may fail to take to sucking. Many other cultures wait three days to begin nursing. They believe that the **colostrum**, the pre-milk substance produced by the mammary glands, is bad. Western doctors, meanwhile, find that it is full of nutritious fat and should be given to the newborn. In many cultures where breastfeeding is the norm, so is supplementation with other liquids, solid foods, or both. Forty years ago in the United States it was acceptable to give some food to young babies. A couple spoons of liquid cereal to a one-month-old were supposed to help her "sleep like a baby" through the night. Today, parents are told to hold off on "solid" foods (pureed and strained) until the baby is four to six months old, and avoid cow's milk until one year. Doing so earlier, the pediatricians say, may cause food allergies later in life or more immediate digestive difficulties. In Bali, however, newborns are given boiled rice and flour porridge and banana from the get-go. The Warlpiri of Australia introduce solids early, offering the infant tea-soaked pieces of cloth and later small pieces of lizard or boiled beef fat. The Fulani of West Africa supplement breast milk with cow and goat's milk as well as other women's milk (that of relatives or co-wives). When the baby is one month old, the Fulani start feeding their babies millet gruel flavored with tamarind, fruit pulp, red peppers, or sugar. These are only a few examples.

The ability to and manner of breastfeeding tie into other activities in which the mother engages. Let's consider work. Among the Ifaluk of Micronesia, women are not expected to work for three months following the baby's birth. The mother's sole "job" during this period is to nurse and bond with her infant. In many other cultures around the world, women carry their infants in a sling while they return to work. This enables them to continue breastfeeding on demand. In other places, babies are left with older children, other new mothers, or elders while their mothers return to subsistence and other activities. In these cases, either the caretakers nurse the babies themselves, or bring the babies to their biological mothers at feeding times. Alternatively, in Western cultures, lactating women returning to the office may hook up their electric breast pumps in the restroom or other semiprivate spaces in order to leave bottles with the nanny or daycare facility.

How long to breastfeed and in what context also vary from culture to culture. In many places a new pregnancy is immediate cause for **weaning**. In the United States, work schedules, public pressure, and values of independence, time management, and convenience influence weaning. In the United States, only 55 percent of all mothers nurse their infants, and 40 percent of those do so for less than two months (DeLoache and Gottlieb 2000:9). Others may nurse for as long as two years, but generally only once or twice a day after the first year. In many other societies, children are breastfed until they are four or five years old. With the introduction of formula and Western values, the age of weaning is becoming younger and younger in most parts of the world today. From beliefs about the nature of motherhood and babies, to patterns of sleeping, eating, and working, breastfeeding is not entirely natural and instinctual; it is clearly a culturally directed activity.

While the biological baseline of motherhood may be universal, being a mother in practice is far more than "natural." Similarly, primate societies are less "natural" and more intricate and fascinating than Charles Darwin ever imagined. Matrifocal units and stable females are the basic building block of primate society. Mothers are critical and mothering is hard work. But there are many styles of mothering and no instincts and no blueprints for such complicated work. Mating and sex serve the purpose of making offspring; they are not the only building blocks of collective existence. Power, authority, status, or domination occur in complex and negotiable situations. Friendship and friends are fundamental.

Kinship groups like the matrifocal units discussed in this chapter appear in many forms in this book. We talked about our early ancestors and matrifocal families in Chapter 1; they are one style of partnering in Chapter 5 and part of "modernization" and the feminization of poverty in Chapter 10. Single-parent and female-headed households are the fastest-growing lifestyles on the planet.

In the next chapter, we will look at different forms for families and a number of ways to find partners in human societies. We will see romance, resistance, more alpha males, and matrifocal units, as well as another view of the social life of the human female.

Some Evolutionary or Revolutionary Books to Read

Are there more female primatologists than male ones? Or is this just a figment of media imagination? What really happened when primate research collided with primate females? Shirley C. Strum and Linda Marie Fedigan brought together scholars from different places, disciplines and genders to comment on the controversies in *Primate Encounters: Models of Science, Gender, and Society* (2000).

Sarah Blaffer Hrdy writes with a unique combination of feminism and evolutionary biology. In her hands, female primates are activist mothers and lovers. Look for *Mother Nature: Maternal Instincts and How They Shape the Human Species* (1999) and the new edition of *The Woman That Never Evolved* (1999). Two field studies depict the personal and intellectual growth of the researcher as well as the complexity of primate societies: Barbara Smuts, *Sex and Friendship in Baboons* (1999); and Shirley Strum, *Almost Human: A Journey into the World of Baboons* (1987).

Having sex and raising infants are the nitty-gritty of evolution. Anthropologist Meredith Small offers an appealing and popular interpretation of research on finding and selecting a mate and rearing the human primate children that result in her books *Female Choices: Sexual Behavior of Female Primates* (1993); *What's Love Got to Do With It? The Evolution of Human Mating* (1995); and *Kids: How Biology and Culture Shape the Way We Raise Our Children* (2001). For a more detailed look at how breastfeeding is influenced by culture in the United States today, see *Mother's Milk: Breastfeeding Controversies in American Culture* (2003) by Bernice L. Hausman.

Chapter Five

Patterns of Partnering from Romance to Resistance

o other topic in *A World Full of Women* is as pervasive and personal as partnering. The words *marriage* and *family* call up images, memories, and value judgments that are difficult to sort out. In all human cultures, most women typically marry and bear children. Regardless of what women personally want to do or actually succeed in doing, we live our lives against the backdrop of the social structures, rules, and expectations for a particular point in history and within those cultural frameworks. There is no right way or wrong way. But there are strategies. "Women's strategies are directly related to the structure of power and authority in the domestic group and to a woman's position with relation to the developmental cycle. . . . Women quarrel with or dominate other women when it is in their interest to do so; they share and exchange with other women when it suits their own goals" (Lamphere 1972:111).

Marriage is one of the major strategies on the planet. All human groups recognize and establish rules and values surrounding marriage. Within the institution, some individuals find salvation, romance, or eternal validation; others find slavery, violence, or psychic death. Marriage as an option in one's life is different from marriage as inevitable or marriage as a career. One thing is clear: It's still work.

In some societies, virtually everyone gets married; many people do it often. Even when getting married or staying married is difficult for us, it is still held up as the ideal thing to do. Even when there are no ceremonies or registration procedures, we still say people are married. In many places and in many times, emotional qualities in marriage are absent or incidental. In effect, exchanges between wives and husbands are "numbed down." A woman's relationships with her children may be more intense and long-lasting and partnering may be only a convenient way to have children. In some cases, the quality of interactions between husband and wife are prescribed by gender ideologies, not by individual personalities. Often, as we shall see in this chapter, friendships, kinfolk, and other women are as important as husbands.

The most common reasons for getting married are to have someone with whom (1) to share work, resources, and status; and (2) to raise children. This makes sense: Men need the services and bodies of females to make babies. Women need help from someone committed to them and to their babies. Kinship systems will not work without marriage.

Varieties of Arrangements

The chapter is inspired in part by the many different experiences my friends, students, colleagues, and I have had with the marriage systems in the United States. Studying anthropology has taught me that the world offers many alternatives and that all women everywhere have to deal somehow with patterns of partnering. So I have picked some key examples of partnering across the globe. They are:

- *the matrilineal Iroquois of Native North America*
- *matrifocal or "mother-centered" households*
- *marriage patterns in Catholic Latin America*

- *traditional patriarchal and patrilineal families of China*

- *African systems of kinship, marriage, and multiple mates*

- *romance as relationship in the United States and increasingly throughout the world*

Each of these cases has a woman-centered point of view. Several themes are woven loosely throughout this chapter. Marriage is mostly about economics, or how people earn a living, and about structures or rules. Women use many strategies to deal with these facts of life. Friendships and feelings matter, but they may have little to do with a spouse.

It matters where we live with our partners. "Your house or mine?" is more than an idle question. Predictably, a bride's life has different meanings if she lives with her kinfolk or his after the wedding. Anthropologists call this *postmarital residence patterns.* There are three kinds in this chapter: matrilocal residence patterns, such as the Iroquois; patrilocal residence patterns, such as the Chinese; or neolocal residence patterns, such as Americans know in our own experience. In primate species, females are rarely required to move from their natal group. As we saw in Chapter 4, males are generally more mobile and females stay as anchors. Humans, however, regularly practice living patterns that send daughters away to become wives. This has consequences for women. Residence patterns are deeply connected to gender ideologies and the treatment of women.

Another theme is how women turn people into relatives. We give birth; this creates **consanguineal kin,** or relatives connected to us through blood. When we marry we have **affinal kin,** or relatives connected to us through marriage. Human beings also create **fictive kin,** informal and formal kinship connections based on the parallels of relationships through birth; adoption is a good example. We also define partners in many different ways.

The Five Fires of the Longhouse

Across the southern region of the Great Lakes, in what is now the United States, lived a group of five tribes called the Iroquois. The Iroquois practiced **matrilineal kinship.** That is, they traced their kinship to each other through women and used this principle to structure their entire social life. They also lived in **matrilocal residences.** This means that a group of women and men related to each other by blood lived together in the same house; when they married, their husbands joined them there as guests. The matrilocal dwellings were called **longhouses.** In effect, Iroquois women owned the houses, the fields, the crops they produced, and a number of very interesting political rights and responsibilities.

The longhouse of the Iroquois is a critical example of women-centered architecture. The longhouse was not just a dwelling; it was the metaphor for their political and spiritual lives. Figure 5.1 shows the floor plan of a longhouse. There were two entrances, one at each end. Berths, benches, or partitioned rooms along the sides accommodated individuals, couples, children, sleeping, and storage. The winter supplies of corn, fur rugs, equipment, or tools and other prepared foodstuffs

Figure 5.1

Iroquois Longhouse

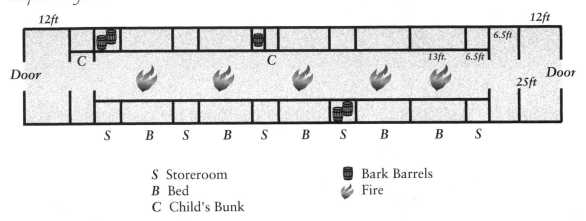

S Storeroom   Bark Barrels
B Bed   Fire
C Child's Bunk

Source: Lewis Henry Morgan, *League of the Ho-De-No Sau-Nee or Iroquois* (1851), volume II, 295.

were stored in the rafters. The middle aisle, with cooking fires, was the indoor social center. Kids played there and adults worked there. A typical longhouse was perhaps 20 feet wide and 150 feet long. They were grouped in permanent villages.

The members of a matriline—that is, the senior women, their daughters, the daughter's children, their brothers, and their unmarried sons—built and owned the longhouse. In other words, those who lived in the longhouse were linked through the females of the clan. Husbands lived there, too, but as outsiders; their homes were with their own matriline.

The women of the longhouse held garden plots and tools in common. They planted, weeded, and harvested corn, beans, and squash, and gathered abundant wild plants. They did all the processing, storage, and distribution of food. It is said that Iroquois women provisioned men's war parties. If the women did not approve and give food, the men could not go to war.

A nineteenth-century lawyer in New York state named Lewis Henry Morgan wrote some extremely significant documents on the Iroquois. We will hear more about Morgan later, but first listen to his interpretation of Iroquois's patterns of partnering:

> From the very nature of the marriage institution among the Iroquois, it follows that the passion of love was entirely unknown among them. Affection after marriage would naturally spring up between the parties from association, from habit, and from mutual dependence; but of that marvellous passion which originates in a higher development of the powers of the human heart, and is founded upon a cultivation of the affections between the sexes, they were entirely ignorant. (Morgan 1851:313)

Morgan's assumption that humans "naturally" feel passion in marriage was one of his Victorian conceits. No one really knows how people felt, certainly in private, in other cultures or in the past. But this particular form of matrilineal kinship and matrilocal residence allows us to discuss how husbands and wives acted in public.

For starters, having a husband or a wife in Iroquois society (and other matrilineal groups like them) was not crucial for regular meals and a roof over one's head. Kinfolk, not spouses, provided those. Iroquois did not have nuclear families as we know them nor the expectation of romance or romantic love as the basis of marriage. Iroquois wives and husbands did not share domestic economies with each other. Iroquois children belonged to their mother's lineage and clan. So there was no such thing as custody arguments, illegitimacy, or abandonment. You can see that the kinship system and the architecture made divorce easy. The first Catholic missionaries to this region were horrified to see Iroquois women who placed their husbands' belongings outside the longhouse and declared themselves divorced. Women also took temporary "husbands" (or lovers) when their own were absent.

Children called their mother's sisters "mom" and their grandmother's sisters "granny," or the Iroquois equivalent. They knew who their biological kin were, but the terms were broader than those in English. So were the circles of responsibility. Anthropologists think that mother's brothers or grandmother's brothers, "uncles" who were clan members, took "fatherly" interests in the lives of their sisters' children. In other words, neither biological fathers nor mothers carried the task of childrearing alone. Women worked in cooperative work groups, lived together, and raised their children in concert.

After contact with Europeans and the changes that resulted, Iroquois households began to form on the European model of patrilineal, nuclear families. They lived in single-room log cabins. Today, in some areas, worship services and community gatherings are held in longhouses. No one lives in them.

Anthropologists and feminists have discussed the status of Iroquois women for decades. They are a major source of evidence in the debates about the power of women in the world. If we believe that women are inevitably subordinate to men, then we have to explain away people like the Iroquois. If we think the Iroquois had a matriarchy, then we want to know how it worked and what insights it offers us. Generations of scholars have projected their own lives on this group in ways that have influenced world history.

"Mother-Centered" Models in the Caribbean

Once we get past the idea of nuclear families as normal, natural, or standard, we often find female-focused kinship units or **matrifocal** households. Like primates, humans have kinship systems in which primary links are between mothers and children. Anthropologists have documented many varieties of cultural settings around the world in which women are mothers, **heads of households**, key decision makers, and financial support for their families.

There are systems of matrifocal kinship in West Africa, the Caribbean, and among other groups of people descended from Africans in the Diaspora to the New World. There are rural villages and poor urban neighborhoods around the world where men cannot find work or have migrated to find work; in any event, they are unavailable as husbands. In Europe and North America, professional and working women often head our own households. There are divorced women, lesbian mothers, single mothers, and the hundreds of thousands of other women who do not fall into the stereotyped nuclear family. Matrifocal households are not limited to lower-class, economically distressed groups or just to societies that are changing rapidly. They seem to occur where women live—by choice or by necessity—economically separate from husbands. Matrifocal patterns of partnering are fluid. Please note that a society may have matrilineal or patrilineal descent, monogamy or polygyny, and still have matrifocal units at its core.

Some social scientists think of matrifocal households and, by extension, the women who head them, as deviate or pathological. They say we are "at risk." Others have viewed the phenomenon of female-headed households as an adaptive strategy to poverty, unemployment, or male work patterns. Others are surprised to find so many social systems in which women as mothers are central.

In the Caribbean, where matrifocal families are customary, couples frequently do not live together in the same household. Nonetheless, they regard themselves as partners. This style of marriage or conjugal bonds is often called **visiting relations** or **consensual unions**. A woman and a man may be in a meaningful, often long-term and committed relationship. They may be parents as well as partners, but they do not share the same household. Women may share affection, love, and mutual respect with their partners. But getting married, if or when it occurs, is likely to be for older people in their thirties or forties, after the children are grown.

In matrifocal, or "mother-centered," households, kinship is not defined by marriage but by blood or consanguineal ties. There is a saying that "blood is thicker than water." In matrifocal families, mothers, children, and siblings are blood; husbands and fathers are water. Matrifocal families are, like all marriage and kinship systems, a way of channeling resources and a way of raising kids.

Male and female relationships are characteristically unstable in matrifocal households.

> *Male and female informants readily acknowledged the shifting allegiances between men and women. Men were known to keep several girlfriends at one time, and marriage, common-law or legal, was no guarantee that monogamy will follow. Women also admitted to keeping an eye out for a better partner and said they would initiate a change if they so desired.*
> *(Prior 1993:314)*

The key feature of matrifocal households is women as mothers. Motherhood, not marriage, turns women into adults. Men are not marginal. First of all, they reside somewhere as brothers and sons. Second, they have a claim on a woman through children and money. Men have a kind of power in that they may have more than one woman; women cannot eliminate men from their lives. Women must work in local economic systems that offer them only low pay and frequent unemployment. As workers, women have low status.

> *These women are members of a culture that may value women as mothers, but women in general do not necessarily enjoy a high status. In other words the mother role is valued, but women are overall subordinate to men. Male informants felt it was their right to physically coerce or punish women as they saw fit, but a man would almost never physically abuse his own mother. (Prior 1993:316)*

Working-class women in the West Indies say that getting married restricts their alternatives. They would be financially dependent on one man. He would have to hold a steady job and agree to support them and their children. As wife, a woman would have to give up a great deal of support from kin group and female relatives.

> *Working class women know they cannot always depend on males in the role of husband–father for economic and emotional support, so they take what they can get from their conflicted situation. They may form a series of "friending" relationships with men for sex, presents, and status. While a man may not be able to provide for a woman economically, her status in her circle of friends is enhanced if she can "hold a man" and keep him satisfied sexually. (Moses 1981:509)*

Neither men nor women believe this is the ideal pattern. To the contrary, women may say that men should take care of them and make the decisions. Men say that they should be providers and protectors. But men migrate or cannot find work, and women have to take over.

Getting children seems to be more crucial to a woman's life than getting a husband. A woman's aunts, grandmothers, other female relatives, or close friends may adopt or foster her children; these are called "borrowed children." Children born to a woman before she marries are called "outside children." "Inside children" are those born to a current spouse or mate. Mothers and daughters, more than mothers and sons or wives and husbands, are the domestic foundation through time.

If having a husband is not one's primary job, then how do women earn a living? Anthropologists separate the cultural patterns brought from Africa from those brought from Western countries like Spain, France, or England. There are long-established and documented African traditions of women controlling internal markets, of economic independence of wives and husbands from each other, and of a sexual division of labor quite different from Western ideas.

> *The fact is that West African and Afro-Caribbean societies have been able, in some contexts, to achieve sexual equality still quite unheard-of in Western societies, for all of their vaunting of individual freedom. The independence and authority exercised by a West African or Haitian market woman in regard to her uses of her own capital, or in regard to the*

economic influence of her husband, has few parallels in the Western world, where individual prerogatives are commonly seen as flowing from individual male wealth, embedded in a nuclear family organization. (Mintz 1981:531)

The Afro-Caribbean patterns contrast sharply with the European-derived patterns of the same geographical area, where a wife customarily takes her husband's name, his social standing, and perhaps his orders.

A particular type of house is characteristic of matrifocal families in the West Indies or Caribbean. The **houseyard** is a West Indian residential unit and a female social space, a cluster or compound of buildings unified by a matrifocal head. Figure 5.2 is an example of Miss Joy's yard.

Figure 5.2
Miss Joy's Yard

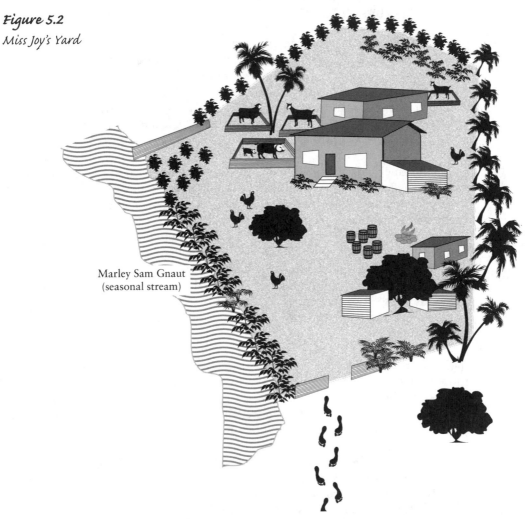

Marley Sam Gnaut
(seasonal stream)

Source: Lydia Mihelic Pulsipher, "Changing Roles in the Life Cycles of Women in Traditional West Indian Houseyards," Janet Momsen (1993), 53.

Here is an explanation.

> *The relationships of those who occupy a particular house in a yard are varied and include the following possibilities: a mother and her young children (occasionally visited at night by one of their fathers), an older woman and several of her adult children (sometimes male, but more often female) and their children, adult (uterine) siblings and their children, a single adult with "borrowed children," a lone single adult, a sexually cohabiting couple with only their common children, or with their common as well as "outside" children, or a couple living alone (usually elderly) who have no common children. (Pulsipher 1993:50)*

A great deal of research points to a growing number of matrifocal families in the United States and around the world. For decades scholars have talked about the phenomenon in African American families; some have seen this as adjustment to the conditions of slavery; others as pathology or an unfortunate matriarchy. Still others see it as necessary adjustments to class, gender, and race.

We must not either romanticize or dismiss this pattern of partnering. Matrifocal lifestyles do not mean that women live separate lives from men or have control over their lives. It does not mean that women are free from racism, sexism, or the hidden injuries of class. Women may still be abused, mistreated, poor, or oppressed in matrifocal families. Women in matrifocal situations do not automatically acquire status and power. It does mean, however, that women are not trained, nor do they expect, to be dependent on husbands for their intimate or economic lives.

Beyond the Virgin Mary in Latin America

In this section, we want to examine ideologies of gender and the realities of marriage in several settings in Latin American societies. The literature on women's lives in Latin America is full of stories about, analyses of, and reasons for unhappy marriages, male irresponsibility, and female suffering.

> *Rich or poor, in towns and villages across the highlands of Guatemala, rarely a day passes without another woeful tale of offenses, abuses, and bad habits of men. . . . Marcela's common-law husband gambles every night and refuses to marry her because he has another wife—and five children—in the next town. Dona Violeta is called a widow, but everyone knows she was abandoned by her husband after the birth of her third child. Carmen had to send her children to live with her mother since their father left her and her new husband refuses to raise another man's offspring. Dona Magdelena's husband drank up her wages, beat her when she complained about it, then spent the next two weeks with his lover, leaving Magdelena penniless. (Ehlers 1991:1)*

What is the problem with these men? Why are these women putting up with it? One of the most common models that has been suggested for understanding the marriages typical of Latin America is a dual complex called **machismo** and **marianismo.** Since its introduction in the early 1970s, this model has been criticized by anthropologists and other Latin American scholars.

The term *marianismo* refers to the Virgin Mary in Christian theology and usually denotes an attitude of saintliness, passivity, and suffering in silence. Women are believed to be morally superior and spiritually pure. *Machismo* is the name for a belief system about men's relationship to women. The word, derived from *macho,* or animal, refers to the qualities of a "real man." This male superiority complex promotes men as virile, husbands as kings, and homes as their castles. Sexual aggressiveness, excessive drinking, violent behavior, and other types of risk-taking are part of the ideology.

According to this model, marianismo promotes a sacred rationale for female subordination. In the face of macho men, women must maximize their lot in life by using feminine power within their households. They benefit from their status as wife and mother and accept stoically what they cannot change.

What's wrong with this theory? In an essay entitled "Against *Marianismo,*" Marysa Navarro argues that "[m]arianismo is an ahistorical, essentialist, anachronistic, sexist, and orientalist fabrication" (2002:270). Marianismo is a stereotype that does not accurately reflect the reality and variety of women's lives. Human beings, female or male, are not just a collection of ideal roles; we are not just the victims of gender ideologies. The core issue is work and earning a living.

> In Guatemala's patriarchal society, the sexual division of labor excludes women from valuable income-producing activities, thus giving them no choice but to accept irresponsible male behavior. Among Mayas and ladinos, the prevailing ideology of male domination in the economy minimizes the contribution women make to family survival and their ability to manage without a resident man. In this system, men are valuable scarce resources who can misbehave with impunity, assured that their wives and mistresses need them for economic reasons. (Ehlers 1991:2)

In this view, women compete with each other for a limited amount of a good thing: husbands who earn money. They put up with men because they have few other choices. As we shall see in Chapter 10, processes we call modernization and economic development may mean that men make more money as women make less.

Many anthropologists think that economics and how women organize resources for survival, not the role assignment of martyred suffering, are the determining factors. Anthropologists Carole Browner and Ellen Lewin examined the Virgin Mary complex and strategies for survival in two groups of working-class Latin American women. What is a strategy?

> We define a strategy as a pattern formed by the many separate, specific behaviors people devise to attain and use resources and to solve the immediate problems confronting them. (Browner and Lewin 1982:63)

The first group Browner and Lewin looked at was women in Cali, Colombia; they are called Caleñas. The other women live in San Francisco; they are called

Latinas. Whether they live in Cali or San Francisco, women have little access to good-paying jobs. So they need either husbands or other economic resources.

> *In Cali, mothers have few alternatives other than to rely on men for sub-sistence, and Caleñas use their femininity and sexuality in efforts to estab-lish what they wish to be permanent conjugal unions. Latina mothers also generally rely on husbands to meet subsistence needs, but in contrast to the Caleñas, Latinas can and do seek public assistance in the event their conjugal relationships prove unreliable or unstable. Freed of the worry of satisfying immediate needs, Latinas on welfare devote themselves to building intense ties with their offspring, whom they hope will care for them later in life. Unlike Caleñas, Latinas place little emphasis on conju-gal affiliation but instead adopt a stance of self-abnegating martyrdom in efforts to cement bonds with their children. (Browner and Lewin 1982:61)*

The women of Cali, Columbia, reported to the interviewers: "It's a rare hus-band who doesn't beat his wife, who doesn't have mistresses, who is loving." The interviewer asked them: "If he's so bad, why do you stay with him? Why is it im-portant that you be with someone?"

One women responded: "Well, in the first place, there's the respect that the children get coming from a family in which the parents are married. . . . Say I left my husband for another. I could end up with someone who didn't want to sup-port my children. They wouldn't be his children, you know. My husband is very poor, but he's more or less responsible toward the children."

Others said, "For the sake of the children." "It's better to be with someone you know, at least you know how you're going to suffer, than to be with someone you don't know."

And another said, "Certainly it's good to live with a husband. Not only are the children more respected, but you are more respected in the barrio besides. You can hold your head up and not feel ashamed of your life."

Latina women in San Francisco say: Love is "only an illusion, nothing more." "If your children know what you've given up on their account, they are bound to do what you want them to for the rest of their lives." "Some women don't mind if their husbands do X [drink excessively, sleep with other women, stay out all night, hit them, or other offenses to domestic stability]. But if my husband ever did X, I would take my children and leave him for good." "Everyone always says, 'for the children, for the children.' But you know what you end up with when you stay for the children? More children!"

Here is a husband's point of view: "When men pay for everything, they can have things the way they want them. But once a woman has her own job and her own money, she begins to feel like more than just a woman, and she starts to make demands and want things too."

In both cities, the anthropologists asked this question: "What do you like best about your husband?" In both cities, the most common answer was: "He brings his paycheck right home." "He gives me what I need to live on." For women in both cities, marriage was a lottery. Everyone played but no one knew who would win.

Marriage may be the only viable economic strategy under the circumstances. Having a husband is the best way to have children. Husbands provide money for the children. He is her job, even when the pay is not good nor the benefits all that great.

A woman's faith in romantic love and monogamy, her need for resources to raise children, and her conformity to a life as True Woman and Ideal Mother conflict with physical abuse, abandonment, and "the other woman." In this picture, partnering may be unavoidable, but it is also unhealthy. Marriage may make women sick.

Duties and Obediences in China

For thousands of years, the people of China organized family life around the principles of **patrilineal descent,** or tracing inheritance and identity through lines of males. No one argues with the assessment that traditional Chinese life was **patriarchal,** or officially under the control of men. For thousands of years, Chinese girls left their parents' homes and went to live with the family of a husband they had typically never met. This type of postmarital residence is called **patrilocal.**

Traditional China means the People's Republic of China before the Communist Revolution. But the core patriarchal values and practices did not end by governmental decree or so-called modernizations. So they continue in the lives of people of the countries and subcultures who share this historic worldview.

The lowest moment of a woman's life in traditional China was her wedding day. Cut off from her first or natal family, the young bride was an outsider and the object of deep suspicion in her new husband's household. She could not expect her husband to side with her against his family. The only way to earn a place for herself was to have sons. She would have to placate her mother-in-law and sisters-in-law, ally herself carefully with other young brides, and make deferential friendships with older women. She would learn to use discretion in gossiping about her household or listening to the gossip of others while, at the same time, establishing herself in the invisible but influential women's community. Treated well, other wives offered advice, comfort, peacemaking, and gradually some protection. Eventually, the accumulation of age and common residence started to pay off. As the young bride matured, her husband started to seek advice from her. Her sons honored her. By menopause she could expect to wield considerable power and to be protected in her old age.

In a system as structured as traditional Chinese life, the effect of personalities was especially strong. Imagine what happened to a bride with few social skills who antagonized her mother-in-law. Imagine a rebellious bride who ignored the informal women's community; who would help her then? Imagine a bride who carefully and quietly did her work, banking courtesies and obedience against the day she was no longer a bride but a mother and mother-in-law. We would not be surprised to find that some women became tyrants and domestic despots; others remembered their pain and provided support to younger women in their turn.

There are many Chinese stories about wicked mothers-in-law. In one tale, the mother-in-law placed her foot-binding cloths in the bridal chamber; in another she required the new bride to launder them by hand. From their own experiences, older women knew the tricks to keep a husband and wife apart, even in the privacy of a couple's bedroom. When women can gain power or even minimal comfort only through men as husbands and sons, they predictably use gossip, guile, and circuitous tactics.

It is difficult to find examples of strategies or resistance to this very controlling system of marriage. There are legends about women who found power in some clever manner. There are many fewer stories about women who found romance, love, autonomy, or independence. Anthropologist Andrea Sankar researched a fascinating set of stories about a movement of Chinese women who chose not to marry and who supported themselves. This option was not open to very many women; so the stories show how the marriage system worked and could be manipulated.

From approximately 1865 to the 1930s in the Pearl River delta of China, there was a sisterhood of women called "self-combers." They took a vow to dress their own hair in a style different from the fashion of married women. They were able to find jobs in the silk industries of the region. They could reach into boiling water, pick up, and unwind the delicate silk thread from the cocoon or perform the other tasks of making silk. These jobs, however difficult or painful, gave them economic alternatives to the arranged marriages and submission to Confucian authority that most Chinese women faced. Note the association of single women with spinning.

These working women banded together in sisterhoods or unions to manipulate the marriage customs for their own benefits. Here are some examples: Some women lived with their brother's families, contributing wages and helping to care for their nieces and nephews. Other women went through a marriage ceremony but did not reside with their husbands after marriage. In some cases, the "bride" sent money to the husband's family, in effect buying her freedom. Married women used the hair-combing vow as a type of divorce. They pledged to remain with the sisterhoods and sent their wages back to their husbands as the price of autonomy. Some sisterhoods pooled their earnings and bought other women to substitute as concubines, to replace their members as wives and mothers. Some families encouraged a daughter's hair-combing vow because they could profit from her earnings. Other women moved out of their parents' house and built a **spinster** house, usually with other women like themselves; this gave them independence, a retirement home, and a way around the ideology that unmarried women brought spiritual damage to their families. However threatening the presence of unmarried women was, their wages apparently compensated and quieted the elders.

Family members nagged the woman about violations of sexual morality. Unmarried women caused Chinese men to worry. They were, by definition, forward, assertive, or lewd; they were probably having affairs with married men; in short, they were out of control sexually. Accusations and belief systems about women as sexually wild and out of control are common when women operate independently outside the legal and religion-sanctioned marriage systems.

Sometimes the emotional bonds forged in the sisterhoods were sexual. Chinese writers tended to ignore females who made love to each other, although they fiercely condemned men who had sex with other men: Such acts did not perpetuate "the Chinese family."

> *In traditional Chinese culture marriage was for production, reproduction, and the maintenance of ancestor worship. Parents or relatives arranged marriages because they understood that it was important for marriage partners to have a successful life. They believed such business was too serious to be left only to sexual attraction. Folk wisdom warned against the instability of love matches. (Sankar 1985:80)*

In fact, the existence of the sisterhoods was a way to avoid marriage and still provide oneself with secure work and retirement; it was not about finding a fulfilling sexual or romantic life. As a result, the lesbian relationships among the women of the sisterhood were typically volatile or temporary. Lives based on romance and abiding passion are problematic in such a system, no matter who does it.

Women who managed to resist marriage often found security, companionship, and affection in the sisterhoods. These were like labor unions or social clubs and ranged in size from small groups of three to seven members to larger associations of up to forty members. These ties of sisterhood were often the major relationships for women; this is particularly true as the chaos of war and violence swept women, families, and local communities asunder. Today sisterhoods still exist in cities of Southeast Asia, Hong Kong, and the People's Republic of China.

A Circle of Wives: African Experiences

The marriage system in which a man has more than one wife is called **polygyny** or polygynous. The word translates as "many women." Anthropologists note that it is fairly common around the world. We fail to note, however, that our analyses are done from a male point of view. Women involved in patterns of polygyny have, by definition, only one husband but one or more co-wives. From a woman's point of view, this system is called **monandry,** or having one husband.

> *Because women in 99.5 percent of cultures around the world marry only one man at once, it is fair to conclude that monandry, one spouse, is the overwhelmingly predominant marriage pattern for the human female. (Fisher 1992:69)*

From a statistical point of view, monandry is the most common form of marriage on the planet. Moreover, women who live in polygynous systems share the status and work of wife with other women. But there are no terms for this pattern.

Polygyny as a marriage system has one of its most vivid expressions on the continent of Africa. This practice is often thought to oppress women. Many contemporary scholars of African life point out, however, that polygyny fostered an ethic of independent action for African women.

In fact the double standard of morality characteristic of monogamous marriages was not the rule. It was quite acceptable in many societies for women in polygynous households to have lovers. Social organization being communal, rather than composed of nuclear family units, ensured a certain amount of socioeconomic security and cooperation among members of the polygynous household. Polygyny also guaranteed the social and economic responsibility of males for their children. As a result women did not have to struggle for their survival or bear the sole responsibility for their children's care, but could at the same time have a certain amount of independence from absolute male dominance. (Steady 1981:16)

At this point, most people ask, How do people involved in polygyny feel about it? How does it work on a personal level? The actions resulting from feelings of jealousy are a major problem. A husband in a polygynous situation has to act fairly and use good managerial skills. Yes, a man may enjoy having a wife kneeling to him as she presents him with a drink. Yes, he may enjoy women vying for his favors, available to him at night, every night. But this may be at the price of quarrelling among his wives. Wife 2 parades her children in front of Wife 1 who has none; Wife 3 decides to sweep while Wife 2 is eating a meal. Wife 1 sings songs that seem to insult her other co-wives. What if two or three wives are pregnant at once? Can he separate them into different households? Yes, but this is expensive. Can he act as judge, listen to each case, and beat them on occasion? Yes, but they will find means to retaliate.

There were, contrary to appearances, some advantages to plural marriages. Sometimes senior wives provided the **bride price** so husbands could acquire another and junior wife. If a husband were going to have a new sweetheart, the first wife could keep a firm eye on her and keep the family income under one roof. This is one way women could exercise some control.

A compelling reason for women to cooperate in plural marriages was to have a "helpmate" or a co-wife to assist in the household work. Traditional housework involved tedious preparations like grinding or carrying foods from market. In fact, female companionship was a major appeal of polygyny. If the marriages worked out and the co-wives liked each other, they would have someone to gossip with. Co-wives as allies and friends meant control over their joint husband, household, budget, and children. They might even find other wives to wait on them!

Polygyny is as much about women's relations to each other as it is their relations to men. Her husband's other wives may well be the most hostile, controlling, cooperative, or loving relationships a wife ever experiences outside her natal family. Polygyny worked best when women liked and conspired with each other. Generally, the senior wife set the tone. Like a mother-in-law in other settings, she could use her power as friendship and cooperation or as dominance and meanness. She had power but a later wife may have been her husband's love match. There are many stories about married women who left husbands because of co-wives. The stories conclude, "The man was all right, but those other women were impossible!" By contrast, wives may get along splendidly. In one West African story, a man wakes up to find his three wives vanished with all their children. They have decided they like each other best and can support themselves in a joint business venture. He whines, "Who's going to fix my breakfast now?"

Many authors talk about the central values and practices in African kinship. These include the centrality of children, multiple mothering, fostering, and the primacy of kinship ties over marital ties. Children in ancestor-worshiping cultures mark the connections between the dead, the living, and as yet unborn; they promise continuity of generations in a more articulated fashion than we normally understand it. Consanguineal kin, or those related by blood, are closer and more dependable than spouses are.

> *If we examine the perceptions of contemporary African women, it is evident that they see themselves as working for their own and their children's benefit, not for their husbands. It seems probable that earlier generations of African women held similar views. Although a woman may have contributed to her husband's accumulation of wealth and status, in practice men seldom exercised direct control over wives' productive activities and could not appropriate their produce in many places, even where there were ideologies of male ownership. (Potash 1989:193)*

Mothers in so-called polygynous households are usually the central figure in family life and households whether they reckon kinship through the mother's line or through the father's line. This means matrifocal units are still the core of emotional life. It also means that women have, at least before colonialism, significant economic independence. Men as husbands have limited authority in their wives' households. A man as brother is extremely important to his sisters and his sisters' children, all of whom share the same matrilineage, property, and ritual responsibilities.

Moreover, the polygynous kinship systems of Africa allowed women to have wives. How is this possible? Taking a wife was a mark of wealth and success. So women who had the means and resources took wives too. Women, that is, biological females who worked as wives to female husbands, did the same things all wives do. They worked at status enhancement and were a major asset in helping their female husbands accumulate wealth. They freed their husbands from domestic work. The female husbands could have the status and power that men had by becoming like men.

This was not necessarily about having sex (although men worried about and commented on that possibility). This is about kinship and using the rules of marriage to advance oneself. Nigerian sociologist Ifi Amadiume grew up in and did research in the Igbo area with a group called Nnobi. She explains:

> *In indigenous Nnobi society, there was a direct link between accumulation of wives, the acquisition of wealth and the exercise of power and authority. The ultimate indication of wealth and power, the title system, was open to men and women, as was the means of becoming rich through*

control over the labour of others by way of polygamy, whether man-to-woman marriage or woman-to-woman marriage. The Nnobi flexible gender system made either possible. (Amadiume 1987:42)

The strategic uses of kinship went beyond female husbands. For the Igbo, land was the basis of how people earned a living and men needed heirs in patrilineal societies. So men without sons converted a daughter into a kind of man—the kind who could inherit land. So a woman became a male daughter and landowner.

In many areas of Africa, women grew and sold their own crops, manufactured products for sale in the local markets, and managed their own money. Women who became successful traders took "wives" for themselves. Adult women could become "husbands," that is, pay a bride-price to gain rights in the labor of women.

If women are expected either to exercise power or to symbolize power, they must be conceptualized as male, or at least not take on the subordinate status of wife. . . . What more effective symbol than a reversal from the expected roles of wife and mother to those of husband and father. (O'Brien 1977:122)

Among the highly stratified states of West Africa, women as wives in polygynous households often had formal relationships with each other. Girls were often betrothed and married soon after puberty to men much older than themselves. The groom's kinfolk paid a bride-price to the bride's kin. This bride-price gave the new husband and his family the right to claim her children for their lineage (the only way to have children in a patrilineage is to buy or otherwise acquire the services from a woman who is not a relative). Wealthy men had several wives; typically, each wife had her own house in the compound and a plot of land to cultivate. She could sell the products in the market and keep the proceeds, generally to assist her children with their education.

The longer a wife was married, the more benefits and freedom she was likely to enjoy. This included intimacies, both sexual and economic, with other women. Taking co-wives as lovers was safer and easier than meeting men outside the compounds. Women did not inform their husbands about these arrangements. Husbands tended to hear gossip and to feel threatened about them but did not have the power to order them stopped. In some groups, women staged a ritual to create a formal and permanent bond between them. By doing this, women probably extended and confirmed their economic networks, enhanced their position in the community, and improved their emotional life (Blackwood 1985a, b).

African polygyny reminds me very forcefully of the contemporary blended family and multiple marriages in the United States. Divorced people often have assorted relationships with an ex-husband's new wife, their new children, her ex-husband, their children, as well as the new mate's former spouses, lovers, and children. Everyone has strong feelings about these arrangements. Sometimes we act strategically, creatively, or romantically. Sometimes we are mean and resistant.

Love Marriages and Lavish Weddings

Isn't it romantic? Their eyes met across the bar. He smiles. She smiles. They fall in love and live happily ever after. Falling in love, soul mates, destiny, fate, true love, being madly in love, transcendence, intimacy, and desire are themes that run throughout Western notions of romance. This discourse of **romantic love** permeates Western culture. From movies to novels, magazines to music, soap operas to greeting cards, romance is everywhere.

The notion of romantic love has always been around; it is ancient. Passion and desire are emotions experienced by women and men in many cultures. Descriptions across cultures look remarkable similar: The heart beats faster. The face flushes. One experiences a feeling of being out of control or of losing one's mind or heart. William Jankowiak defines romantic passion as "any intense attraction involving the idealization of the other within an erotic context" (1995:4). This is a broad definition that can be applied to many cultures throughout time and place. While this general idea and the physiological sensations associated with passion and infatuation are similar, the cultural and historical context of **romance** make it particular. Romance is defined and judged differently across the world. It is a changing concept, emerging from, reacting to, and reflecting other cultural phenomena, such as property laws, gender ideology, religious beliefs, racial perspectives, and economic concerns. As these change, so do the forms of romance.

The ideas of romance and romantic encounters in many cultures are associated with affairs or rebellion against authority. They offer adventure, excitement, or defiance. Falling in love is rebellious and subversive. It may be a powerful form of resistance. Around the world, we see examples of romantic passion, but they usually surface outside of marriage, often flying in the face of parental and societal expectations. In other words, most people can think of someone who fell in love with a person he or she was not supposed to marry. In fact, romance in the West has a long history of focusing on pre- or extramarital affairs. Romance manuals of the medieval, European court instructed people on how to conduct love affairs outside of marriage. Marriage and romance were in opposition.

Today, for most couples in the United States, ideas of romance, of intimacy, of falling in love, and of being in love are central to formal and informal relationships. These relationships range from casual affairs to committed relationships. Romance and intimacy are predominant themes in many homosexual and heterosexual relationships. The goal of a romantic pursuit ranges from getting someone "into bed," to a "long-term" relationship, to marriage.

Marriage as an institution is not the same as the set of feelings called romance or romantic love. The association of romance with marriage in Western Europe appears as early as the seventeenth century. In the eighteenth century, **companionate marriages** based on compatibility rather than economic or familial concerns gained popularity in both Europe and the United States. Love, idealized and transcendent, became ascendant in the nineteenth century. Romance became more popular, and unrealistic expectations about marriage grew. The connection of romance to love and marriage is also in part a reaction to women working outside of the home. Some argue that romance woos women back to the kitchen and into unequal relationships with men. At other times marrying for love has been considered an act of rebellion against patriarchal structures.

Typically, "falling in love" and individual preference have not been the primary reasons for getting married. Economic realities, the desire for children, legitimate sexual access, and the duties of kinship have been. A more predominant pattern for marriage in the world is for the families to help the young people find a spouse. Sometimes there are outright **arranged marriages**. Other times, there are expectations so subtle and pervasive that everyone just goes along with them. Women sometimes go into these marriages kicking and screaming. Sometimes they run away. And sometimes they request them.

Arranged marriages sometimes offer surprising benefits. A shy or noncompetitive person can end up with a good partner. Many people in arranged marriages expect to fall in love later, and many actually do. Strongly situated in familial and economic networks, arranged marriages may be more stable. While the expectations and adherence to arranged marriages vary from place to place, they all place a greater emphasis on family obligations and building community than do romantic marriages where the couple is center stage. In the cultures where they exist, arranged marriages are often set in stark contrast to nonarranged marriages, sometimes called **love marriages** or **elopements**. The following are two examples of what arranged marriages can be like. In each case, the woman to be married plays a different role, faces different expectations, and has different grounds for satisfaction. In each, the connections among love, passion, and marriage are arranged differently.

Psychology professor, Monisha Pasupathi identifies herself as the product of a love marriage between her Brahmin father and European American mother. She questions the image of arranged marriages as oppressive to women. Her father was the only one of his siblings to choose his own spouse. Raised in the United States, Pasupathi is expected to choose her spouse, though many of her paternal cousins in India and the United States opt for arranged marriages. One of her cousins in India decided to pursue an arranged marriage after she completed her MBA. Pasupathi writes,

> *When the time came to search for a husband, my cousin contributed some criteria for the search process, stipulating educational level, asking for someone who would be flexible about whether she worked or not, someone easygoing with a sense of humor, who was vegetarian, and did not smoke. As is quickly evident, these kinds of criteria would not look out of place in an American personals advertisement. (2002:212)*

In this case, the bride's parents contacted the parents of potential grooms and suggested compatible bachelors. In the end, Pasupathi's cousin had the final say as to whom she would wed. This kind of familial involvement is likely to ground the marriage in more realistic expectations. The presence of a kinship-based support system also helps make the marriage more stable.

In some cultures, arranged marriages are highly stable. In others, they are expected to serve only as first marriages for young women. The Kalasha of Pakistan recognize that a woman may leave the arranged marriage of her youth to pursue a later marriage with a husband of her choice through elopement. Of course there are advantages to staying in arranged marriages. If the woman is unhappy, she can seek redress from her family. It also means that the husband must work harder to please and keep his wife. If a husband seems reluctant to meet his wife's requests, she might counter with the question, "Do you think I stay here because I am in love with you?" (Maggi 2001:207). When a woman elopes, she has essentially "made her own bed" and must lie in it. Elopement also jeopardizes the woman's relationship with her natal family, since she is breaking an agreement that they worked hard to arrange. This in turn affects her family's relationships with other families. In addition, when a woman elopes into a second marriage, she must leave her children with her first husband's family. These consequences are powerful deterrents against elopement. Still, the Kalasha consider the ability for women to elope out of their arranged marriages and into marriages of their own design as one of the foremost ways that women are free.

In every culture, the core values associated with gender, kinship, economics, and marriage are represented in the motifs and symbols of the wedding. Weddings in the United States are no exception. Here, in the increasingly lavish wedding, love is idealized and the couple takes center stage. Ultimately, the American wedding compresses our ideals of independence, intimacy, romance, and capitalism into a single event. As economic production and familial reproduction are nudged to the background, the idea of the self-sufficient couple as consuming force is pushed to the fore. The wedding itself expresses the culmination of romantic pursuits and ideals of the nuclear family and **neolocal residence** (setting up a new home irrespective of where your relatives live). This type of wedding is becoming ever more popular across boundaries of class, ethnicity, and sexual preference.

In *Cinderella Dreams: The Allure of the Lavish Wedding*, Cele C. Otnes and Elizabeth H. Pleck (2003) write about the wedding in American society. They reiterate that the lavish wedding is the ultimate synthesis of romance and capitalism. Current American wedding trends are a booming industry, both at home and abroad. From dating to the engagement ring, the wedding dress to the reception, the couple is mired in consumerism. Consumer culture seizes the physiological and emotional sensations of romance, infatuation, and passion to sell everything—from hair color to cleaning products, cars to diet pills. They promise magical transformation, eternal happiness, and sexual pleasure.

Picture a typical wedding. Following the ceremony, there is the reception. And at the center of the reception, is the cake. Often costing hundreds, if not thousands of dollars, the cake stands there majestically, a tower of ethereally iced layers. Atop perch a plastic bride and groom, perfect and unchanging in their respective white gown and black tux. The wedding cake announces the central motif of the American wedding: The new couple is elevated by confectionary romance, isolated from the rest of society, friends, family, coworkers, and the progression of time itself. By no coincidence, it is traditional for the bride and groom to share the first slice of their happily-ever-after cake. The guests follow suit, but all too often report that the cake itself is dry and tasteless. This foreshadows the disappointment many couples face when, as it is said, "the honeymoon is over."

The cake serves as a metaphor, echoing what many find to be the reality of marriage. As you may recall, Western romance has historical roots in nonmarital relationships. What happens once the romance of courtship and wedding are over? Romance might whisk a couple up to the altar, but once there, it is up to the couple to do the work of building their relationship. The couple is expected to rely heavily on one another: providing unconditional support and respite from every-day pressures, perhaps raising children together, and growing ever closer and more intimate. The idealization of love, marriage, and monogamy continues. As one of my friends said, "Being in love is the only thing that makes the institution of marriage bearable."

These representations of romance in partnering are one of the most powerful and influential forces in the world. Western ideologies of partnering and romance are exported in myriad of ways, from missionary zeal to consumer products and entertainment. In *Invitations to Love: Literacy, Love Letters, and Social Change in Nepal* (2001), Laura Ahearn explores the influence of development and literacy on notions of love and marriage. Love letters in this region of Nepal are a recent introduction, made possible by the increased rate of literacy in the 1990s. As such, romance is intimately related to development. The structure, content, and use of love letters emerges from the intersection of local and Western concepts of love, passion, courtship, and marriage.

In the village of Junigau (the site of Ahearn's study), people historically wed in one of three manners: through arrangement, **capture marriage**, or elopement. By the time of Ahearn's research, capture marriages had all but disappeared and elopements had become more popular than arranged marriages. Western con-

Elaborate wedding cakes depict notions of romance in the United States.

cepts of love, romance, and companionate marriage have found their way into village culture. Romantic discourse is embedded in the schoolbooks, magazines, and novels that villagers read. There are even guidebooks that offer instruction on composing effective love letters. Romance has become equated with education, economic success, and development, in part indicated by the level of literacy that enables the exchange of love letters in the first place.

Ahearn notes that the ideas of romance expressed in Nepali love letters express new forms of agency in some respects, but not others. Men write about love as a powerful desire that overtakes them. Here are some excerpts from a letter written by a male university student:

> *Life is an infinite circle. . . . In the whole "world" there must be few individuals who do not bow down to love. Sarita, I'm helpless, and I have to make friends of a notebook and pen in order to place this helplessness before you. . . . Love is the union of two souls. The "main" meaning of love is "life success." I'm offering you an invitation to love. If you are capable of accepting it, then accept; otherwise, in this, my time of suffering and life's last moment, please return this revealing letter. (Ahearn 2001:213–214)*

Sarita, the recipient of this letter, hesitates in returning the affections of her suitor. All the while, she finds herself becoming increasingly mired in the exchange of love letters. Women's reputations are jeopardized by such letter exchanges. Fearing they will be perceived as breaking the mores of sexual conduct, thus bringing dishonor to their families, women like Sarita may succumb to elopement. Love overtakes men. Elopement overtakes women. Sarita elopes not because she wishes to, but because of the circumstances. When Ahearn asks her what she means by circumstances, Sarita responds,

> *Circumstances—well, very, a lot of dishonor has occurred. . . . People say, "She's pregnant, they do bad things"—that's what others say, right? And that's NOT true, there's NOTHING bad that we've done. Dishonor has occurred because rumors have begun to spread all over the place. And after such talk, if the boy breaks it off . . . and if someone comes from somewhere else to ask permission to marry the girl, someone—either the boy's brothers and other relatives, or other, will say, "No, that . . . that girl used to have a 'love.' So-and-so's daughter used to have a 'love,' it is said, and that boy left her." And then the boy's father will say, "WHAT?!? You won't marry that one! Kill the negotiations!" Yes, that's what I mean by saying dishonor has occurred. That's what I mean by saying that I seek to marry only because of circumstances, see? (Ahearn 2001:242)*

At the same time, couples view love-based unions, with their emphasis on individuality, spousal choice, and **modernity** as avenues to success. As this example from Nepal illustrates, Western romance carries meanings of what is modern, progressive, and successful with it, just as development projects and other imports bear the standards of Western partnering ideologies. These ideas are embraced, refashioned, and resisted in local ways. These ideas can have unforeseen effects.

This leaves us with a number of questions: Are the ideologies of romance a form of resistance to, escape from, or conformity to monogamous and neolocal marriage patterns? Are women oppressed or liberated by the romantic ideologies of partnering? Are the ideas of love and romance universal? Was Morgan wrong when he said that the Iroquois felt no such emotions? Is romantic love a gender ideology? If so, whom does it serve? Is romance another form of women's work?

You may have noticed that I omitted discussion of a prominent feature of partnering: wife-beating and wife-battering. We will cover this important topic in Chapter 9, in the context of violence against women around the world. This discussion of "marriage and family" leads us into the next chapter, to systems that segregate the lives of females and males in highly structured ways and buttress their segregation with elaborate ideologies and myths.

Reading from Romance to Resistance

All good ethnographies cover topics like "marriage and family." However, not all of them cover women's lives with sensitivity and insight. Here are four suggestions. Sally Price has a second edition of *Co-wives and Calabashes* (1993), a readable ethnography about the Saramaka Maroons, descendants of Africans brought as slaves to the Dutch colony of Surinam. Gender is complex and fascinating in this matrilineal and polygynous society. After having two kids, Diane Bell finished high school, went to college, and got a doctorate. She has published widely in anthropology, history, law, and women's studies. Her book, *Daughters of the Dreaming* (1993, 2d ed.), is a tale both of her fieldwork in the central Australian desert and of women's lives in an absolutely fascinating setting, rich in ritualism and spiritualism against all odds. For wives' strategies for economic advancement, read Garcia Clark's *Onions Are My Husband: Survival Accumulation by West African Market Women* (1994). Wynne Maggi's *Our Women Are Free: Gender and Ethnicity in the Hindukush* (2001) is a fascinating ethnography about Kalasha women in Pakistan. Her discussions of women's agency, freedom, and marriage choices merit further reading.

Shulamith Firestone's classic, *The Dialectic of Sex* (1970), is an important read for anyone interested in feminist perspectives on romance. Two books about wives in European and American history reveal the patterns of the past and how they both entrap and empower women. Stephanie Coontz counters the mythologies about American marriage and families in *The Way We Never Were: American Families and the Nostalgia Trap* (1992). In *A History of the Wife* (2001), historian Marilyn Yalom traces wives from Biblical times, through Greek and Roman civilizations, the Middle Ages, Victorian England, and into contemporary culture, and shows what wifedom inherited from the past—the medieval cult of love, what has been discarded—legal servitude to a husband, and what we are currently inventing—same sex marriages. *Modern Love: Romance, Intimacy, and the Marriage Crisis* (2003) by David R. Shumway looks at marriage, relationships, and popular American culture in relation to discourses on romance and intimacy. Shumway's insightful discussion of intimacy deepens our understanding of the culture of marriage and relationships in the United States.

Chapter Six

A Two-Bodied World

Cultural Systems for Separating Females and Males

he problems with the Christians start, said Father, as with women, when the hudud, or sacred frontier, is not respected. I was born in the midst of chaos, since neither Christians nor women accepted the frontiers. . . . When Allah created the earth, said Father, he separated men from women, and put a sea between Muslims and Christians for a reason. Harmony exists when each group respects the prescribed limits of the other; trespassing leads only to sorrow and unhappiness. But women dreamed of trespassing all the time. The world beyond the gate was their obsession. They fantasized all day long about parading in unfamiliar streets, while the Christians kept crossing the sea, bringing death and chaos. (Mernissi 1994:1)*

In many human cultures, women and men live apart from each other in fascinating and complex ways. These **sexual segregation** or **gender separation systems** are historically based styles of living and social organizations in which the lives of women and the lives of men are substantially segregated. In these groups, people manipulate the biological facts of sex and reproduction and the social necessities of kinship. They invent or embroider whole arenas of social life around the notion of gender.

This chapter contains three examples. The first takes place in the rain forests of the Amazon in a group called the Mundurucú. The second example concerns selected groups in the culture area of Melanesia. The third example comes from some of the nation states of the Muslim Middle East. We will conclude with Moroccan sociologist Fatima Mernissi, who grew up in a harem in Morocco, one of these systems of separation. The opening paragraph of her autobiography, quoted above, sets the themes of this chapter.

Why do such segregated systems exist? There are as many theories as there are anthropologists, ethnographers, historians, or other commentators. As you will see, mythologies, ideologies, or sacred scriptures justify but do not explain the segregation of sexes. Insiders and outsiders or participants and observers usually have strong opinions and deep emotions about such gender-differentiated lives. No one is safely objective. There are no agreements about what these systems ultimately mean or how they came to exist. Sometimes, but not always, these systems appear to be cases of male control or dominance. Much of the time, however, they look like an elaborate game of creativity wrapped in the symbols and perceptions of a two-bodied world. Each example in the chapter contains these multiple perspectives.

On one level, these dramatic systems are still about partnering, kinship, family, and marriage; the same work still gets done. So this chapter is an extension of Chapters 4 and 5. We have merely turned up the volume on one characteristic, gender separation.

The following themes appear in each. First, significant items of material culture symbolize the sexual segregation systems. This includes such objects as trumpets, flutes, veils, masks, banana fiber skirts, string bags, and many others. Body decorations, costumes, and clothing are often pronounced between genders. Living quarters are physically separated: men's houses, women's houses, or men's sides, women's sides.

Second, each example centers on assertions that there are only two genders and men and women are not equal or interchangeable. Our human "natures" are different. People in these kinds of cultures have elaborate mythologies which establish sacred justifications for how relationships between the sexes are supposed to be. They apply the myths to conception as well as life after death. They have to work out the practical considerations in separating genders. What happens to young boys, born to women, who must grow up to be men? What if women question the system or have their own system? Who does the work and who gets the credit? What about having sex? What about personal feelings, emotions, or sentiments, such as love?

Third, women are powerful in unexpected ways.

Amazon: Women of the Forest and the Flutes

In 1952 two young graduate students at Columbia University, Yolanda Murphy and Robert Murphy, married and went to South America to do fieldwork in anthropology. The research they did together in the rain forests of Amazonian Brazil led to one of the first ethnographies that actually looked at and saw women's lives. The Murphys did not listen just to what men said about women. Nor did they have the kind of marriage in which she wrote about women and he wrote about the "real" culture. This is why their book, *Women of the Forest,* has become an icon in women's studies.

There are three points in time for Mundurucú gender relations. First is the mythic past, when women owned and played sacred musical instruments. Second is the ethnographic present, the moment the Murphys witnessed, of uneasy truces, fear, and anger between women and men. The third moment is the future. The Murphys arrived as traditional Mundurucú life was changing to resemble that of other poor people within the nation state of Brazil.

In the past, the Mundurucú, like other groups deep in the forests of the Amazon, made gardens, collected wild fruits and nuts, hunted, or fished for a living. The heavy task of clearing the land for gardening was men's work; they helped in planting the manioc shoots. But all the rest of the planting, harvesting, and food processing was done by women. Manioc, the bitter staple of their diet, was inedible without the time-consuming, physically laborious, and exhausting work of women in processing the tubers.

The Mythic Past of the Mundurucú

The Mundurucú tell a tale, a myth about sex, sacred objects, men's groups, and women's work. In the distant past, three women were collecting firewood when they heard music in the distance. They traced the source of the sound and found flute-like trumpets. Once they had tried them, the women wanted to do nothing more than play the sacred instruments all day long. Their husbands and brothers grew suspicious, followed them, and discovered their secret. They tricked the women into bringing the trumpets into the village and seized them from the women. After all, they said, we men are the only ones who can go hunting to catch meat for ceremonials and offerings to the trumpets. The men took the trumpets to their men's house where the women could not touch them. The women returned to their own dwelling houses and cried for what they had lost.

This story outlines the mythic past of Mundurucú males and females and justifies the separations of the present. Women once owned and played with the sacred trumpets. Men wrested them away. Men hunt; meat is the only proper food for honoring the ancestors. Women make manioc cakes; everyone eats them every day, but they are unfit for offering to the ancestors. The men live in men's houses with each other and the trumpets. Women live in dwelling houses where men enter at will. So women cannot refuse the sexual needs of men.

Such stories of power and gender reversals laced with sexual and phallic symbols are common, although not universal, in the world. They act as spiritual permission or as a supernatural charter for how separate sexes are supposed to, or allowed to, treat each other. They justify but do not explain.

The Ethnographic Present

In the 1950s, Mundurucú men were uneasy and fearful in their control. The male creed said that women were inferior and ungovernable. But women also threatened men. After all, they once owned the trumpets and found private pleasure in them. Men were insecure: They could deny formal authority to women, but they knew the oppressed had potential power. According to the Murphys, the two genders were not just ranked higher or lower than each other. These were not individuals in role conflict. They were opposing armies.

Men wanted women to be passive and retiring, to close off their eyes and mouths. Women were not supposed to participate in political or religious affairs nor question the ways of men. A woman who violated these rules was said to be wanton and promiscuous, a Mundurucú nymphomaniac. Men used gang rape to punish any woman who violated their taboos. These ranged from acting seductively to spying on the sacred flutes. So women had to work and travel in groups of two or more. If a woman walked alone outside the village, she was assumed to be heading for a rendezvous. Just being alone made her available and gave men the right to stop her and demand intercourse. The Murphys called this a classic example of phallic sadism.

Mundurucú men asserted that they possessed the crucial ingredients for siring offspring. But women actually bore and nursed the children. This fundamental contradiction was partially resolved by a kind of folk-science about reproduction. The Mundurucú believed that seminal fluid coagulated and formed the fetus. So a woman needed to have a number of sexual contacts with a man before she could become pregnant. In this reasoning, men provide all the raw material to make a child; women merely did the work of carrying them. One consequence of this belief was that women's frequent extramarital affairs were not counted toward conception or pregnancy building; only her husband's efforts mattered. Folk beliefs like this reduce women's work in reproduction to something resembling an incubator.

In their dirt-floored communal dwellings, there was no "housework" as we know it. The major work of Mundurucú women was making manioc. The tubers from the manioc plant grew year round in the poor soils of the forests. But manioc is bitter and nauseating unless carefully processed. So groups of women worked long and hard to peel, chop, and grate the tubers. They hauled water by hand and poured it over the pieces to leach out acids. They toasted the lumpy manioc flour over a fire until dry. In addition, they gathered, gardened, and cared for children. All the work was competently supervised by experienced older women. These women served as midwives, advised on matters such as hammock-making, and exercised a mild but undisputed authority.

As women processed the manioc, they gossiped. This activity must not be overlooked or trivialized. Gossip is the primary form of social control in face-to-face groups such as villages, companies, neighborhoods, or sororities. Most of it is the exchange of valuable information about other people's activities and behaviors. Gossip may be thought of in this context as personal strategies, apprenticeship learning, or social control.

Everyone ate manioc every day, but they preferred to eat meat. Men hunted only irregularly and with unpredictable results, but they garnered attention and recognition for it.

> *Hunting is central in Mundurucú culture because it is men's work, and not vice versa. In actuality, gardening provides a larger proportion of the sheer bulk of Mundurucú food intake and the subject of greatest labor investment, albeit mostly female labor. (Murphy and Murphy 1974:62)*

The architecture of their domestic life was one of the most telling features of how women and men related to each other. A traditional Mundurucú village had a number of dwellings and one men's house. The dwellings were open; they had no compartments and no privacy. Females regardless of age and boys below the age of puberty lived there. Household members hung their sleeping hammocks at the quieter ends of the dwelling and used the busy center for cooking, nursing babies, and visiting back and forth. Children and dogs wandered in and out. Men dropped by for food, sex, or visiting their babies, but they were marginal to life within the dwellings. Men took the young boys away from the communal dwellings at some point before puberty. Both women and men agreed that the only enduring bond was between mothers and daughters. Sisters and the residential bonds of shared work and shared children came next. Despite patrilineal descent and the male myth of control, the reality was matrilocal and matrifocal, mother-centered living arrangements.

The women of Mundurucú lived in deep solidarity with each other. They shared farming, manioc flour-making, common dwellings, and caring for each other's children. Women traveled in bands for protection. When men asserted authority and the power of the myth, they only increased women's cohesion with each other and their hostility toward males. Women dropped their eyes or averted their heads around men.

In one sense, this behavior can be interpreted as submissive, although at another level it is a primary form of defense. Women guard their emotions before men, communicate as little as possible of their subjective states, set themselves off with reserve. The woman who casts down her eyes when near men is not really saying that she is inferior, but that she is apart and distant, that she is not to be interfered with. She becomes symbolically impenetrable. (Murphy and Murphy 1974:137)

The Murphys described the women as "secular" and "pragmatic." Women knew about the trumpets and ritual equipment hidden in the men's house, but seemed indifferent both to the objects and men's anxieties about them. Women said that men were lazy. In fact, women were more loyal to housemates than to husbands.

Under these circumstances, why would women bother with marriage? They fed children with their own labor and shared domestic quarters with other women. Marriage, however, was simply the normal state for adults and the smallest building block in a functioning society. For women, marriage appeared to be an investment, a status, a presumed or usual activity. It was not compelled by feelings. A woman understood that intercourse was the way to get and keep a husband and that male sexual satisfaction was the goal. So adultery was a form of revenge on an erring husband, not a means of enjoyment for a woman.

Most of the women complained to the Murphys about frequent childbearing. They blamed men for the pregnancies, miscarriages, and stillbirths they experienced through adulthood. They told the anthropologists about several birth control remedies made from roots. The same concoctions could also be used to induce abortions. They kept all these matters secret from men; it was simply none of their business.

The Future Arrived

Everyone has heard about the deforestation of the Amazon basin, the development policies of nation states like Brazil, and the profound and irreversible changes of modernization. The village traditions of the Mundurucú were already under pressure when the Murphys arrived. Brazilians were clearing the forest for plantations, agriculture, and ranching. Some villages were already involved with the cash and consumer economy, missionary stations, and wage labor. What happened to women, men, and systems of separation when the entire economic and social base shifted?

The Mundurucú moved into smaller households. There were no longer dwellings arranged by gender, no more sacred instruments to support the oppression of women, and no more groups of men making demands. Nuclear families became the unit of work and common meals.

Women still do most of the work, simply because in smaller couple-centered households, there is no one else. Husbands will "help," but at the expense of women's vital connections with each other. Preparing manioc flour is easier with new equipment but bereft of cooperation, amiability, and female socializing. Men will take care of babies more often, simply because there is no one else to do it. In contrast to the old forest dwellings, small households have few back-up baby tenders.

Mundurucú women want husbands to live with them and provide for them. They want Western consumer goods: metal pots, pans, knives, axes, clothing, ornaments, canned foods, and the things they know women in big cities have. They want hand-turned, mechanical grinders for manioc. This simple tool speeds the processing a hundredfold and alters the sexual division of labor in manifold ways. So Mundurucú women urge their husbands to take wage labor jobs to earn cash. They nag and sweet-talk them into harder work or debt. Husbands work for hourly wages when they can and use the money to buy Western consumer goods. Religious and festive gatherings will be at the mission station and in the bars of small towns. Men will be able to buy alcohol.

Are women better off with all these changes? Cohesive women's work groups and female-centered living arrangements are gone. The source of solidarity in the forest dwellings came from shared kinship, space, and workloads. One does not retrieve profound connections in shared visits between houses. Senior women no longer provide leadership. Men, as husbands, are the heads of households.

> *Instead of asking ourselves who has it best, perhaps we should be asking the Mundurucú woman. The answer here is quite unequivocal: with few exceptions they prefer the nuclear family arrangements of the new communities. They do so because trade goods are more readily available, and they prefer their men to help them. On one level, this is exactly what the women want—they seek aid and relief in the drudge work of manioc growing and processing. . . . And though there may have been little absolute improvement in their situation, the gap between them and the men is perceived by them to have narrowed. The women may not have been elevated, but the men surely have been reduced. (Murphy and Murphy 1974:202)*

Yolanda Murphy and Robert Murphy had gone to Brazil as two individuals and left as "time-tested veterans of the connubial state" (1985:75). Yolanda Murphy had been absorbed into village sisterhoods as a friend and advocate. The women "looked upon her as a person with the same basic problem as theirs: men" (1985:70). Robert had been an outsider even to Mundurucú males. He slept, quite literally, with his wife, and didn't know how to hunt. The couple may have lived in the same quarters, but they hadn't lived in the same world.

Melanesia: Birth and Semen

The gender separation systems of Melanesia are probably the most dramatic in the world. Accounts and analyses of aggression and antagonism between men and women pervade anthropological research. The social order in most (although not all) of Melanesia seems to be divided by gender.

A first pervasive theme is that males and females are radically different in their physical and psychological being and that the fluids, essences, and powers of women are dangerous and inimical to those of men. This premise renders cosmic and natural the terms of men's domination of religion and ritual, and the limited coparticipation of men and women in domestic life. (Keesing 1982:7)

In ordinary life, men and women are separate. They work apart and spend leisure hours apart. Their tasks and family responsibilities are different; so are their authority and powers. In many cultures of New Guinea, rules of residence separate husbands and wives into different houses. In many places, women go to menstrual huts or birth huts. Young boys are often removed from the company of all women, including their mothers, and taken into the men's houses. There, initiation rituals for the boys dramatize the dangers of pollution or injury caused by women and teach the boys ways to purify themselves. Males have strong anxieties about sex and the polluting powers and dangerous "natures" of women. Many rituals and myths reflect an ideology of mutual danger. Each gender would be safer if they could only avoid the other. But such a life is impossible. Baby boys would die without their mothers, husbands and wives must share work and food, and everyone is at the mercy of their sex drives.

Here are some characteristic statements from the highlands of New Guinea that give the flavor of gender relationships there:

Women: "No wonder that log defies your efforts—you cannot even raise your own tiny penises!"

Men: "Stand aside or close your legs lest our huge logs burst your dragging vulvas."

Men: "Women are rubbish."

Women: "Men are no good." (Meggitt 1964)

Blood Fears and Womb Envy

Many Melanesian men believe, often fervently, that contact with women and their generative powers, particularly menstrual blood, is dangerous. Females free themselves of contamination at regular intervals because they menstruate. So men have rituals of bloodletting that imitate females. They start in puberty and may continue throughout their lives or until the dangers they imagine are gone.

The technique of male menstruation is as follows. First the man catches a crayfish or crab and removes one of the claws, which he keeps wrapped up with ginger until it is required. He also collects various soothing leaves, including some from a plant whose fruit has a smooth skin of deep purple color. From dawn onwards on the day he has fixed he eats noth-

*ing. Then late in the afternoon he goes to a lonely beach, covers his head
with a palm spathe, removes his clothing, and wades out till the water is
up to his knees. He stands there with legs apart and induces an erection
either by thinking about desirable women or by masturbation. When
ready he pushes back the foreskin and hacks at the glans, first on the left
side, then on the right. Above all, he must not allow the blood to fall on
his fingers or his legs. He waits till the cut has begun to dry and the sea is
no longer pink. (Hogbin 1970:88)*

This fellow, temporarily saved from the dangers of female pollution, wrapped
his penis in leaves and returned to the men's house. There he rested for three days
while the soreness wore off.

Accounts from other areas of New Guinea report that men inserted sharp-
edged reeds in penises, noses, or other body orifices to induce bleeding. Sometimes
groups of men went off together to have their purifying periods. Sometimes they
lacerated their genitals, pierced the septum of their noses, raised ridged scars
across their bodies, or otherwise permanently marked their bodies.

But having regular periods is not enough. Women create babies in their own
bodies, they give birth and nurse infants. So in some groups, men have created initiation ceremonies and other rituals that mimic or mirror female powers of reproduction. These male cults are ripe with pseudo-procreative symbolism. They
emphasize the passage of male children safely through puberty and the growing of
boys into men through the agency of other males. Some groups sponsor initiation
ceremonies in which older men ceremonially give birth to the younger ones.

In many of the male ideologies, semen is the equivalent of breast milk. So men
nourish or feed boys with semen, or male milk, through fellatio or anal intercourse. This is what anthropologist Gilbert Herdt calls "ritualized homosexuality"
(1982, 1984, 1987a, b). Men insist that the elaborate ceremonialism and symbolic
structures help prepare young boys for adulthood, the dangers of sexuality, marriage, fatherhood, hunting, and the endemic warfare that characterized many areas
before contact. We should not be surprised that in some groups men keep sacred
flutes in their men's houses and recount stories of having wrested them from the
women. The sounds of the flutes are said to be the voices and visitations from the
spirit world. The threat of gang rape or death hangs over the head of any woman
who witnesses the ceremonies, discusses the flutes, or challenges the deception.
From all accounts, rape appears to be a common and predictable feature of
women's lives. There are few models of companionable, shared lovemaking.

These cults of manhood show us how a culture constructs men and the principles of maleness. Boys become men, not through an ordinary process of matura-
tion, but through elaborate rituals of isolation, ordeal, instruction, revelation,
fear, and suffering. Females may make babies, but only males can make men.

*The rites celebrate, not the unity and power of society, but the unity and
power of men. They celebrate and reinforce male dominance in the face
of women's visible power to create and sustain life, and in the face of the
bonds between boys and their mothers which must be broken to sustain
male solidarity and dominance. Women's physical control over reproductive*

processes and emotional control over their sons must be overcome by
politics, secrecy, ideology, and dramatized male power. (Keesing 1982:22,
23)

This kind of analysis opens the door for female-centered viewpoints. It is reasonable to note that Freud's penis envy, which women are said to have, is matched here by cases of womb envy. It is possible to read the ethnographic accounts and see groups of men who want the privileges and powers of reproduction which only females have. This means that the men do not just want to control women, but (dare we think it) to become women. One can "read" the ceremonies as men's attempts to appropriate women's bodies, emotions, feelings and, above all, the monopoly on creativity.

On the other hand, it is possible to read these accounts and dismiss symbolism and the intricacies of the human mind in favor of an argument about power. The ideologies of danger and the cults of manhood can be interpreted as instruments of subordination and systematic deception.

There are four areas in which males are not otherwise assured of power
and control. These all have to do generally with female resources—fertil-
ity, childcare, labor, and periodicity. . . . The social solidarity rests upon a
power structure entirely in the hands of males, a power structure sup-
ported where necessary by a variety of acts that are magical, pure and
simple, and designed to keep power in the hands of males. (Langness
1974:19)

Whatever the psychology of envy, the net social effect is one of control and confiscation. The dilemmas of this system of gender separation are exceptionally poignant and instructive. While separation from women is cosmically ordained, men must still depend on them. They eat the food women grow and harvest. Even the sons and nephews of the next generation are courtesy of excluded and demeaned females. Men have painfully tried and failed to produce and reproduce themselves without women. Even with the best protections and regular periods, men are still in danger.

Looped String Bags

It is difficult to detect the substance of women's lives in places like Melanesia. Men lead such dramatic lives. In addition to the vivid ceremonialism discussed above, men typically wear striking costumes, decorate themselves in theatrical styles, and are more conspicuous. The ideologies of gender give them top billing. Sometimes even anthropologists defined women by what men say women do or by complicated analysis of kinship or social organization.

The most defining feature of women's lives is, quite simply, the looped string bag or **bilum** they carry everywhere. The contrast of this piece of equipment with the drama of men's lives is striking and illustrates the scale of gender separation. Figure 6.1 shows the techniques and hours of work that women put into a bilum.

Both men and women carry looped string bags everywhere, every day, throughout the Highlands of New Guinea. Women always wear the large bilums with the

Figure 6.1
The Making of a Bilum Bag

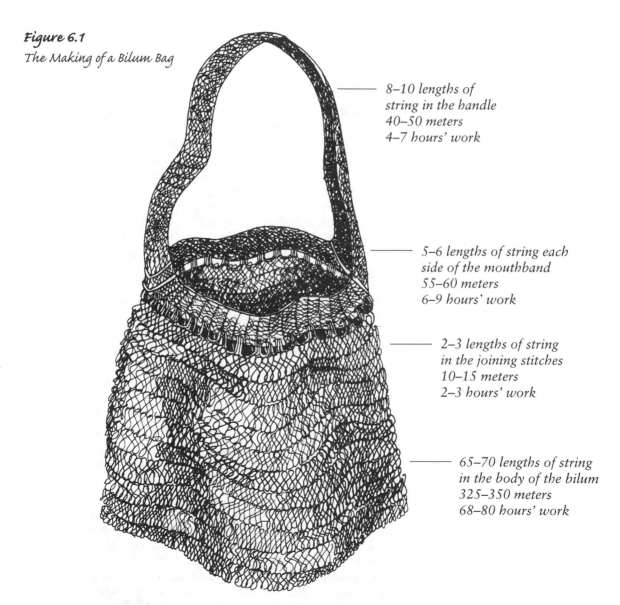

8–10 lengths of string in the handle 40–50 meters 4–7 hours' work

5–6 lengths of string each side of the mouthband 55–60 meters 6–9 hours' work

2–3 lengths of string in the joining stitches 10–15 meters 2–3 hours' work

65–70 lengths of string in the body of the bilum 325–350 meters 68–80 hours' work

Source: Maureen MacKenzie, *Androgynous Objects: String Bags and Gender in Central New Guinea* (1991), permissions from Harwood Academic Publishers.

strap suspended from their foreheads. The bags hang down their backs, and their necks or shoulders carry the weight. Men wear smaller bilums slung from their shoulders or across their chests. All are constructed from a single strand of spun plant fibers. Bilums make women beautiful. The bags themselves are aesthetically pleasing and display meticulous attention to detail and design. Bilums have hundreds of purposes. They serve as

> *container, baby carrier and cradle, pocket, quiver, attire, dancing regalia, ornament, amulet, toy, trade commodity, wealth item, marker of identity, spirit catcher, shrine and source of all cultural resources. (MacKenzie 1991:6)*

Women and men say, bilums are our mothers. The analogy between the bellies of pregnant women and the expanding open-looped bilum filled with babies and garden produce is unavoidable. Bilums are external wombs, cradles in which babies sleep, nurse, and live for most of their first year of life. In some cultures of Melanesia, placentas are called bilums; they too nourish babies.

Women are not fully dressed without bilums. Social events, ritual transactions, or stages in the female life cycle are not complete without an exchange of bilums. The string bags are "widow's weeds" for formally mourning a dead husband. Young girls show readiness for adult responsibility by looping a bag; old women wrap themselves in many bags down to their knees. Women loop in menstrual huts and in birth huts—where such customs exist. In particular, they loop with each other as they gossip and talk.

> *Women carry around with them an unfinished bilum, looping as they walk to and from their gardens and market; as they attend local village meetings; or closer to home, as they cook food sitting around the hearth side. In fact, no matter where a Telefolmin woman might be, whether sitting or walking, her hands are rarely idle, her fingers are perpetually working in the continuous tasks of spinning fibers and looping bilums. (MacKenzie 1991:61)*

A strong case can be made for the curative, even spiritual qualities, of repetitive hand tasks such as weaving, looping, knitting, cross-stitching, quilting, and other crafts women typically do around the world. Such self-soothing activities are not just productivity or work in the raw economic sense.

Sometimes men make bilums or decorate the large ones made by kinswomen. In some places, young male initiates receive a string bag from maternal uncles. The bag contains what they will need to protect themselves from the power of women. These and other customs only enhance the association of women with string bags.

In Chapter 1, we discussed women's work in carrying and constructing containers. This was probably an unsung but fundamental contribution in becoming human beings. The women of Melanesia who loop, make baskets, pottery, and other containers are one of the best examples of the carrying complex anywhere in the world. In fact, the bilum bag is an official symbol of the nation of Papua–New Guinea in the post-independence period.

Wok Meri: "Mothers of Money"

The traditional ways in which women and men in Melanesia are separated extend into the present. Men monopolize business enterprises in the new money economy just as they controlled ceremonial transactions like initiations and bride wealth in the old traditional systems. But beginning in the 1960s, women in some groups in the Highlands of New Guinea developed a savings and exchange system called **Wok Meri,** or "the work of women." Both males and females agree that Wok Meri groups started because women were angry about males who squandered money on gambling and alcohol. So women formed networks of autonomous groups ranging in size from two to thirty-five. They recruited each other from the traditional kinship units. These lineages and clans staged important traditional rituals to mark the life passages and routinely borrowed shells, pigs, and produce from each other.

The prime mover in each Wok Meri is a "big woman," a senior female who establishes and maintains ties with other "big women." Big women organize and lead meetings or ceremonies. They help young women save money and hire young men as bookkeepers, truck drivers, or advisers. Wok Meri groups invest their money in such businesses as trucking, running small stores, wholesale trading, or coffee-bean production. Wok Meri is not a movement to maintain or create new systems of separation for men and women. Instead, Wok Meri emphasizes the collective actions of established kinship networks with females as the link. It allows women property rights relative to men. But the importance of Wok Meri extends beyond economic relations into the entire fabric of social and cultural life. Through Wok Meri, women have established their presence in ceremonial and commercial arenas of Highland New Guinea life.

> *Wok Meri ideology, rituals, and symbols reveal women's analysis of their own importance and capabilities, the stereotype of the male personality, and their evaluation of men's social responsibilities and the manner in which they fulfill them. These data are noteworthy because we know little about Highland women's perceptions of themselves and of men, although there is a large body of literature about Highland men's perceptions of women as polluting, dangerous, disruptive, and in need of control. In Wok Meri women express in words, actions, rituals, and symbols their own interpretation of gender roles. (Sexton 1986:141)*

In Wok Meri ceremonies, women claim to be the "mother of money." They are declaring both ownership and their role in producing income. Their rituals reenact both childbirth and betrothal ceremonies. They give birth to "daughters" symbolized by bags of coins and string bags. Women say, "We are like coffee trees that bear fruit that we can trade and sell. So too, women bear children, the daughters of coffee, who marry and link men, women, children, and clans in reciprocity and exchange."

In the midst of so many symbolic interpretations about women's dangers and men's painful rituals in New Guinea is a practical instance of banks, capital development, credit, and lending institutions organized for and by women. Women keep men out of financial transactions because, they say, only women linked through birth and blood can be trusted with money.

Islamic Middle East: Veiled Separations

The Islamic world is gendered. A variety of systems, concrete and symbolic, separate the lives of women from men. These are sometimes called **purdah**. Anthropologist Lila Abu-Lughod uses the phrase *mutual avoidance* to describe the rules or principles that dominate the separate social lives of women and men in the Islamic Middle East (Abu-Lughod 1985:638).

The literature on women in the Middle East is particularly problematic. First is the obstacle of Orientalism, a **Eurocentric** and **ethnocentric** view of the Middle East as a monolithic "Other," the object of cliches and colonial ownership. Outsiders often attribute strange sexual moralities or judge the men in these countries harshly for the treatment of "their" women.

> *Moreover, the Middle East is staggeringly diverse in modes of economy, culture, ethnicity, race, language, class, ideology, and religions. The intersection of class, ethnicity, and religion, for example, is a dynamic that confounds our scholarship a great deal. The ways in which indigenous religions, economies, and cultures have interacted with British (and many other) imperialisms further compound analyses. (Hale 1989:246)*

Second, within the limited frameworks Westerners bring to this topic, women are seen as objects and cardboard cutouts. Everyone knows the stereotypes of belly-dancers, mysterious, sexy, veiled women out of the *Arabian Nights*. We have seen pictures of women so shrouded that they are only shadows with eyes. Many Westerners believe that Islam is a monolithic, omnipresent force whose purpose is to lock up women. Scholarship in the West often assumes that women are only fixtures of households, domestic domains, tribes, or ethnic groups. Men who worked in the area often left collecting data about women up to their wives. In short, we have observed women in the Middle East through our own veils.

Fatima Mernissi, whose autobiographical quote opened this chapter, directs Western women not to compare themselves with Middle Eastern women. She says that all of us live under systems of domination and separation, that both the Muslim East and the Christian West are based on systems of sexual inequality. If a woman like Mernissi is to be liberated or a feminist in the modern Arab–Islamic world, she must be anticolonial and anti-Western. So the assumptions developed in Western women's movements are not applicable at best. At worst, they are patronizing and intrusive.

This said, we must still find a way to discuss this widespread and important system. The symbol most people associate with gender separation in the Islamic Middle East is "the veil." This is a generic term for coverings of the female form that range from a dress with long skirt and sleeves to a total body covering (sometimes including eyes and hands). Sometimes a "veil" is only a filmy scarf draped across a woman's lower face.

> *There are few, if any, other regions of the world where one element in the culture still symbolizes so much to scholars and observers as does the veil in the Muslim Middle East. It is used as a symbol by nationalist apolo-*

gists and by Middle Eastern and Western feminists alike. It conjures up
the exotic, erotic, the process of seclusion, the harem, marginalization,
modesty, honor and shame, social distance, gender segregation, and, of
course, the subordination of women. (Hale 1989:247)

Why do women "veil" themselves? What does it mean? There are immense individual differences. Some women say that veils, in whatever form, are practical.
In olden times, veils kept blowing sand away. Others say veils are progressive or
modern. They keep strangers from staring. The custom of wearing veils is in ac-
cordance with religious beliefs; it promotes self-respect and modesty. A veil is voluntary. It's because men cannot handle the uncovered power of women.

The reasons why women
wear veils may be as hidden
or as highlighted as their
bodies are.

Whatever interpretations one may have heard, it is widely assumed that veiling is related to the commands of the Prophet Muhammad and the religion of Islam. A widely quoted verse from the Qur'an, the sacred scriptures of Islam, commands:

> *And tell the believing women to lower their gaze and be modest, and to display of their adornment only that which is apparent and to draw their veils over their bosoms, and not to reveal their adornment save to their own husbands or fathers or husband's fathers, or their sons or their husband's sons, or their women, or their slaves, or male attendants who lack vigor or children who know naught of women's nakedness. And let them not stamp their feet so as to reveal what they hide of their adornment.*
> *(Qur'an, Surah 24)*

This quote would seem to give scriptural authority to the practices of wearing veils and other prescriptions for modesty. However, veiling or other forms of seclusion are not necessarily symbols of female subordination. Women have many different interpretations of what they mean and how an individual fits into these customs. A good way to approach this topic is to let women who have lived these features of sexual separation speak for themselves.

Bedouin Veils

Anthropologist Lila Abu-Lughod lived for two years with the Awlad Àli Bedouin in Egypt. Semi-nomadic **pastoralists** in the process of settling down, they combined sheep and camel herding with trade. Abu-Lughod herself came from an Arabic and Muslim background; her father introduced her in an appropriate manner to the Bedouin group. Since young women never live alone and kinship always defines identity in such groups, she embraced and immersed herself in the small, intimate community of women as an adopted daughter.

The Bedouin women she knew lived neither in harems nor in seclusion. In truth, they could not afford such luxuries. But the principles of sexual segregation, distinct from the systems of seclusion in urban areas, were nonetheless real. The Bedouin social world was divided into two parts. Women and children were in the first part and men in the other. In the past, separate lives were marked by nothing more substantial than a woven blanket through the middle of their tents. Or women wore veils and men averted their gazes. Controlling one's eyes or mouth is an effective form of separation.

Women in Bedouin society are secluded and, by American definitions, subordinated. But women do not hold these images as their own. They speak of female communities that give them strength and personal feelings of power. They speak of passion in their relationships to men. There is love, anger, yearning, sensuality, and occasionally, something we might call romance. Above all, there are secrets women share with each other, not with men.

Abu-Lughod makes two compelling points about the consequences of the Bedouin separation systems for women. First, the community of women created under these circumstances is almost a feminist fantasy come true. Women's lives with each other are intense and close. Within that intimacy is freedom for personal expression.

> *Individual development among women does not occur in opposition to male development; indeed cultural ideals of the feminine "personality" resemble the masculine and include enterprise, boldness, pride, and independence. Because of the denial of sexuality among Awlad Àli, women do not orient themselves toward men or try to please them. Instead they value competence, self-sufficiency, and respectful distance. They orient themselves toward other women. (Abu-Lughod 1985:657)*

Cut off from men is not cut off from life. Women can be informal, relaxed, and honest with each other. Moreover, they share common and inevitable suffering: babies who die, husbands who take a second wife or abandon them, or arranged marriages that please others but not themselves.

Her second point is more subtle. She calls this "veiled sentiments." Bedouin women do not ask for autonomy or social and economic independence. Instead they write poetry to speak their yearning for bonds of affection with men, men as lovers, husbands, and kinsmen.

> *More often than not, the poems voice sentiments of sadness, unfulfilled longing, or suffering caused by painful losses or sense of abandonment. What is striking is that most often, the poems seem to concern love relationships with men—the very relationships whose importance is continually minimized in ordinary social interaction. Women—who otherwise vehemently denied attachment to their spouses, seemed unconcerned with their marriages, and admitted no interest in sexual matters or in members of the opposite sex—recited poems that expressed their vulnerability to and emotional dependence on men. (Abu-Lughod 1985:654)*

Her interpretation of Bedouin women's poetry is ironic and compelling because marriage is a set of crises for them. Men and women spend very little time with each other. Married couples don't "live together." Moreover, their private lives seem to be intimately public. For example, Abu-Lughod writes about the key moment in a young bride's life, her wedding night and the blood of honor (1993:90). In this story, the entire camp has been riveted by the approaching nuptials. Young girls and female relatives sing and recite their poetry to the bride:

> *May she be good*
> *And bless us with children and wealth*
>
> *May she be a real Arab*
> *To enter the community and not make trouble*
>
> *Make her dear mother happy, Lord*
> *Hanging her cloth upon the tent ropes*
>
> *I'm confident in the loved one*
> *You'll find it there intact . . .*

Reread the last two stanzas again. They refer to the "blood of honor," which brides must manifest at their wedding. The verses express the hopes that her virginity is "intact." A bloodstained handkerchief or cloth would be proof. The groom is supposed to use his finger to acquire the evidence of honor.

Amidst noise, singing, and high-energy expectations, the groom was ushered into a room alone for the first time with his bride, Selima.

> *It seemed like forever (though later they said two minutes, stopwatch timed). My heart was beating and my camera trained on the door when it was finally flung open. I jumped as the guns went off and the men rushed away. The women streamed in to surround Selima, dazed and limp in the arms of a relative, singing and dancing with relief. The cloth with its red spot of blood, a faint mark, was waved above our heads. Selima's maternal aunt exclaimed, "Praise God! Blessings on the Prophet! How beautiful!" (Abu-Lughod 1993:191)*

Here we see that women are in control of other women's morality. Succeeding at the standards of virginity and other women's work of modesty brings honor and dignity to everyone.

Female Faces and Female Spaces

Anthropologist Unni Wikan accompanied her husband to the town of Sohar in Oman, Arabia. Because she spoke Arabic, she was able to talk to women about the customs of seclusion and separation. In this region, some women wear a dark mask or **burqa** across their faces. Most women wear a length of fabric as shawl or scarf over their hair, and loose clothing that covers them modestly.

The facial mask was the most striking aspect of their attire and their separation from men. To a Westerner, such customs are irresistible, and Wikan wanted to understand why and how the masks were situated in women's lives. The women she came to know told her in dozens of different ways: "It is not that we wear burqa because it is shameful to go without it, but because it is beautiful to go with it!"

There are elaborate rules of wearing the facial mask. Married women remove it only before Allah and their husband. At home, when the chances of encountering a stranger are slim, they wear it perched on top of their heads for convenience, like others wear sunglasses. But women often wear the facial mask when it is not required; older women apparently feel it is part of their personality. The colors and styles of women's clothing are strictly conventional. But a woman controls her burqa, and with it she makes a fashion statement and exploits her freedom to the fullest.

> *First, the burqa beautifies in a spiritual sense. Donning her burqa, the woman signals her moral excellence in a tangible way. She communicates a beautiful aspect of her person and, in the act, she herself becomes beautiful. But furthermore, the burqa itself—as a symbol of all things beautiful, female modesty and grace, decency, and poise—is intrinsically*

> *beautiful. Like a jewel, it adds to what is already there. No matter how*
> *beautiful the woman, it cannot fail to make her even more so. Because*
> *she and it are both beautiful. (Wikan 1982:101)*

The Sohari women did not question the canons or premises of sexual modesty and segregation. Those were facts of life, like the sun rising or regular meals. Not everyone might agree, but Wikan's field research left her with a sense of powerful women in constricted situations.

> *There must be few contemporary societies where law and customary rules*
> *combine to define so powerless a position for women as in Oman. They*
> *have little say in the choice of spouse, cannot leave their house without*
> *the husband's permission, are debarred from going to the market to make*
> *a single purchase, often may not choose their own clothes, must wear*
> *masks before all males who are marriageable, and so forth. And yet I*
> *have never met women who seem so in control of themselves and their*
> *situation. Omani women impress with their self-assurance and poise.*
> *(Wikan 1982:185)*

Husbands and wives do not spend much time in each other's company. Where several women share a husband, it may be only a few times a week. Where men migrate to work, a wife may see a husband only a few scattered weeks per year. Yet every account speaks of the rich communal lives women share with each other and their successes at wringing meaning from cloistered worlds. Each man, on the other hand, must worry continually about how the conduct of wives, daughters, and female relatives reflects on him and his honor in the face of other men. Men believe that female relatives, mothers, sisters, daughters, and wives may stray sexually; they are potential sources of dishonor and humiliation. No action of his can erase this stain. So a man must be ever vigilant of women's chastity.

In her ethnography about women in the country of Yemen, Carla Makhlouf interprets veils and the customs of veiling as allowing symbolic statements and subtle manipulations of social situations. Elaborate veiling, she says, does not reduce all women to anonymous shadows. Yes, the full body veiling allows modesty, but it is also provocative.

> *What is seen after being concealed is all the more attractive, for the veil*
> *clothes women in an aura of mystery and contributes to the imagery of*
> *the ideal woman. By making all women look alike, the veil provides a*
> *certain freedom of movement: a veiled woman could go with men and*
> *have affairs without being caught. (Makhlouf 1979:33)*

Makhlouf questioned women in Yemen again and again about customs of veiling and seclusion. And still they denied that their veils caused or reflected their subordinate status. Women objected to their veil on the grounds they were cumbersome or meaningless. Most of all, women saw veils as both the symbols and the objects that prevented them from open, sincere interactions or associations with men. Veiling prevented friendship.

Harems and Other Female Worlds

In the **harem** in which Fatima Mernissi grew up, men and women lived separate existences in marked social spaces. At the courtyard level, life was formal, proper, and strict; men made the rules. Upstairs, however, life was dominated by an emotional quality she identifies as tenderness, freely and unconditionally given. Widowed aunts, assorted relatives, and their children all resided there.

> *The number of relatives living with us at any one time varied according to the amount of conflict in their lives. Distant female relatives would sometimes come to seek refuge on our top floors for a few weeks when they got into fights with their husbands. Some would come to stay, with their children, for a short time only, just to show their husbands that they had another place to stay, that they could survive on their own and were not desperately dependent. (This strategy often was successful, and they would return home in a stronger bargaining position.) But other relatives came to stay for good, after a divorce or some other serious problem, and this was one of the traditions Father always worried about whenever someone attacked the institution of harem life. "Where will the troubled women go?" he would say. (Mernissi 1994:16)*

The kind of harem Mernissi grew up in was certainly not the imperial Turkish harems or those of the *Arabian Nights*, which have obsessed Westerners, with **polygamy**, slave women, eunuchs, and the romanticized trappings of empire. Those were gone. She grew up in a domestic harem, which she characterizes as rather dull and strongly bourgeois.

> *In these domestic harems, a man, his sons, and their wives lived in the same house, pooled their resources, and requested that the women refrain from stepping outside. The men need not have many wives, as is the case in the harem which inspired the tales in this book. What defines it as a harem is not polygamy, but the men's desire to seclude their wives, and their wish to maintain an extended household rather than break into nuclear units. (Mernissi 1994:35)*

Young Fatima asked her maternal grandmother about the sacred frontiers that women and foreigners were forbidden to cross. Her grandmother replied that any space you entered, a courtyard, a room, a balcony, even a street, had invisible rules. The rules were like the foundations of a building, the laws of mathematics, or the legal codes of Islam and the nation. Stick to the invisible rules and nothing bad can happen, she explained. But then her grandmother added, "It's too bad. The rules were not made to help women."

As an adult and a professional, Fatima Mernissi kept asking, why do these systems of segregation for males and females exist? Her own answer comes from personal experiences, scholarly research, and a singular concentration on the question. She concluded that men somehow come to believe that the presence of women and their uncontrollable essence or "nature" are too dangerous. Passive men cannot control themselves sexually (or believe they cannot); women are lusty creatures who tempt them and lead them astray. That is why the Qur'an allows elderly women to go about unveiled.

Mernissi points out that Islam does not say that women are "naturally" inferior. Quite the contrary, Islam says: Women are dangerous and powerful and must be restrained with customs about modesty, with separated social and material spaces, and with legal and mythical sanctions. Why? Because men need these protections; they fear they will lose control over their minds and fall prey to disorder and chaos. Chaos, she says, is represented by an unveiled woman.

Mernissi presents a strongly researched and reasoned analysis of male and female relations in Islamic society. She finds historic reasons to believe that before the Prophet Mohammed's time, women had considerably more self-determination than they do now. Marital unions were less subject to family control. After the prophet's death, the systems of seclusion grew. The key, she says, was keeping a husband and wife from falling in love with each other.

> Does love between man and wife threaten something vital in the Muslim order? We have seen that sexual satisfaction is considered necessary to the moral health of the believer. There is no tension between Islam and sexuality as long as that sexuality is expressed harmoniously and is not frustrated. . . . Heterosexual involvement, real love, is the danger which must be overcome. (Mernissi 1975:62)

These accounts by women who grew up in, speak the languages of, or participated in the practices of seclusion are full of comments about the positive and paradoxically freeing nature of veils and seclusion, symbolic or real. Muslim women often see the patterns of seclusion as a source of pride and prestige, not as a source of oppression. Indeed, harems, the ultimate form of seclusion, required huge economic assets and large staffs. Only a rich husband can afford such conspicuous consumption. Many women interpret concealing cloaks, veils, or masks as a liberating invention. It is a safe way out of enclosed living spaces, a kind of portable safety. Many Muslim feminists want to find ways to interpret the Qur'an and still remain within the fold. So in the Muslim Middle East, men and women endlessly debate the sayings of the Prophet. Both sides take comfort in holy words.

Conclusions: What Do Systems of Separation Mean?

Where do these sexual tensions and gender divisions come from? Why are there human cultures with a gender civil war in their midst? For some observers, the answers to the questions asked above is that men need these systems. Here is what the Murphys wrote.

> If the men's house symbolism has any function at all in Mundurucú society, it is to conceal from the men the fragility of their own superiority; it

> perpetuates an illusion. Their position is a vulnerable one. They are tran-
> sients in their houses and their communities, their own sense of unity is
> uneasily maintained, and the collegiality has begotten an even stronger
> unity among the women. Perhaps Margaret Mead summed it up best
> when she said, in a passing remark: "If men really were all that powerful,
> they wouldn't need such rigmarole." (Murphy and Murphy 1974:226)

Egyptian feminist writer and physician Nawaal El Saadawi argues the same points. She says that veils actually protect men from women who are more powerful. It is male honor and morals that have to be shielded. Fatima Mernissi notes that the English word "sexist" carries the connotation that males are favored over females. On the contrary, she says, we should look at what men are losing in systems of segregation. "It is my belief that, in spite of appearances, the Muslim system does not favor men; the self-fulfillment of men is just as impaired and limited as that of women" (Mernissi 1975:105).

Many skilled observers have noted, sometimes ruefully, that nothing in human social life is so potentially explosive as sex or as universal as gender. It is little wonder that in some places and in some times women and men want to claim the ultimate credit for giving life or want to control the awesome power of sexuality.

So we might conclude that gender is the most fundamental organizing principle on the planet, the one most capable of elaboration and codification. We might conclude that systems of separation only intensify the connections between women and men, and that any system which oppresses women will correspondingly oppress men. We might conclude that these elaborate systems are another form of control over women's sexuality and reproduction, for whatever motives men might have. We might offer symbolic or psychological explanations for these phenomena. Or we might conclude that things are not always as they seem.

The systems of separation described here lead us into the next chapter. There we shall see females and males who have crossed these boundaries. Just as political borders change or shift, so do the boundaries between the genders or the sexes. While the accounts in this chapter appear to draw strict lines between females and males, between men and women, the borders do not always hold.

Check Out These Books

In the past two decades, certain progressive young Arab women voluntarily donned veils. The movement rapidly expanded and continues to gain momentum. It sparked controversy within Islamic culture and from Western feminists. The young women embraced veiling as an affirmation of cultural identity and a strident feminist statement of their own. Read about veils and liberation in Fadwa El Guindi, *Veil: Modesty, Privacy and Resistance* (1999). In her new book, Fatima Mernissi, a leading social scientist and feminist writer from Morocco, offers the radical view that women in the West are just as much segregated and separated as women in Islamic societies; the systems that bind us just look different: *Scheherazade Goes West: Different Cultures, Different Harems* (2001).

On systems of separation in Melanesia, I recommend two classic ethnographies. The first is Maria Lepowsky's engaging study *Fruit of the Motherland: Gender in an Equalitarian Society* (1993). She says that gender does not always tear men and women apart. Annette Weiner moves the lives of Trobriand women to center stage—*Women of Value, Men of Renown* (1976)— as she shows how women give birth but also give death. Bundles of banana leaves are the key.

Chapter Seven

A Third Sex?

Gender as Alternative or Continuum

ost of us have grown up with what anthropologists call a *natural attitude* about gender. This means we believe that:

1. There are two sexes: male and female, girl or boy. People are born this way and they remain in one of these two categories all their lives. We assume that half of the world have penises and the other half have vaginas. So, in essence, genitals are gender.
2. This is a "natural" dichotomy because god, science, doctors, mothers, or other authority figures said so. There are no exceptions. No one is allowed to pick a sex, convert to the opposite gender, invent a new sex or gender, or mix them up together in daily life.
3. "Naturally," the objects of one's sexual desires are from the "opposite" sex or gender. "Normal" people wear the clothing and exhibit the personal habits of the gender into which they were born. Only during well-defined ceremonial occasions with symbolic and elaborate rules is it permissible to dress up as a person of the "opposite sex."

The core concept in this chapter is that sex and gender are not necessarily, essentially, or "naturally" limited to two forms or two styles. The categories **third sex** and **third gender** are convenient ways to describe human alternatives to the "natural attitude" and to illustrate how gender, sex, and sexuality can be constructed. Some of the studies presented here show structured, culturally patterned systems in which males adopt female clothing or other attributes and do women's work. Similar comparative examples illustrate cases in which women elect to take on male responsibilities and qualities. The examples invite questions about same-sex friendships and cross-sex or cross-gender activities.

Alas, we cannot cover all the research in the depth it deserves, but we can ask a few questions. Why would men want to be women or be like women? Or vice-versa, what advantages does a female have in being or acting like a man? Can a person convert to another gender? Can a culture invent a third or even a fourth gender? How do they do it? Why? What does this mean for the study of women, of gender, of sex?

Western social scientists have typically believed that all human groups perceive sex and gender as dichotomous or binary. But this may be only a projection of our own cultural orientations, hopes, or fantasies. When we look at other groups around the world, we see many potentials and possibilities. Yes, social scientists generally agree that two sexes are needed for reproduction. But we also understand that life has meaning beyond reproduction, and there are more forms of sexuality than the kind needed for egg and sperm to connect.

This chapter is confusing because we are crossing a lot of borders you may have taken for granted or assumed were fixed. We will skirt the edges of an exciting and rapidly growing literature on homosexuality. Moreover, there are not-yet-fully explored connections between gender alternatives, homosexual lifestyles, and spiritual power. You will notice how often the topic comes up.

One purpose for this chapter is to move beyond dualism, beyond the two-bodied world, beyond masculine and feminine, and to explore how sex and gender may be fabricated in other settings. Dualism is limited whether it is nature or nurture, public or private, body or mind, good or evil, or boy and girl. None of these arbitrary divisions explains what anthropologists see in many human cultures around the world.

Making Out and Making Up Sexes and Genders

My students usually have a thousand questions at this point. They want to know why some people seem different. What are the causes, they ask, for men acting like women or for women who love each other? They hint that people in this or other cultures may be immoral, wrong, or sick. They want to apply television talk shows, new research in genetics, and personal experiences to confusing but fascinating situations. I would like to clear the air and as much as possible present a sensible outlook on these questions. Please understand that this is a new field and scholars are still working on the concepts and definitions we need.

Let's begin with three broad clusters of potential for human beings around the world. The circles in Figure 7.1 summarize these points. The first circle shows biological sex; the second circle is about cultural definitions; and the third circle is about the individual psychology of desire, eroticism, or identity. This drawing does not reflect all the possible permutations or complexities of human existence. It merely introduces some alternatives beyond the two-bodied world.

Biological Sex and Intersexes

Sexual and gender identities are composed of many steps and stages. Some of them happen even before the midwife announces, "It's a girl" or "It's a boy." First, each of us acquires a set of chromosomes that establish a baseline for classification by sex. The X chromosome is female. The Y chromosome is male. This means that a person with XX is female and a person with XY is male. But chromosomes may combine in other ways. Here are some known possibilities: XXX, YYY, XYY, XXY, and XO. Individuals conceived with such genetic patterns may be difficult to classify in binary systems.

After the chromosomes are set, there are various stages of fetal development in which reproductive structures form. Some of these, like penises and vaginas, are outside the body and will be visible. The rest of the reproductive structures, like ovaries and uteruses, are inside the body. Most of the time, the reproductive structures match each other and the chromosomes; sometimes chromosomes, internal structures, and external structures simply do not match.

During a number of points in fetal development, the endocrine and hormonal systems must mature and correlate with each other in complex ways. They must kick in at the right time and in the right way because these are the coordinating systems for aspects of psycho-sexual development in later life. Sometimes, for various reasons, a fetus is exposed to masculinizing or feminizing hormones; these may influence development in a number of ways.

Figure 7.1
The potentials for sex, gender, and desire.

BIOLOGICAL SEX

KEY

 Female

 Male

 Intersex

 Man, boy, husband, father, brother, son

 Woman, girl, wife, mother, sister, daughter

 Androgynous

 Homosexual

 Transsexual or Transgendered

 Heterosexual

 Cross-dresser

GENDER, SOCIETY & CULTURE

IDENTITY & DESIRE

An estimated 5 percent of human births result in anomalous or unusual features. Sometimes babies are born with genitals that appear to be both male and female, or depending on how these matters are interpreted, with genitals of neither sex. Generally scholars say that such individuals are **intersexed.** Intersex is another category of phenotypic or biological sex in addition to the dichotomous categories of male and female. This means that humans are born in every society whose biological sex does not neatly fall into one of two categories (Katchadourian 1979). These possibilities are marked in Figure 7.1.

So we have reasons to doubt conventional wisdom or the natural attitude about two and only two genders. But the incidence of babies with unusual chromosomal combinations or atypical sex organs is too random and too small to account for the patterned social customs of crossing the boundaries of gender described in this chapter. So biology is only one basis for a third gender. If biological sex is malleable, then gender as a social construction must be even more so.

Social and Cultural Genders

Biology is just the beginning. At birth, midwives or their local equivalent say to a laboring woman, "Congratulations, you have a beautiful baby (fill in the blank)." This diagnosis opens the cultural processes of **gender attribution.** People in every social group expect certain behaviors from infants and children according to the category they are assigned at birth. So from this point on, it's pink or blue, guns or dolls, skirts or pants. Then, in early childhood, around the ages of two to four, little kids somehow decide or come to have the knowledge of which gender they are, boy or girl or other. This is called **gender identity.** Generally, most people come to the same conclusion as their chromosomes and the midwife did. In other words, their biological sex accords with their personal identity and the social category or gender to which they were assigned.

However, some people in many different human cultures remain convinced their bodies are one gender but their souls, spirits, or personalities are a different one. Anatomically correct males may be certain that a more authentic female lives inside them and wants to come out. The reverse is true for some people born as females; they believe themselves to be true or real males trapped in an alien body. In each case, these individuals feel very strongly that their body is the mistake, not their personality. Generally, we call such individuals **transsexuals.** Sometimes they respond by adopting the dress and work of the opposite sex. Sometimes they become a third sex or make other creative adjustments.

In recent years in Euro-American cultures, such individuals have often sought surgical and hormonal interventions that would give them the body that most closely approaches their personal identity. Males take female hormones, grow breasts, and ask to have their penises removed. Females take male hormones, grow beards, and ask for hysterectomies. They generally change their names, clothes, and hobbies to those resembling the desired gender. Their friends and relatives switch personal pronouns. I need to note that such surgeries seem to be based on the notion that there are two genders, and that problems can be solved by moving into the other one.

Objects of Our Desires

There is still more. A human being takes its chromosomes, hormones, a gender assigned at birth, and a gender assumed in childhood, and goes out into the world to engage in a lifelong process of noticing, defining, and finding its objects of desire. Sometime before or during adolescence, people focus on sex, how and with whom to do it. If biology is plastic and cultures offer a number of options, then sexual desire, preference, orientation, or identity are even more elastic. The last circle in Figure 7.1 shows some possibilities for linking our sexual identities with what we desire or to whom we are attracted.

Margaret Mead and Ruth Benedict, of course, pondered the problem of how an individual picks up cultural cues; they noted that sex roles often crossed traditional boundaries. They opened the doors for fuller analysis of the cultural contexts of same-sex behaviors and cross-gender roles and meanings. As they taught us, "womanhood" and "manhood," or "masculine" and "feminine," are inconstant and unstable.

In Western culture, we are supposed to experience ourselves as female or as male and to display the clothing, mannerisms, or habits of those two ends of the continuum of gender. The popular and professional literature contains a variety of terms to describe people who transform, transcend, or challenge gender rules: sexual deviation, sexual aberrancy, female incongruity, hermaphrodites, men-women, inverts, homosexuals, transvestites, transsexuals, made-women, made-men, prostitutes, transgenders, and eunuchs. Many negative social judgments surround the practices described in this chapter. They include concepts like abnormal, deviant, perverted, sinners; they also include verdicts based on the natural attitudes, such as freaks of "nature" doing "unnatural" acts.

Having sex with another person is not always what it seems. Some groups with which we are familiar tend to define people in categories centered on who is having sex together: heterosexual, homosexual, or bisexual. The Western criteria for gender basically revolve around who to have sex with and who to marry. Other societies define sex as the act itself, insertive, receptive, or reciprocal, for example. Others seem to define forms of sexuality as age-appropriate rather than gender-appropriate. Others prescribe certain actions for marriage; the rest of your life is your own. Others say that only marriage between an anatomically correct male and female who have sex in the missionary position is "natural." Some cultures exhibit features, beliefs, or customs that researchers in this field call "sex-positive"; they can tolerate variety. Other have such punitive restrictions on gender and sexuality that we label them "sex-negative." Others have elaborate categories that label and place people in boxes.

The feminist and gay movements of the last quarter-century have taught us that the personal is political. We have learned that what goes on in bedrooms or kitchens or boardrooms is structured by larger social relations of power, by history, and by the unseen hand of culture. The French anthropologist Claude Lévi-Strauss contributed the idea of raw versus cooked. Biology is the raw material and culture cooks us until we're done. The recipes in different cultures translate our biology into social experiences.

Crossing Over and Cross-Dressing

The most accessible examples of sexual alternatives and gender constructions are probably the universal practices of **cross-dressing.** Dressing up in the clothes, hairstyles, or makeup of the "opposite sex" has a longer and more vivid history than most of us credit. The older term, no longer in vogue, is "transvestism," which means "clothing across." American popular culture is filled and overflows with cross-dressing and cross-dressers. Traditions of drag queens, female impersonators, and similar forms of gender bending are alive and well in the vast entertainment industries.

Many scholars argue that gender-bending is the cutting edge of artistic consciousness, that gender is overdetermined, and that all binary thinking has problems, whether it is yes–no, self–other, Democrat–Republican, or black–white. Arbitrary definitions and distinctions like male and female cannot hold in cultural transformations. Other times and places in the world reveal a similar fluidity of gender. When people cross the borders of gender, they first adopt clothing from the other category. Then they add work patterns and spiritual, sexual, erotic, or artistic activities.

The kind of traditional healers anthropologists call shamans often dress in clothes of the opposite sex, or become what the pre-Buddhist folk religions of southeast Asia named halfman–halfwoman. Shamans journey to the spirit world through altered states of consciousness or trances. This means that they are crossing more boundaries than merely gender. Their strength in healing and the quality of their spiritual life, in fact, depend on transcending or crossing ordinary borders of consciousness, sex, and gender.

Military Maids

Private Lyons Wakeman of the Union army wrote home in 1863. "I don't believe there are any rebel bullets made for me yet. Nor do I care if there is." But Confederate germs, not bullets, killed him, and he was laid to rest in the Chalmette National Cemetery downriver from New Orleans. One hundred and thirty years later, Private Wakeman's letters reveal another part of the story. Citizen Sarah Wakeman of upstate New York, the oldest of nine children, was working as a maid. So in 1862, at the age of nineteen, she ran away and joined the 153rd Regiment, New York State Volunteers, for a $152 enlistment fee and $13 dollars a month in pay. She listed her occupation as "boatman." Sarah was one of an estimated 400 such women who served in the Civil War; they dressed like and were treated as male soldiers (Burgess 1994).

It is difficult to document how many women have joined the military or worked successfully in men's jobs. In July 1777, courts in England began prosecuting "female husbands": women acting as men in military ranks who were married to women. Dozens of ballads and songs were sung about soldiers and sailors who followed their husbands into battle in the name of love or money. Historian Julie Wheelwright has found court cases, journals, newspaper reports, and many other accounts of women who abandoned dresses for trousers to escape unhappy marriages, to live with other women, to follow male lovers into battle, or to enter male occupations for economic reasons.

The thread that pulls these stories together is women's desire for male privilege and a longing for escape from domestic confines and powerlessness. Many vividly describe a lifelong yearning for liberation from the constraints they chafed against as women. They were unconventional women who spent their lives rebelling against their assigned role before they pursued a male career. Most could only conceive of themselves as active and powerful in male disguise. Some were lesbians who bravely risked ostracism and punishment by symbolically claiming the right to women's erotic love through their assumption of male clothing. Many,

Pauline Cushman served as a Union spy during the Civil War.

*when the initial purpose for their masquerade had been served, continued
to pass as men or deeply longed for a return to their male role. Happy
endings are all too rare in their stories. (Wheelwright 1989:19)*

Some women lived as men all their adult lives; the military was the only life
they knew. Others had a temporary adventure. Working-class women were probably used to hard physical labor, and upper-class women were often seeking an escape. The point is this: Women have long disguised themselves for safety when
traveling, for access to male privileges or jobs, and for convenience or comfort.
Given the sheer number of folktales, legends, stories, and examples, there is every
reason to believe that women have lived male lives in many times and places
where female lives were restricted.

In Western history, women who cross-dress, act like men, or claim male privileges have evoked severe displeasure and serious legal or religious sanctions. Joan
of Arc's persecutors worried more over her male attire than her victories in battle. In pre-Christian Iceland, cross-dressing was grounds for divorce. In the nineteenth century in France, many legal codes prohibited women from dressing like
men or entering the military in disguise. However, when women in these situations record their feelings, they say that living as a male was the most exhilarating and liberating experience of their lives.

Intersexed Children: A Case for Consideration

In a routine repair surgery, surgeons accidentally burned off the penis of a normal
baby boy, eight months old. This child was "normal" in that he had 46 chromosomes and XY genes in the conventional locations; he had a twin brother and parents who were raising him as a male. More than most of us realize, physicians
encounter such cases of ambiguous or severely traumatized genitalia. Their solution
to this particular case has become a classic reported in the pediatric, psychiatric,
and sexological literature (Diamond and Sigmundson 1997; Money 1994; Money
and Ehrhardt 1972).

A team of physicians assembled and recommended to the parents that their
child be raised as a female. This decision was in keeping with the medical standard
that in cases of extensive penile damage to male infants, the child should be
switched to female. The medical management philosophy is based on two beliefs
that bear strongly on the definitions of sex and gender explored in this chapter: (1)
At birth, individuals are psychosexually neutral; (2) healthy psychosexual development is dependent on the appearance of the genitals.

The parents acquiesced. As a result of these recommendations, surgeons removed the child's testicles and began a lengthy series of procedures to construct
more feminine genitals. They advised the child's mother to dress and treat the
child as if she had a new daughter and to keep the past a secret. Frilly dresses, gen-
der-stereotyped toys, and later, makeup played a major role in their adjustments.
The management team at Johns Hopkins University Medical School seemed quite
pleased with both their theories and the results. The parents took the child there
for annual check-ups and occasional reconstructive surgery. She had her own

endocrinologist to prescribe and monitor the hormones that produce breasts, a changeless voice, and a hairless face, although never a menstrual period. Later, a female psychiatrist was added to the team to act as a role model and foster female identification. "John" seemed to be accepting life as "Joan."

Put aside your intuitive problems with believing that females are people without penises; that a vagina is merely a hole, an opening, or a passive receptacle; or that a male's ability to father children has no meaning apart from the appearance and "normal" functioning of a full-sized penis. What happened to this experiment in gender and sexuality?

Joan knew she was different from what others wanted her to be. Kids teased her about her girl clothes and boy looks. No one wanted to play with her. Once she got expelled from school after she got into a fight. The pressure to act like a girl—or the doctors' ideas of how girls should act—was unremitting. Joan was frustrated when no one listened to her feelings; they would chastise her when she acted like boys act—or the doctors' ideas of how boys act.

The local psychiatric team remarked on Joan's preference for her twin brother's toys, gadgets, tools, men's clothing, rough sports, and urinating standing up. Just a tomboy they said. Perhaps they didn't know about her refusal to wear "feminine" clothing and makeup or her insistence on shaving just as her father did. The sex-reassignment team enlisted the help of male-to-female transsexuals to convince John that he was really Joan with a treasured vagina. All these surgeries and check-ups meant a constant—intrusive—scrutiny of her genitals and exposed her to ridicule when she didn't think "like a girl."

When Joan was twelve years old, the team gave her female hormones. She said they made her feel funny. All girls your age feel funny from hormones, the doctors told her. By the time her breasts had developed at age 14, Joan knew she was really a boy. Somehow she had known this all her life. She began to live as a male and adamantly refused to return to the hospital for further treatments. When the parents and the doctors realized it was live as John or kill herself as Joan, they told him the full story.

John remembers: "All of a sudden everything clicked. For the first time things made sense and I understood who and what I was" (Diamond and Sigmundson 1997:300). He went back to the operating table for a double mastectomy, the construction of a phallus, and male hormone treatments. But John was relatively happy—happier than he had ever been. Yes, he had an unseen physical disability. He had lost his biological potential for siring children, and his re-reconstructed genitals would never respond well. But he had his own identity. His brain (a major sex organ) knew he was a male. He was popular in school, grew up, and married a woman with small children, whom he then adopted. The simplistic propositions that genitals are gender and that sexual-gender identity is a question of clothes and toys at an impressionable age are gross simplifications of complex physiological and social realities. From this specific situation, we see that "Joan" developed as a boy—despite all the pressures against that. He developed as a heterosexual; for him, girls were not something to be, but to be with sexually.

About one in every 1,000 births are babies with ambiguous genitalia resulting from a variety of chromosomal and hormonal abnormalities. As things stand now, such individuals are designated as females; surgeons consider it easier to turn ambiguous genitalia into vaginas than into a penis. But in an atmosphere of ambiguity and choice, many reconstructed females are unhappy with their enforced identity. They may have a Y chromosome—the most overt mark of a male—or they may have been bathed in male hormones while still in utero, creating a "psychosexual bias" prenatally. Enough people are experiencing these debates through their bodies that they have formed a support group, the Intersex Society of North America. They worry about so many surgical and pharmaceutical interventions and ask: Why not leave these intersexed children alone? Let them decide who they are. Their point is that gender is overdetermined, too stereotyped, and too binary in contemporary cultures. This seems to be another argument for the third sex and third gender categories, or at least for individual flexibility.

When Boys Will Be Girls

In a variety of human societies, individuals who were not born female decide nonetheless to live as women do. These biological males dress and act in the manner their own culture prescribes for biological females. One term for this phenomenon is **gynemimesis,** derived from the Greek words *gyne* or woman, plus *mimos,* mime or mimicking.

Dressing like women is the first and most obvious way to express a new gender identity. Then men do women's work, form communities with each other, or alter their bodies in some way to match their idea of women's bodies. Sometimes there is shared sexuality, either in ritual or lifestyle, as prostitution or as preference. Sometimes there is body mutilation; transforming the male body ranges from systematic removal of body hair to removal of penis and testicles or surgical construction of a vagina.

Why do men do this? What is so meaningful or attractive about being female? In situations in which women's status is high and the social rewards seem to be great, then becoming a female makes some sense. Sometimes, however, becoming or imitating a woman is moving against the grain. What is the purpose of taking on the devalued and seemingly constrained roles of women? No one is certain why this phenomenon appears so regularly; we do know, however, that cross-cultural settings give us the best opportunity to observe. In the following section, we will see a specific example of gynemimesis and gender alternatives from India. This example offers another way to understand how the continuum of gender constructs the choices people make in their lives.

Neither Woman nor Man: Hijras of India

The **hijras** of India are men who adopt female dress and other features of female behavior. They form a kind of intersex or third sex. Ordinarily they live together in groups and earn a living by performing at and blessing certain key rituals like weddings, births, and other festivals. They collect alms or offerings as well as payments for these performances. They worship Bahuchara Mata, one of many mother goddesses venerated in India. In devotion to this goddess, some men submit to castration or emasculation, removal of the penis and testicles. In their traditions, this act gives them the power to curse or to bless male infants. For hijras, surgery and worship of the goddess buttress their claims of special power and a place in Indian society.

No one knows how many hijras live in India; estimates range from 50,000 to 500,000. When anthropologist Serena Nanda asked them about their social identities, some replied, "We are neither man nor woman." Others said, "We hijras are like women." All of them explained that sometime in childhood or adolescence, they realized they would not be able to fit into the typical continuum of gender definitions in India; nor were they going to be able to act as a husband and consummate the heterosexual marriages arranged by their families. Many said, "We were born this way."

Hijras wear women's clothing and take on other defining aspects of female identity. Not all hijras undergo the surgery or even perform publicly. And some

Hijras often earn a living by performing and blessing certain key rituals.

earn their living as prostitutes, although their claim to spiritual power rests on their renunciation of male sexuality and the embrace of "otherworldly" religious practices. But all have renounced the conventional Indian version of "real men."

The surgery is a **rite of passage,** moving a person from one status to another through rituals. The symbolism is painfully clear: The person who performs the surgery is called a midwife. The operation is conceived of as both birth and rebirth. The soon-to-be woman or hijra has the ritual status of a pregnant and post-partum woman. When the forty-day recovery period after the surgery is over, the hijra community dresses her as a bride and presents her to the goddess, Mata.

The new initiate into the community will find established relationships and the possibilities for others. The teacher–pupil relationship between a guru and her disciple is a mutual obligation of aid and loyalty. In addition, hijras form networks of **fictive kinship.** They use biological relations as a metaphor or symbol for creating new formal and informal connections. We might also think of the surgery and the status of hijra as a form of career development. It is difficult to earn a living in India. But the hijras offer a niche for survival and an occupation with exclusive privileges and rights. The surgery offers physical and religious validation, a new family, and an economic monopoly over certain ritual occasions. Hijras think of themselves as females; therefore, they want what every good Indian woman is supposed to want: a husband and children. They also want to choose their own mates and enjoy the kind of romance and love they see in movies.

Hijras dress as women, style their long hair, pluck out facial hairs, and use female pronouns and kinship terms. They sit in "ladies only" seats and count themselves as women in the census. But most make no real attempt to pass as women. They would have to follow standards of demure modesty and public restraint required of women. Instead, hijras offer caricatures or burlesques of standard females with heavy sexual overtones.

> It is not at all uncommon to see hijras in female clothing sporting several days growth of beard, or exposing hairy, muscular arms. The ultimate sanction of hijras to an abusive or unresponsive public is to lift their skirts and expose the mutilated genitals. The implicit threat of this shameless, and thoroughly unfeminine, behavior is enough to make most people give them a few cents so they will go away. (Nanda 1985:38)

Although Indian men may dress in women's clothes or find religious justifications for a third sex and gender, women in India do not cross those lines easily, if at all. There are no comparable groups for females wearing men's clothes and performing men's work.

Two-Spirits in Native North America

By sharp contrast, in the traditional and preconquest societies of the New World, both females and males had opportunities to negotiate alternative identities or roles. In the following sections, we will look at individuals whom contemporary Native Americans call **two-spirits.** This is a generic term in English for people who are lesbian, gay, transgendered, cross-dressers, transvestites, transsexuals, or otherwise have "marked" lives in the bands, tribes, or nations where concepts of multiple genders occur.

Although many languages in Native North America had words for two-spirits, two terms have been used historically in English. They are **berdache** for men who voluntarily adopted female dress, mannerisms, speech, and social roles, and **amazon** for females in Native North American cultures who adopted men's dress and occupational status. It is important for us to note that these words are outdated labels that originated in Western thought, languages, and colonial practices. Europeans who brought very different and bifurcated systems of politics and religions to this continent had trouble understanding these ancient roles. In addition, Western observers projected their own negative judgments about women onto those they called Indians. Although the terms "berdache" and "amazon" appear in a number of publications, including this book, they may not accurately reflect patterns or values of gender variance in the contemporary communities of Native North Americans. The term "two-spirits" better integrates the sexual, gendered, political, artistic, and spiritual meanings of crossing the borders.

Many Native North American societies were as gender-equal as we are likely to find. Women's and men's tasks were complementary and each gender was respected for the contributions they made. In many Native American tribes, female status was often high; therefore, males who moved in that direction assumed that status.

Anthropologist Walter Williams traveled widely among contemporary Native American groups. He identified himself as a gay anthropologist who wanted to learn how other cultures accommodate the gender and sexual variations that create so many anxieties in Euro-American societies.

Williams used the term "berdache" for a morphological male who does not live out the standard male role. He may be stereotyped as feminine but is more accurately thought of as androgynous. Such a man does some women's work and mixes clothing, behaviors, and social expectations for women and men simultaneously. In the past, elaborate myths and folk traditions supported men in these choices. They were frequently renowned for spiritual, intellectual, or artistic achievements. They used their special powers to bless ceremonies, predict the future, assign personal names, or assume spiritual responsibilities. Many of these men had reputations for hard work and loving generosity, especially to children.

Parents and other family members recognized the unique characteristics and personalities of the two-spirits. Lame Deer, a Lakota shaman, speaks:

> *We think that if a woman has two little ones growing inside her, if she is going to have twins, sometimes instead of giving birth to two babies they have formed up in her womb into just one, into a half-man/half-woman kind of being. . . . To us a man is what nature, or his dreams, make him. We accept him for what he wants to be. That's up to him. (Quoted in Williams 1986:25)*

Lame Deer suggests a number of causes or reasons for becoming a two-spirit: election by the spirits, prenatal or biological influences, or individual psychology as expressed in dreams. Above all, he notes: This lifestyle was acceptable.

In North America, such men helped women in their work, provided good company, and assumed many heavy tasks. They took no time off for menstruating, birthing, carrying a baby, or nursing. Since these men did women's work, they typically married men. Getting married means expanding one's kinship base, having someone to share work with, and bringing other's experiences to survival tasks.

Females, a Man–Woman, and Zuni Pueblo

The research on two-spirits in Native North America is strongly associated with the first generation of female anthropologists, particularly Ruth Benedict, who worked at Zuni Pueblo in New Mexico. Anthropologists often regard Zuni Pueblo as a nearly perfect social order: democratic, pluralistic, and holistic. No groups dominated other groups. Moreover, Zuni Pueblo was classically matrilineal; the household or family group centered on a mother and her daughters. These women, with their sons and brothers, traced a common descent back to a mythical female ancestress.

Zuni is commonly referred to as a theocracy, in which authority was vested in priests and religious concerns dominated private and public life. Religious societies maintained their own kivas, or round underground ritual chambers, and sponsored regular services that featured dramatic and colorful masked dancers. The people of Zuni are also known for extraordinary artistic productivity, such as pottery, murals, jewelry, and weaving. These products are created in a process that Zunis compare to giving birth.

In Zuni life, the sexual division of labor was as complementary as human beings are capable of. It is obvious that Zuni women enjoyed high status and economic independence. As examples, women plastered the outside walls of the houses men built. Men grew corn; women stored and distributed it. Men did not enter the granaries, because corn was sacred at a large number of symbolic levels. Even art was divided by gender: Women made pottery and ceramics and used the small belt loom to make long objects like scarves and belts. Men made tools for their personal use, jewelry, and wove larger items like blankets and their wives' woolen leggings! Men carried a special responsibility for "things of the universe" that is, the welfare of the earth and all living creatures.

Women produced life; women then fed those lives. But life was not just babies. Life was corn and the spirit world. So women sprinkled ground cornmeal on the masked gods and joined the medicine societies to learn techniques for curing serious injuries and illnesses. Ruth Benedict said of the Zunis:

> *The Zuni are a ceremonious people, a people who value sobriety and inoffensiveness above all other virtues. . . . Pleasant relations between the sexes are merely one aspect of pleasant relations with human beings. . . . They do not picture the universe, as we do, as a conflict of good and evil. They are not dualistic. (Benedict 1934a:116)*

Zunis did not have a "natural attitude." A two-spirited Zuni man did woman's work and wore women's clothes. He negotiated his status with his own character and personality. Typically, a young boy might demonstrate qualities that were known to lead into this status; he liked playing with girls and doing their domestic activities. His female relatives remarked on this. Sometimes he had experienced unusual dreams or a strange illness. The transition became final at adolescence, when he adopted the outward markers of women's dress.

Anthropologist Will Roscoe began his research with a group called Gay American Indians, who were sponsoring a history project. This led him to the archives of major museums in the United States. Like Walter Williams, he tapped into collections of oral traditions. He wrote, in effect, an ethnographic biography of a well-known Zuni two-spirit named We'wha. Here he describes We'wha's work.

> *Assisting the women of his household, We'wha daily set out piles of hewe' and steaming bowls of mutton stew for an appreciative family. He learned to keep the house neat, according to fastidious Zuni standards, by spraying water on the dirt floor and sweeping it several times a day. In certain chores performed by women—fetching wood, carrying water from the well in jugs balanced on the head, plastering the walls of houses, threshing wheat, winnowing grain and beans, and tending the waffle gardens along the banks of the river—We'wha's strength and endurance was especially advantageous. (Roscoe 1991:39)*

When We'wha visited Washington, D.C., the newspapers commented:

> *The princess is an eccentric child of nature. Although she is moving at present in the highest circles of Washington, she yet has lapses from the conventionalities of life and goes back to the freer notion of life on the plains. The general style of the princess is massive. Her broad face, her worn features and the peculiar parting of her hair give her a masculine look among the pale-faced society ladies. (for Washington Chronicle, April 18, 1886)*

In the style of that time, We'wha was called a priestess, a princess, a maiden, and a girl. He knitted continuously while in Washington; this was unremarkable in that setting; after all, he was a woman. But at Zuni Pueblo, knitting would have attracted confused attention, since only men knitted!

So, was We'wha a male or a female? The Zunis said a not-man but also a not-woman. Here's where it may be helpful to think of two-spirited people in Native North America or people who adopt similar customs around the world as a third sex or an alternative gender. Zunis did. They had many powerful initiations and ceremonies for validating these statuses; they could distinguish between biological sex and gender identity.

Zuni men–women often formed long-term emotional and sexual relationships with regular men, sometimes in contexts that must be described as marriage. By the same token, females could choose to do Zuni men's work and wear their clothes. They were spoken of as "manly" or "like a man–woman." Unfortunately, we know much less about these women than we do about the men.

A well-known Zuni two-spirit: We'wha.

A Fourth Sex? Cross-Gendered Females

Two-spirits are a category in Native North America that included men, women, not-men, and not-women. Unfortunately, there is little ethnographic evidence about two-spirited women. Most authors agree that men in transgendered statuses were more common than females were. The two-spirited world appeared to be more articulated and institutionalized for males than for females.

> *Throughout most of North America, there was no recognized female counterpart to the male berdache. Yet women willing and able to traverse the sex boundary do not seem to have been in short supply. Wherever ethnographic attention has been turned to this subject, the impression is given that for every boy who dreamed of the burden strap, there was a woman who actually picked up the bow. (Whitehead 1981:90)*

Many Native American groups had alternative gender categories for women as two-spirits; there were special names for "women who passed for men, dressed like men, and married women." In some groups, there were words that translated as "manly hearted women." The Yuman Indians said, "She wished only to become a man."

Gone-to-the-Spirits

An intriguing account of a woman who dreamed of a bow and arrows comes from the historical and anthropological literature for the Kutenai.

> *Gone-to-the-Spirits carried on activities customarily pursued only by men among her people. In 1811 she is described in historical narratives as assuming the roles of courier, guide, prophetess, and warrior. Again in 1825 she is seen momentarily as a person of prominence among the Kutenai; and finally in 1837, she appears as a peace mediator between the Flathead and the Blackfoot, before meeting her death at the hands of the latter. During these years she dressed in masculine garb and lived as "husband" of a succession of individuals of her own sex. (Schaeffer 1965:193)*

Her sexual or gender career began when she married a French-Canadian man and accompanied him through the Rocky Mountains on several trading or exploring expeditions. According to journals and letters of that period, the couple parted, and when the former wife returned to the Kutenai, she announced,

> *I'm a man now. We Indians did not believe the white people possessed such power from the supernaturals. I can tell you that they do, greater power than we have. They changed my sex while I was with them. (Quoted in Schaeffer 1965:196)*

In honor of her sexual metamorphosis, she changed her name to Gone-to-the-Spirits. Then she dressed in men's shirts, leggings, and loincloths; she carried a bow and arrows as well as a gun. Gone-to-the-Spirits went on raiding parties. Her hunting skills provided fish and game for her family. She proposed marriage to several young women; they declined. Many of her peers thought she had lost her mind. Soon, however, Gone-to-the-Spirits attracted her first wife.

> *A young man, well dressed in leather, carrying a Bow and Quiver of Arrows, with his Wife, a young woman in good clothing, came to my tent door and requested me to give them my protection; somewhat at a loss what answer to give, on looking at them, in the Man I recognized the Woman. She had become a prophetess, declared her sex changed, that she was now a Man, dressed and armed herself as such, and also took a young woman to Wife, of whom she pretended to be very jealous. (Quoted in Schaeffer 1965:203)*

Another trader and journal-keeper in the region, called the pair "bold and adventurous amazons" whom he mistook at first for man and wife. Some sources describe Gone-to-the-Spirits as quite large and heavy-boned; others say she had a delicate frame. Perhaps size is relative to perceived gender. All accounts note her determination to live as the men of her time did. They also discuss her abilities as a "prophetess." She practiced healing and divinations of a shaman. Some tribes called her "Manlike Woman" and spread her reputation for prophesy and other supernatural powers.

Many other accounts from Native North America tell about women taking on male roles such as hunting, leading war parties, seeking revenge, and marrying women. Woman Chief of the Crows was captured in childhood by the Crow Indians and raised by a warrior. She lived and died as a brave and a chief. She hunted successfully, took three wives, served in the tribal council, acquired fame, honor, standing, and a reputation for daring and extraordinary luck or power. Clearly, she was judged by her accomplishments.

Ironically, the women who went as wives to these female chiefs and manly hearted women are totally invisible in the literature. The men who wrote these accounts uniformly assumed that anyone who is a man or pretending to be a man automatically needs a woman. In fact, they had no firm boundaries between wives and servants. Therefore, once they accepted a women who acted like a man, it was easy to assume that "he" needed a wife.

Women hunted for the same reasons men did: They had children to feed. Other times women went to war for revenge, defense, necessity, or in response to a vision. Living as a man was, under many circumstances, a practical and socially responsible course of action. Native Americans seemed to be amazingly dispassionate about females who hunted, warred, lived like a man, and courted women.

> *A woman who could succeed at doing the things men did was honored as a man would be. Few, if any, tortured rationalizations were brought to bear upon her achievement. What seems to have been more disturbing to the culture—which means, for all intents and purposes, to the men—was the possibility that women, within their own department, might be onto a good thing. (Whitehead 1981:108)*

In other words, Native American men seem to have had more trouble with their peers becoming or acting like women than with women becoming or acting like men.

The Cultures of Women-with-Women

The examples from Native North America challenge the concepts of owning a woman in marriage, being married as the central role in a woman's life, the idea of "two shall be as one," or other romantic fantasies. A woman's social status and affiliations were not dependent on a husband.

> *The important consideration in the Indian view is that they were still fulfilling the standard role of "mother and wife" within their culture. The traditional gender role for women did not restrict their choice of sexual partners. Gender identity (woman or amazon) was important, but sexual identity (heterosexual or homosexual) was not. (Williams 1986:247)*

Information on women's same-sex relationships among Native Americans is difficult to tease out of the sources that condemned women's same-sex lives as much if not more than men's. Women were expected to marry; but they also had bonds, some of them sexual, outside marriage. In the sexual division of labor and kinship, females were goddesses, spirits, mothers, healers, sisters, prophets, grandmothers, shamans, wives, and daughters. Men were gods, spirits, fathers, diviners, warriors, uncles, shamans, brothers, and husbands. So women spent a lot of time in each other's company. They grew up in a woman's culture and practiced a wide range of women's rituals and activities. In Native North America sex was private, not sinful or dirty. Sex was for making babies, and women made their most definitive contributions in having babies. It is said that the Arapaho thought that dying in war and in childbirth were equal honors.

The core elements of women's identities came from a community of those moved by the same spirit. Those related through the spirit world were closer than those related by blood. In fact, relationships to the world of gods, goddesses, spirits, and metaphysical or occult forces grew out of and transcended sex, sexual identity, or eroticism.

> *Within such systems, individual action was believed to be directed by Spirits (through dreams, visions, direct encounter, or possession of power objects such as stones, shells, masks, or fetishes). In this context it is quite possible that lesbianism was practiced rather commonly, as long as the individuals cooperated with the larger social customs. Women were generally constrained to have children, but in many tribes, childbearing meant empowerment. It was the passport to maturity and inclusion in woman-culture. An important point is that women who did not have children because of constitutional, personal, or Spirit-directed disinclination had other ways to experience Spirit instruction and stabilization, to exercise power, and to be mothers. (Allen 1989:109)*

For Native Americans, power did not mean control or the ability to coerce others to get one's own way. Power was supernatural; it was wisdom, awareness, mindfulness. Power often came from females or the female qualities in everyone. Power came through the vision quest, trance states, objects, and abilities to see, hear, heal, or hunt. Power was in the myths, dances, ceremonies, and art. People called "medicine women" or "manly hearted women" had exceptional powers. Like men who learned this kind of power, women probably became **androgynous.** They shared features of both male and female.

The anthropological study of women is relatively recent. And seeing women outside of traditional female roles is even more so. This is one reason why we have more information on men in alternative gender roles than we do about women. Anthropologists who saw women only in domestic roles, such as food processing, child-rearing, or kinship obligations, probably could not see nonheterosexual activities. The universal customs of marriage presume and privilege heterosexual lives. Women are "naturally" expected to marry and have children. The natural attitude puts serious legal and social constraints on female expressions of sexuality and power. More to the point, if women act in secret or in concert with others to break taboos or reject conventional and ascribed marriage patterns, they hope to go unnoticed. We often do not see women living out parts of their lives with other women. We are not prepared emotionally or intellectually to notice adolescent girls' structured sexual experimentation or adult women's lifelong friendships with each other. The social construction of being a lesbian (our current socio-political term) or being a woman-loving-woman (Ruth Benedict's phrase) varies enormously from time to time and place to place.

> *The range of lesbian behavior that appears crossculturally varies from formal to informal relations. . . . Examples of such would be adolescent sex play and affairs among women in harems or polygynous households. Formal lesbian relations are part of a network or social structure extending beyond the pair or immediate love relationship, and occur within such social relationships as bond friendship, sisterhoods, initiation schools, the cross-gender role, or woman-marriage. An examination of social stratification suggests that, in societies where women have control over their productive activities and status, both formal and informal relations may occur. Where women lack power, particularly in class societies, they maintain only informal lesbian ties or build institutions outside the dominant culture. (Blackwood 1985b:10)*

In a number of tribal settings, lesbian or women-centered friendships were an ordinary part and parcel of kinship, economics, and religion. In some groups, young girls typically play with each other's bodies before marriage. Among Australian aborigines, equalitarian gatherer–hunter societies, adolescent sex play for girls was structured within kinship categories for determining proper marriage partners. Thus a youngster could have mutually stimulating play with another girl as long as they were cross-cousins—that means linked to each other by parents who were siblings of the opposite sex, her mother's brother's daughter or father's sister's daughter. In fact, female cross-cousins would marry each other's brothers; these girls were destined to be sisters-in-law. These early sexual friendships set up bonds that may have translated into shared mothering, food gathering, or other extensions of friendship.

In a number of societies in West Africa, teenage girls engaged in sexual play with each other as an ordinary part of adolescence. Later, as married women, they kept these activities secret from their husbands. Many opportunities were available for women in polygynous households. In many parts of Africa, female initiation societies included sexual play and erotic exchanges. This research points to a broad view of female sexuality and puts sensuality, touching, caressing, and verbal expressions of love before intercourse. In these African examples, women experience warm, nurturant, early mothering, genital sensuality in childhood, and institutionalized female friendships in adolescence.

Cross-cultural research on women's friendships, the meaning and structuring of them, and their replacement of or coexistence with relationships of men and marriage, is just beginning. It is important to break free of ethnocentric polarizations and the rigid categories of homosexual and heterosexual to which we assign people. These categories do not explain what women's lives are often about and they ignore our creative responses to conditions we cannot control or did not produce.

Conclusions beyond the Categories of Sex, Gender, and Desire

So how do we account for the border crossings we have seen in this chapter? A person's morphological sex or her or his sex as assigned at birth can function independently of gender status, behavior, and erotic attractions. Gender and sexuality appear to be immensely flexible. Why? Many writers, anthropologists and others, say that third genders are varieties of institutionalized homosexuality. But as we have seen in India and Native North America, adopting women's work and social habits seems to be more about defining characteristics than the choice of a sexual partner.

Another theory for the third gender involves the limitations of the gender roles available in any given culture at any time. Unusual or peculiarly talented individuals may want to be less or more aggressive, nurturant, artistic, athletic, or dressed-up than their cultural milieu generally allows. The best way or the only way to achieve these personal goals may be to borrow or adopt the desired behaviors from the other gender, to mimic, or to form new or autonomous genders. If work is assigned by gender (and it is), then careers and subsistence may only be possible by taking on the marks and status of another gender. Hence women as warriors.

By contrast, some anthropologists lean toward a theory that cross-dressing and gender-bending may be religious matters. In this approach, spiritual power is available to individuals who unite or transcend the oppositions of female and male. There is wholeness or oneness in androgyny, in creating new gender categories, or in eroticism apart from reproduction. The two-spirits of Native North America were not threats to rigid gender ideologies. Indeed, they transcend the division of human beings into female and male. Like the deities or spirits, they also cross the lines.

The idea of a third sex or third gender is a striking counterpoint to the Western ideologies of women and men as polar opposites, sexuality as reproduction, or sensuality as sinful. It offers a vision of reconciliation for our masculine selves and our feminine selves that goes beyond sexual politics.

There are elaborate and publicly supported ceremonies and displays for people who want to cross-dress in New Orleans.

Important Books beyond the Natural Attitude

In a national dialogue over sexual identity issues and cultural values, gays and lesbians in the United States are inventing and embellishing "marriage" and "family"—see Kath Weston's *Families We Choose: Lesbians, Gays, Kinship Between Men, Between Women* (1991). Adolescents and college-age gays are also pushing at old boundaries and tired categories, as discussed in Gilbert Herdt and Andrew Boxer's *Children of Horizons: How Gay and Lesbian Youth are Forging a New Way Out of the Closet* (1996). They have found common ground and alternatives in the two-spirited people of Native North America. For an intimate look at how two-spirited people define themselves, how others treat them, and how scholars interpret their cultures, see Sue-Ellen Jacobs, Wesley Thomas, and Sabine Lang's *Two-Spirit People: Native American Gender Identity, Sexuality, and Spirituality*

(1997) and Sabine Lang's *Men as Women, Women as Men: Changing Gender in Native American Cultures* (2000).

To explore same sex relationships across cultures, read Serena Nanda's *Gender Diversity: Crosscultural Variations* (2000), an eye-opening account of the differences in how sex/gender diversity are experienced in seven different places. Or read Gilbert Herdt's *Same Sex, Different Cultures: Gays and Lesbians across Cultures* (1997) for the ever-changing sexual landscapes across the breadth of human culture and sexual experiences.

Chapter Eight

Life's Lesions

Suffering and Healing

*M*aria, a woman living in Mexico City, speaks:

> *The doctors always asked me what is wrong, and I always tell them, and they tell me that with the medications they prescribe I will get better, but I never get better. Then they tell me I am nervous. But I tell them that I am not nervous and I feel the same. When I go to the doctor I get nervous because I am being told that I am suffering from nerves. By saying this, they make me nervous and they make me tremble. . . . My husband's angers make me sick, and every time he changed jobs, his behavior also changed. Three years he took up with another woman and this harmed me a lot. At that time I began suffering from colitis. Also my children are a bit wild. All this makes me nervous.*

Kaja, an anthropologist, responds:

> *During the course of all my studies in Mexico, both men and women laid bare their lives to me and spoke openly about their pains. When speaking about their sickness, they incessantly referred to their day-to-day experiences, which always revolved around their relationships with their mates, children, parents, and neighbors. Their discourses persuaded me that what I identify as* **life's lesions***—which are embedded in existential conditions, contradictions, and moral evaluations—are as virulent as any pathogen found in nature. (Finkler 1994a:xii)*

Her years of fieldwork research in hospitals and in Spiritualist religions in Mexico revealed several key points to anthropologist Kaja Finkler (1994a, 1994b). Women are the majority of healers in the Spiritualist churches and the majority of the patients in doctor's offices and hospitals. Women report experiences of pain and sickness more than men do. Women's sufferings are real, but they are not life-threatening. The symptoms are subacute, hard to diagnose, and even more difficult to treat. Yet women live longer than men do. These paradoxes are true worldwide. She concludes that adversities, hostile social relationships, moral contradictions, and unresolved anxieties are inscribed upon women's bodies. That's what makes women sick.

Every woman Finkler interviewed lived under stressful conditions. But who has a stress-free life? All of us know women who sound like Maria. Some of us feel like Maria. Her story touches a live nerve. It is not that men don't experience profound suffering. Of course they do. But to the extent that our physical bodies differ and that our life experiences are shaped—gendered—by contrasting forces, women and men act and react in different ways. "There are obvious differences between male and female patterns of sickness and health. Not surprisingly, these stem in part from biological differences between the sexes. But as we shall see, the situation is more complex than might at first appear. All societies continue to be divided along the 'fault line' of gender, and this too has a profound effect on the well-being of both men and women" (Doyal 1995:1). Women's lives can literally make us sick.

In Mexico, women typically talk about "nerves" and "fright" (a nasty surprise) as causes of ill health. Something happens suddenly that seems unbearable and has many moral ramifications and unforeseen consequences. What do Maria and the other women like her do when this happens? Typically they seek out help from family, friends, and informal social networks. They look for medical or religious assistance, spiritual healing, or practical cures. The doctors in Mexico tell women like Maria to eat a better diet, more fruits, vegetables, and animal proteins. But they cannot afford such a diet. Doctors say, get more exercise. But they already work hard. Another physician says that her problems are "only nerves." Priests tell them to obey their husbands or ignore the gripping poverty they are trapped in. When various physicians cannot or do not bring a cure, women seek help from alternative medicines and a large variety of folk practitioners. They buy aspirin, antacids, shots, pills, and over-the-counter medicines they hear about. Sometimes they take all these actions all at once. They often move away from the Catholicism in which most were raised and join an Evangelical, Pentecostal, or Spiritualist church. Women in Mexico—as everywhere in the world—talk about the same symptoms: depression, sleeplessness, nerves, anxiety, and tiredness. Overriding everything they feel or do is their search for explanation, acknowledgment, and validation. What they suffer from hurts. Surely someone, somewhere, will know what to do.

Women's Wounds

This chapter is about women's wounds. These kinds of pain won't automatically kill a woman, but they may make her feel very sick or crazy. Here are a few of life's lesions women suffer from that are mentioned in this book: poverty, social class, husbands, no husbands, parents, no parents, loss of children, too much fertility, not enough fertility, loss of meaning or of life's dreams, loss of bodily autonomy, loss of home or homeland, violence, abuses, discriminations, oppression, and betrayals. Add in diseases, afflictions, and sicknesses of the body, soul, or personality, and even then, you will still be able to suggest additional situations of suffering.

This chapter is not about women's relationship to Western medicine, biomedicine, drugs, surgery, hygienic practices, the pill, or any of a thousand topics in international public health. As fascinating and valuable as these approaches may be, they come out of Western experiences and are oriented to authoritative systems of knowledge. For many women, such systems are alien; for just as many, they are not available. By contrast, women across the planet seek out health and an end to suffering in many different ways. We want to find a way to see women's experiences through anthropological or comparative lenses. So I propose the following themes and offer some ethnographic examples to illustrate them:

- *Life's lesions are embodied, that is, expressed in women's physical bodies.*

- *This kind of suffering is real. It's not "all in her head." It cannot be ignored and should not be depreciated on the erroneous grounds that it is made up or imaginary. The idea of a separation between mind and body is largely irrelevant.*

- *Women tend to frame experiences of suffering and seeking help around ordinary social roles such as mother, wife, lover, sister, daughter, friend, or community member.*

- *Women's pains center in and mediate the life stream along the continuum of birth and death.*

- *Women tend to take a flexible and relative view of categories such as biological, medical, religious, spiritual, therapeutic, or healing and move fluidly among them. The spiritual and physical, supernatural and natural, and therefore religious and therapeutic are integrated. Women often speak about a variety of personal relationships with assorted other-wordly beings such as spirits, angels, ghosts, souls, goddesses, gods, or saints (to name a few).*

- *Women often seek out creative or expressive domains such as poetry, song, handwork, performances, ceremonials, trances, or altered states of consciousness. Women practice small-scale personal and practical rituals or other inconspicuous means of acknowledging suffering and healing.*

The systems we now call biomedicine and organized or world religions were once linked. In fact, in many parts of the world today, science and religion, nature and supernature, and the mind, body, and spirit are still linked within explanatory and practical cosmological models. Imagine a continuum. At one end are the formal institutions we all participate in and know about on a number of levels: the administrative and financial structures of biomedicine, science, and world religions. This is "the establishment": complexes tied to global economies and vast bureaucracies such as the World Health Organization or the World Council of Churches, and identified in such powerful individuals as the Pope or the Surgeon General of the United States. In our personal lives, we have (or don't have) insurance companies, HMOs, religious affiliations, retirement plans, and so on. At the opposite end of the continuum are healing traditions, folk religions, over-the-counter medicines, alternative medicines, self-medication, herbalists, midwives, and an emphasis on expressiveness and connections. Some people make all of this a question of "belief systems," orthodoxies, and conformity. But it is much more. Anthropologists typically observe that the continuum has complex and multiple dimensions, and most humans participate in activities and organizations along this continuum in dynamic and ever-changing ways. You will notice that boundaries between religion and science, healing or curing, or knowledge or knowing tend to blur when we take up the large questions of women's lived experiences.

Paths to Authority

Humans have many sources of knowledge and wisdom: intuition, revelation, common sense, books, teachers, doctors, theologians, dreams, trances, angels, therapists, and mothers (among others). Women typically practice what anthropologists call **embodied knowledge.** It's the response to the question, "How do you know?" with an answer of "I feel it in my gut." Or, "What's wrong with her?" "She has a broken heart." It is the equivalent of telling your mechanic that the car is making a funny noise or intuiting a problem in your body before a medical diagnosis. Embodied knowledge is also the ability to do something practical. Women often experience and practice knowledge as narrative, stories, and first-person accounts. Women embrace knowledge as experience, revelation, and intuition. But these qualities cannot be "proved." They are not "scientific." Women typically learn and pass knowledge on through apprenticeships and informal instruction with each other. Along with embodied knowledge, women are interested in practices that are effective, that work.

The efficacy of a healing treatment or a religious ritual, the ability to transform the current circumstances in a convincing manner, is one way that authority is granted within informal systems of knowledge. Authority has the power to compel people to believe and act in certain ways. Practitioners of biomedicine, religion, and alternative forms of healing engage in different means of positioning their beliefs and practices as systems of **authoritative knowledge.** As Brigett Jordan says, "The power of authoritative knowledge is not that it is correct but that it counts" (1993:153). Often, formal systems of authoritative knowledge have other forms of power supporting them. They may have momentum from centuries of existence. They may be supported by rulers and armies. There are known penalties for going against these systems: one may be gossiped about, banished, or excluded. People or groups involved in the reward systems of authoritative knowledge are called **gatekeepers.** The gatekeepers may suppress other forms of knowledge, outlawing them or identifying them and their practitioners as ignorant, primitive, illogical, or trouble-making. They may limit access to the knowledge to a minority of trained specialists, increasing other people's dependency and reliance on the experts. And so it goes—certain systems of knowledge become official and ascendant. They are considered legitimate; and others are not.

The journey to authority is complex, however. It is not simply a matter of forcing people to abide by a system of knowledge through formal means. There are many reasons why people integrate certain forms of knowledge into their lives and not others, and many ways of making a system of knowledge count. People follow certain doctrines because they believe that they work or because they accurately represent their experiences. People also follow systems of authoritative knowledge because they find meaning and satisfaction within them. As we will see throughout this chapter, many women pursue healing and religious strategies because of their visceral, or embodied experiences. These are utterly convincing—not only to the women at the center, but also to those men and women who follow their lead.

Gendering Religions

The **world religions** are major sites for authoritative knowledge. These belief systems, which cover large geographical areas and are associated with contemporary nation–states and international politics, expanded through military, economic, migratory, colonial, evangelical, or other means. They include Christianity (Catholicism, Protestantism, and Pentecostalism), Islam, Judaism, Hinduism,

Confucianism, Buddhism, and Taoism. Within the world religions and the countries associated with them are a number of smaller and less visible traditions. These religions predate and exist apart from, in resistance to, or in accommodation to colonial, national, or world religions.

Human religions have their own sexual division of labor. Men generally get to do the thinking and women generally get to do the feeling. Thinking includes scholarship, scriptures, theology, philosophy, doctrines, and dogma. Feeling involves mourning the dead and celebrating the stages and transformation of giving life. In another typical division of labor, when religion is a job, men get it. Where religion is defined as public ritual, career tracks, and bureaucracies, and is allied to government or the establishment in some way, men are paid to do it. Women are usually incorporated in the same symbolic manner that is characteristic of marriage. Within the establishment religions, women are often decorative, supportive, auxiliary, or compliant.

Women's spiritual lives are often secret, muted, or marginal when we view them through the lenses of state government, world religions, and male scholars. In many societies, women's religious practice is inconspicuous in contrast to the **conspicuous worship** practiced by men. It is easy to associate public displays, elaborate physical structures, and overt economic investment with a religion's core values. The inconspicuousness of women's religions, however, should not be taken as evidence that they do not exist or are not meaningful or central to the female (and sometimes male) participants. Consider the Zuni, an indigenous people of the Southwestern United States. Will Roscoe found that

> *Zunis considered women inherently complete or* dehya *because they created new life. Their sacredness was centered in their bodies. As a result, women, in effect, initiated themselves. Through menstruation and childbirth they apprehended the mysteries of life and death at their source and experienced their own rebirth. From the Zuni point of view, there was no need for society to intervene to induct women into religion. This has led many observers to conclude that the Zunis had no rites of passage for women and that women were excluded from religious life. . . . A closer look reveals that Zuni women were no less concerned with the supernatural, their lives no less imbued with ceremonialism than were men's. (1991:136–137)*

Women often seek spiritual fulfillment, answers to life's questions, and cures to life's ills via their own channels and religious formulations. Sometimes women "tame" or "domesticate" the systems of male control and ideology so they can live within them and find meanings for their lives. And sometimes women find or create alternative religions for themselves. We will call these *women's religions.* Women's religions focus on women's lives and their relationships to social, natural, and supernatural experiences: life, childbirth, miscarriage, infertility, illness, death, sex, relationships with people, animals, nature, spirits, gods, and goddesses. As such, women's religions center on acknowledging suffering and seeking healing. They exist in and around formal, institutionalized religion and biomedicine. Women in many cultures act as religious-healing specialists, including midwives, fortune-tellers, diviners, seers, mediums, shamans, and herbalists. Their activities often allow women to achieve status, prestige, and financial awards outside their domestic units or apart from mainstream religions and dominant cultures.

Women's religions often exist in societies in which women already have relative autonomy, for example in matrilineal, matrilocal, or matrifocal groups. Or they spring up in societies like those of the Americas and Asia, which are so complex, new, or rapidly changing that women can find openings even within the establishment religions. Women's religions can coexist with structured antifemale gender ideologies and gender dissonance. Religious activities may offer women space for achievement and self-expression or serve as a locus of resistance and separation. Women may create a sense of female community, sometimes deep in the heart of separatist or patriarchal ideologies. In these cases, women typically assert the primacy of direct experience with the ordinary and spirit world over established religious bureaucracies or doctrines built on reason or other canons of what constitutes "truth."

Anthropologist Susan Sered works in Israel at the crossroads of three world religions: Judaism, Christianity, and Islam. She began to question how women defined and organized their religion and spirituality in societies dominated by such patriarchies. She interviewed women and investigated women's rituals at shrines, at maternity hospitals, and in situations in which sexual segregation was firmly established. She then began to look for examples of women's religions around the world for a comparison. Sered found ethnographic and historic materials from many groups in which women dominate both in leadership and in membership. They are healers, spiritual guides, midwives, herbalists, or other practitioners. In each women's religion Sered discusses, women relate in some complex fashion to patriarchy, male dominations, or world religions. Although men participate in most of these religions, the consciousness and awareness is female-centered.

Sered also found that experiences around motherhood or mothering are omnipresent. Within women's religions, the reality of motherhood—achieved, desired, or lost—shapes the lives of adult women. Motherhood is the pivotal motif or metaphor. This does not mean that women's religions necessarily create good mothers, better mothers, or a universal standard for being mothers, or even that every woman involved is a mother. But we must note (once again) that most women give birth and have intimate physical and psychological connections with children. This inevitably means that women are connected to each other, to children, to food and feeding, to ancestors, and to death. Beyond giving birth, the most common experience women share is loss of children. Sered writes,

> *My argument is not that child death leads women to "escape" into religion. My argument is that child death encourages women to ponder existential and theological questions. As part of that process, some women change their religious beliefs and affiliations. In sum, although Western-style mother-love is not universal, child death is something with which women in all cultures must grapple, albeit in different ways. Encouraging motherhood, rejecting motherhood, and the loss of motherhood are important to women, and all of these themes surface in women's religions. (1994:90)*

The variety of experiences women have with fertility, motherhood, and loss is a primary example of the relationships among physical, spiritual, and social health. These concepts of lived experience and embodiment are expressed throughout women's religions around the world.

Many religions grew creatively from the terrible experiences of slavery, colonialism, and the **African Diaspora** in the New World. Women are the majority of participants and leaders in these groups. In Brazil, many religions combine parts of African and Native American tribal traditions with folk Catholicism and spirit-centered practices. These Afro-Brazilian religions center on public rituals for curing illness and misfortune. Spirits enter and possess women's bodies in dramatic ceremonies. You might be familiar with names such as Candomblé, Umbanda, or Macumba. Throughout Central America, old women organize mourning and other rituals around their ancestors. The Black Caribs in contemporary Belize are the best documented of these groups.

In the many nations of Africa, women are taking elements of local traditions in art, music, trance, or dance and combining them with pieces of the world religions to create lively cults. The *zār* cult of northern Africa and the Middle East, one of many examples, involves curing or healing through possession states and trances. *Zār* are impulsive spirits who enter women, particularly married women. Other women in the cult help the newly possessed tame the zār spirits with dancing, food, and woman-centered rituals. The most notable feature of these groups is women as **adepts**. The term means "uniquely skilled" and is applied to the leadership styles of women, which contrast dramatically with leadership in "organized" religious bureaucracies (see Jules-Rosette 1979). In Sierra Leone and most of West Africa, groups of women control their own organization, called Sande

Women assisting each other as the "spirits come down."

Secret Societies. Older women of Sande initiate teenage girls into this all-female society and teach them about childbirth and other aspects of being adult women. Sande groups protect their members from men and nonmember females.

In four examples Sered found in Asia, it is clear that localized and female-centered spiritual traditions predate the arrival of any world religions and, today, exist apart from them. These women's religions are strongly tied to kinship and healing. In northern Thailand, where households are matrilocal and matrilineal, spirits are relatives, too; they belong to the kin group. Members of the cults are all matrilineal descendants of the founding ancestress. In the indigenous religion of the Ryukyu Islands (of which Okinawa is the largest), women dominate the official and mainstream religion. Priestesses conduct rituals for households, villages, and families, and female shamans deal with personal healing and divination. In Burma, the indigenous or pre-Buddhist religions involved careful handling of *nats*—spirits, gods, or ghosts—at rituals for curing sicknesses, at harvests, planting, births, initiations, deaths, or weddings. The *nats* entered and possessed the bodies of women. In Korea, women conduct household rituals for the gods and seek out female shamans to help them with misfortunes and sicknesses within their families.

Sered reports on four women's religions from the United States. Christian Science is a religious movement whose members believe in the power of faith to cure sickness. Mary Baker Eddy organized this religion in Boston in 1879. She taught that matter, and therefore illness, is only an illusion. The Shakers were an eighteenth-century migration of believers from England to rural America. Their leader, Ann Lee, or Mother Ann, witnessed her four children die in a poor town in England. She led a group of followers to America; they believed her to be a completion or complement of Jesus. The rural communes they built emphasized agriculture, handmade crafts, celibacy, and ecstatic worship or "shaking."

Kate and Margaret Fox were sisters living in New York state. In 1848 they made contact with the spirit of a murdered salesman. This event is said to have been the beginning of the popular movement called Spiritualism. Nineteenth-century Spiritualism was a loosely organized religious movement based on belief in the survival of human personalities or souls after death and in their ability to communicate with those left behind, usually through a medium or channeler. Spiritualism or beliefs and practices that involve communications with dead people are very common phenomena around the world. Women are said to be more adept or receptive than men are. Today Spiritualist groups flourish around the world and emphasize healing through spiritual powers.

A contemporary religious movement in the United States, called the *Feminist Spirituality Movement,* is linked to feminism and the secular women's movement. Women borrow from the rituals, symbols, and mythologies of many cultures, particularly those of the ancient Middle East, Mediterranean, and Western European traditions. They emphasize goddesses, matriarchies, and female energies within women's bodies. Parallel to feminist spirituality is *womanism* or the *Womanist Movement,* a contemporary spiritual movement of African American feminists. Womanism draws on such sources as literature, African American folklore, Christianity, and feminism. Womanists speak of creating new styles of partnerships with men.

There are other examples of female-centered spirituality from many times and places, for example, celibate Christian women's communities, women's healing cults, New Orleans Voudou, Haitian Vodou in urban America, and many others. It is important to know that groups like this exist and that they validate women's life experiences in many ways. We will discuss several of these in more detail later in the chapter.

Healers and Healing

In anthropological studies of religion from around the world, women routinely act as curers, healers, nurturers, and mediators. Once again, as a warning against generalizing, it is not exclusively women who perform healing roles across human cultures. Men do them, too, but in different ways, if only because men have had more access to the formal structures. Western biomedical practices are part of systems of authoritative knowledge, but they exist side by side with woman-centered systems of healing.

> As nurturers, healers protect, comfort, and guide patients to restored health in the same way that mothers care for their children. And like dependent children, patients look to healers to meet their physical and emotional needs. . . . As mediators, healers cross symbolic boundaries, particularly those separating the human world from that of spirits and ancestors, and intervene with the latter on behalf of their patients or clients. In yet another sense, healers mediate between forces that cause illness when the body experiences imbalance: hot or cold, excess emotion like fright or anger, harmful natural qualities like the wind or magnetism associated with eclipses, and so forth. (McClain 1989a:73)

The most common aspect of women's religions are explaining, acknowledging, and alleviating suffering. Women around the world are not simply resigned to pain, bad luck, or an evil fate. Something—even something unorthodox—can be done. Healing in women's religions is eclectic; women pay little attention to authorities or explanations that preach the one and only true way. Two aspects of healing seem to be particularly striking in women's religions. First, women's healing rituals acknowledge that suffering is real. When the dominant mode of reality or the authoritative systems of knowledge are modeled on men's perceptions and experiences, then women may feel "crazy" about themselves. We ask, am I hysterical, neurotic, a malingerer, a hypochondriac? Is it all in my head? Women's religions offer communal, even public affirmations that there is genuine suffering and the need for healing, even for conditions that have no names in conventional religion or science.

Second, the healer herself has suffered; she knows about pain and loss and fear in her own gut. She is not an authority and has probably received her training through observation, participation, and apprenticeships. Only experience and the willingness to enter these feelings in order to help others make her an expert. This brings suffering and healing into the context of community and interpersonal relationships. Most women as healers work, out of necessity, in informal and domestic settings. They treat relatives, neighbors, and each other for illnesses that are not life-threatening. They make the decisions to consult specialists, either indigenous or biomedical.

Think of the support groups you know about: Mothers Against Drunk Driving, Compassionate Friends (and other groups for loved ones of deceased children), Reach to Recovery (and other groups for those coping with cancer), or Al-Anon (and other groups for supporting relatives and recovery around drugs and alcohol use). Hundreds of such groups have grown up to validate and support some very painful problems and losses. They exist apart from and meet needs that authoritative systems of medicine and religion cannot.

Anthropologists also may have neglected very crucial areas of women's religious or spiritual activity. For example, there is magic, or techniques for making good things happen for us. Getting a mate to notice us, love us, or marry us; and getting the children we want or don't want are everyday acts women practice in many locales. The box on page 204 shows examples of love magic from Santeria. These practices have an enviable reputation for success. I have often been asked for help of this kind or have needed it myself. Unfortunately, I wasn't raised in a coherent tradition of women's magic.

Women everywhere practice **divination**, or knowing about the unknowable, imaginative techniques for acquiring information or knowledge where empirical facts are not available. Men do this, too, but not as predictably. Women regularly foretell or foresee the sex of an unborn child, a person's future happiness, the outcome of a journey or business decision, the location of lost articles, or the source of illness. To learn about the future, to understand the past, and to seek advice or wisdom are akin to therapy at its deepest levels.

Midwifery

The quintessential healers in human societies are **midwives**. Pregnancy, birth, and babies have been women's work in the majority of times and periods on the planet. In many groups around the world, women as mothers are not trivialized or isolated, and pregnancy is not an illness. Long before authoritative systems of knowledge about pregnancy and childbirth existed, women placed their experiences and skills into the service of others.

> *Descriptions of traditional midwives from India, Pakistan, Bangladesh, Nigeria, Tanzania, Brazil, Mexico, Guatemala and Jamaica describe them as mature women who have themselves born children. All descriptions indicate that they achieve their status rather than having it ascribed by birth. The successful ones command great respect, have more clients and are very close to the families under their care. In the Sudan they are regarded by the children they deliver as a second mother, or the "mother of all people" in Iraq. In Guatemala midwives are regarded with deference and respect. They are addressed with an honorific title, asked to godmother and given gifts. All the children a midwife has delivered greet her with bowed head and kiss her hand. (MacCormack 1982:11)*

In many places, spirits call women into the service of midwifery. In Sierra Leone, the ancestors direct certain women personally to perform these valuable tasks for other women. In some African spirit-possession cults, birth is compared to baptism. That means that a midwife makes new members of the church as well as ritually purifying pregnant women through confession and exorcism so they can safely give birth. Afro-Caribbean women in Jamaica and other places may experience birth as a state of altered consciousness. In fact, giving birth can be a spiritual or religious experience. Midwives are often considered spiritual experts for

Love Magic

Santeria is an African religious tradition that uses some Roman Catholic rituals and symbols. Yoruba people, brought to Cuba as slaves for sug-arcane plantations, originated these practices. Santeria calls on the Yoruba spirits, *orishas,* and selected Catholic saints. Santeria was the religion of oppressed peoples who had every reason to hide their elaborate ceremonies and belief systems which involved initiations, sacrifices, divination, and spirit possession. Here are a few of the many spells available to the women of Santeria.

To get married: Gather some of his semen on a piece of cotton. He must not know what you intend. Form the cotton into a wick. Make an oil lamp from a hollowed-out lily bulb. Write his name on a little piece of paper in the form of a cross. Place it in the bottom of the bulb. Add quicksilver and a series of oils [recipes vary] and float the cotton in it while invoking Oshún to intercede and convince him to marry you. Light the lamp at nine o'clock for five nights and call forth the blessings of Oshún. This spell is said to be infallible.

To get pregnant: Enlist the aid of the beautiful moon goddess, Yemayá, patroness of motherhood. Bring her a pomegranate cut in half and smeared with honey. Write your name on a piece of paper and place it between the two halves of the pomegranate and reunite them. Invoke Yemayá and ask her to bless you with health and fruitfulness as the pomegranate is rich in seeds. On the first day of your new menstrual cycle, burn a blue candle in her honor. Do this every day for a month. It is common to become pregnant during this month.

Source: Adapted from Migene Gonzáles-Wippler, (*Santeria: African Magic in Latin America*) 1981.

whom there are no male equivalents. This may explain the fears projected onto midwives or official jealousies and appropriation of women's reproduction powers.

Traditional midwives give a variety of services far beyond what those in Western biomedical culture have ever imagined. They commonly diagnose the pregnancy by touch, estimate the date of delivery, and teach the woman about each stage of pregnancy. They give full-body massages during pregnancy and birth and for periods afterward. They may cook, care for a woman's other children, or offer rich companionship and reassurance. They prepare herbal remedies, call on supernatural powers, and cure stretch-marks or nausea. They give advice on sex, birth control, abortion, baby care, and breastfeeding; they may stage appropriate or comforting ceremonies. Women who are prepared for giving birth and supported by friends and relatives generally have an easier time (see Davis-Floyd and Sargent 1997). In these cases, embodied knowledge may well be power.

A Healer by Trade

Mama Lola, or Alourdes Margaux, is a priestess in the Haitian Vodou tradition. She is one of hundreds of professional healers active in the urban Haitian communities in the United States. Anthropologist Karen McCarthy Brown (1991) wrote an elegant biography of Mama Lola and her woman-centered ways of healing.

No one has any idea of how many healers like Mama Lola are out in the world working. There is no certification, no accreditation, no registry, no statistics. We only know that healers in the informal intersection between medicine and religion are legion. Some are good, some are great, some are trivial or even harmful. Mama Lola enjoys a serious reputation in her New York community for being effective, trustworthy, and discreet. It is also known that she is not interested in large profits from her healing work. She also does not want to attract official attention, so she ministers, like many women in similar circumstances around the world, to a small group of Haitians. Vodou leaders, mostly men, operate on a grander scale than Alourdes, with great ceremonies of dancing and drumming.

Vodou is a new religion that grew out of the agony and chaos of Haiti's eighteenth-century plantations. It blends several distinct African religions, which slaves brought to the island, with the French Catholicism the colonists carried to the island.

> *Healing is at the heart of the religions that African slaves bequeathed to their descendants, and Alourdes's Vodou practice is no exception. She deals both with health problems and with a full range of love, work, and family difficulties. Like healers in related traditions found throughout the Caribbean and South America, Alourdes combines the skills of a medical doctor, a psychotherapist, a social worker, and a priest. (Brown 1991:5)*

The high-spirited performances of the Vodou spirits have a dramatic and theatrical quality. The spirits speak and play with the faithful. They hug them, hold them, feed them, or chastise them. Individual problems or group discontents are aired in the communications with the spirits. Strife is healed and misunderstandings rectified. At the rituals and ceremonies, the followers bring gifts of food and entertainment to the Vodou spirits, and their earthly community is bonded and strengthened. Healers like Mama Lola call out assorted spirits who live in close quarters with humans. Here Mama Lola speaks of how these contacts feel to her:

> When the spirit going to come in you head, you feel very light, light like a piece of paper . . . very light in your head. You feel dizzy in your head. Then after, you pass out. But the spirit come, and he talk to people, and he look at the table you make for him. . . . Then he leaves and . . . you come from very, very, very far. But when the spirit in your body, in your head, you don't know nothing. They have to tell you what the spirit say, what message he leave for you. (Brown 1991:352)

There is much to heal from both in Haiti, the poorest country in this hemisphere, and in the United States and Canada for the thousands of immigrants who have come. People suffer from the twin diseases of poverty and racism, which result in chronic poor health, low resistance to diseases, and high infant mortality. As Brown says,

> There is no Vodou ritual, large or small, individual or communal, which is not a healing rite. It is no exaggeration to say that Haitians believe that living and suffering are inseparable. Vodou is the system they have devised to deal with the suffering that is life, a system whose purpose is to minimize pain, avoid disaster, cushion loss, and strengthen survivors and survival instincts. (Brown 1991:10)

Visiting Spirits

A striking feature of women's activities in organized religions, in women's religions, or in female spirituality is the category of beings we typically call spirits. When these energies, forces, entities, or spirits enter people, anthropologists call it **spirit possession.** Supernatural personalities can contact or enter people while they are in an **altered state of consciousness** or a trance state. These are usually called *possession trances.* Unlike cases of demon possession and exorcism, possession trances are generally invited during the course of ceremonies, rather than at random moments. The rites, beliefs, and community that engage in such trance behavior is known as a *possession cult.*

Spirit possession, in some form or another, is reported throughout the world. There are many varieties of experiences along a continuum of spirit possession, spirit mediumship, and **shamanism.** Those who help others through spirit visitations are called various names depending on the context: mediums, channelers, shamans, seers, or diviners. Frequently, those who can go into these states of nonordinary reality or altered consciousness can come back and use their experiences to help themselves and other people. The idioms of spirit and spirit possession are widespread; they coexist with the psychotherapy-counseling idioms and other ways of dealing with conflict, manipulating social identities, and consolidating personal identities. Erika Bourguignon (1991) looked at 488 societies around the world; 90 percent of them reported one or more institutionalized, culturally patterned forms of altered states of consciousness. Over half of those attributed the altered state to spirits.

Spirit possession is a system of illness and trance rituals indigenously interpreted in terms of the influence of an alien spirit. *Alien* here simply means "not of one's own ego" or somehow different from what we think of as "self." Spirits come from outside; so being possessed is not just an internal sate. In these trance-like states, women are removed from the socially constructed world of everyday life and separated from their socially constructed selves. Furthermore, they actually become spirits. This fact is important. It means that members of the audience and other participants witness an individual woman's transformation into a spirit being. "Deities are seen to be physically present on earth, and seen to look like—to wear the bodies of—women" (Sered 1994:192). Spirits may themselves be male, female, or gender-neutral. They may be old or young, married or single. Spirits appear in many forms and change shapes regularly. Through women's bodies, women and men are able to see, hear, feel and converse with the spirits. This is another form of embodiment.

The association of women with intense feelings and ecstasy in contexts of self-knowledge and helping is strikingly widespread in the world. Many scholars think that women are particularly adept at accommodating possession states. Men also have these abilities and use them on occasion, but the patterns look different. When broader gender structures favor an egalitarian relationship between men and women, as among foragers, men *and* women are more likely to engage in trancing behavior. Where gender roles are more strictly separated, women tend to become members of a community of adepts or mediums. Their cults are forced to compete with or accommodate themselves to dominant religions.

Ritualized Rebellions and Extraordinary Emotions

Possession cults, far from being different or exotic, are another form of women's adjustment and health-seeking. They are also about direct experience with the nonordinary or spirit world, with ecstasy, sensuality, or sexuality. There is a major difference between knowledge based on prophesy, vision, revelation, or other forms of direct personal experience and religions based on male authority, sacred scriptures, creeds, or received wisdom.

> *For the possessed, possession is real. However it manifests itself—in trance, in acute hysterical dissociation, in schizophrenic reactions, in multiple personality, in tantrums, or in love—possession provides an existential validation for the belief in a class of spirits who are able to enter and take control of a human being or animal. The belief that one has been or can be possessed is an important determinant of the subjective life of the individual. . . . The spirits or demons capable of entering and seizing control of an individual serve more than an explanatory function. They enable the possessed to articulate a range of experiences which*

the Westerner would refer to as "inner," "psychological," or "mental."
(Crapanzano and Garrison 1977:141)

In spirit possession, anthropologists expect, for example, that the individual's sense of personal responsibility would be different. For example, the psychological explanations associated with a breach in the individual's moral code—dispositions that the Westerner might express in terms of guilt—can also be articulated in terms of spirits. The individual does not chastise herself or himself, as the Western depressive does. The spirit does it. Spirit possession gives a person an idiom for self-expression different from the internal, past-oriented psychological idiom of the Western world from which the case history itself developed. Possession is a form of communication; it has rhetorical force, that is, it speaks and people listen.

The spirits as elements within an explanatory and experiential idiom are polysemic [they stand for or illuminate many things on many levels]. They refer to psychological realities, to social ones, and to biological ones. They become the idioms in which anxiety, conflict, illness, and recovery are couched. The rhetoric of spirit possession may be used for self-promotion, self-assertion, realignment of marital relations, and commonly, escape from an unpleasant situation and control over those in the rituals and ceremonies that arise around possession states.

It is difficult to talk coherently about spirit possession and the groups that form around it. The specific shapes and activities of the groups, cults, religions, and spiritual practices vary tremendously. But so frequent is the association of women with spirit possession that it begs for an explanation. One prominent theory talks of women trapped by the double standards of male–female relationships or by the socioeconomic conditions of colonialism. In this classical explanation, spirit possession is the assertion of rights among socially marginal people. Women with inferior or ambiguous status have a powerful means to protect their gains, bid for attention, or induce their husband, village, or boss to honor the obligations inherent in their admittedly unequal relationship. The cults are ways in which powerless people (predominantly women) work out their anger of and fears about more powerful people.

Persons afflicted by the spirit receive extra attention and sympathy. After all, someone entered by a capricious spirit cannot be held to blame for her actions. The spirits themselves can not be controlled; they may return at any time. I. M. Lewis calls them "cults of affliction" because they grow out of deprivation and circumstances in which women's aspirations or intelligence outstrip their opportunities for expressing them. He says that in these cults of affliction women find release from and alternatives to male-dominated societies and husband-dominated marriages.

> *For all their concern with disease and its treatment, such women's possession cults are also, I argue, thinly disguised protest movements directed against the dominant sex. They thus play a significant part in the sex-war in traditional societies and cultures where women lack more obvious and direct means for forwarding their aims. To a considerable extent they protect women from the exactions of men, and offer an effective vehicle for manipulating husbands and male relatives. (Lewis 1971:31)*

Lewis notes that the possessing spirits typically visit marginal or peripheral people, lower-class or otherwise socially powerless women and men. Typically those possessed are women in male-dominated societies. But poor women living in male-dominated contexts are probably the plurality if not the outright majority of the world's population. There's nothing marginal about sheer numbers or obvious needs. Neither are possession cults peripheral to the participants.

So the affliction argument does not go far enough. There are other reasons to seek out these groups, particularly for help in coping with illness and grieving. For example, many women of Luvale in Zambia have experienced terrible losses, such as barrenness, miscarriages, and babies dead at birth or in infancy. Others have illnesses that are difficult to understand, refuse to go away, or cause pain, depression, or weakness (Spring 1978). Women become adept in trances or possession states. They call on their female ancestors to help them conceive or carry a living baby to term. Women form bonds with each other, with living descendants, and with their deceased ones to become mothers and to heal from the losses of motherhood. At several levels, possession is therapeutic. It works like group therapy or as an expressive and aesthetic form, a ritual dramatization of conflicts.

It must be noted here that discussion about spirit possession is not questions about beliefs or belief systems. Foremost, they are questions about structured experiences that women are having. Mama Lola's work illustrates the relationship between spirits and healing and the poverty and racism experienced by Haitian immigrants. Here are two concrete examples of spirit possession. The first example centers on an individual woman in Korea. Her story is not unique to her; it happens at other times to other women. The second example is from Sudan, North Africa, and concerns the women of a large village.

From Housewife to Shaman

Korean housewives often feel that their domestic or traditional roles are suffocating them. Many women can identify with this problem. As a result, some Korean women suffer what Americans tend to call a "nervous breakdown." Koreans say that such women are "harshly fated." The resolution to the crisis is prescribed in Korean folk therapies or ethnopsychiatry.

Youngsook Kim Harvey traced the spiraling development of this breakdown and its resolution in the lives of six Korean women. She reports the following stages:

1. The victim experiences severe conflicts within herself, with being a housewife, and with important members of the family, such as her husband, mother-in-law, and/or sisters-in-law.
2. The victim feels overwhelmed and helplessly trapped by these struggles.
3. The victim falls ill with vague symptoms and is granted some released time from household responsibilities.
4. The illness persists, and the family reduces or completely eliminates its normal demands on the victim while mobilizing its resources to rescue her from her sickness.

5. Under these circumstances, the victim recovers and resumes her usual functions.
6. Now reassured by her recovery, her family resumes their old patterns of interacting.
7. The cumulative strain of living with the conflicts again becomes unbearable, and the victim again becomes sick.

This cycle will be repeated several times until the victim and the family reach an impasse.

So the illness builds. At first, the symptoms are vague: tiredness, faintness, dizziness, headaches, aches in her limbs, insomnia, or heaviness in the heart or tightness of her chest. These do not respond to Chinese herbal treatments or Western medications. In time, the woman begins to have strange dreams or visions. She is socially disruptive. Her family and neighbors regard her as immoral or crazy. They think she talks too much.

> *Worst of all, as far as the community is concerned, victims may speak too frankly and accurately about things going on in the community that would normally not be openly discussed. They may, for example, say that the chronic illness of a young housewife is due to bottled-up resentment toward her abusive mother-in-law or toward her husband, who will not curtail his gambling or extramarital affairs. Or they may refer to the well-known, but never publicly discussed, history of a man who repeatedly fails in his business ventures and puts the blame for his failures on the disturbance created in his household by his nagging wife. They sometimes reveal adulterous affairs among neighbors that, in all likelihood, everyone has known about but no one has openly acknowledged. (Harvey 1980:44)*

At this crucial moment, a shaman diagnoses the afflictions as possession sickness. As the shaman says, the victim has been "caught by the descending spirits." Although the families are embarrassed and defensive, they believe that the spirits are particularly attracted to those who suffer in this fashion. Eventually family members prevail on the victim to accept her calling as a shaman, a psychic healer.

In this quote, a Korean woman who went through this personal transformation talks about a spirit visit she received.

> *I went looking for my spirits one day about two months after my mother called me out of death. . . . No, I wasn't hallucinating, but I was, I think, in a state of possession. I had my eyes closed and was muttering something when, vaguely at first and then more clearly, an old woman appeared before me. She said, "Oh, I'm so-and-so, I'm seventy-four years old and my birthday is August 2. I became a mudang [female visionary and shaman] when I was nineteen. I've three sons. Come see me." I told her I didn't know where she lived, but she would not answer me. She just left. But I saw the very spot where she lived very clearly in my mind and the way to the place. (Harvey 1979:153)*

As a shaman and not a victim, this Korean woman grew into spiritual authority, earning power and full health. She struck a firm bargain with family members. Because the spirits have called these women to be shamans and healers, the situations that provoked the breakdown (such as an abusive husband or cruel mother-in-law) are neutralized. Better still, the women are paid for their healing and counseling services. Income, independence, and a new status help cure the breakdown and offer the chance to aid others as well (see Kendall 1985).

Wombs and Wounds

The zār cult is the most widespread traditional healing practice in Africa. Anthropologist Janice Boddy spent nearly two years in ethnographic fieldwork in a Muslim village in northern Sudan documenting these practices. People gather in the evening for the ceremonies. The smells of incense, prepared foods, and many bodies fill the air. Women drum in complex syncopation with elaborately decorated goatskin drums, or even washtubs. As the rhythm intensifies, women move their bodies to chants called "threads"; their singing is called "pulling the threads." Some rise to dance and "descend"—the metaphor for doing the steps indicating that spirits have possessed them. While they are possessed, women wield swords menacingly, smoke cigarettes, swagger about, pray in the postures of men, drink alcohol and animal blood, wear men's clothes, brag and burp, and raise their voices loudly. Because they do these things, they are said to be possessed. All such behaviors are forbidden to the ordinarily dignified and proper matrons of the village.

During the long nights, older women supervise, stay vigilant, interpret events, and tend younger women who descend to the spirits. The villagers say, "She has a spirit" or "She is with spirit." Spirits are often called red winds. Red is for blood; wind is for capriciousness and ambivalence, for being always present but seen only in its effects. Because the women are possessed by alien spirits, they are not held responsible for their actions. Spirits have identities, personalities, and desires just like people do. The spirits usually identify themselves in some way; they make demands, issue orders, and act up or act out, as we say. In these performances the zār spirits appear to make demands on a possessed woman's husband and family members. Through her, they make provocative comments on village issues such as the increasing influence of Islam or encroaching Western economic domination. With exceptional spontaneity and imagination participants draw on a repertoire of symbols, actions, and familiar spirits. The ceremony is full of surprises. The performances are often improvisations on well-known themes. But a woman may suddenly be seized by a spirit new to the village or unknown to her. Outside the zār ceremonies, women do not act this way.

In this large village, two-thirds of the married women between the ages of thirty-five and fifty-five are involved in spirit possession activities. The majority of those who acknowledge possession are competent, mentally healthy people who are responding to stressful situations in a culturally appropriate manner. Possession affects women who are known to have unstable marriages, to be divorced, to be divorced more than once, to be separated, or whose husband has withdrawn financial support or taken another wife. Possessed women have lost more children than have the nonpossessed, have had less reproductive success, have had more miscarriages, have never been pregnant, or have fewer surviving male children. Women who mourn the loss of a beloved adult daughter, for example, are particularly vulnerable. Zār spirits favor women who do not or cannot approximate the village's high ideals of marriage and fertility. Since these problems mount with age and sustained blows, it stands to reason that older women are the most likely to be possessed. As Boddy notes, motherhood and its dramatic failures are always at the forefront.

> *Each pregnancy is a source of anxiety for a woman; each prolonged and undesired reproductive hiatus, a test of nerve. . . . Not unexpectedly then, fertility problems recognized by the villagers are both physical and social in origin, going beyond apparent sterility, stillbirth, miscarriage, infant mortality, and early childhood death. They include experiencing lengthy intervals between pregnancies, bearing a daughter as the first child, and having daughters only or daughters who survive and sons who do not. (Boddy 1989:174)*

The truth of this village in Sudan, as in many others like it, is that females are in a predicament. There are so many ways to fail, so many ways to be inadequate, so many sources of sorrow. Not just the fact of infertility, but the social contexts for being a mother, material security, and attaining and securing a valuable social status in later life are involved. Women begin their lives as virgin brides, the idealization of femininity. With luck and skill, they may end their lives as grandmothers, outrageously frank, renowned as earthy and strategic players in the game of life. A woman hopes to have born and raised not too few or not too many children whose own betrothals and marriages she has managed. She has her eye on her grandchildren and no longer needs her husband's good will as much. But dangers lie between virgin and grandmother.

Women in the village say that zār spirits are like husbands. They place restrictions on her behavior; they cause suffering. Moreover, the spirits disagree among themselves. There seems to be no pleasing them. When she pleases one group, another is disgruntled.

> *Characteristics such as these are typical of spirits regardless of whom they possess, and in this, women say, they are like husbands. Sometimes you get a good one who treats you well and never neglects to provide you with expense money, sometimes you get a bad one who never sends a pound. Often a good one will have a change of heart and, occasionally, for no reason at all, a bad one behaves rather well. (Boddy 1989:265)*

Spirit possession is both an illness and a story or narrative about illness (what anthropologists often call a text). Suppose a woman becomes ill, however it may be defined in this cultural context. She has headaches, stomachaches, extreme tiredness, anxiety or depression, apathy, loss of appetite, and nonspecific aches and pains. (Sound familiar?) Her family and friends try various remedies. But when over-the-counter drugs, prayer, Western treatments, Islamic medicines, and all the try-everything techniques fail, possession is suspected and a "cure" is organized. For her, a diagnosis of possession is a dramatic shift. Spirits come from outside: outside women's bodies or personalities, outside the village. Therefore, she is not responsible for her illness. She also has an explanation for it and some relief or amelioration. "Unlike Western psychotherapy which encourages the patient to accept and integrate previously dissociated feelings as part of herself, zār therapy works by convincing her to recognize them as separated from herself in the first place" (Boddy 1989:255).

Her illness does not originate within herself but from the social context in which she is too firmly embedded. The outside spirits are not projections of her psyche or other Western notions. Instead they form what is for this village a logical circle. In possession, a woman's experiences are reframed. She is not an infertile woman; the spirits have seen fit to usurp her capacities. According to the villagers, possession is a form of dissociation, a radical discontinuity of personal identity. It is induced by the appropriate ritual conditions; it is practiced by witnessing this happening to other women as well as being guided by discussions and by others who help with the trances. Women don't become possessed during their periods. Unmarried women are not supposed to be possessed. In this way, possession is often compared to intercourse. Adepts say that women learn not to resist the entry of the spirits into their bodies; they learn to accept, accommodate, and ultimately find release or ecstasy.

Boddy is at pains to note that this situation is not about male conspiracy or dominance. She considers it a case of women so oversocialized that there is too little room to be what we call a person, an individual. Women's behavior is simply controlled much more rigorously than is men's. "The central problem which possession addresses, in hundreds of idiosyncratic, counterhegemonic ways, is the cultural overdetermination of women's selfhood" (Boddy 1989:252). In this context, "overdetermined" means that women are trained to assume a moral self-image more narrow than their experiences of life offer them. Overdetermined means extensive genital surgeries or "pharaonic circumcision" and onerous codes of modesty and chastity. The primary overriding life goal assigned to women (whether they want it or not) is motherhood. Under these circumstances, there are too many ways to fail and to suffer through no fault of one's own. The village women have fallen deeply into the cracks of morality: the painful differences between what ought to be and what actually is. Islam does not address this paradox, these life lesions. The zār spirits, however, do.

Interestingly, the zār spirits demand that their female hostesses treat themselves as special. Women are ordered to eat good foods, find clean and sweet-smelling things, bathe with scented soaps, use expensive perfumes, wear lovely clean clothes and gold jewelry, braid their hair neatly, and refrain from strong emotions. Although their identities remain quite distinct from those they possess, spirits want to enjoy a sensory life through their human hostesses. Looking at possession from the outside, we see that the zār spirits free a woman and take her into a bigger, broader world. They do this by validating and embodying her personal experiences apart from the conflicts of a cultural consensus that subordinates her.

Spirit performances subtly suggest fresh interpretations of a woman's life. One's culturally overdetermined self is more happily repositioned at the center of the village; at best, the painful events or deprivations of one's life are transcended. Under the circumstances Boddy describes, it is easy to see women's resistance, even creative rebellions, to these controlling forces they have experienced in ordinary reality. In accommodating the spirits, Boddy says, women are conscious of and speaking about their own subordination. She suggests that spirit possession is a feminist discourse—veiled and allegorical—on women's harsh life experiences. Participating in zār is a form of cultural resistance, however muted or indirect.

Both the zār spirits and human beings, both men and women, are creatures of Allah and subject to his laws. Although only a handful of men are ever possessed, they are the audience, and to some extent, the object of the performances. In possession, villagers see alien spirits acting through each other. In a culture in which one's dreams and visions have value, women experience the reality of this other world of spirits in an orderly and directed way. It is possible to define these trances in biomedical terms, but that is not the villagers' way. For them, this is a social reality enacted in ritual. They are literally "carried away," taken on an excursion into another reality, another world. Being possessed is not a cure; it doesn't make a women fertile, pregnant, or reunited with lost loved ones. But it may give her a life, an identify, an explanation, and a healing validation beyond that.

To Conclude

We see patterns in these accounts. Mama Lola's healing work is done because the need is there even when the Catholic Church is not. If women are barred from full participation in Islam—no matter how relevant this morality is to their lives, so men are barred from full participation in the zār cults, and yet must conform to its demands. Women are central and men peripheral when it comes to physical, social, and cultural reproduction: the worldliness of village life. In Korea, when all other paths are blocked, a spirit way may open up for some women to achieve practical success. Never mind that not all women who try this route succeed.

In Mexico, if established religion and biomedicine offer surcease of pain, fine. But most of the medical and religious authorities from whom women seek help are, in fact, no help. Finkler thinks that the ideologies of romantic love in Mexico (and elsewhere) work to keep women in subordination, that is, sick. With industrialization, women lost economic complementarity and independence as the mortar cementing marriages together. Dependency and the notion of romantic love replaced these older ways. When women moved away from or are removed from extended families, when they become dependent on the goodwill of one man, they become vulnerable. Women like Marie are sometimes able to alter, to leverage, their personal economic situations. When economic possibilities open up, their ideologies and expectations about marital relationships change. Their health improves dramatically.

This suggests that subordination, dependency, and institutional neglect are associated with women getting sick. Can poverty kill; is it a disease? Many scholars think so.

Two out of three women around the world presently suffer from the most debilitating disease known to humanity. Common symptoms of the fast-spreading ailment include chronic anemia, malnutrition, and severe fatigue. Sufferers exhibit an increased susceptibility to infections of the respiratory and reproductive tracts. And premature death is a frequent outcome. In the absence of direct intervention, the disease is often communicated from mother to child, with markedly higher transmission rates among females than males. Yet, while studies confirm the efficacy of numerous prevention and treatment strategies, to date few have been vigorously pursued. (Jacobson in Koblinsky, Timyan, and Gay 1993:3)

These observations lead us directly into the next chapter, which is about the ultimate consequences for women of the patriarchal trinity: Christianity, colonialism, and capitalism. It is also about women's response, resiliency, and resistance.

A Field Full of Books to Read

Because women's embodied and spiritual lives unite in the subject of eating, and because women express our social relationships and our bodies through food, I suggest reading *The Anthropology of Food and Body: Gender, Meaning, and Power* by Carole Counihan (1999). Barbara Ehrenreich and Deidre English collaborated on two slim books which Feminist Press continues to publish: *Witches, Midwives and Nurses: A History of Women Healers* (1973) and *Complaints and Disorders: The Sexual Politics of Sickness* (1973). They remain, for the price and for fun of reading, the most accessible introductions to women as healers and women as patients.

For two books on women-centered religions, read the classic *City of Women* by Ruth Landes (1994), on the Candomblé religious movement in Brazil; or Jeannette Rodriguez's *Our Lady of Guadalupe: Faith and Empowerment among Mexican-American Women* (1994). A controversy rages among women and social scientists about the archaeology of goddess-centered religions. Some people claim that men and women lived together peacefully before recorded history and that society was centered around women, with their mysterious life-giving powers. Then a transformation occurred, and men thereafter dominated social life. Read Cynthia Eller's *The Myth of Matriarchal Prehistory: Why an Invented Past Won't Give Women a Future* (2000). In *Women at the Center: Life in a Modern Matriarchy* (2002), Peggy Reeves Sanday counters the claim that matriarchies do not exist. She presents a detailed ethnography of a woman-centered society in Indonesia. Especially interesting is the relationship between the local culture and rituals of women and the practice of Islam.

Chapter Nine

Who Owns Her Body?

Challenges to Cultural Relativism

ut can we ultimately take a stance of cultural relativism to systems that systematically use pain, fear, and deception to dominate boys and subordinate, demean, and oppress women by threat of rape and murder? Anthropologists will not all share my views. I, for one, find the systems described here to be expressions of cruelty, inhumanity, oppression, and error, as well as of cultural creativity. (Keesing 1982:37)

This quote from anthropologist Roger Keesing refers to the vivid initiation cults for young boys and the elaborate systems for separating women and men in Melanesia discussed in Chapter 6. These customs disturbed Keesing. He wondered how to reconcile his personal and his professional responses.

Anthropologists say that people in human cultures act out of sets of customs that are deeply twined with their history, environment, ways of making a living, and belief systems. Here is the first challenge to **cultural relativism**. Are all cultures and ideologies equal? Are all customs neutral or justifiable because some culture or another does them? Can we be objective about these customs? Should we be objective? Are some things just wrong? What about individual choices and rights?

The core idea of cultural relativism in anthropology means that we do not judge others by our own standards. Anthropologists commit to describing and analyzing other cultures and cultural systems on their own terms, often in their own languages. Franz Boas, founder of the first anthropology department and teacher of Margaret Mead, Ruth Benedict, and many others, first articulated this principle for anthropologists. But when we apply the anthropological principles of cultural relativism to the study of women or to our hopes for better lives, tensions start to build.

Here is the second challenge to cultural relativism. Flatly stated, the treatment of women in human societies transcends cultural boundaries. Patterns of hurting women and girls or using them for sex and reproduction in what appear to be bitter and destructive ways take on striking similarities wherever we happen to be on the planet. What we call domestic violence, for example, looks roughly the same in any household regardless of its cultural contexts.

The phenomenon of *gendered violence* seems to go beyond cultural relativism and suggests a kind of gruesome universality about owning, using, and hurting women. Anthropologists face an agonizing dilemma.

> We respect the right of other peoples to hold values different from our own, and it is not our place to criticize them for behavior that is acceptable in their society but that is unacceptable and the subject of political agendas in our own. On the other hand, we are uncomfortable with analyses that are restricted to describing and explaining violence toward women and with explanations that seem almost to justify practices that we personally find abhorrent—practices that may result in the suffering, maiming, suicide, or murder of women who have befriended us and whom we care for and respect. We are caught between our own ethnocentrism on the one hand and the sterile aloofness of extreme relativism on the other. (Counts, Brown, and Campbell 1999:xviii)

To illustrate the dimensions of these dilemmas, I have selected two very broad or worldwide conditions of gendered violence.

1. Wife beating and wife battering. This is the most common form of family violence across the planet, and is the obvious conclusion to chapter 5 on patterns of partnering.
2. Asymmetrical and gendered sexual services, including prostitution, sexual slavery, and rape or sexual violence around the world. Once again this category of treatment falls unequally and unevenly on females; in significant ways, it transcends cultural definitions, standards, or practices.

Then we will take up three case studies that challenge our ideas of cultural relativism in other ways. These include gang rape on American campuses; the disappearance of daughters in Southeast Asia; and female genital surgeries in Africa.

Human Rights and Cultural Relativism

Someone, somewhere, in most human groups, inevitably believes that he or she can, does, or should control the bodies of women. Ruling groups, gatekeepers, policymakers, the power elite, the patriarchy, tribal elders, religious authorities, relatives, kinfolk, cults, congresses, commissions, or committees, in whatever form they take, tend to worry about controlling women's bodies. Their concerns generally come to light in the areas of sexuality and reproduction. Please note, this is not predictably an issue of men controlling women. Women often participate in systems of controlling each other; this has been a difficult phenomenon for feminists and the women's movement to explain.

Everywhere on the planet, women's bodies are restricted and controlled in ways men's bodies are not. Men's bodies are much less subject to rules than women's bodies are. Every human society has elaborate covert and overt rules women are supposed to observe.

The reasons for excluding women from full public participation or enforcing peculiar customs vary, but they usually sound something like this: Women are too emotional. Women don't really know what they want. Women are a source of danger and pollution. Women cause a lot of trouble between men. Being around women is just too tempting, too exciting, or too provocative for men to handle; therefore, women need to be restrained. It is extremely common around the world for men to believe that sexual contact with a woman somehow weakens them.

In a number of human cultures, the problem is women who somehow fall outside established categories. Widows, divorced women, or teenage mothers may have no defined status, no place, or no position. What happens to a woman who wants to control her own sexuality or her own income? Circumstances vary, but the principle remains: Who is she if she is not connected to a man or to legitimate kinship groups?

Unfortunately, neither feminists, anthropologists, or other thinking people have easy answers, good theories, or workable solutions to the problems presented here.

What reasons can we offer? Who gets the blame? Capitalism, colonialism, Christianity, culture in the abstract, evolution and biology built into our bodies and brains, the "nature of mankind," or some specific men? More to the point, there is no such animal as "womankind," so we cannot speak as if women somehow had an answer. There are millions of women who live different social existences in a variety of social settings. For one woman, working as a prostitute and sending the money home is daughterly duty done; for another, it is liberation, a nest-egg, or tuition money. Yet a third woman finds only degradation and death. How do we understand their lives: by the codes we live by, by the codes they live by, or by universal codes of rights and responsibilities that transcend culture? Can we be pro-female and culturally relative at the same time?

The examples in this chapter reflect these tensions; they are uncomfortable and raise more questions than they answer. There are not two sides to these stories; there are dozens. No one, least of all me, is objective. Everyone lives in complex and shifting structures of histories and cultures. We all have feelings, opinions, beliefs, and experiences. These examples will elicit strong feelings and many personal, moral, or intellectual judgments, some of them conflicting. It is acceptable, although very uncomfortable, to feel this way.

The Western feminist in me says that all women have a right, even a responsibility, to control our sexuality, to have autonomy over and within our bodies. At the same time, I recognize that women in other places, in other times, have not believed in the same principles I do. The anthropologist in me thinks that reproduction and sex are always embedded in collective lives and community structures, regardless of how these are defined and regardless of how support and control are acted out in the lives of individual women. These parts of me are in conflict.

It is easy to talk about human rights, to discuss the rights of women, minorities, ethnic groups, or homosexuals, for example. But the very idea is a distinctly Western European cultural concept forged in particular histories and personalities. Do we have "the right" or the responsibility to make other groups on the planet adopt the principles of individualism or majority vote we espouse? Can we make other countries treat their citizens as individuals, in some way we understand as "equal"? Is this a kind of imperialism or another colonialism?

Are women's rights different from or the same as men's rights? Do human rights include women's rights or do "human rights" actually refer to men? If women have rights, what are they? Is this just another "women's issue"?

The "Nature" of Violence

Part of this chapter is about violence against women. Yes, women are capable of violent acts and do act violently on occasion. But violent acts on the planet are strongly gendered. Frequently, and in predictable and patterned ways, some men hurt some women and some children (see Table 9.1). Students beg to know why, to have answers. Many ask about the origins or meanings of culture-bound mistreatment of women. For some the question is, Why do men do it? Or why some men and not others? For others the question is, Why do humans do it? But "It's just the custom" is no longer the answer.

Table 9.1 *Gendered Violence through a Woman's Life*

Phase	Type of Violence
Before Birth	Sex-selective abortions, battering during pregnancy, coerced pregancy (through rape in war, for example).
Infancy	Female infanticide, emotional and physical abuse. Food and medical care are withheld or limited.
Childhood	Molestation, incest, and sexual abuse; differential access to food, medical care, and education; child pornography and prostitution; genital surgeries; gendered neglect—may be weaned earlier. Less food, fewer visits to health clinics for well-baby care or to hospitals for critical care. A heavy load of domestic duties—sibling care, cleaning, cooking, water-carrying.
Adolescence	Date rape, courtship violence, economically coerced sex, sexual abuse in the workplace, rape, sexual harassment, forced prostitution, and sexual servitude. Girls who are unschooled and an economic burden may be married off by arrangement, often for cash. "Honor" killings; dowry deaths.
Reproductive	Abuse and murder by intimate partners, wife-battering, wife-beating, marital rape, dowry abuse and murders, psychological abuse, sexual abuse in the workplace, sexual harassment, rape. Abuse of women with disabilities. Too early child-bearing and coerced pregnancies.
Elder Years	Abandonment and exploitation of widows, elder abuse (which affects mostly women).

Source: Adapted from United Nations Population Fund, *The State of world Population 2000. Lives Together, Worlds Apart: Men and Women in a Time of Change.* 2000:28.

Here is a summary of major explanations that scholars offer. First, some point to genetics, neurology, chemistry, and physiology. They see violence coming out of the operations of human brains. Second, others believe that social conditions, such as poverty, unemployment, and substance use, generate frustration, stress, and family strains. Third, yet others point to the violence that occurs in the power relations between men and women, individually and in groups (Van Hasselt, Morrison, Bellack, and Hersen 1988). There is significant merit in each approach.

Here is the only answer that I have been able to work out for myself. If this answer is unsatisfactory to you, please search for another one and let me know.

First: People do violence *because they can*. This means there are chances, occasions, and structures of opportunity. Ideologies that justify and sustain violence create the openings. There is violence because there are differentials of size, strength, power, and access to the means of violence between men and women.

Second: People do violence *because it feels good to them*. Violence is connected to rushes of feelings, sensations of release, relief, and meeting needs. Sometimes we call this "acting out" or finding an outlet for anger. There may be chemicals and hormones associated with these feelings; adrenalin, serotonin, dopamine, or testosterone are examples.

Third: People do violence *because it works*. Acts of violence help people achieve their goals—whatever they are.

A Worldwide Case:
Wife Beating and Wife Battering

Three women—scholars in various fields—published the first international, cross-cultural, and ethnographic book on the topic of domestic violence. In *To Have and to Hit*, they define **wife beating** as a man deliberately inflicting physical pain on a woman within a male–female relationship or partnership. This is "normal," that is, expected in the customs of the culture. The men who beat the women in their lives do so with cultural authorization and approval. Women do not like the beatings and would prefer to have husbands who did not beat them. But women are not always meek or passive; they often have strategies to defend themselves.

Wife battering, on the other hand, goes beyond the physical reprimands that characterize wife beating. It includes the possibilities of severe injuries, maiming, and death. Battering is usually not acceptable to members of social groups; there are few or no cultural approvals or authorizations. Sometimes bystanders may intervene in ways they would not consider for wife beating. In other groups, mistreatment of wives, up to and including murder, is not remarkable; that is, no one comments and there are no effective sanctions (Counts, Brown, and Campbell 1999:3).

The definitions exclude psychological abuse: insults, threats, blackmail, or verbal assaults. These are not easy to define in our personal experiences and impossible to identify with the current skills of field ethnography. So these anthropologists pologists do not cover individual psychology and motivations. It does not matter whether or not the partners are officially married; they are still involved with each other.

Table 9.2 *International "Domestic" Violence Surveys*

Percentage of Women Reporting Physical Abuse by a Male Partner, 1986–1993

Percent	Country
60	Chile
60	Equador
60	Sri Lanka
60	Tanzania
59	Japan
49	Guatemala
46	Uganda
42	Kenya
41	Belgium
40	Zambia
39	Malaysia
27–36	Canada
28	USA
25	Norway
21	Netherlands

Source: Naomi Neft and Ann Levine, *Where Women Stand: An International Report on the Status of Women in 140 Countries, 1997–1998*. New York: Random House, p. 154.

International surveys give some idea of the prevalence of domestic violence. Table 9.2 shows the percentage of women reporting abuse from a male partner in selected countries. Is mistreating women as partners universal? Basically, yes. The range is from mild physical rebukes to murder. In some societies, violence and mistreatment of women are extremely rare; in others it is a daily and predictable occurrence. Wifely transgressions demand a reaction: A husband's meal is not on time or doesn't taste right. A wife has not paid appropriate attention to her in-laws. She has dressed immodestly or is believed to be unfaithful. The merest suspicion of adultery is enough. Worldwide, the worst crimes wives commit are disobedience and insubordination.

> *The latter two wifely offenses are widely viewed as egregious and are punished with the extreme severity typical of righteous indignation. Surprisingly disproportionate vehemence and violent rage are seen as justified, because of the firm belief that the entire social fabric would unravel if such wifely behavior were countenanced. A wife's assertiveness or her flirtations with autonomy are viewed as equivalent to insurrection and as a threat against the sacred social order. (Counts, Brown, and Campbell 1992:3)*

When women are economically independent or contribute substantially to subsistence and household economies, they are beaten less. After all, an injured woman cannot work as well or may require money for medical care. Younger women are more likely to be mistreated than older women. Older women who have extra-domestic support, adult children, particularly sons, and some degree of autonomy are safer from abuse. Wife abuse and domestic violence are linked to specific kinship structures. For example, in some cultures, a man must be seen to be in control of his wife or his standing with male peers and family members suffers. In some cultures, older women as senior wives or mothers-in-law may promote and assist in mistreating junior brides or daughters-in-law.

The most crucial factor in wife abuse is probably *social isolation*. Rules for post-marital residence make good examples. A woman who must live in her husband's community and kin group, away from her natal kinfolks, is the most vulnerable. Marital privacy, that is, the social isolation of a couple with each other, is a critical factor in mobile societies like the United States. Women suffer when domestic life is separated from public life, as in nuclear family systems. Table 9.2 illustrates the dangers of dying or suffering from "accidents" at home.

The dangers of violence are greater when they are veiled in privacy and secrecy. When women live as isolated individuals, they are far more vulnerable. Women need everyday, communal, and public connections to each other. Women are socially isolated when their communities offer few or no alternatives and institutions. Where judges, lawyers, and policemen beat their wives regularly, women cannot expect legislative relief, justice, or help.

Do women somehow even the score? Yes. Women may leave their husbands or boyfriends. Others strike back with weapons or words; shame and gossip can be powerful instruments of social control. Some women attempt suicide, poison a man's food, or bring the wrath of supernatural entities down on him. Others take lovers or flaunt their autonomy. Yet others deprive him of that which he claims to have beaten her for: her respect and attention.

What about husband beating and husband battering? Aren't women guilty too? There are those who claim that women beat their husbands just as much as they themselves are beaten; in other words, domestic violence is symmetrical. This is a painful issue for feminists who prefer to see women as victims rather than as perpetrators; it is a controversial issue in popular American culture, with its fixation on male bashing and backlash. But the cross-cultural evidence simply does not support a claim of gender equality in beatings and batterings (Dobash, Dobash, Wilson, and Daly 1992).

Researcher Daniel Levinson has done an extensive cross-cultural study of family violence drawn from a world sample of ninety cultures or societies worldwide taken from the Human Area Relations File (1988, 1989). Husband beating was reported in 26.9 percent; by contrast, wife beating occurred in 84.5 percent of the same groups. When Levinson looked at the number of households within each group, he found that husband beating occurred in only 6.7 percent of those societies he sampled, and wife beating occurred in the majority of households in 48.7 percent of the groups.

So women beat their husbands on occasion, but not in the same frequencies as men beat their wives. In fact, there are no societies reported from anywhere in the world in which women beat husbands but husbands did not beat wives. There are, however, many societies in which men beat women unilaterally, in which couples typically have mutually violent partnerships, or in which women fight back or act in self-defense. So beating is not symmetrical. Battering is even less symmetrical. Men batter, kill, and maim women in domestic partnerships with far greater impunity and frequency than women do.

Another Worldwide Case: International Sexual Services

In Chapter 1 we talked about sex as work and sex workers as women who want job benefits in their chosen profession. In this chapter, I want to present a continuum of sexual services that range from kept women to female captivity. Once again, we note that men may be prostitutes, but it is not the mirror image, the same phenomena, or in the same frequencies as that which happens to women. The continuum from voluntary **sex-work** to female **sexual slavery** and rape is quite specific to females. Sexual service is gendered work across the planet.

There is a long, slippery gradient between voluntary sex-work and sexual slavery. Women work at prostitution to support themselves and their families in one of the most readily available jobs in the world. At the same time, illegal traffic in women and children as a cheap labor supply in international prostitution may be a form of slavery. What are the dimensions of the problem?

> *There are no comprehensive studies of the problem of prostitution worldwide, its incidence and impact on different societies; nor are there any statistics on how many persons, including children, may be involved. Even less information is available about the men who benefit from the trade, as either clients or procurers. It is widely believed that prostitution follows only domestic work as women's major employment in many areas of the third world. (Reanda 1991:205)*

Please note that no knowledgeable person seriously suggests that so many children and young women go into prostitution for personal fulfillment and sexual satisfaction. Serving men sexually is one of the leading forms of employment and survival for women on the planet.

The questions about prostitution are thorny. At the heart of the debate is work and sex, two of the most vital issues of gender on the planet. Are prostitutes criminals or are they promiscuous? Is prostitution about vice or lasciviousness? Why does women's sexuality have to be a problem? Are men's sexual needs and women's availability somehow rooted in our human "nature" and biology? Or is the willingness and ability of men to pay for sex a part of ideological, institutional, and behavioral controls and exploitation of women? Is prostitution just another form of work and prostitutes another example of invisible workers?

Sexual Tourism

The travel, tourism, and international hospitality industry is either the second largest economic enterprise in the world or the first. The figures vary; either way, this is an impressive facet of capitalism, development, modernization, or colonialism. The international tourist industry has formed around leisure services and cultural experiences as consumer goods. Prostitution is a core element, and the sexual services of young females are increasingly valuable to the industry and to many countries in the world.

Since the 1970s, tourism has become one of the leading strategies for development or modernization everywhere in the world. Tourists bring in lots of money. Countries pressed for cash (and what country isn't) look to the infrastructures of international travel. Women and sex are prominent enticements of tourist destinations. That means that bosses and managers must ensure a continuous supply of labor.

In a remarkable study of sexual tourism in Southeast Asia, Thanh-dam Truong talks about her personal experiences and the questions that led to her research. Note the layers of her conflicts about cultural relativism in just one paragraph.

> *Being Vietnamese, I witnessed the spread of prostitution in my adolescence in South Vietnam during the Indochina conflict. Forced urbanization campaigns, carried out for military reasons in the 1960s, uprooted millions of peasants in an effort to destroy the rural bases of communist guerrillas. Many rural women were drawn into the cities and to areas surrounding US military bases, where a service economy instantly sprung up and revolved around personal services provided to US military personnel. Brothels and sex establishments mushroomed in these areas and enriched many of their owners. The profitability of prostitution made the entrenched Confucian ethics of the society and its codes of sexual conduct almost irrelevant for many. Where there was a certain awareness of the fragility of our social fabric during a period of major upheaval, the internal causes of prostitution were rarely discussed. It was far easier to blame American imperialism in order to defend one's own cultural integrity. From 1968 to 1973, as a student in the United States, I was exposed to the anti-war movement and the pertinent debates prevailing at the time, of which the controversy surrounding prostitution was one. At that time notions about prostitution were reversed. With some exceptions, the*

blame was placed on the loose sexual mores of Vietnamese women, or on the backwardness of Vietnamese men who found it legitimate to sell women, including their female kin. (Truong 1990:x)

For American servicemen, the sexual services of prostitutes were part of "R and R," rest and recreation. Many military bureaucracies, including the United States, organize and supervise brothels or support institutionalized prostitution. When the war in Vietnam ended, businessmen replaced military men in Thailand and other places in Asia. Today, hundreds of thousands of women serve men sexually. They are called "Comfort Women," "Hospitality Girls," or "Go-go girls." Planes land, busses stop, and cruise ships dock. Soldiers, businessmen, and other travelers debark for sex tours advertised and promoted internationally.

Although prostitution is illegal in many countries, governments sanction or overlook its presence. Escort services, sex holidays and resorts, sex therapy centers, telephone-sex calls, and dating services are only a few examples. Some observers say that legally sanctioned overseas employment agencies and international mail-order bride agencies are often fronts for traffic in women across international borders. There are many reports of violence, deception, blackmail, and contracts to sell daughters.

Thailand is often cited as a country in which women hold their families' purse-strings, work in their own businesses, or hold wage-labor jobs. The country is also credited with one of the most elaborate, repressive, and lucrative commercial sex operations in the world. The tourist industry, coupled with the longstanding sexual practices of Thai men and ideologies about women, provide the climate for sex as a growth industry.

The traditional duties of Thai females include the care of younger siblings or aging relatives. A daughter or sister who prostitutes herself can provide her family with otherwise unobtainable consumer goods, build them a house, or save the family land. Although such a daughter cannot earn merit within Buddhism by giving food to monks or going to temples on holy days, a prostitute can earn merit through contributions of cash. Monks will not discuss how much of their living comes from the dutiful daughters of prostitution. There are accounts in Thailand of middle-class women, including university students, who are part- or full-time prostitutes.

In the past, Thai men took many wives, major and minor. Although neither polygamy nor prostitution is legal, the practices and ideologies continue. In the reigning gender ideologies, men (particularly elite ones) are given the right to rule over women. In this quote, Chiang Mai, age fifteen, explains sexual tourism and her role as a prostitute in Thailand.

At first I was very scared, but after a while I got used to it. None of the girls thought about running away because they came for the money, every one of them was there out of necessity. . . . If there weren't any girls working at the country's border, would the foreigners bother coming in? Another point is that the girls make money, the men have a good time. It's a business. Even though I don't like working that way, just think, if the girls are caught, where else can they go to earn money? (Quoted in Muecke 1992:896)

The stories of women who enter prostitution in Thailand sound similar to those in the Philippines, Korea, or many other countries. Rural families saddled with debts make a contract for their teenage daughter; someone promises her a good job and gives them a lot of money. In some places, these contracts look like traditional arranged marriages; they give similar rights to the labor contractors that husbands received. Or young girls flee homes where abuse, poverty, or alcohol make life on the streets seem safer or easier to them. The real prostitution may be in ideologies of family loyalty, religious obligations, business bottom-lines, and governmental denials. For example, the Thai government blames prostitutes for the spread of HIV–AIDS and other sexually transmitted diseases. Yet women in the sexual service industries are more vulnerable than the men who pay them, more at the mercy of asymmetries in relations of power. Table 9.3 shows the world spread of sexual tourism.

Sexual exploitation turns women into objects, mere bodies, or commodities. It normalizes violence against women and other forms of socially patterned oppres-

Table 9.3 *Sexual Tourism and the Sex Trade in the 1990s*

Countries Sexual Tourists Live in and Leave From

United States	Canada
Japan	China
France	Germany
Great Britain	Norway
Sweden	Singapore
Saudi Arabia	Kuwait
Australia	

Major Destinations for Sexual Tourists

Dominican Republic	Costa Rica
Brazil	Morocco
Hungary	India
Bangladesh	Indonesia
Philippines	Kenya
Thailand	Cambodia
Vietnam	

Source: Joni Seager, *The State of Women in the World Atlas, New Edition.* London: Penguin Books, 1997: p. 54.

sion against women. It is big business and it affects women in ways it does not affect men.

> *Prostitution is a male consumer market. The intense public focus on women's will, her choice or her "right to prostitute," deflects attention from the primary fact that prostitution exists first because of male customer demand. Sex industries are in place—from trafficking to brothels—to provide female bodies to satisfy that market demand. What matters in terms of the prostitution market and male demand is that there are female bodies provided for sex exchange. How or why they get there is irrelevant to the market. (Barry 1995:39)*

In the light of prostitution as transnational business, the distinction between "voluntary" and "enforced" servitude is difficult to sustain. More and more scholars are growing into a painful awareness that domestic violence and child

For many women, self-defense training is a strong source of empowerment.

abuse are horribly and intricately linked to prostitution. Many, some say most, prostitutes in the world are victims of incest, violence, or rape (UNPF 2000:29). In this view, prostitution is a status of servitude in which women are coerced, blackmailed, threatened, and abused. Thus made vulnerable, they can be separated from familial and institutional assistance and blamed for their conditions. This gives credence to those who call international patterns of prostitution a form of female slavery.

Sexual servitude and violence against women are global. They cut across cultural boundaries. The women quoted above argue that we cannot excuse sexual slavery or violence on the grounds of cultural relativism nor can we buy into arguments about protecting the privacy of household life or of men's rights.

For the remainder of the chapter, we will take up three culturally grounded examples that challenge how we think about the treatment of women in human society. Each of these case studies illustrates a different view of the central question in this chapter: Who owns her body? Each example challenges cultural relativism anew.

Case Study Number 1: Rape on a University Campus

The first case study hits close to home. Anthropologist Peggy Sanday has studied and written about violence and rape cross-culturally. She argues that men are not "naturally" programmed to rape any more than women are "naturally" programmed to be motherly. In extensive cross-cultural research, she found societies that were largely free of rapes and others she characterized as "rape-prone." Sanday argues forcefully that rape is part of certain cultural complexes that include interpersonal violence, ideologies of male dominance, and systems of gender separation. Her most chilling ethnographic example of how rape is patterned comes from fraternity row on an American college campus (1990).

At the University of Pennsylvania, a female student reported a gang rape by a number of the brothers at a fraternity. When Sanday investigated the case with an anthropological eye and began to collect similar accounts from other campuses, she discovered customs, beliefs, and a subculture that condoned and created conditions for gang rape and other forms of sexual violence against women. Through testimonies, court transcripts, interviews, and comparative materials, Sanday reconstructed the "group-think" and gender ideologies that made gang rape normal and even commendable behavior for many men on fraternity row. Their activities served as powerful bonding mechanisms among fraternity brothers and were buttressed by elaborate rituals, social class privileges, and the systematic denials of college and university administrators.

Lois Forer presided as trial judge. Here she speaks about the fraternity males charged with gang rape.

I was amazed to learn that the attitudes, language, behavior, and literacy levels of these fraternity members are identical to those of young, underprivileged criminals. Both groups frequently engage in sexual behavior that others call gang rape. Both call it "playing train" or "pulling train" (one man follows another). Both groups consider it a form of male bonding for which the female is merely an available instrument. Both may prepare themselves for this test of manhood by ingesting quantities of alcohol and fortifying themselves with drugs. Both consider this acceptable, indeed, normal conduct. Both are amazed to learn that such actions could be crimes. These fraternity brothers, like slum hoodlums, are often semiliterate and unable to present coherent and intelligible statements in their own defense even though they are high school graduates and students in good academic standing at elite universities. The difference between the two groups is that fraternity brothers are rarely, if ever, prosecuted for their conduct whereas slum youths are prosecuted, convicted, and imprisoned. (Forer in Sanday 1990:xiii)

Anthropologist Sanday and Judge Forer analyzed the reactions of the university administrators. Their responses can be summarized in the immortal words of the women's movement, "They just don't get it." Most simply did not understand how and why their policies penalized women and privileged acts that are crimes in civil contexts. Women's responses to stories of fraternity gang rape ranged from "cut it off" or "hang them high" to defense, understanding, and support of the young men and the social institutions involved. Men talked about "situations that got out of hand." They said, "Perhaps she asked for it." They asked, "What was she doing there in the first place?" They customarily drank a great deal and took turns having sex with an anonymous woman in the presence of each other. For the men accused of gang rape, the identities of the women they assaulted were irrelevant.

Case Study Number 2: Disappeared and Endangered Daughters

Millions of young girls from East and South Asian societies are "missing." The numbers vary, although all are difficult to believe. Some experts estimate that 60 million daughters are missing, others say 100 million. Put another way: For every 120 males living there are only 100 females living. The United Nations Population Fund collected these statistics, compared them to those of the rest of the world, and asked itself these questions: In what regions and countries are girls disadvantaged relative to boys in terms of health and survival? Has the magnitude of female disadvantage changed over the last 25 years? They concluded: Throughout Asia, particularly in India and China, the two most populous countries on earth, the disadvantages of being female, already severe, have grown more pronounced. Despite the fact that, overall, childhood deaths continue to decline and the status of adult women to improve, the relative plight of daughters has become worse than ever. A United Nations' publication puts it bluntly: "Fifty percent of humanity lives in countries where gender inequality results in excess or surplus mortality of girls" (UNPF 2000:13).

China, India, Bangladesh, Pakistan, and Indonesia report dramatic increases in abnormal sex ratios at birth. There are more males than females born in proportions much greater than chance alone would provide. This means that millions of couples in those countries use new technologies to find out if they are expecting a son or a daughter. If they don't like the results, they opt for a sex-selective abortion. They keep the sons. Their daughters disappear. Even girls who survive through birth face additional risks their brothers do not. Many more daughters than sons die in their early years of life. These countries also report a very high number of deaths of infant girls and girls not yet five years of age. Girls in the most danger are those with older sisters and no brothers. Population data and statistics show clear patterns of "son preference" and "daughter discrimination" (Croll 2000:7). There is a clear pattern of *female disadvantage:* death or illness in females that arises from differential treatment of boys and girls, which may reflect deliberate discrimination by adults in favor of males or other forms of unconscious bias against girls.

The problem of so many females who do not survive into adulthood is still a hidden and largely unacknowledged problem that confounds the experts. It is startling to learn that in India, China, and across East and South Asia, daughter discrimination is actually increasing. Despite rising economic development, declining birth rates, smaller family size, and the generally improved status of women, there is also increased pressure to give birth to and raise boy babies. Not all daughters are equally at risk. Recent studies suggest strongly that the second or third daughter born into a family without sons is in greatest danger. In the past, women were expected to have enough pregnancies to guarantee several surviving sons; their large families could accommodate a daughter or two. But now people want smaller families. That means that unborn daughters are the first to be sacrificed.

Daughters are a liability on several fronts. In India, many parents say that baby girls are a financial burden. Families cannot afford the clothes for the ceremonies performed as they pass through childhood and adolescence and, above all, the dowries that permit them to marry and cease to be a drain on their natal families. Sometimes, it is said, it is better to die before birth than to be born into a life of tears. Sons, by contrast, take care of their parents, validate their existence in many ways, and, at last, light their funeral fires. In rural China, there are many versions of this man's statement: "You must have a son to carry on the family name. If you don't have a son, you won't have anyone to worship the dead parent's soul. It will cut the generations, there will be no ancestors. You raise sons, sons support you in your old age. It is impossible for daughters to take care of the aged because they marry out" (Croll 2000:114). Deliberate discrimination by adults in favor of males, or other forms of unconscious bias against girls, results in illness or death for girls more than for boys. Even with tremendous expansion of medical services and health care technologies, parents can still withhold health care and education on the basis of gender.

In the nineteenth century and well into the twentieth, there were continual reports in Asia of dramatic gender bias; little Chinese girls whose tiny feet were broken and bound with cloth to make them look alluring and to keep them from running away or working. In India, widows were considered economically useless and were sent to their deaths on the same fires that cremated their husbands (Narasimhan 1990). Throughout East and South Asia, female infanticide and abandonment were common. But now sex-identification technologies and sex-selective abortions are supplanting the older forms of infanticide and neglect.

Statistical and qualitative data suggests that daughter discrimination may not be unconscious, as it is sometimes argued. Instead, parents calculate the costs and benefits in planning their children, the number, the spacing, the gender, and how much family resources to invest in a daughter versus a son. From all available statistics, couples in Asia want either a son and a daughter, two sons, two sons and a daughter, or three sons. They use contraception after their families have achieved the desired gender configuration. With current family planning and medical techniques, they can limit both total family size and the number of females. Family planners did not plan on this interpretation when they argued for women's access to contraceptives and good medical care. They didn't expect couples to factor gender preference and female deaths into "the calculus of conscious control."

Ironically, improvements in pre-natal care and family planning, particularly the technologies that allow parents to know the sex of their unborn baby and make decisions about his or her fate before birth, fuel the dramatic statistics. These new technologies have replaced both female infanticide and fatal female neglect. Ultrasound machines, fetal testing, and legal abortion services are widely available. Although government policies in most Asian countries prohibit the use of new technologies for sex identification, the fees for ultrasound help support the underfunded health clinics. In India, clinics or hospitals providing sex identification testing and abortion are relatively cheap and widely available, and the regulatory apparatus is largely absent. In China, the national family planning program mandates a "one child policy" to combat overpopulation. The official one-child policy became the unofficial one-son policy. As a result, many girls are abandoned in orphanages or are fostered in distant places where neglect can be institutionalized.

An advertisement in the *India Express* asked: "Is it a boy or a girl? It is now possible to find the sex of your child in early pregnancy before it is born with the aid of latest sophisticated imported electronic equipment. Amniocentesis and antenatal sex determination have come to our rescue and can help in keeping some check over the accelerating population as well as in giving relief to the couples requiring a male child" (Croll 2000:94).

India has the highest "masculinity ratio" in the world. Throughout the twentieth century, census reports have recorded a steady decline in the number of females in the population. Even if a daughter survives sex-selective diagnosis and abortion, she may be neglected to death. *Neglect* means that she receives less food, nutrition, health care, or physical attention. Son preference is so strong in some areas of India and amongst some groups that daughters must logically suffer in order for families to carry out what they think of as their proper functions. Hence, the greater the scale of son preference, the more intense the discrimination against daughters is likely to be. For example, there are significant differences in the numbers of boys and girls admitted to city, county, and township hospitals in China and in the cost of their treatment.

Those people at the United Nations who studied son preference and daughter discrimination offer their best plausible answer: Sons have economic value, daughters don't (UNPF 2000:12). To parents, sons can repay their parents' investments in health care and education, which are quite costly. Sons don't require a dowry. All the reforms and improvements in the last half of the twentieth century have not touched the greater social or cultural value attached to sons. Women's lives may have been changed, but only if they survive their early years as daughters.

Today's girls are not necessarily tomorrow's women. There are several reasons that threats to the survival and development of female infants have received little attention. First, gender and women's studies have been more concerned with the social construction of gender, gendered divisions of labor and adult women's status, employment, health and reproductive rights, or domestic violence than with girls or the safety of girlhood. The second reason is a failure to print gender, that is, boy or girl, on top of the word "children." The experience of childhood is not the same for females as it is for males, and aggregate figures that lump all children's health care, education, and familial investment together lose sight of females in Asia and allow them to disappear. The simultaneous increase in Asian women's status, education, and employment opportunities and in daughter discrimination suggest that the status of "daughters" may be different from or independent of female adults as daughters-in-law, wives or mothers.

"Children" are not children, an ungendered collective category. In both China and India, couples go to enormous lengths to have sons. They may defy their government, their bodies, and, no doubt, even their emotions, to take radical measures against their daughters during pregnancy, at birth, or in infancy and early childhood. For them the key question at conception and throughout the pregnancy is gender: Sisters are less welcome than their brothers are. This is another example of the "do anything" principle.

Case Study Number 3: Genital Cutting

At the beginning of a new millennium, millions of females in dozens of countries still bear scars of the cutting done to their genitals earlier in their lives. Various writers estimate that more than 100 million women and girls have experienced some form of female genital surgery. Some place this number at over 114 million (Toubia 1995; Toubia and Rahman 2000). In addition, about two million girls are "eligible" for the procedure each year. Some form of genital cutting is practiced in approximately twenty-eight countries in Africa. But the procedure is not limited to Africa. Medical and social service practitioners are finding circumcised women in immigrant populations now living in North America, Europe, South America, and Australia. On occasion, families want the surgeries performed on their daughters, and medical personnel face new challenges regarding Western laws and customs and cultural communication when that happens.

Some people call these procedures *female circumcision* or *female genital mutilation*. The operation itself has many varieties, which defy easy categorization and labeling. For that reason I avoid the blanket term *female genital mutilations* because it implies intentional harm and evil intent. In **clitoridectomy**, the clitoris and all or part of the labia minora and/or all parts of the labia majora, the inner folds of skin or "lips" of the external genitalia, are removed. The extent of removal and the results vary. In the most extensive type of surgery, **infibulation**, the remaining sides of the vulva are stitched together to close up the vagina and leave only a small opening for urine and menses. Sometimes the operation is only token.

There is no reason to believe that such surgeries contribute to the health and survival of women and children. The cuttings carry risks. Practitioners with minimal training operate under unhygienic conditions. Possible complications include obstruction of the flow of urine or menses, infections, chronic pelvic inflammation, infertility, and obstructed labor. New incisions made during childbirth must be made across inelastic scar tissue. Some will need repeated stitchings with each pregnancy. Sometimes girls bleed to death or die from infections. In the West it is believed that genital cuttings compromise sexual fulfillment and orgasmic potential, but there is no way to document this belief.

Female genital surgeries have been customary in various periods and places in Western history. In London in the nineteenth century, doctors removed the clitorises torises of women—a "harmless operative procedure" to cure "diseases" such as hysteria, excessive masturbation, nymphomania, restlessness, melancholy, or failure to appreciate domestic life. In countries such as Germany and France, clitoridectomies were a medically approved treatment for "female weakness" or a disinterest in marital intercourse. Well into the twentieth century in the United States, clitoridectomies were recommended for "deviant behaviors," "nervous breakdowns," and "hysteria" (Gruenbaum 2001:9). Again, incidence and numbers are impossible to know, but the obvious conclusion is that someone somewhere wants to control women's bodies. The threat of such surgeries may have operated to keep women "in line."

"Why do these surgeries?" is the first question anyone asks. But no one has a simple answer and the debates are complex. Female surgeries belong to no one ethnic group or religion exclusively: Muslims, Christians, Jews, and followers of traditional African religions practice it. For some, the cutting is a female rite of passage. For others it is not. Women say that they plan to circumcise their daughters as they themselves were cut, that the cuttings are the only rituals they control. Yet other women say that they will not arrange for the surgeries for their daughters or will perform only a symbolic cutting. Many women from these countries living abroad go to elaborate lengths to perform the surgery themselves or have it performed on their daughters. At the same time, African women have sought asylum, or sanctuary and political protection, in France, the United States, and other Western countries to avoid the operation.

There are reasons that are not reasons: It's a good tradition; it is a religious practice; or it promotes cleanliness and increases marriage prospects. Parents of young girls are often deeply concerned about their daughters' marriageability and protections within marriage. Although many have claimed that the purpose of female **circumcision** is to control and destroy female sexual pleasure, there is no convincing evidence for that. Yet for others, female circumcision is related to morality or sexuality. Some believe it makes a woman's body more beautiful and pleasing for both her and her mate. The European and American perspective on sexual pleasure is as culturally bound as any other, and, in any case, our customs have not always promoted the best possible sexual health for girls and women.

These practices are easy to denounce. Many international reform efforts call for an end to the surgeries. It is more difficult, however, to develop an understanding of the cultural contexts in which female genital surgeries are still practiced. The situation requires more than a few horrible facts or a philosophic position for or against practices that are not under our control. Loving parents and supportive women in the community approve of the cuttings. Families celebrate the event. Many anthropologists believe that we can understand the cultural and historical contexts for the operation as much as we understand the medical, sexual, and physical consequences.

> *It may be our hubris as anthropologists that we cannot—or dare not—imagine ourselves so immersed in any culture that we would buy its multiplex rationalizations—its meanings—however subtle and persuasive and coherent they may be. And yet we submit ourselves to cesarean sections and mechanized childbirth to produce the "perfect" baby; inculcate in our daughters, albeit implicitly, that they must diet, exercise, dye, and depilate to achieve the "perfect" body; we tweeze and pluck and color and conceal to attain the "perfect" face. We work hard at being women, spend considerable sums of money, suscept ourselves to bunions and bulimia and worse. (Boddy 1991:16)*

The international responses to female genital cuttings vary. There are radical "Eradication Now!" campaigns. There are public health programs that call for "harm reduction" and educational programs that offer culturally acceptable alternatives when abolishing the practices seems impossible. For impassioned people who oppose the practice without compromise, such reforms are only an obstacle. They say that we should stop making cultural excuses for the human rights abuse of women and children. Some scholars and political activists say we should draw the line at these "crimes," "brutal rituals," or "torture." Novelist Alice Walker, whose novel *Possessing the Secret of Joy* explored the life of an African woman who underwent the surgery, calls it genital mutilation and the sexual blinding of women. She followed her novel with a film and another book, *Warrior Marks*. Walker passionately denounces any form of cultural relativism or situational understanding.

> *Clearly, female genital mutilation is a painful, complex, and difficult issue, which involves questions of cultural and national identities, sexuality, human rights, and the rights of women and girls to live safe and healthy lives. But this complexity is not an excuse to sit by and do nothing. Who cares if African women and children are subjected to violence?* **We should all care.** *(Walker and Parmar 1993:95)*

From another direction entirely, African women often ask, what good is all this attention to veils, clitorises, sexual fulfillment, and orgasms that Western women worry about when we need access to banks, capital, legal status, land titles, and clean water? Let us handle men our way. Stay off our backs and out of our underwear and marital beds. They note that many foreign groups have the approach of "them" helping "us." The most serious voices caution against unwelcome and ineffective interference. These voices ask, who owns the problem? Who sets the agenda? (Gruenbaum 2001; El Saadawi 1980).

Since the early 1980s, organized efforts for change have accelerated dramatically as international and nongovernmental organizations have become involved and as African women themselves have moved into leadership positions. The World Health Organization, United States Agency for International Development, and a number of human rights organizations have opened up an international dialogue. Many grassroots organizations have developed. They link up with one another and with the international initiatives to curb the practice or to practice it with less severity in the form of a symbolic cutting and shaving. Their goals are to talk openly, to substitute safer surgical practices, to create noninvasive rituals, to empower parents as the agents of change, and to mount sensible public health campaigns. It has taken time for the momentum to build and for strong leadership in the countries in question to arise. What is true is that both grassroots changes and global changes are possible, although not in a straight line nor in accord with narrow principles.

Women's Rights and Critical Cultural Relativism

So who owns a woman's body? Father, mother, government, husband, boss, religion? Can a woman own her own body all by herself? Is there any hope for alleviating some of the gendered violence and damaging gender ideologies discussed in this chapter? Alas, I still have no easy or final answers.

Two things in particular do seem to matter in shifting the unequal equation that results in partner violence, wife beating, and wife battering (Counts, Brown, and Campbell 1999). They are sanctions and sanctuary. A *sanction* is an authoritative response, ratification, validation, or support for a given action. Saying that "a man's home is his castle," "it's only domestic violence," or "boys will be boys" are public sanctions, tacit endorsements of customary activities that support the hurting of women and children. If colleges treat rape on college campuses as the equivalent of cheating on an exam rather than a criminal act, they are sanctioning violence against women.

But sanctions can work in the opposite direction as well. Obviously, some cultures have strong sanctions *against* wife beating. They offer positive sanctions for treating wives well. A social work professional who conducts therapy groups for battering men told me that he requires the men in the program to use only the first names of their wives or girlfriends. They are not allowed to depersonalize or privatize the relationship. They cannot assert ownership. That means they are not permitted to say "my wife" or "my girlfriend." On one American college campus, the women students published names and developed other strategies to address the men who had raped or attacked them. I realize that these are small-scale and controversial actions, but they suggest the collective possibilities of sanction, of ensuring that "no means no" with help from our networks. Many small-scale groups have ways to address beating and battering. People in these groups do not reward or excuse battering men. They do not keep secrets. They gossip and make public announcements about the men who beat and batter.

Sanctuary means a safe place to be and people committed to women's safety. Battered women's shelters are a good example of sanctuaries. So are systems of female solidarity and cultural patterns such as matrilocal residence. A woman who lives with or near family members who will not sanction violence against her is safer than a woman who lives far from a vigilant network. Anything that enhances personal autonomy, economic opportunities, or links to other women contributes to women's safety. Where there are places of refuge, systems of community solidarity and mediation, or intimate interventions against men who batter, women are safer.

The human rights movement was once seen as a defense against the actions of oppressive governments. But now it includes the previously dismissed category of "women's issues," the tragedies and pain caused not by sovereign states but by relatives and intimates. At international conferences that discuss and debate the improvement of life on this planet, the mistreatment, death, and maiming of women in the name of culture and cultural relativism are high on the list of topics discussed.

Delegates to these international gatherings tell stories of "honor killings." If a woman has been accused, justly or not, of some infidelity—from flirting to an affair—even if she has been raped, she has "defiled the honor" of the man who claims her as his property. That's been reason enough for hundreds of socially approved homicides in Pakistan and Bangladesh each year. Delegates talk about coerced sexual relations in South Africa, the "catch-and-rape gangs" of roving young men, some infected with HIV. An estimated nine out of ten new HIV infections are the result of these systematic rapes. In war-torn countries, displaced war orphans and the children of the poor are often forced into prostitution, which endangers their health and safety.

The question of **dowry deaths** in India is always on the agenda at international conferences. There, a **dowry** may amount to the equivalent of a year's salary or the price of a house. Weddings are actually commercial transactions, a transfer of capital. A bride's family may have trouble accumulating such a payment. The practice of dowries has fostered substantial violence toward women. A bride is found soaked with kerosene and burned to death in her kitchen. Sometimes these are ruled suicides by the authorities. The husband is then free to marry again and collect another dowry. The hardship of providing dowries alone prejudices families against female children, but national laws and restrictions against the dowries have not changed the strength of the custom. Nor has heightened education or economic opportunities for women made a difference (Van Willigen and Channa 1991).

As the interconnections of the world's people increases, the health and safety of women and girls becomes a global concern. None of the examples in this chapter fit into the old anthropological notion of "absolute cultural relativism," in which anything that is acceptable in any one culture must be viewed as acceptable by an outsider seeking to understand the practice. We anthropologists can no longer suspend our values without consideration of the values of *universal* human rights. We debate among ourselves what role we play, individually and as a group, in studying vulnerable populations, sites of inequality, and even violence. "I regard cultural relativism not as an ultimate ethical stance but as a mental technique to assist people to avoid negative judgments of, say, food preferences, manners of greeting, or marital customs. Such a perspective is clearly necessary for carrying out ethnographic field research" (Gruenbaum 2001:26).

One answer is "critical cultural relativism." Critical cultural relativism prompts us to understand the plural interests within any society and to understand the power relationships between these groups; for example, young and old, rich and poor, the able and the less abled, husbands and wives. Then we critique, not criticize, the behavior of these groups from the standpoint of more or less generally agreed upon human rights. Since we cannot claim or hope to achieve objectivity, the best we can do is subject our home culture and that of others to critical cultural relativism.

In this way, a broad spectrum of the human community has come to a shaky agreement that genital surgery of girls and women is wrong, because the harm it causes outweighs the social good or cultural values it represents. *Harm* takes place when there is death, pain, disability, and loss of freedom that results from the action of one human being upon another. *Harm* is the map to use when we explore the territory between universal rights and cultural relativism. *Avoidance of harm* has become a key concept in the development of ethical guidelines in medical and social science research. The international, cross-cultural, and interdisciplinary dialogues that place wife beating and battering, the sale of daughters, or female surgeries within the context of avoiding harm negotiate this terrain carefully. They try to avoid the pitfalls of scientific or discipline superiority, listen carefully to multiple voices, and represent them in the broadest manner possible.

The cultural "right" of a man to discipline, slap, hit, or beat his wife or children is widely recognized across a myriad of different cultures throughout the world where male dominance is an accepted fact of life. But since the Vienna Conference of 1993 and the United Nations Beijing Women's Conference of 1995, the issue of domestic violence is now on the agenda of every human rights conference on the planet. In this spirit, anthropologists often serve as brokers in the intercultural dialogue about human rights. We have moved beyond the idea of a value-free social science to the task of developing a moral system at the level of our shared humanity that must at certain times supersede cultural relativism. A broad spectrum of the human community—active feminist agitations, indigenous grassroots organizations, and international human rights tribunals—are coming to the agreement that change is both possible and desirable.

Some Powerful Books to Empower Us

Begin with books of articles that cover the world, global leadership, and multiple and overlapping agendas such as international human rights laws, feminist studies, family law, and anthropology. Imaginative multi-disciplinary studies on key topics include Charlotte Bunch and Niamh Reilly's *Demanding Accountability: The Global Campaign and Vienna Tribunal for Women's Human Rights* (1994) and *African Feminism: The Politics of Survival in Sub-Saharan Africa* (1997), edited by Gwendolyn Mikell.

Consider books on specific topics mentioned in this chapter; some can change the way we think about sex, gender, and human rights. Include *Sex Work: Writings by Women in the Sex Industry* by Frederique Delacoste and Priscilla Alexander, eds., 2nd ed. (2000) and a contrasting book, *Global Sex Workers: Rights, Resistance, and Redefinition,* edited by Kamala Kempadoo and Jo Doezema (1998). Peggy Sanday's book, *A Woman Scorned: Acquaintance Rape on Trial* (1996), is an analysis of America's sexual culture. Bettina Shell-Duncan and Ylva Hernlund's book, *Female "Circumcision" in Africa: Culture, Controversy, and Change* (2000), and Ellen Gruenbaum's *The Female Circumcision Controversy: An Anthropological Perspective* (2001) explore the role that activists and scholars should and should not play. I have quoted extensively from Dorothy Counts, Judith Brown, and Jacqueline Campbell, who produced *To Have and To Hit: Cultural Perspectives on Wife-Beating* (2nd ed., 1999), and Elisabeth Croll's *Endangered Daughters: Discrimination and Development in Asia* (2000).

Chapter Ten

Invisible Workers

Women as the Earth's Last Colony

J magine a woman who works with poor people in India and who won an international peace prize for helping them.

Did you guess Mother Teresa? She was a Roman Catholic nun who worked with poor and dying people of Calcutta. She won the European Nobel Peace Prize in 1979.

Or did you guess Ela Bhatt? She founded the Self-Employed Women's Association of Ahmedabad in 1972. SEWA is a trade union for women who work in the informal sector outside the regular wage economy. Many people think that SEWA is the most successful women's grassroots organization in the world. A Hindu by birth and a lawyer by profession, Ela Bhatt received Asia's top award, the Ramon Magsaysay Foundation Prize, in 1977 for her work with poor women.

Women's work is often invisible within the Eurocentric view of the world, within agencies for international development, and to those who profit from women's work. So the purpose of this chapter is, literally, to make women's work visible. The work of women discussed in this chapter still looks like the four kinds we saw in Chapter 1: production, reproduction, status-enhancement, and emotional work.

First, we will look at some somber statistics on the working and living conditions for women worldwide. Then we turn to the processes of "modernization" and "development" in international agencies like the United Nations. We examine the consequences of colonialism and capitalism on some arenas of women's lives and consider the critique of capitalism in the works of Frederick Engels, Karl Marx, and Eleanor Leacock. Last, we will take up two examples of women's resistance and grassroots movements.

The stage setting for this chapter is **colonialism:** the processes and policies in which a nation-state acquires, extends, or retains its political, social, cultural, and economic dominance over other peoples or territories. World history in the last 500 years has been shaped by European nations that established hegemony over "their" colonies, immense groups of people unrelated to them by geography, history, language, or culture.

The European colonizers believed they were doing the "natives" a favor by bringing them the benefits of civilization. The people whom they subjected were said to be "primitives," "savages," pagan, underdeveloped, natural, or romantic. Mostly they were of a different color. Since colonized people did not belong to the culture of empire with its superiority complexes, they became "the Other." The culture of empire exported and projected its own assumptions about the world and what was "natural" onto those they controlled.

By the turn of this century, European countries had taken over more than 85 percent of the globe. This is why people used to say that the sun never set on the British Empire. After 1945, colonies began to achieve independence from colonial rulers, some through formal political processes, others through bitter wars and revolutions. After World War II, newly independent nations in Asia, Africa, and Latin America adopted the term **Third World** to distinguish themselves from the "First World," the Western democracies, and the "Second World," the Soviet-bloc nations.

The term "Third World" contains some contradictions. For example, it is often viewed as a synonym for poverty or used to belittle and judge other people. Many Third World countries, however, have higher standards of living than do entire segments of First World countries. Capitalist and democratic nations like the United States have huge populations of very poor people. In rural areas and urban centers alike, the poorest are inevitably female. Meanwhile, the Second World, the Soviet-bloc nations, no longer exists; but there are women and men living in the new countries created out of upheaval. Moreover, the **Fourth World** are groups descended from the empires and tribal peoples that existed before world colonialism. Sometimes Native Americans refer to themselves as the **First Nations,** the cultures of this hemisphere who inhabited North and South America before Europeans arrived and who observe tribal traditions and ethnic identities in contemporary multicultural settings. There are women in all these groups.

A dominant ideology of European colonizers was a belief in an economic system called **capitalism.** In this system, private individuals and corporations invest in and own the means of production. They distribute and exchange wealth. So a capitalist is a person who has capital—money, assets, land, factories, investments, and other means of production. Capitalism contrasts with socialism (in which governments own and distribute wealth) and the economic systems of communal or tribal societies that existed prior to capitalism.

Whatever the benefits or advantages of capitalism, it is not a system that has been uniformly kind to women. Long after subjected groups gained independence from their colonial masters, women's lives did not change for the better. Indeed, there is considerable evidence that they only got worse. In 1970 Ester Boserup published an eye-opening book in which she asserted that there were no good explanations for the existence and increase in poverty for women in the Third World. She said that modernization and development initiatives that claimed to improve the lot of people in underdeveloped countries had, paradoxically, deeply negative effects on women. Expensive and highly touted projects either failed to address women's issues or failed to see women as workers. By any calculation, women were working harder for less return. Females were poorer, sicker, and more exhausted than they were before help arrived.

So, for purposes of this chapter, women are the last and the largest colony on earth. We are "the Other." Our labor or work is appropriated, devalued, or ignored. Women are treated as part of nature, a resource like air, water, and land that exists to be used up. And most important, women around the planet share characteristics with each other that are not shared with men, regardless of the countries any of us live in.

Characteristics of Women's Lives in the Last Colony

What do we mean by invisible workers? The United Nations summarized the principal trends in women's lives on the planet for the decades 1970 to 2000. Here is what they concluded.

More than three-quarters of the world's women live in so-called developing regions. The absolute majority of them are poor. Everywhere in the world, workplaces are segregated by sex.

Women do domestic tasks such as fetching water and firewood. Women process and prepare food. In developing countries, particularly in rural areas, there is often no safe water to drink, much less water to cook and wash with. People don't have basic sanitation or electricity. Table 10.1 shows woman-hours per week spent in carrying water in selected countries.

Women care for children. There is no country in the world, regardless of its ideologies, in which men as leaders, men as husbands, or men as fathers provide more than a fraction of the care children require. This principle holds true regardless of how much any citizen, mother or wife, son or daughter, might need.

Parenting is a female task, and males have proved highly resistant to doing women's work anywhere on the globe. When food is in short supply, crops fail, or parents lose their jobs, children go hungry. But their mothers usually go hungry before that. Women and children may not get the right kinds of food to nourish their brain, their growth, or the sheer physical labor exerted to get that food.

Table 10.1

Water is work.

Woman-Hours Per Week Drawing and Carrying Water, by Country

Villages in Mozambique
  15.3 hours per week in the dry season
  2.9 hours per week in the wet season

Farming villages in Senegal
  17.5 hours per week

Rural areas of Botswana
  5.5 hours per week

Baroda region of India
  7.0 hours per week

Villages in Nepal
  1.5 hours per week for girls age 5-9.
  4.9 hours per week for girls age 10-14.
  4.7 hours per week for females 15 and older.

United States and Canada
  0.0001 hours per week

Source: United Nations, *The World's Women 1995: Trends and Statistics* (1995), 50.

Forever Working

Through the decades 1970 to 2000, women's opportunities in wage employment in agriculture, industry, and the service sectors in many countries did not increase. Occupational segregation, unemployment, and underemployment also failed to improve. So women have increasingly turned to work in the informal sector. In some countries, informal sector earnings showed dramatic increases. Self-employment may be considered the major form of work for women in the world. This kind of work is not secure and pays far less than the formal sector, generally less than the minimal wage. Although women bear the costs of setting up their informal activities, they often do not control the benefits; fathers, husbands, and sons may take the profits as their own.

The major occupations available for women in the world are street-selling, factory assembly lines, piecework, cash-cropping and commercial agriculture, prostitution or sex-work, and service in domestic settings, like maids who change the sheets on hotel beds. Many jobs are physically demanding and the working conditions are dangerous. Women are predictably and consistently paid less than men for any job.

Women produce 75 percent or 85 percent or 90 percent of the food crops in the world; estimates vary, but they are always high. Women usually have no title to the land they work and depend on. They cannot get credit, cash, or build equity by owning property. Women contribute most of the labor to raise cash crops that increasingly encroach on land needed for food. **Cash crops** such as cotton, tea, sugar, cocaine, jute, or rubber cannot be eaten. Husbands or male relatives often sell these crops, keep the money, or distribute it at will. In this way, women are treated as skilled and necessary workers, but still dependent and invisible.

The statistics-keepers at the United Nations say that work in the informal sector is extremely difficult to measure. This is another way in which women are invisible. When the second shift or the double days are calculated (and this is not consistent or easy), then women work harder and for more hours than men do.

The United Nations produced a chart called "Value of Unpaid Housework to the Gross National Product." The statistics-keepers at the UN calculate the contribution of women's unpaid housework to the formal economic sector. To use the United States as an example, they estimate that if domestic labor and housework (including the most common kinds, child care, house care, husband care, and elder care) were acknowledged, the economic productivity of the United States would increase by about 25 percent. This is another view of invisible work (United Nations 1991:95).

According to the United Nations, not a single country in the world, no matter how the statistics are gathered or reported, contains men who come anywhere close to women in the amount of time spent in housework. Housework is cross-culturally and universally defined as food processing and meal preparation, child care, shopping, household cleaning, and management (1991:102).

Meanwhile, fewer women are getting married. Cohabitation is increasing. The average household size is decreasing in most regions. Women-headed households are a growing worldwide phenomenon. People living in female-headed households are poorer in general than people living in other kinds. Collectively, the birth rate seems to be falling, yet more single women are giving birth to children than ever before.

Men often migrate; they leave to find work elsewhere. This means a high divorce rate or informal divorces; some husbands do not return or send money back. A significant proportion of the world's households have no adult male worker; the estimates vary from 40 percent of households to 80 percent. Something has happened to men as husbands. These are major changes since 1970.

Poor women do not and probably never did live in the style middle-class people in the United States call "staying at home." Poor women's work is underreported and underestimated, especially when they do it to support their families.

These statistics and the quality of life they represent are often summed up in the phrase, the **feminization of poverty.** This is a term for the social and economic conditions characterized by women-headed households with few or no legal protections, double-day housework, and caring for children, combined with low wages in the formal or informal economic sectors. Such female-headed households are regarded as the largest definable group of poor people worldwide. This may also be called the pauperization of women.

Death and Poor Health

Women worldwide make the same observation about their health: "I feel very, very tired, most of the time." Women also get beaten and hurt a lot of the time.

The most revealing statistic about women's health is probably **maternal mortality.** This is a figure calculated on the basis of how many women die during pregnancy and giving birth within a year; it is expressed as the number of female deaths per 100,000 births. All countries keep these records. Combined with figures on infant deaths, the deaths of women in pregnancy-related events are the single best indicators for a nation's health status and commitment to women and babies. Rates of maternal mortality show a greater disparity between the developed and developing regions than any other health indicator. Table 10.2 shows some of the death rates for women in a selection of countries. Over 200,000 women die each year from illegal abortions (Seager 1997:38).

Pregnant women in developing regions face a risk of death in pregnancy that is 80 to 600 times higher than women in developed regions. Why? Women die when they give birth without knowledgeable helpers or where there are few backup services for emergencies or difficult pregnancies. Pregnant women die of anemia and endemic malnutrition. Women who have already had many children die.

According to the World Health Organization, AIDS is now the leading cause of death for women twenty to forty years old in some major cities of Europe, South America, and the United States, as well as in significant areas of sub-Saharan Africa. *Sexually transmitted diseases* (STDs) like syphilis, gonorrhea, or HIV are the most contagious conditions on the planet. STDs affect women more harshly

Table 10.2 Death
by motherhood.

Maternal Mortality in Selected Countries

These figures represent the number of women who died in some pregnancy-associated event per 100,000 live births 1980–1998.

Sweden	5	Bolivia	390
Ireland	7	Costa Rica	29
Denmark	10	Cuba	27
United States	8	Peru	270
Ghana	210	Chile	23
Mozambique	1,100	China	65
Central African		North Korea	110
Republic	1,100	South Korea	20
Egypt	170	Nepal	540
Algeria	140	Bangladesh	440

Source: United Nations. *The World's Women: Trends and Statistics* 2000:79–83.

than men, but treatment programs are few and far between. The number of women contracting HIV is growing faster than the number of men contracting it (United Nations 1995:74; United Nations 2000:14).

In the developmental literature, women are often put in an appendix as "special considerations." Or women qualify for assistance in economic development projects "where applicable." In national and international programs, the term "family" is a euphemism for women. There are no programs anywhere in the world with the word "family" in the title that target men. Any situation that affects women negatively affects children even more so.

Depressing statistics like these are available from a number of sources besides the United Nations; I have not made them up. Note the photograph entitled, "According to Statistics, She's Not Working."

International Strategies for Solving the Problem(s) of Women

Students offer various suggestions. Why not give poor women charity? Why not help their husbands get jobs? Why not send women to school for job training? Why not pass a law saying that banks have to give out loans to poor people? Why not encourage landowners to treat women better? Why not motivate poor women to work harder? Why not reason with the governments and tell them how much the work of women contributes to national economies? Why not provide birth control services? Why not ask for a grant from a private international foundation? Why not elect better officials? Why not lobby governments to provide better services? Why not do a research study, conduct a national survey, or appoint a task force to study these serious problems? Here is a long answer.

In 1975 the United Nations declared an International Women's Year; the response was enthusiastic. But the problems were larger than the UN had imagined, so the year lengthened into a decade. Demands came from many sources for more integration of women into development projects. Many countries started women's bureaus, agencies, departments, commissions, and organizations.

The founders of the Decade of Women acknowledged that myths about women and work make the situation worse. The primary myth was: Men produce the world's food; women prepare it for the table; women work to supplement the family's income. Women contribute a minor share to the world's economic growth. In short, women don't work; they stay at home and take care of children. But myths are not facts. So the informal slogan of the Decade of Women became

Women do two-thirds of the world's work, receive 10 percent of the world's income, and own 1 percent of the means of production.

According to statistics, she's not working

Carrying firewood for the daily cooking in Kathmandu, Nepal. UN PHOTO/John Isaac.

Improving statistics and indicators on women
INSTRAW

INTERNATIONAL RESEARCH AND TRAINING INSTITUTE
FOR THE ADVANCEMENT OF WOMEN (INSTRAW)
César N. Penson 102-A, P.O. Box 21747, Santo Domingo, Dominican Republic
Tel. (809) 685-2111, Telex 326-4280 WRA SD.

High Fashions for Low Incomes

Here is a capsule appraisal of how officials in various development endeavors have constructed women's work. Agencies like the World Bank, the United States Agency for International Development, the World Health Organization, and the legion of nongovernmental agencies establish projects in underdeveloped countries. From about 1950 and into the 1970s, women in the Third World were treated as passive and needy; they were thought of as incompetent mothers. So most international development schemes attempted to change women's child care and reproductive activities. This meant food handouts, nutritional counseling, and family planning, a *welfare approach*. It challenges no one and blames mothers, so it remains popular (Moser 1993:231).

Then the United Nations' Decade of Women, from 1976 to 1985, selected *equity for women* as its goal. Women were supposed to be active participants in development goals. The UN acknowledged the difficulties for women who lack the political and economic autonomy men have, so this viewpoint challenged women's subordinate positions. As a result, it is unpopular with national governments who think that Western feminists are behind the idea. The equity viewpoint is often known by its initials: WID or Women in Development.

The second wave of WID toned down the notion of equity in favor of *antipoverty*. The problem for women, developers said, is not inequality and oppression. Women are just poor. This approach appeals most to nongovernmental and private organizations who like to sponsor small-scale projects in which women earn some money.

The third wave of WID has been about *efficiency*. This centers on the belief that when women participate in economic systems in a more businesslike manner, their income will improve. Efficiency will automatically ensure equity as well. This approach relies on an elastic concept of women's time and workloads. This competency model assumes that women will extend their workday to compensate for a decline in social services. Hence it is a very popular approach in development circles.

The latest fashion in development for women is called *empowerment*. The most articulate versions come from women in the Third World themselves. They state that male oppression is no different or no worse than colonial, postcolonial, or neocolonial oppression. They say that gender ideologies or sexism are not as dreadful as class prejudices and racism. This viewpoint seriously challenges Western feminism as well as national governments, international development agencies, and private organizations. Some watered-down versions of empowerment see power as something that can be handed to cooperative women as a gift rather than a quality of self-reliance, if not resistance.

Work and Housewifization

One of the toughest barriers to solving problems and improving the lives of women is **housewifization**. This awkward term comes from "the housewife," who is the primary model for female labor in the postcolonial and capitalist world. In fact, some feminists say that the relationship between capitalist systems in the First World and the Third World mirrors the relations between husband and wife in the West.

The operative principle is this: Women are defined primarily in terms of familial roles. Our work is only an extension of our domestic life. Hence we are invisible "outside the home." The idea of "the housewife" emerged in the First World during the nineteenth century in the same cultures that invented the family wage laws and colonialism. It was the reigning paradigm for women's lives in the United States during the 1950s when doctrines of "modernization" and international development were implemented.

What matters is not the actual work a woman does; it is the conditions, in particular, the relations of power, under which she does the work. In the international sexual division of labor, women are housewives and men do paid work.

> To be defined as a housewife does not mean that women de facto work only in the home—in any case, what would "home" mean? A wind screen, a hut, a pavement? It means that they have to do any work at any time and at any place, not paid or poorly paid, and that this low pay is justified by the fact that they are considered to be materially dependent on a male "breadwinner," irrespective of whether or not there is such a man, or whether or not he is capable of providing "bread" for the family. (Mies 1986:9)

Many programs for development, particularly those in agriculture, education, and occupational training, see women in nurturing and homemaking roles. So they emphasize "home economics" as a remedy to world poverty. The housewifization of international development projects reinforces the primary Western middle-class ideology that mothering is a full-time job and the only work women have. The worst part is that these ideologies ignore the resources mothers require for children as well as the competencies and skills they may have.

> The care of children is of course a major concern of women everywhere; however, the need is not for lessons in "mothercraft" from self-appointed outside experts, but for the means of feeding and maintaining the children. This means generating food and income by their own work in agriculture or other activities. A major finding of a study of poor women in Tamil Nadu, India, was that most of them defined their role "as a woman" not in the expected Western terms of being a wife and mother, but "to earn and support the family." (Rogers 1986:91)

Women may work harder and even make more money. But that matters little if they cannot control the products of their labor. Many male workers benefit from systems of low or unequal pay for women's work. For most women in the world, life as just a "housewife" is inconceivable. They have never had a choice to "stay at home." The men they know are poor too.

Women's status and freedom everywhere is linked to whatever local accommodations are made to the global economy. In this, the last decade of the twentieth century, women's jobs are factory work, housework, sex-work, growing or serving food, child care work, and jobs in the service sectors. Here are two examples of the most common jobs women are likely to have around the world.

Housework Revisited

A common and commonly invisible form of work for women around the world is working in other people's homes; the term for this is **household worker**. Household workers are people recruited from outside the employing household to perform some portion of its reproductive work. The tasks may be done indoors or outdoors; they involve equipment and machinery as well as emotional and psychological work. Such employees are also called servants, domestics, nannies, maids, housekeepers, menials, or retainers. As my dictionary reports, the opposite is master.

In a world of refugees, migrants, emigrants, landless, dispossessed, and outright poor people of so many kinds, recruiting household labor is easy. Housework includes home care of frail elders, children, or sick people, as well as cooking, cleaning, yardwork, shopping, driving, and the myriad tasks of running a household. It bears an uncanny resemblance to work many of us do as mothers, wives, or daughters. The difference is the economic relationship.

> *At root in all cases is an employer-worker relationship. Household worker labor is put to the tasks of reproduction rather than production. While housework does not produce capital directly, workers perform socially necessary household maintenance, food preparation, child care and socialization, and other reproductive tasks for a wage. The value of household workers' labor is transferred to members of the employing household, permitting them to allocate their time and energies in other ways—to more remunerative or prestigious productive work, leisure, or investment in social relations. The essential point is that the workers' labor is utilized to maintain and advance the position of members of the employer household. The labor for which employers pay frees them for other, generally preferred, activities. (Sanjek and Cohen 1990:3)*

Somebody must do this work. If we don't do it ourselves out of duty, love, habit, or similar motivations, then we must compel or hire others to do the work. Household work is not only largely invisible to men; it is also invisible to the women who use it.

The relationship of household worker to employer is characterized by its solid inequality. Household workers can lose their jobs at any moment; they must follow orders. There is always a power differential between employer and employee; it may be gender, age, class, ethnicity, race, or citizenship and migration status. So the customs of hiring household workers also ratify power relations and reinforce inequality in each local society where it is found. In societies with social ranks and classes, household work carries a stigma. Somehow, it is associated with dirt, with uncleanliness. Like other women's work, it is necessary but devalued.

Caring for, cleaning up after, or feeding others, especially infants and children, is also emotional work. That is why employers often pretend to have fictive kin relationships with employees. Despite all rhetoric to the contrary, such workers are not kinfolk. They are not "one of the family," "a daughter," or most telling of all, a maid. Calling a household worker by her first name, the way Americans address children, only hides the employee–employer relationship. We might call this maternalism or patronizing.

Housework is status enhancement for someone else—women's work we discussed in Chapter 1. People who can afford to transfer jobs in their households to someone else have more resources to invest in other activities, like play or social relationships. They may do volunteer work, give elaborate parties, or take up exotic hobbies. The household worker does not enhance her own status; her work enhances someone else's status. A household worker still has to do her own household work after her paid household workday.

Working Daughters: The Feminization of Factories

A large portion of what we call modernization and economic development in international settings depends on women's work in factories. In contemporary jargon, the factories are called "export processing zones," "Free Trade Zones," "flexible labor systems," or "offshore manufacturing." The early women's movement called such worksites "sweat shops." By whatever name, the factories of transnational companies depend entirely on sources of cheap labor. Workers make computer parts, electronic equipment, textiles, apparel, footwear, toys, and other consumer goods sold all over the world. Anthropologist Aihwa Ong did ethnographic research in some of these factories in Malaysia. Here she comments on the labor practices of the multinational corporations that own the factories.

> To achieve global dominance, Japanese and Western companies bypassed high production costs, labor militancy, and environmental concerns at home by moving to Southeast Asia or Mexico. Such rapid shifts with respect to labor markets and their attendant maneuvers in new financial markets enhance the flexibility and mobility that allows corporations to exert greater labor control worldwide. . . . The most important recent experiment in corporate production is its flexible combination of mass assembly and subcontracting systems, of modern firms and home work as linked units dominated by transnational capital. (Ong 1991:282)

How does this translate into the lives of women? Eighty percent of the workers on the floor are young Malaysian women from rural villages. They assemble computer parts. All the managers and executives are male, usually from Japan, India, or other "developed" countries. Female workers in relative isolation from each other work under male eyes, pressured to produce in work speedups and penalized for trips to the locker rooms. Dress codes, moral instructions, and policies about menstruation, pregnancy, and privacy are based on management's ideologies about "women's nature." The managers of the transnational companies say that their female workers "naturally" have nimble fingers and docile personalities.

Women who work in the factory zones are generally between sixteen and twenty-four years old. If they have a child, they will be dismissed. The jobs are full-time, the shifts are long. The work is so stressful that few expect to survive, physically and psychologically, beyond a few years. Managers assume, correctly, that young women have to accept these conditions and that factory work is only an interlude until they can do better.

These young women are called *factory daughters;* they constitute the lowest-paid and the lower half of the total industrial work force in developing countries. Policy makers and businessmen consider them a secondary labor force; they say women only work until they can get married. So young women are daughters at home and "daughters" at work. Ong concluded: Yes, women are free to work, but subject to male authority. Yes, women's work is necessary, but civil treatment is not.

Many countries look like Malaysia. Families in China, Taiwan, and other areas of Asia still regard daughters as poor long-term investments who should pay back their natal families for the gift of life and childhood care. Proper, respectful daughters go to work in factories and give the money to their parents. A daughter's income may help her brother through his education. The families claim their daughters' labor; the daughter receives some affection and security.

In the Special Economic Zones of China, women and children return from job or school to work on electronic parts, toys, clothes, or artificial flowers. In Hong Kong, extended families contract with large transnational companies for piecework. Businessmen say that "family production units" ensure a disciplined and docile workforce and "peaceful industrial relations." The building blocks of this entire economic system are daughters. In the Philippines, where wages are among the lowest in Asia, the garment industry is built largely on the base of women who sew at home in their villages. Corporate executives speak in glowing terms about "the Asian family" in which children (factory workers) obey their parents (managers).

Along the United States–Mexican border, housewives do their "homework" for international corporations that pay them little or only by the piece. When there are not enough young women, their biggest labor pool, companies hire children.

Factory workplaces are typically sexualized. Managers promote Western images of sex appeal and sexual availability. Women can get jobs and keep or lose them on the basis of using sex as a strategy. Simultaneously, sexual harassment, rape, and other forms of control over women make factories look much like harems.

On the other hand, industrial employment for some young girls may be a glimpse of freedom. They can live away from home, have boyfriends, save for marriage, help out parents, escape a poor village, and have some discretionary income. In a few cases, they can get some education. Women in these situations rarely think of themselves in terms of global sisterhood or even a collective force. Their work is like marriage and family; factory daughters may be aware of their condition but unable to negotiate or escape.

Contrary to Western feminist expectations, most working daughters did not seek more equal relations at home and would gladly trade their "bitter" independence for the security of a college student who has a family to look after her needs. (Ong 1991:298)

Factory daughters do not challenge the industrial system; factories are only a stepping-stone. These young working women hope to graduate from the assembly line altogether; many consider prostitution as a step up and marriage as a wonderful dream.

The new international division of labor and the feminization of industrial work look like older-style patriarchal families. Women in factories speak about their immense tiredness, injuries, dangers, poor sleep, and missed periods. Factory daughters say that they don't mind hard work. "But we would like to have justice, recognition, and respect from our bosses."

A Marxist–Feminist Thinks about Women and Work

Since the landmark research of the 1970s, anthropologists and scholars in other disciplines have discussed, debated, and argued at length about women's status. Many assumed that male dominance was simply a fact of life, the painful part of "it's only natural." Some anthropologists pointed to cultures that seemed reasonably good compared to the United States; other scholars offered studies of groups in which women's position was worse.

Sometimes anthropologists picked one dimension as the comparative key to women's lives. We analyzed rituals, symbols, availability of birth control or health care, matrilocal households, and how much husbands helped. Sometimes we defined the key to women's status as elections, promotions, equal opportunity, equal employment, or other state-controlled arenas of our lives. We argued whether women had ever been equal to or superior to men; this is the substance of the debates about matriarchy, for example. Then we argued about equality in our own countries, within our own homes, with fathers, husbands, or bosses.

To answer these personal and professional questions, many anthropologists, sociologists, historians, and other social scientists (many of them feminists) have followed a path that leads from the Iroquois women in Native North America to the factories of the industrial and post-industrial revolutions.

Let's turn once again to Lewis Henry Morgan, who wrote about the Iroquois, men and women who lived in matrilineal groups and matrilocal longhouses. His book, *League of the Iroquois*, published in 1851, is thought to be the first complete ethnography ever written. As he described the Iroquois, women owned the fields not as private property, but as the necessary means to produce food for their matrilines and villages. Whatever land women needed and could effectively put under cultivation, they "owned." They didn't "own" the land in the sense of buying and selling or in the sense of alienating the land from its productive, food-growing purposes. Nor did any one woman "own" land as an individual. If a person or a group did not use the land for food production, then someone else could use the land. In other words, no one could "buy" or "sell" land and build a shopping mall on it. No one can miss the comparison to capitalism here.

Meanwhile, in Europe, groups of men were making revolutions; these began with the French Revolution in the 1790s and continued throughout the nineteenth century. These groups of men protested the class and economic structures of their time. They asked: Why did a few men have most of the money while the majority of other men literally starved on the streets or worked for wages that did not begin to feed their families? The two most powerful theorists to come out of that period are Frederick Engels and Karl Marx, from whose name are derived the theories called Marxism.

To Marx and Engels, the best examples of how humans should relate to each other came from the women of the Iroquois Confederacy. Their worst examples came from English factories, their exploited workers and capitalist owners. When Engels read Morgan's book, he realized that Iroquois women were not the property of their husbands. He saw the institution of monogamous marriage as the basis for treating women as private property. For him, this was the beginning of the patriarchy and repression of women. Engels proposed a more elegant version of housewifization.

> *With the patriarchal family and still more with the single monogamous family, a change came. Household management lost its public character. It no longer concerned society. It became a private service; the wife became the head servant, excluded from all participation in social production. . . .*
>
> *The modern individual family is founded on the open or concealed domestic slavery of the wife, and modern society is a mass composed of these individual families as its molecules. . . .*
>
> *In the great majority of cases today, at least in the possessing classes, the husband is obliged to earn a living and support his family, and that in itself gives him a position of supremacy without any need for special legal titles or privileges. Within the family he is the bourgeois, and the wife represents the proletariat. (Engels 1972:137)*

Both Marx and Engels believed that the transformation of matrilineal and matrilocal cultures such as the Iroquois into patriarchal and capitalist societies was a great tragedy. Here is Frederick Engels's most famous declaration of his position.

> *The overthrow of mother right was the* world historical defeat of the female sex. *The man took command in the home also; the woman was degraded and reduced to servitude; she became the slave of his lust and a mere instrument for the production of children. (Engels 1972:120)*

Engels believed that the custom of monogamous marriages put control of sex in the hands of men as husbands so they could be assured of their own paternity. In the past, during the stages of history Engels characterized as mother-right, women controlled their own sexuality, including the right to sell it or give it away as they chose. But monogamy made women property and their work invisible and unpaid.

Eleanor Leacock

The theories of Karl Marx and Frederick Engels have had an enormous impact on the development of feminist thinking about women's work in all the social sciences during the last quarter-century. Their theories, however, would have made much less sense were it not for anthropologist Eleanor Leacock, who retold these grand narratives and put women into the foreground.

Eleanor "Happy" Leacock was attending Columbia University when World War II ended. She audited Ruth Benedict's course on personality and culture.

> I still quote her phrase, "You can't beat your culture." Cross-cultural knowledge certainly enables one to gain a useful perspective on one's culture, but it is folly to think one can transcend it. I tied Benedict's point in with a dictum of Engels that was oft-quoted in my undergraduate days: freedom lies in the understanding of necessity. As I saw it (and see it), one aims as best one can to understand the constraints within which one lives, and to define realistically the actual alternatives one has to choose among. I was pregnant when taking Benedict's class, and soon to be plunged into the agonizing dilemma faced by young couples who challenge the structure of gender but are trapped in the structures of child rearing: Which of the attendant problems are caused by the structure itself and which by personal limitations in commitment and understanding? (Leacock 1993:14)

Leacock had married while still in college, and had two children by the time she went to Labrador for fieldwork with the Montagnais–Naskapi. This group is sometimes called Algonkins or Algonquins after the language they speak. Earlier ethnographers believed that the group owned private or family hunting territories and generally practiced patrilineal ownership and kinship.

But Leacock reconstructed the movements and relationships among bands for two generations back in time. Instead of hunting territories, she found equalitarian communities where individuals and groups of cooperative relatives used trap lines. She showed that the male-centered hunting territories and patrilocal living patterns came into being after European colonies, laws, and customs came to Canada. In earlier, precolonial times, women lived in matrilocal households. They also held considerable power and autonomy. The situation she described mirrored the neighboring Iroquois. For Leacock, this meant that Engels and Marx had read Morgan and the Iroquois wives correctly. There was no prehistoric, universal, or essential pattern of male dominance.

In 1972 Leacock wrote an introduction to a new edition of Engels's classic work, *The Origin of the Family, Private Property and the State*. In this highly influential piece and research that followed, she made three points that bear directly on this chapter.

First, she used her own fieldwork to show that in hunting–gathering and horticultural societies, women and men, husbands and wives, were *relatively equal*. Such groups had diffused or consensual decision making, and both women and men did work of comparable worth. In what Marx called "primitive communism," people had relatively equalitarian social lives compared to societies formed irrevocably on class differences. Leacock noted that cultures who trace descent through the female line or have matrilocal residence tend to give women more status.

> *The significant point for women's status is that the household was communal, and the division of labor between the sexes reciprocal; the economy did not involve the dependence of the wife and children on the husband. (1972:33)*

Leacock's second point was that oppression is not somehow "natural," nor is it just in our heads. The origins of oppression for women in contemporary life are not in "nature" or biology, sex or gender differences, nor the results of symbolic and cognitive processes.

> *In all of her work, the underlying theme is clear, and clearly supported: human nature, flexible to a fault, is not inherently hierarchical. Women's oppression, thus, is not due to some universal will to power or innate quality of maleness, but due to concrete trajectories—locally variable, always reversible or open to transformation—of political, social, and economic change. (Gailey 1993:74)*

So Leacock argued against any theory of universal female subordination. Capitalism, market conditions, missionaries, colonial governors, development agencies, and national or state governments determine gender relations, she said; they are not the solution to the problems they have created. Monogamy, private property, and social classes are all part of capitalism and the patriarchy, she insisted; they are all political. The objections of Leacock, Marx, or Engels to monogamous marriages are not criticisms of men or husbands, individually or in groups, but in the powers assigned to them in such customs as the family wage laws.

In other words, the statistics cited at the beginning of this chapter have not always been true. Most pointedly, Leacock said, women are not automatically relegated to second-class status because of childbearing and childrearing.

The third major point Leacock made is this: At key moments in human history, women lost autonomy and equalitarian status as economic systems changed. This occurred when the concepts of private property, monogamous marriage, and class or ranked societies came together. For Leacock, the oppression of women comes with the "transformation of their socially necessary labor into private service through the separation of the family from the clan" (Leacock 1972:41). So here is a summary of her major points:

> *Whatever the status of women in any given society at any given time, it just got worse with the introduction of colonialism, capitalism, and Christianity or other patriarchal institutions.*

Women's Powers as the Roots of Grass

Faced with the awesome difficulties outlined above, what do women do? Women resist, organize, and invent new forms of social cooperation. **Grassroots movements** are a prime example. The name poignantly suggests their origin. Grassroots organizations spring up where national governments have been unwilling or unable to provide basic services like accessible water, electricity, schools, health clinics, transportation services, or access to banks or land ownership. These communal or cooperative women's movements are often concerned with immediate survival issues like food, fuel, credit, physical safety, child care, and health. Ordinary people, mostly women, and always distinct from the elites who hold power, have formed literally thousands of these small-scale organizations around the world. Many are spontaneous, addressing an immediate problem. Others become significant bureaucracies and agencies. All provide apprenticeships and allow women to assert personal power. Considerations of space allow us only two examples of the thousands of women's grassroots movements and collective actions.

Mothers, Family Values, and the Military

In Argentina in 1976, a military coup brought a change of leadership. Young people who objected to the new military regime started to disappear. A young man was seized from the doorstep of his mother's house. A couple was kidnapped from their car. A young teacher never returned from her school. Several medical students were taken from hospitals late at night. One woman lost four daughters, two of them pregnant, and two sons-in-law. Their relatives could not locate them or find any word of their safety.

Maimed bodies turned up. Tales of torture in military prisons began to circulate. Gradually, Argentine citizens began to realize that the kidnappings took place with the knowledge and cooperation of other countries, businessmen, those in the legal system, and indeed, virtually with the blessings of the Catholic Church. In futile rounds, families went to the military headquarters, to courts, and to prisons. But government officials lied or refused to respond. Slowly, the despairing families began to see a pattern of kidnapping by military authorities, of a state-organized system of oppression and terrorism. Finally, women turned to each other.

But what kind of power do women have against the entire establishment of a country, against a military dictatorship? As Maria del Rosario remembers,

> In April 1977, after a year of going in groups from one place to another, one of the mothers, Azucena Villaflor de Vicenti, said, "Let's go to Plaza de Mayo and when there's enough of us"—a thousand she said—"we'll go together to Government House and demand an answer." (Quoted in Fisher 1989:28)

But how could they recognize each other in the large crowds? Again Azucena had an idea. She asked the women to wear one of their children's old diapers as a head scarf. She said mothers always keep little things their babies wore. So women wore baby diapers or other white head scarfs to identify themselves.

The mothers began to walk together in the Plaza de Mayo. The military responded swiftly. As another mother, Aida de Suárez, remembers,

> They started to call us las locas [the madwomen] . . . Of course they called us mad. How could the armed forces admit they were worried by a

*group of middle-aged women? And anyway we were mad. When every-
one was terrorized we didn't stay at home crying—we went to the streets
to confront them directly. We were mad but it was the only way to stay
sane. (Quoted in Fisher 1989:60)*

In December of 1977, the military kidnapped fourteen of the mothers, including Azucena and two nuns. The women never saw them again.

The mothers appealed to every international forum. The pope granted an audience but never replied to their questions. The bishops and many of the priests in
the Argentine church hierarchies preached resignation and passivity. Most refused
to say masses for the disappeared children. Only foreign journalists seemed to understand the meaning of a mothers' march every Thursday afternoon. Women in
white head scarves became the only visible evidence to the world that the government of Argentina was lying.

In 1978 the military government stepped up harassment, arrests, and threats.
Unable to attack the mothers in the face of the world press, the junta closed off the
Plaza de Mayo at the end of 1978. Through 1979 the women made lightning
strikes on the plaza; they hurried in and made their statement as best they could.
Sometimes they sang the national anthem because soldiers had to lower their
weapons.

On the first Thursday of the New Year of 1980, the mothers returned to the
Plaza de Mayo to stay. If they were taken prisoner or killed, they decided, nothing mattered but to march for their children. As Maria del Rosario said,

> *The beatings and threats continued, but that year we returned to the
> square and they were never able to stop us again. (Quoted in Fisher
> 1989:108)*

As Aida de Suárez said,

> *In some ways we were always there. If there were twenty of us, there
> were twenty. If there were fifty, there were fifty. From 30 April 1977
> we've always been there because this square is ours. On Thursdays at half
> past three this square belongs to us. (Quoted in Fisher 1989:108)*

Among the Thursday marchers were grandmothers searching for grandchildren, the babies of their disappeared ones. A number of young women had been
kidnapped while pregnant. Their captors waited to torture and kill them until
after they gave birth. Stories began to circulate of babies sold or adopted into the
families of the military. Many women had grandchildren they had never known.
So the grandmothers of the Plaza de Mayo came into being.

Without intending to, these women had also developed an organization, a
grassroots collective. The Mothers might accept that their children were dead,
even that their bodies might never be returned or identified. But they would never
accept official denials of their very existence and the meaning of their deaths. In
August of 1979, the women registered themselves as the Mothers of Plaza de
Mayo. Soon the organization acquired a meeting house. Forensic archaeologists

and geneticists helped them establish formal programs to locate missing relatives through gene tracing, and to identify bodies, the causes of death, and the guilty parties, where possible. Today the Mother's organization provides counseling, financial assistance, and programs to work for the quality of social justice they feel their children died for.

These women challenged a regime who talked about family values and the duties of motherhood. The Mothers wanted the murderers named, acknowledged, and brought to justice. They wanted men held accountable for their actions. They wanted justice and mercy from the Catholic Church, which they believe acted as an accomplice. They wanted the unions to speak out. By 1982 thousands of people had joined the Mothers at the Thursday marches. In 1983, the military rule fell. By that time, 30,000 people, all of them someone's children, had disappeared.

The women say, we're only mothers; all the disappeared are our children. As a result of the Mothers of the Plaza de Mayo, women in white scarves are marching in other Latin American countries. Argentina is not the only place with dictators and disappeared children.

Self-Employed, Organized, and Cooperative

In Ahmedabad, the state of Gujarat, western India, in the early 1970s, some women carrying freight on their heads noticed that men who were members of textile unions had advantages they did not have. So they approached the Textile Labour Association, India's largest union of textile workers, and there found Ela Bhatt, heading the women's wing of the union. She had an answer for their questions: "You need to organize."

Fully half of the workforce of India's cities are what international development reports call informal, marginal, unorganized, or peripheral workers. Ela Bhatt calls them *self-employed workers*.

> *Self-employed is a broad term covering all the workers who are not in a formal employer-employee relationship. It means women who work at home—weavers, potters, garment and quilt stitchers, patchworkers, embroiderers, bidi [cigarette] rollers, incense stick makers, milk producers, spinners, basket and broom weavers, metalworkers, carpenters, shoemakers, painters, sculptors, and toymakers. It includes women who sell or trade their services or labor—agricultural workers, headloaders, handcart pullers, waste paper collectors, acrobats, cleaners, and construction workers. And it includes the multitude of hawkers and vendors who carry out trade in the streets and markets from their baskets or cartloads of wares. Both traditional and modern occupations come under SEWA's definition of self-employed, from the bartering of goods to capitalistic piece-rate work. (Rose 1992:17)*

Why are these women self-employed? Because they have no education, skills, jobs, or access to resources such as a bank account or because they had migrated into cities from the even more desperate countryside. Under these circumstances, women exercise extraordinary ingenuity. They do not remain "unemployed" when no appropriate "job" can be found. Women combine many kinds of work to bring in small amounts of cash. They trade and barter for food or clothing. They exchange services, sell consumer goods, collect wood or produce, and recycle materials for money.

Besides piecing together family income from hard work and cleverness, they spend most of their earnings on their family, on food, clothing, and meager shelter. The women of SEWA say that about one-third of poor families are supported solely by self-employed females. If a woman has a husband and if he has a job (big ifs), he typically contributes only a portion to household expenses.

The first problem the women attacked in their organizing drive was fair credit. Understand that self-employed women typically earn only enough money for day-to-day maintenance. They must spend part of that as working capital, for example, to buy raw materials, rent stalls, or pay bribes, fines, or fees. When they borrow money on a daily basis, they must pay exorbitant interest rates; as much as 10 percent per day is not unusual. Beyond the expenses of daily business, families have emergencies and social obligations. A baby needs medical treatment or a family member dies and must be buried. The national banks of India wanted nothing to do with female customers who could not sign their names, wanted only small loans, or practiced a different set of manners. Borrowing money from landowners, traders, or businessmen only left a self-employed person deeper in debt. Wages dropped even as women added hours of work.

The solution was obvious: Women needed their own bank. So they formed one, ignoring all the professionals who said it could not be done. As women carried heavy loads on their heads through the city, they talked to other women. They pooled small amounts of cash from many women. They put their pictures on their bank books and left them at the bank rather than risk taking them home. From the earliest days the atmosphere in the lobby of the bank was informal. Women laughed, cried, smoked, and talked with their banking sisters. One woman gave birth at the bank. Ela Bhatt tells these stories about the woman-centered services:

> One of our members was married to a policeman. They had not been speaking to each other several years, but lived together in a sort of quiet hostility. She cooked for him, and he gave her money to run the family. She wanted to buy a used sewing machine, and earn her own money. Her husband used to be a tailor and had a machine in the house, but how could she negotiate with him? So the bank went to his office and negotiated the price for him to sell it to her. What other bank would do this? (Rose 1992:173)

> In 1975 when the bank was not taking many risks, a vegetable vendor came who was under such economic pressure that she was absolutely desperate. Her husband was an unemployed textile worker, and he would somehow roam about and fill his belly each day, but it was a very difficult

situation for her and her children. The bank decided to extend her a loan of 50 Rupees, and someone went with her to buy green masalas like coriander, mint, ginger, garlic, and chillies. That day SEWA cared for her children, who were sick and hungry. The woman earned 6 Rupees profit that day and her children had dinner. Each day she parlayed the loan into more profits and within a week returned 51 Rupees to the bank. It was hardly any risk for the bank, and it literally meant life or death for that woman. After that we started extending those 50 Rupee loans to many women. (Rose 1992:173)

Now women say, "SEWA is our mother and the bank is like our mother's place." The doors are always open for her daughters. Women can tell secrets, find help, learn new skills, or borrow some money. The bank is their only door to the formal, bureaucratized, and institutionalized world of money. A poor woman can borrow working capital at low interest rates and make loans to buy tools and raw materials she needs. Since most of their depositors could not travel long distances to make regular deposits, the bank went to them. When women escaped the high-interest debts that were never paid off, they began to save and invest their money. The SEWA bank is the best model for women worldwide.

Ask Ela Bhatt why women should have assets in their own names, why every district should have a woman's bank, or why loans to women nurture life and leadership. She will reply,

Because women's income is used mostly for "bread, clothes, and house," the more cash income which goes into her hands, the faster the family's quality of life goes up. And secondly there is an increasing number of women headed households, and in times of crises, assets are the only things which help them. (Quoted in Rose 1992:198)

Women are poorer than men amongst the poor. They are the worst victims of all socio-economic decay, degradation, and distortions. Yet I envisage poor women as being in the vanguard of development processes and movements. (Quoted in Rose 1992:263)

Building SEWA has not been easy. It has grown from a loan network and trade union to a women's movement. SEWA operates as a shadow government for women, providing services that the formal sector and the developmental agencies cannot or will not. It is the international model for women's banking and self-help financial services. Figure 10.1 shows all of the helping hands of SEWA.

As you can see from the diagram, SEWA has grown from banking to many other arenas. It includes cooperatives for vendors, artisans, and service workers. SEWA remains for women only; they say that men do not share or understand women's problems. The primary values of SEWA are nonviolence, arbitration, reconciliation, and a quiet, fiercely determined resistance to exploitation, whether from husbands, colonial powers, or the government of India. The women of SEWA say: "We not only want a piece of the pie, but we also want to choose the flavour and to know how to make it ourselves."

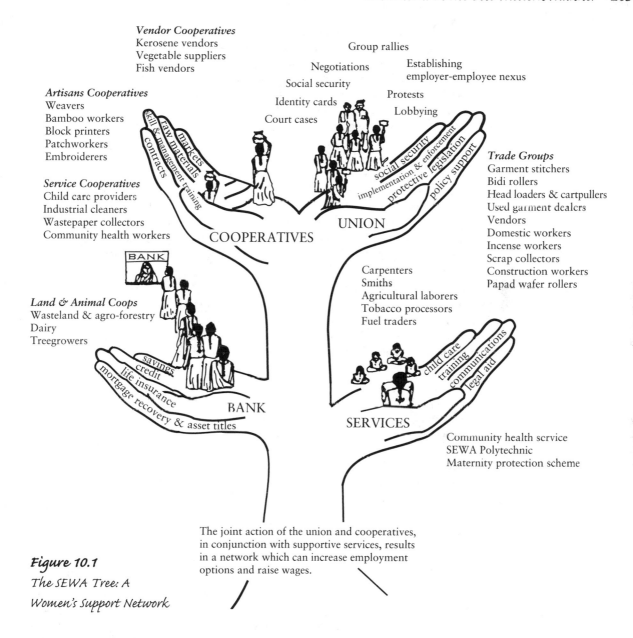

Vendor Cooperatives
Kerosene vendors
Vegetable suppliers
Fish vendors

Group rallies

Negotiations

Establishing
employer-employee nexus

Social security

Artisans Cooperatives
Weavers
Bamboo workers
Block printers
Patchworkers
Embroiderers

Identity cards

Court cases

Protests

Lobbying

markets
raw materials
skill & management training
contracts

social security
implementation & enforcement
protective legislation
policy support

Trade Groups
Garment stitchers
Bidi rollers
Head loaders & cartpullers
Used garment dealers
Vendors
Domestic workers
Incense workers
Scrap collectors
Construction workers
Papad wafer rollers

Service Cooperatives
Child care providers
Industrial cleaners
Wastepaper collectors
Community health workers

COOPERATIVES

UNION

BANK

Carpenters
Smiths
Agricultural laborers
Tobacco processors
Fuel traders

Land & Animal Coops
Wasteland & agro-forestry
Dairy
Treegrowers

savings
credit
life insurance
mortgage recovery & asset titles

child care
training
communications
legal aid

BANK

SERVICES

Community health service
SEWA Polytechnic
Maternity protection scheme

The joint action of the union and cooperatives,
in conjunction with supportive services, results
in a network which can increase employment
options and raise wages.

Figure 10.1
*The SEWA Tree: A
Women's Support Network*

Conclusions in the Post-Modern Manner

Sometimes, sitting at my computer in blue jeans and T-shirt, I am uncomfortably aware of the little tags in so many things I buy. They say: Made in China, Malaysia, Philippines, Korea, or India. Then I read some of the articles and books listed in the bibliography. My colleagues talk about capital accumulation, the politics of post-modernity, the ethnography of work and cultural struggles. I sit awed by the work of invisible women. Read what Eleanor Leacock says about this on the next page.

> *Third World women suffer manifold forms of oppression: as virtual slave labor in households, unpaid for their work as mothers who create new generations of workers, and as wives or sisters who succor the present ones; as workers, often in marginal jobs and more underpaid than men; and as members of racial minorities, or of semicolonial nations, subject to various economic, legal, and social disabilities. All the while, women bear the brunt, psychologically and sometimes physically, of the frustration and anger of their menfolk, who, in miserable complicity with an exploitative system, take advantage of the petty power they have been given over the women close to them. Perhaps the most bitter reality lies with the family, which is idealized as a retreat and sanctuary in a difficult world. Women fight hard to make it this, yet what could be a center of preparation for resistance by both sexes is so often instead a confused personal battleground, in which women have little recourse but to help recreate the conditions of their own oppression. (Leacock 1981:311)*

Marx, Engels, some feminists, and many others believed that socialist societies would free women from private service to husbands and the unpaid drudgery of domestic labor. Like Lenin at the beginning of the Russian Revolution, they paid lip service to liberating women from household oppression. But socialist dogmas and communist rules have not achieved the reformation in women's lives they once proclaimed.

Now the scholars and theoreticians say the "modern" period is over and we live in a state called **post-modern** and in a condition of **post-modernism**. These are difficult concepts to define. "Post-modern" has come to mean the emotional, social, and intellectual currents that began in the 1950s and 1960s in capitalist Western countries and are characterized by such concepts as pluralism, multiplicity, differences, ambiguity, fragmentation, and discontinuity. These stand in sharp contrast to the simple constructs about culture Margaret Mead and other anthropologists proposed.

The ideologies that sustained colonialism and capitalism are unstable, dead, or dying, the post-modernists say. From the idea of modernization as a straight line of progress from backward to progressive, the Enlightenment notions of reason and freedom, the Marxist stories of class conflict and the state in service of the people, to Freud's theories about drives and repression, the old narratives fail to explain the qualities of contemporary human existence. Post-modernist critiques of contemporary life highlight issues of power, desire, ethnicity, gender, sex, and race. The motto of post-modernism may well be, "Everything is political". All theories about the world must account for systems of power, particularly those that fall so heavily on our physical bodies, sexuality, and unconscious minds.

Are there positive indications for gendered survival in the world—something that contrasts with the bleak pictures painted in this chapter? Joni Seager, who compiled *The State of Women in the World Atlas* (1997), offers statistics and indexes about women in the world. Amid the predictable bleakness and invisible work, some trends offer hope. The United Nations Development Programme has created a gender-sensitive development index (GDI) that measures some quality-of-life issues, including life expectancy, educational attainment, and income, as well as national policies for making women more visible in national planning. Since 1970 the GDI values for the countries of the world have improved, although the pace has been uneven at best. Scandinavian countries rank very high. They have adopted gender equality and women's empowerment as conscious state policies. The status of women has deteriorated most sharply and consistently in Eastern Europe, where the transition from state socialism to a free market economy has come at a high cost. The numbers of women holding public office have plummeted. Poverty rates, domestic violence, pornography, and sexual exploitation are skyrocketing. As women's employment decreased dramatically, so has state support for health care, child care, food and housing subsidies, and availability of abortion.

Is there good news? It's uneven and sometimes depends on how one reads the statistics. Literacy and education are increasingly available to women. Perhaps a quarter of the world's adult population does not read or write. Of those, about two-thirds are women. In twenty of the world's poorest countries, three-quarters of adult women are not literate. High rates of women's illiteracy are a direct reflection of discrimination and restricted educational opportunities. Like maternal mortality, the statistics reflect the cultural traditions and assumptions that constrain women. The good news is that literacy is a spreading social goal and that women are becoming more and more literate. A dramatic example is the United Arab Emirates, where women's literacy has leapt from 7 percent in 1970 to 76 percent in 1990 (Seager 1997:120, 74). Reading and writing have long been instruments of power; for women, literacy is a form of freedom.

There's good news in the spread of micro-credit lending banks. SEWA (founded in 1974) and the Grameen Bank (founded in 1983) are probably the best known, but there are dozens around the world imitating their successes. Women's World Banking is a global network of more than fifty affiliate institutions tailoring financial services to women. In 1995 they issued more than 200,000 loans to more than 500,000 clients, averaging the U.S. equivalent of $300 (Seager 1997:79). Beyond this formal network are at least hundreds of small-scale, informal, grassroots women's groups that operate credit arrangements to circumvent the formal credit structures that have penalized and excluded women. Some loans are as small as $1.50 U.S. Even that tiny sum can make a big difference in a woman's life. Of all the development initiatives and economic programs in the agencies and governments of the world, women-centered banking may well be the best.

There is good news when women of the world gather to meet each other, to argue with each other, and to learn from each other. There's also good news in the growing number of treaties, accords, conventions, and tribunals that have addressed the state of the world's women. The Convention on the Elimination of All Forms of Discrimination Against Women (CEDAW) grew out of the decades of organizing within the United Nations (Seager 1997:104). The UN produced the Nairobi Looking-Forward Strategies for the Advancement of Women in 1985. The Vienna Declaration grew out of the United Nations World Conference on Human Rights in 1993. It was an historic call to eliminate violence against women in public and in private life (Bunch and Reilly 1994). There are others. The practical effectiveness of these agreements is open to question. They do, however, place a floor under expectations of fair and universal treatment. Women's pressure groups can hold their governments responsible for the spirit of the accords, if not the letter. They do not have to reinvent the issues each time, to document their own oppression instead of fighting it. These declarations confront official denials and can be used to leverage policies and policy makers. The writers of these declarations say, "Women's rights are human rights."

The best news is the sheer numbers, tenacity, and spread of grassroots organizations in the world: centers for women, associations of feminists, women's studies institutes, women's networks to fight violence or promote peace, rural women united, lesbians and gays marching, Green women involved in environmental politics, networks for reproductive freedoms, committees for working women, alliances to assist refugees, bookstores, caucuses, theater groups, and media in myriad forms. Here's a tiny sample of such organizations: Boston Women's Health Collective, Taipei Women's Rescue Foundation, Federation of Nigerian Women's Societies, Women's Solidarity Commission (Poland), Center for Women War Victims (Croatia), Voices of Women (Sri Lanka), Friends of Women (Malaysia), Colectivo de Lesbianas Feministas (Costa Rica), Third World Movement Against the Exploitation of Women (Philippines), Alliance for Arab Women (Egypt), National Feminist Assemblywomen's League (Japan), Korean Women Workers' Association, Red Thread (Guyana), Mongolian Female Lawyers Association, and hundreds and hundreds more.

Chimpanzee mothers and baboon females showed us the examples of matrifocal units, generations, and connections that flow from mothers. Anthropologists provide models of women, men, and children living in a vast array of cultural alternatives for being human. Women of color testify to the ravages of racism, and in so doing, offer visions of women and men together in a world free of slavery and hatred. Spirits visit women and women's religions in the heart of patriarchies, and women take that healing to others. Radical separatists in lesbian communities point out that "women have no country of our own" and then work to establish autonomy and authenticity for themselves and others. Women's shelter movements around the world work to provide sanctuaries and safety in women-centered environments. Today many women all over the world echo Virginia Woolf's immortal call for "a room of one's own." We have models of deep and abiding friendships among men and women from primates to world assemblies for peace. And ordinary women everywhere form simple groups to meet their basic needs. We grow like roots of grass.

When we ask, "what can I do," the answer comes. Find a group, join it, support it, form one if necessary, make common cause with people who share your visions. Or as Margaret Mead said toward the end of her life, "Never doubt that a small group of thoughtful and committed citizens can change the world; indeed, it's the only thing that ever has."

Reading, Writing, and Resistance

For a generation, the essential feminist text on the international women's movement was Robin Morgan's *Sisterhood Is Global*. Now it is out in a new edition. Here are two books that offer dynamic examples of women's work and gendered suffering. Grace Chang's *Disposable Domestics: Immigrant Women Workers in the Global Economy* (2000) shows how the work of immigrant women in the caregiving industries and the vast expansion of service sectors have become central to capitalism. Paul Farmer, Margaret Connors, and Janie Simmons wrote a passionate and compassionate account of the intersection of HIV, classism, racism, and sexism: *Women, Poverty and AIDS: Sex, Drugs and Structural Violence* (1996).

Women's biographies and oral histories bring the global home. Among many excellent ones, try Jyotsna Sreenivasan, *Ela Bhatt: Uniting Women in India* (2000); Judith Harlan's *Mamphela Ramphele: Changing Apartheid in South Africa* (2000); or Ellen Cantarow's *Moving the Mountain: Women Working for Social Change* (1999), which is the oral histories of three political activists in civil rights, suffrage, and labor organizing.

Numbers add up. Read Marilyn Waring's *Counting for Nothing: What Men Value and Women Are Worth* (2000). Or order the best international collection of statistics and use them to illustrate and illuminate the issues about which you care passionately: from the United Nations, *The World's Women 2000: Trends and Statistics*. Beyond the depressing statistics on poverty, sickness, violence, and death are women as micro-entrepreneurs. Paola Cianturco and Toby Tuttle wrote *In Her Hands: Craftswomen Changing the World* (2000) about the international movement of craft cooperatives run for and by women.

Glossary

The purpose of this glossary is to define technical terms as well as common words with distinct meanings in anthropology or related disciplines. Official, dictionary, common-sense definitions and woman-centered definitions are included. These helpful working explanations are distilled from many sources.

abortifacients: Drugs, potions, or other substances that cause or are believed to cause a pregnancy to end. See **emmenagogue.**

adept: A person skilled or proficient in a special area of knowledge, wisdom, or activity. In this context, the term refers to women with spirit, spiritual, or spiritualist contacts.

affinal kin: A kinship tie that involves marriage as the defining link; this contrasts with consanguineal or blood relatives. Affinal kinspeople include spouses and all their relatives; in-laws are examples of affinal kin.

African diaspora: The dispersal of people and cultures from Africa during the last 500 years, primarily through the practices of slavery and, primarily into the New World (the Caribbean, North America, and South America).

agency: The power to act and make decisions. Recognizes that people are not pawns, but active participants in their culture and everyday lives.

agriculture: Complex cultivation of a limited variety of crops using a plow, domesticated draft animals, or farm machinery. May include irrigation systems, livestock breeding, and/or large-scale production of cash crops, plantations, and agribusiness.

alpha male: A term used to mark the highest-ranking male in a primate group. The term is also used for the hero in romance novels.

altered state of consciousness: A state of nonordinary reality such as sleep, dreaming, coma, intoxication, trance, psychosis, deep meditation, visionary episodes, or psychedelic experiences. Altered states are induced by a variety of factors, including hypnosis, fatigue, drugs, sensory deprivation, sensory overload, organic brain injury, fasting, biofeedback, psychological stress, or communal fervor. All cultures tend to define some of these altered states of consciousness as valuable and desirable and others as negative and undesirable.

amazons: The original term probably meant "moon-woman" but now is widely used for women as warriors. In Greek legends, the writer Homer tells of Amazons who aided Troy during the Trojan wars. Portuguese explorers named the Amazon river after they encountered women warriors in Brazil. Here the word refers to oral and written traditions about women who passed for men, dressed like men, and married women, primarily in the cultures of Native North and South America. See also **two-spirits.**

androgyny, androgynous: Unisex, sexual neutrality, or sharing features of both male and female.

arranged marriage: A marriage partnership organized by relatives of the bride and groom. Often includes choosing spouses, betrothal, and the exchange of gifts between families. The participation of the bride and groom in this process varies cross-culturally.

authoritative knowledge: For any particular area of social life, there are systems of knowledge, explanation, or power that become ascendant and official. Examples of this are: traditional midwives versus the "science" and technology in hospital deliveries; Papal Decrees versus common sense, revelation, or intuition.

berdache: A Euro-American term for socially constructed patterns of gender alternatives among some Native American societies. It usually refers to males who assume female dress, mannerisms, speech, and social roles. The Native American name for these individuals (as translated into English) is **two-spirits.**

bilum, bilums: Looped string bags that are the most visible and symbolic object in women's lives in most of Melanesia.

biocultural markers: The specific times in the female life cycle in which physiology and biology intersect with cultural programming. Human cultures may mark puberty, marriage, childbirth, or menopause.

breastfeeding: Feeding a baby milk from the mother's breast. Breastfeeding techniques and beliefs are in large part culturally determined. Also called nursing or suckling.

bride-price, bride-wealth: Cash or other goods paid to a bride's family by the groom's family around the time of the wedding. This is generally a transaction between the bride's father and the groom's father.

burqa, burka: Facial mask worn by women in the Muslim Middle East. Burqa is the spelling of the Arabic word in Oman.

capitalism: An economic system in which investment in and ownership of the means of production, distribution, and exchange of wealth is made and maintained chiefly by private individuals or corporations. This contrasts with state-owned wealth. Capitalists are people who have capital (money, assets, land, investment, and so on).

capture marriage: A form of marriage where the groom and his family take the bride from her family home by force. The bride's family sometimes agrees to this. Capture marriages bypass more formal and lengthy marriage arrangements.

cash crops, cash cropping: Agricultural production that is not for subsistence, family consumption, or sharing, but is grown and marketed for money. Examples of cash crops include heroin, cocaine, spices, tobacco, rubber, and cotton or other fibers.

circumcision (sunna): Removal of the prepuce or hood of the clitoris, with the body of the clitoris remaining intact. See also **female genital surgeries.**

clitoridectomy (excision): Removal of the clitoris and all or part of the labia minora and/or all or part of the labia majora. See also **female genital surgeries** and **infibulation.**

code switching: In linguistics, the practice of changing languages or linguistic codes depending on social context. Here, it is applied to culture and women's cultures. Women are able to switch between the cultural systems or codes in which they participate depending on social context, goals, and needs.

coitus interruptus: The technical term for "pulling out" or ending intercourse before male ejaculation. Common form of birth control.

colonialism, colony: In the last 500 years, the history of the world has been characterized by European nations that had policies (colonialism) of extending or retaining their power or authority over other areas of the world (colonies) that were unrelated to them by geography, history, language, or culture.

colostrum: The substance produced in the mammary glands during pregnancy and for a few days after birth that precedes breastmilk. It is high in fat and nutrients, and is thicker and more yellow than breastmilk. Women in many cultures discard the colostrum as "bad." Western medicine encourages giving it to newborns.

companionate marriage: Marriage based on criteria of compatibility and shared commitment to a lifestyle rather than economic concerns. Arose in the seventeenth century in the United States and Western Europe and is increasingly spreading around the globe.

complementarity, complementary gender roles: The idea that the sexual division of labor between genders completes or finishes off the other part. Some theorists use the term in the sense of equality, as in two sides of a coin; others for gender separation systems of ranking and hierarchy as forms of cooperation.

consanguineal kin: Relatives connected to us by ties of blood; people related through parents, siblings, or both.

consensual unions: Female–male partnerships with children that resemble marriage but exist outside legal or religious ratification. These may also be called visiting relations or common-law marriages.

consort, consort pair, consortship: Terms from primate studies that indicate an exclusive although not permanent mating relationship between female and male adult primates. Sometimes such couples are called a pair bond, and the process of getting together is called a **courtship** or **pair-bonding.**

conspicuous worship: Overt religious ceremonies, rituals, and practices. These are supported by large outlays of wealth, involve intricate forms of material culture, and occur in public spaces.

co-sleep: A practice where parents and children sleep in the same bed or mat.

courtship, courting: The time period during the life cycle and the social practices among animals (including humans) in which males present their case for mating and in which females solicit, reward, and establish appropriate responses.

cross-dressing: Widespread customs in human cultures of adopting the clothing, hairstyles, or other social attributes of other genders in daily, ceremonial, or ritual contexts.

cultural relativism: A viewpoint in anthropology that holds that the norms and values of each culture or subculture have their own validity and cannot be used as a standard for evaluating other cultures; that while human cultures are very different from each other, they are all equally valuable.

differential reproductive strategies, differential sexual strategies: The Darwinian notion that females and males act differently from each other in sex and reproduction, and that males and females have separate strategies for maximizing investments in and outcomes of mating.

divination: A procedure or ritual used to find out the otherwise unknowable, such as future events, the sex of an unborn child, or the source of illnesses attributed to supernatural causes.

double day: An entrenched division of labor by sex in which women are in charge of children, household, and domestic lifestyles, in addition to any full-time or part-time wage-labor jobs. See also **second shift,** the term popularized in the United States.

doula: A Greek word meaning "a woman who serves women" or a helper in doing women's work. A doula is an experienced woman, a friend, or a close female relative. Such women are also called childbirth companions or labor assistants, although they may provide service for other life stages and conditions.

dowry: A payment in money, land, or other goods to the groom or groom's family by the bride's family.

dowry death: A common term in parts of India that refers to husbands or family members killing or trying to kill a wife in connection with her **dowry** or another dowry they may hope for after her death.

egalitarian, equalitarian: Used to describe gender or other political relationships where people have more or less equal access to power and resources.

elopement: Marriage organized by the bride and groom alone, without regard for the formalities of arranged marriage or other family or community interests. In some contexts, elopement is considered a romantic coup and is driven by concepts of romantic love. At other times, elopement may be a way to avoid the expense of elaborate wedding ceremonies.

embodied knowledge: Information, intuition, or knowledge that comes from direct personal experiences and is generally coded or perceived in parts of the body or mind.

emmenagogue: Drugs, potions, or other substances used to bring on a period or to establish regular menstrual cycles; this may also mean ending a pregnancy in its early stages.

estrus, estrous cycle: Estrus is a noun; estrous is an adjective. Technical terms for ovulation and the external markings in female primates. The skin of the genital area swells and turns pink, hence we say, "in the pink" or "pink ladies." Occurs normally midway in the thirty-five day menstrual cycle and signals ovulation and sexual interest for primate females. Corresponds to "in heat" or "horny."

ethnocentric, ethnocentrism: Means "group-centered." The tendency to use the norms, values, and beliefs of one's own culture or subculture as the basis to judge others. This concept is often contrasted with cultural relativism.

Eurocentric, Eurocentrism: One of the ways to be ethnocentric; this one refers to the notion that Europe, a small geographic region and peninsula of Asia whose peoples and ideologies experienced rapid expansion during the last 500 years, is really the pinnacle of human evolution and world culture.

exchange value work: The production of commodities or services for sale, for the market; work as the exchange of goods or services for money or other financial considerations.

family wage, family wage laws, family wage ideology: Social, business, and legal customs formed around the belief that male workers are paid to support a wife and their children. Young, single women are not paid the same as men; they are not assumed to be supporting families. Married women are not assumed to work or to need other than a husband's income. This idea originated in industrial, capitalist societies in nineteenth-century Europe.

female genital surgeries: Practices in Africa and parts of the Middle East in which part or most of female external genitalia are removed. The extent and results vary. For specific kinds, see **circumcision, infibulation.** Also called female genital mutilation.

feminization of poverty: A term for the social and economic conditions characterized by women-headed households with few or no legal protections, double-day housework, and child care, combined with low wages in the formal or informal economic sectors. Such female-headed households are regarded as the largest definable group of poor people worldwide. Also called the pauperization of women.

fictive kinship: Common customs in human societies for using biological relations as a metaphor for creating formal and informal connections. Includes adoption, fosterage, godparents, sisterhood or brotherhood, "families we choose," and other arrangements.

First Nations: The name Native Americans use to refer to the cultures of this hemisphere who inhabited North America and South America before Europeans arrived, and who observe tribal traditions and ethnic identities in contemporary multicultural settings.

foraging: An economic system of gathering or collecting foods and processing them. Also called gathering–hunting or hunting–gathering.

formal work sector: The part of the economy included in official statistics such as the GNP (Gross National Product) and for which national records are kept and reported. Includes wages, investments, land transactions, and other economic activities regulated by national laws. Does not include housework, child care, barter, or work done in the informal sector.

formula: A liquid food prescribed for infants, designed as a substitute for breastmilk. Formula comes in powdered, concentrated, and liquid forms. Most formulas are based on cow's milk. Soy-based formulas are available for lactose intolerant children.

Fourth World: The people and groups descended from empires and tribal cultures that existed before world colonialism. Includes indigenous peoples. See also **Third World** and **First Nations.**

gatekeeper, gatekeepers: A term used to indicate any person within an institution who controls access to social, educational, economic, medical, or other kinds of resources or who controls the policies of access or exclusion.

gender attribution: A term that refers to the biological, social, or material criteria people of a social group use to identify each other as males, females, or any other culturally defined gender category. Usually assigned at birth.

gender identity: A term that refers to an individual's own feeling of whether he or she is a woman or man or other. This personal identity is believed to be formed during the first three or four years of life and exists regardless of genetic makeup or other social definitions of sex or gender.

gender ideology, gender ideologies: These are belief systems that encompass the meanings of male, female, masculine, feminine, sex, and reproduction in any given culture. These might include prescriptions and sanctions for appropriate male and female behavior or cultural rationalizations and explanations for social and political relationships between males and females.

gender role: This term describes what men and women actually do, their activity patterns, social relations and behaviors in specific cultural settings. Sometimes referred to as sex roles.

gender separation systems: Historically based styles of living and social organizations in which the lives of women and men are substantially segregated. This usually includes housing, economics, religion, and leisure activities. May also be called **sexual segregation systems.**

genital mutilation: See **female genital surgeries, clitoridectomy,** and **infibulation.**

grassroots, grassroots organizations: The term refers to small-scale social movements formed by ordinary or common people, distinct from the leadership of elites of a country or region, often in rural areas away from metropolitan centers of power. In women's culture, grassroots organizations typically grow up where national and local governments cannot, do not, or will not provide basic social services for women and children.

grooming, social grooming: A term used in primate studies for cleaning, handling, or manipulating the skin, hair, or fur of another member of one's own species. Grooming serves functions of communication, sociability, and group cohesion.

gynemimesis: Derived from the Greek words *gyne,* woman, and *mimos,* mime or mimicking. Refers to men who act, dress, and live as females in the manner their culture prescribes.

harem: Arabic for "forbidden." Refers to Muslim practices of identifying one part of a household as the residence of women. The term harem also refers to all women, mothers, sisters, wives, concubines, daughters, entertainers, slaves, and servants within a gender-segregated household. Often used in reference to animals in which the group consists of a number of females, their offspring, and one adult male. Sometimes defined in dictionaries as one male heading, leading, and mating a number of females.

head of household: A term for the adult who controls the distribution of family resources and the labor of family members. In patrilineal systems, the head of household is assumed to be any husband or the oldest male. Women as single heads of households are the fastest-growing family form worldwide.

hijras: Groups of men in India who form an institutionalized third gender usually marked by adoption of female dress, social roles, and work, as well as ritual responsibilities and male genital surgery.

horticulture: Planting, raising, and harvesting garden crops; generally horticulture is associated with small-scale cultivation using hoes and digging sticks.

household worker: A person who works in other people's homes; an employee recruited from outside the employing household to perform status-enhancing and reproductive work. Also called servant, domestic, domestic worker, nanny, maid, housekeeper, menial, or retainer. The opposite is master.

housewifization: Using wives as the model for female work or labor in contemporary economic systems; used especially in Marxist and feminist analyses of colonialism and capitalism.

houseyard: A West Indian residential unit and female social space; a cluster or compound of buildings with a matrifocal head.

infibulation (or pharaonic circumcision): Removal of the clitoris, the labia minora, and parts of the labia majora, as in the clitoridectomy. In infibulation, the remaining sides of the vulva are stitched together to close up the vagina, except for a small opening for urine and menses.

informal work sector: Activities outside the formal economy not counted or listed in national statistics of productivity or regulated by national laws. Examples include street vending, subsistence farming, craft production, cottage industries, and selling sex.

intersexes: A category of phenotypic or biological sex in addition to the dichotomous categories of male and female. In some contexts, intersexed individuals may be called **transsexuals.**

lithotomy position: The physical position for giving birth to human infants in which the woman lies on her back with her legs in the air. This position is favored in the United States but rarely known or practiced elsewhere.

longhouse: The architectural structure occupied by the **matrifocal** and **matrilineal** household in Iroquois society.

love marriage: A marriage practice set in opposition to arranged marriage in many cultures. A marriage based on love rather than economic concerns or kinship obligations.

macho, machismo: A Spanish word for the belief system about men's relationship to women in Latin America or other Spanish-speaking, Catholic countries. Derived from the word *macho* meaning "animal," macho refers to the qualities of a "real man." A male-superiority complex. See **gender ideology** and **marianismo.**

maidenhood: The culturally constructed period between menarche and marriage, motherhood, or other adult statuses.

marianismo: A controversial belief system about women's relationship to men in Latin America and other Spanish-speaking or Catholic countries. Derived from the Virgin Mary in Christian theology; promotes a sacred rationale for female subordination and suffering. See also **gender ideology** and **macho, machismo.**

maternal mortality rates: A statistic calculated on the basis of how many women die during pregnancy or while giving birth, expressed as the number of deaths per 100,000 births per year.

matrifocal: Mother-centered families, households, or genealogies; groups centered on the primary links between a mother and her children. The basic pattern in primate societies. A common pattern in human societies that may co-occur within a number of different marriage patterns and gender arrangements.

matrilineal, matriline, matriliny: Kinship systems and associated customs in which both males and females trace their descent and inheritance through their mothers and through a female line and female ancestors. Approximately one-third of the world's societies can be considered matrilineal; this pattern is often associated with horticultural societies. See **patrilineal.**

matrilocal residence patterns: A common system in the world where a young couple live with the bride's parents or family members after their wedding. This means the groom must move into his wife's household or nearby. Matrilocal may also mean the home territory of the matrilineal kin group, family, or tribe. See also **patrilocal** and **neolocal residence patterns.**

means of production: The tools or resources a person or group needs to earn a living. These include, but are not limited to, land, education, bank loans, draft animals, tools, inheritance, or capital for investment.

medicalization of childbirth: A system of authoritative knowledge in which pregnancy and childbirth are believed to be a kind of illness, pathology, or medical problem, and in which women are "delivered" by specialists who use technology in hospitals.

menarche: The technical term for the first menstrual period and the beginning of monthly cycling. Menarche or first menses is marked in some ceremonial way in many cultures to indicate a girl's sexual or reproductive maturity.

menopause: Physiological changes that accompany the ultimate cessation of the menstrual cycle and female fertility. The symptoms of menopause vary cross-culturally. Menopause is often associated with the life stage of middle-age.

menstrual taboos: Widespread although not universal beliefs about the dangers that menstruating people represent to themselves and others. Also includes the precautions one must take to protect oneself and others. May also be called female pollution beliefs.

midwife, midwives, midwifery: From Anglo-Saxon meaning "wise woman" or "witch." Generally means women who serve as birth attendants. The most common kind of healer in traditional human societies.

modernity: A shifting and culturally contextualized doctrine that focuses on "Western," post-Enlightenment versions of progress, history, and tradition. Spread by agents of colonialism, development, and other forms of globalization, it advances particularly Western views about technology, marriage practices, gender, religion, commerce, and science, among others. The existence of and response to this doctrine are characteristic of postcolonial situations.

monandry: The most common form of marriage in the world. It refers to the practice in which a woman takes a man as spouse or spouse emulator.

Neolithic: "New Stone Age"; Refers to the period of time after 10,000 B.C. when many human groups settled in villages, used ground stone tools, and produced food by cultivation of crops and the domestication of animals. Scholars often refer to it as a revolution because humans developed a radically new relationship to the environment.

neolocal residence patterns: Customs in which the newly married couple establishes a residence apart from either set of relatives. These independent and privatized households are characteristic of industrial and post-industrial Western countries. They are the residence patterns typical of nuclear families in the United States. See **matrilocal** or **patrilocal residence patterns.**

pair-bond, pair-bonding: A term from primate studies for a female and a male who go off together for a while and form a temporary couple. See **consort** and **courtship.**

parental investment: Behavior toward one's offspring that increases their chances of survival. May include behaviors that favor some offspring at the cost of investing in other offspring. Assumed to differ from females and males in any given species, hence the terms male parental investment and female parental investment.

pastoralists, pastoralism: Societies that depend on herding and breeding animals like horses, cattle, sheep, goats, camels. Because they must move their herds in relationship to the environment, they are usually mobile or seasonally nomadic. Pastoralists generally have a bad reputation with settled agriculturalists, on whom they prey for harvested crops, and with feminists because their kinship systems are typically **patrilineal, patrilocal** or **patriarchal.**

patriarchy, patriarchal: Cultures in which males as fathers or husbands are assumed to be in charge, official heads of household; in which descent and inheritance are traced through the male line; and in which men are generally in control of the distribution of family resources. Also refers to the extensions of kinship into **gender ideologies** and a world system of domination of men over women.

patrilineal, patriline, patriliny: Kinship systems and associated customs in which both males and females trace their descent and inheritance through their fathers and a male line and male ancestors. See **matrilineal.**

patrilocal residence patterns: A common system in the world, in which a young couple lives with the groom's parents or family members after the wedding. This means the bride must move into the household of her husband's family. Patrilocal may also mean the home territory of the husband's family, kin, or tribe. See **matrilocal** or **neolocal residence patterns.**

polyandry, fraternal polyandry: From the Greek words for "many" plus "men." A woman is wife to more than one man at a time. In fraternal polyandry, her husbands are two, three, or more brothers. Polyandry is the rarest system of getting married in the world.

polygamy: From the Greek words for "many" plus "mate." This is a general term for all forms of plural marriage in which a person has more than one spouse or spouse emulator at one time. This includes **polyandry** and **polygyny**, as well as systems of concubinage in which the legal standing of women differs from each other and from their husbands.

polygyny: From the Greek words for "many" plus "women." A marriage custom in which a man has more than one wife at one time.

post-modern, post-modernism: Usually refers to the emotional, social, and intellectual currents that began in the 1950s and 1960s in capitalist Western countries and are characterized by such concepts as pluralisms, multiplicity, differences, ambiguities, fragmentation, and discontinuities. Generally thought to be cultural–ideological domains in which older belief systems, often referred to as narratives, are unstable or disintegrating, or fail to explain the qualities of human existence. Post-modernist critiques and writings highlight issues about power, desire, ethnicity, gender, sex, and race.

post-partum sex taboo: Prescriptions against sexual relations following childbirth. May last as little as a few weeks to up to several years if they are extended over the nursing period.

purdah: This is a term from Hindi, Urdu, Persian, and related languages in South Asia that means "curtain." Today it refers to the practices of seclusion for women in Islamic and Hindu cultures, including harems or women's quarters, the screens placed in households to prevent men from seeing women, or the veils used for the streets and other public places, or other forms for enforcing standards of female modesty.

rites of passage: This term refers to the ceremonies and rituals that mark the passage of a person through life stages. Although cultures may recognize a variety of stages in life, the generally acknowledged ones are birth, puberty, marriage, and death.

romance, romantic love: A culturally defined complex that associates passion, eroticism, and transcendence with the idea of an ideal mate. Varies from one culture to the next and changes as marriage practices, technologies, gender ideologies, and other cultural phenomena change.

second shift: A concept popular in the United States that refers to the entrenched division of labor by sex, in which women are in charge of children, household, and domestic lifestyles, in addition to any full-time or part-time wage-labor jobs. See also **double day,** a term often used internationally.

sexual division of labor: A universal, pan-human, and time-honored practice of *Homo sapiens,* in which necessary work and tasks are divided up according to gender. Men get some of the jobs and women get some of the jobs.

sexual segregation systems: See **gender separation systems.**

sexual slavery, female sexual slavery: This includes involuntary prostitution, incest, kidnapping, the sale of women through marriage contracts, or other circumstances where women or girls cannot change the immediate conditions of their lives, where they cannot

get out of a captive state, and where they are subject to sexual violence and/or exploitation.

sexually proceptive: A term used in primate studies to describe females' simultaneous occurrence of being in **estrus** and sexual interest. Recognizes the active part females play in selecting, enticing, or rejecting certain males as mates.

sex-work, sex workers, sex industry: A form of productive work in marketing and selling sex.

shaman, shamanism: A shaman is a spiritual specialist adept at trance, divination, and curing. She or he derives power directly from a supernatural source, usually through mystic experiences and apprenticeships. An important part of their work is psychic journeying and performance of public ceremonials for healing.

social birth: The event, ceremony, ritual, or marked point in time when an infant child takes on or is given a cultural identity. This is usually different from biological birth.

social paternity: The ascription and assignment of the status of father to a male. May or may not be connected to biological fatherhood.

spinster: A common term for unmarried women in many cultures in which making cloth was a primary contribution to households. This is an example of work attached to marital status for females.

spirit possession: The idea that a supernatural entity or personality can enter and use otherwise ordinary human bodies and personalities. Anthropologists generally regard possession as an **altered state of consciousness,** which is explained in a culturally recognizable manner as the presence of spirits operating within a social group.

subsistence technology: The tools and strategies used to procure food primarily. Includes hunting-gathering (or foraging), horticulture, agriculture, pastoralism, and industrial and post-industrial modes of production.

testimonial: As used here, a written genre that relates a life story culled from individual and collective realities across cultural boundaries. Like oral histories, testimonials are usually produced through the collaboration of a nonliterate narrator and literate author.

third gender: A convenient category to use in discussing structured, culturally patterned systems in various human cultures in which men take on females' dress and work or in which females take on males' dress and work, or in which conventional and dichotomous gender systems cannot account for individuals or groups of people who live apart from them. See **two-spirits, hijras.**

third sex: A category used to describe individuals with anatomical, biological, or physiological attributes that challenge the binary categories of male and female. The third sex category sometimes overlaps third gender categories. See **hijras, intersexes, transsexuals.**

Third World: A term adopted by postcolonial and nonaligned nations of Asia, Africa, and Latin America after World War II to distinguish themselves from the "First World," the Western democracies and former colonial powers, and the "Second World," or the Soviet-bloc nations. See **Fourth World.**

transsexuals: Refers to individuals who somehow change into or move to the "opposite sex" or into a third sex; a type of border crossing. There is no firm agreement on the meaning of this term. For example, the term *transsexuals* may include anatomical males or anatomical females who believe that a person of the opposite sex lives in their bodies; it may include intersexed or transgendered individuals. Responses include cross-dressing, assumption of alternative lifestyles, and in some cases surgical, hormonal, or other body alterations. May include reassignment of biological sex or social gender.

two-spirits, two-spirited: This is a generic term for people who are lesbian, gay, transgendered, cross-dressers, transvestites, transsexuals, or otherwise have "marked" lives in the bands, tribes, or nations of Native North America in which concepts of multiple genders occur.

use value: Services and products made and consumed within families and that do not have a monetary value and are not sold. They have "value" only in private domestic settings.

visiting relations: A term for a woman and a man in a relationship, often long-term or parental, who do not live together in the same household. See **consensual unions.**

wean, weaning: To accustom a child or other young animal to food other than its mother's milk; to withdraw or withhold suckling as a mark of a specific de-velopmental stage in infant growth; to withdraw something pleasurable from a dependent creature.

Western culture: A practical shorthand term for European societies, European-derived, and Euro-American-centered cultural traditions that spread during colonial expansion of the last 500 years. Includes the cultural constructions inherited and reformulated from Greco-Roman cultures, Judeo-Christian traditions, and beliefs in personality, democracy, sexual division of labor, or other systems of thought and practice developed within these cultural systems.

wet-nurses, wet-nursing: A common set of customs in which parents place their newborn child into the care of a lactating woman not its biological mother.

wife battering: This is a category of abuse of women more severe than **wife beating;** it includes the possibilities of severe injuries, disabilities, and death. It does not matter whether or not the partners are officially married.

wife beating: Defined as a man deliberately inflicting physical pain on a woman within a male–female relationship. It does not matter whether or not the partners are officially married.

Wok Meri: Neo-Melanesian word that means "the work of women." These female-centered groups operate savings, banking, and exchange systems in both formal and informal economic sectors in the highlands of New Guinea.

women's culture: A term used to describe female-centered values, activities, and experiences apart from the general culture in which females and males both participate. Women's culture is not a subculture. See **code switching.**

work: Any kind of labor or activity that has some recognizable or measurable social value, however these may be expressed. Includes work as production, reproduction, status enhancement, and moral–morale building. See **use value** and **exchange value work.**

world religions: Widespread, highly structured, and often hierarchal systems of religious practice, which have enormous economic, political, and membership bases. These include Islam, Christianity, Judaism, Hinduism, Confucianism, Buddhism, and Taoism.

Bibliography

Abu-Lughod, Lila 1993 *Writing Women's Worlds: Bedouin Stories.* Berkeley: University of California Press.

——— 1986 *Veiled Sentiments: Honor and Poetry in a Bedouin Society.* Berkeley: University of California Press.

——— 1985 "A community of secrets: The separate world of Bedouin women." *Signs* 10(4):637–657.

Agostin, Marjorie (Ed.) 1993 *Surviving Beyond Fear: Women, Children and Human Rights in Latin America.* Fredonia, NY: White Pine Press.

Ahearn, Laura M. 2001 *Invitations to Love: Literacy, Love Letters, and Social Change in Nepal.* Ann Arbor: The University of Michigan Press.

Albers, Patricia and Beatrice Medicine (Eds.) 1983 *The Hidden Half: Studies of Plains Indian Women.* Washington, DC: University Press of America.

Allen, Paula Gunn 1989 "Lesbians in American Indian Cultures." In Martin Duberman, Martha Vicinus, and George Chauncey (Eds.). *Hidden from History: Reclaiming the Gay and Lesbian Past.* New York: Meridian, pp. 106–117.

Altmann, Jeanne 1980 *Baboon Mothers and Infants.* Cambridge, MA: Harvard University Press.

Amadiume, Ifi 1987 *Male Daughters, Female Husbands: Gender and Sex in an African Society.* London: Zed Books.

Arias, Arturo (Ed.) 2001 *The Rigoberta Menchú Controversy.* Minneapolis: University of Minnesota Press.

Bachofen, J. J. 1967 *Myth, Religion and Mother Right: Selected Writings of J. J. Bachofen.* Introduction by Joseph Campbell; translated by Ralph Manheim. Princeton, NJ: Princeton University Press.

Barber, Elizabeth 1994 *Women's Work: The First 20,000 Years. Women, Cloth, and Society in Early Times.* New York: W. W. Norton.

Barry, Kathleen 1995 *The Prostitution of Sexuality.* New York: New York University Press.

Bateson, Gregory 1958 *Naven.* 2d ed. Stanford, CA: Stanford University Press.

Bateson, Mary Catherine. 1984 *With a Daughter's Eye: A Memoir of Margaret Mead and Gregory Bateson.* New York: William Morrow.

Behar, Ruth and Deborah Gordon (Eds.) 1995 *Women Writing Culture.* Berkeley: University of California Press.

Bell, Diane 1993 *Daughters of the Dreaming.* 2d ed. Minneapolis: University of Minnesota Press.

Benedict, Ruth 1934a *Patterns of Culture.* New York: Mentor.

——— 1934b *Zuni Mythology.* 2 Vols. New York: Columbia University Contributions to Anthropology No. 21.

——— 1923 "The Concept of the Guardian Spirit in North America." *Memoirs of the American Anthropological Association* No. 29.

Bennholdt-Thomsen, Veronika 1988 "Why Do Housewives Continue to Be Created in the Third World Too?" In Mies et al. 1988:159–167.

Beyene, Yewoubdar 1989 *From Menarche to Menopause: Reproductive Lives of Peasant Women in Two Cultures.* Albany: State University of New York Press.

Biesele, Megan 1993 *Women Like Meat: The Folklore and Foraging Ideology of the Kalahari Ju/'hoan.* Bloomington: Indiana University Press.

Blackwood, Evelyn (Ed.) 1985a "Anthropology and homosexual behavior." Special Issues of the *Journal of Homosexuality* 11(3/4).

——— 1985b "Breaking the Mirror: The Construction of Lesbianism and the Anthropological Discourse on Homosexuality." In Blackwood 1985a:1–15.

Boddy, Janice 1991 "Body politics: Continuing the anticircumcision crusade." *Medical Anthropology Quarterly* 5(1):15–17.

——— 1989 *Wombs and Alien Spirits: Women, Men, and the Zār Cult in Northern Sudan.* Madison, WI: University of Wisconsin Press.

Boserup, Ester 1970 *Woman's Role in Economic Development.* New York: St. Martin's Press.

Bourguignon, Erika 1991 *Possession.* Prospect Heights, IL: Waveland Press.

Brettell, Caroline and Carolyn Sargent (Eds.) 1993 *Gender in Cross-Cultural Perspective.* Englewood Cliffs, NJ: Prentice-Hall.

Brown, Karen McCarthy 1991 *Mama Lola: A Vodou Priestess in Brooklyn.* Berkeley: University of California Press.

Browner, Carole and Ellen Lewin 1982 "Female altruism reconsidered: The Virgin Mary as economic woman." *American Ethnologist* 9:61–75.

Browner, Carole and Bernard Ortiz de Montellano 1986 "Herbal Emmenagogues Used by Women in Colombia and Mexico." In Nina Etkin (Ed.). *Plants in Indigenous Medicine and Diet: Biobehavioral Approaches.* Bedford Hills, NY: Redgrave.

Buckley, Thomas and Alma Gottlieb (Eds.) 1988 *Blood Magic: The Anthropology of Menstruation.* Berkeley: University of California Press.

Bullough, Vern and Bonnie Bullough 1993 *Cross Dressing, Sex and Gender.* Philadelphia: University of Pennsylvania Press.

Bunch, Charlotte and Niamh Reilly 1994 *Demanding Accountability: The Global Campaign and Vienna Tribunal for Women's Human Rights.* New Brunswick, NJ: Rutgers University Center for Women's Global Leadership.

Burbank, Victoria 1988 *Aboriginal Adolescence: Maidenhood in an Australian Community.* New Brunswick, NJ: Rutgers University Press.

Burgess, Lauren Cook (Ed.) 1994 *An Uncommon Soldier: The Civil War Letters of Sarah Rosetta Wakeman alias Pvt. Lyons Wakeman.* Pasadena, MD: Minerva Center.

Caffrey, Margaret 1989 *Ruth Benedict: Stranger in This Land.* Austin: University of Texas Press.

Cantarow, Ellen 1999 *Moving the Mountain: Women Working for Social Change.* With Susan O'Malley and Sharon Strom. New York: Feminist Press.

Cassell, Joan 1987 *Children in the Field: Anthropological Experiences.* Philadelphia: Temple University Press.

Chang, Grace 2000 *Disposable Domestics: Immigrant Women Workers in the Global Economy.* Cambridge, MA: South End Press.

Cianturco, Paola and Toby Tuttle 2000 *In Her Hands: Craftswomen Changing the World.* New York: The Monacelli Press.

Clark, Garcia 1994 *Onions Are My Husband: Survival and Accumulation by West African Market Women.* Chicago: University of Chicago Press.

Coontz, Stephanie 1992 *The Way We Never Were: American Families and the Nostalgia Trap.* New York: Basic Books.

Counihan, Carole M. 1999 *The Anthropology of Food and Body: Gender, Meaning, and Power.* New York: Routledge.

Counts, Dorothy, Judith Brown and Jacquelyn Campbell (Eds.) 1999 *To Have and To Hit: Cultural Perspectives on the Beating of Wives.* 2nd Ed. Urbana and Chicago: University of Illinois Press.

Crapanzano, Vincent and Vivian Garrison (Eds.) 1977 *Case Studies in Spirit Possession.* New York: John Wiley and Sons.

Croll, Elisabeth 2000 *Endangered Daughters: Discrimination and Development in Asia.* London and New York: Routledge.

Daly, Martin and Margo Wilson 1984 "A Sociobiological Analysis of Human Infanticide." In Hausfater and Hrdy 1984:487–502.

Davis, Dona 1993 "When men become 'women': Gender antagonism and the changing sexual geography of work in Newfoundland." *Sex Roles* 29(7/8):457–475.

——— 1989 "The variable character of nerves in a Newfoundland fishing village." *Medical Anthropology* 11:63–78.

Davis-Floyd, Robbie and Carolyn Sargent (Eds.) 1997 *Childbirth and Authoritative Knowledge: Cross-Cultural Perspectives.* Berkeley: University of California Press.

Davis-Floyd, Robbie and Joseph Dumit (Eds.) 1997 *Cyborg Babies: From Techno-Sex to Techno-Tots.* New York: Routledge.

Delacoste, Frederique and Priscilla Alexander (Eds.) 1987 *Sex Work: Writings by Women in the Sex Industry.* San Francisco: Cleis Press.

Delaney, Carol 1991 *The Seed and the Soil: Gender and Cosmology in Turkish Village Society.* Berkeley: University of California Press.

DeLoache, Judy and Alma Gottlieb (Eds.) 2000 *A World of Babies: Imagined Childcare Guides for Seven Societies*. New York: Cambridge University Press.

Devereaux, George 1976 *A Study of Abortion in Primitive Societies*. Revised Ed. New York: International University Press.

Diamond, Milton and H. Keith Sigmundson 1997 "Sex reassignment at birth: Long-term review and clinical implications." *Archives of Pediatric and Adolescent Medicine* 151:298–304.

Dobash, Russell, R. Emerson Dobash, Margo Wilson, and Martin Daly 1992 "The myth of sexual symmetry in marital violence." *Social Problems* 39(1):71-91.

Doerr, Edd and James Prescott (Eds.) 1989 *Abortion Rights and Fetal "Personhood."* Long Beach, CA: Centerline Press.

Doyal, Leslie 1995 *What Makes Women Sick? Gender and the Political Economy of Health*. New Brunswick, NJ: Rutgers University Press.

Ehlers, Tracy Bachrach 1991 "Debunking marianismo: Economic vulnerability and survival strategies among Guatemalan wives." *Ethnology* 30:1–16.

Ehrenreich, Barbara and Deidre English 1973 *Witches, Midwives and Nurses: A History of Women Healers*. New York: The Feminist Press.

——— 1973 *Complaints and Disorders: The Sexual Politics of Sickness*. New York: The Feminist Press.

Eller, Cynthia 2000 *The Myth of Matriarchal Prehistory: Why an Invented Past Won't Give Women a Future*. Boston, MA: Beacon Press.

——— 1993 *Living in the Lap of the Goddess: The Feminist Spirituality Movement in America*. New York: Crossroad.

——— 1991 "Relativizing the patriarchy: The sacred history of the feminist spirituality movement." *History of Religion* 30(3):279–295.

El Guindi, Fadwa 1999 *Veil: Modesty, Privacy and Resistance*. Oxford and New York: Berg.

El Saadawi, Nawal 1980 *The Hidden Faces of Eve*. London: Zed Press.

Engels, Frederick 1972 *The Origin of the Family, Private Property and the State*. Edited, with an introduction by Eleanor Leacock. New York: International Publishers.

Etienne, Mona and Eleanor Leacock (Eds.) 1980 *Women and Colonization: Anthropological Perspectives*. New York: Praeger.

Falk, Nancy and Rita Gross (Eds.) 1980 *Unspoken Worlds: Women's Religious Lives in Non-Western Cultures*. San Francisco: Harper and Row.

Farmer, Paul, Margaret Connors, and Janie Simmons (Eds.) 1966 *Women, Poverty and AIDS: Sex, Drugs and Structural Violence*. Monroe, ME: Common Courage Press.

Fedigan, Linda M. and Laurence Fedigan 1989 "Gender and the Study of Primates." In Morgan 1989: 41–65.

Finkler, Kaja 2000 *Experiencing the New Genetics: Family and Kinship on the Medical Frontier*. Philadelphia: University of Pennsylvania Press.

——— 1994a *Women in Pain: Gender and Morbidity in Mexico*. Philadelphia: University of Pennsylvania Press.

——— 1994b *Spiritualist Healers in Mexico*. Salem, WI: Sheffield.

Firestone, Shulamith 1970 *The Dialectic of Sex*. New York: William Morrow and Co.

Fisher, Helen 1992 *The Anatomy of Love: The Mysteries of Mating, Marriage, and Why We Stray*. New York: Fawcett.

Fisher, Jo 1989 *Mothers of the Disappeared*. London: Zed Books.

Franklin, Sarah and Helena Ragoné (Eds.) 1998 *Reproducing Reproduction: Kinship, Power, and Technological Innovation*. Philadelphia: University of Pennsylvania Press.

Frisbie, Charlotte 1967 *Kinaaldá: A Study of the Navaho Girl's Puberty Ceremony*. Middleton, CT: Wesleyan University Press.

Gailey, Christine Ward 1993 "Equalitarian and Class Societies: Transitions and Transformations." In Sutton 1993:67–76.

Garber, Marjorie 1992 *Vested Interests: Cross-Dressing and Cultural Anxiety*. New York: Harper Perennial.

Gelles, Richard and Jane Lancaster (Eds.) 1987 *Child Abuse and Neglect: Biosocial Dimensions*. New York: Aldine de Gruyter.

Gero, Joan and Margaret Conkey (Eds.) 1991 *Engendering Archaeology: Women and Prehistory*. Oxford: Basil Blackwell.

Gewertz, Deborah 1981 "A historical reconsideration of female dominance among the Chambri of Papua New Guinea." *American Ethnologist* 8:94–106.

—— 1983 *Sepik River Societies: A Historical Ethnography of the Chambri and Their Neighbors.* New Haven, CT: Yale University Press.

Gill, Lesley 1994 *Precarious Dependencies: Gender, Class and Domestic Service in Bolivia.* New York: Columbia University Press.

Ginsberg, Faye 1989 *Contested Lives: The Abortion Debate in an American Community.* Berkeley: University of California Press.

Ginsberg, Faye and Rayna Rapp (Eds.) 1995 *Conceiving the New World Order: The Global Politics of Reproduction.* Berkeley: University of California Press.

Goodall Jane 1990 *Through a Window: My Thirty Years with the Chimpanzees of Gombe.* Boston: Houghton Mifflin.

—— 1986 *The Chimpanzees of Gombe: Patterns of Behavior.* Cambridge, MA: Belknap Press.

—— 1971 *In the Shadow of Man.* New York: Dell.

Gonzáles-Wippler, Migene 1981 *Santeria: African Magic in Latin America.* New York: Original Products.

Gruenbaum, Ellen 2001 *The Female Circumcision Controversy: An Anthropological Perspective.* Philadelphia: University of Pennsylvania Press.

Gutmann, David 1992 "Beyond Nurture: Developmental Perspectives on the Vital Older Woman." In Kerns and Brown 1992:221–233.

Hahn, Robert (Ed.) 1987 *The Anthropology of American Obstetrics.* Special Issue of *Medical Anthropology Quarterly* 1(3):319–334.

Hale, Sondra 1989 "The Politics of Gender in the Middle East." In Morgan 1989:246–267.

Harlan, Judith 2000 *Mamphela Ramphele: Changing Apartheid in South Africa.* New York: Feminist Press.

Harvey, Youngsook Kim 1979 *Six Korean Women: The Socialization of Shamans.* St. Paul, MN: West.

—— 1980 "Possession Sickness and Korean Shamans." In Falk and Gross 1980:41–52.

Hausfater, Glenn and Sarah B. Hrdy (Eds.) 1984 *Infanticide: Comparative and Evolutionary Perspectives.* New York: Aldine.

Hausman, Bernice L. 2003 *Mother's Milk: Breastfeeding Controversies in American Culture.* London: Routledge.

Herdt, Gilbert 1997 *Same Sex, Different Cultures: Gays and Lesbians Across Cultures.* Boulder, CO: Westview Press.

—— (Ed.) 1993 *Third Sex, Third Gender: Beyond Sexual Dimorphism in Gender and History.* New York: Zone Books.

—— 1987a *Guardians of the Flute: Idioms of Masculinity.* New York: Columbia University Press.

—— 1987b *The Sambia: Ritual and Gender in New Guinea.* New York: Holt, Rinehart and Winston.

—— (Ed.) 1984 *Ritualized Homosexuality in Melanesia.* Berkeley: University of California Press.

—— (Ed.) 1982 *Rituals of Manhood: Male Initiation in Papua New Guinea.* Berkeley: University of California Press.

Herdt, Gilbert and Andrew Boxer 1996 *Children of Horizons: How Gay and Lesbian Youth Are Forging a New Way Out of the Closet.* Boston: Beacon Press.

Himes, Norman E. 1970 *Medical History of Contraception.* New York: Schocken.

Hochschild, Arlie R. 1990 *The Second Shift: Working Parents and the Revolution at Home.* New York: Avon.

—— 1997 *The Time Bind: When Work Becomes Home and Home Becomes Work.* New York: Metropolitan Books.

Hoch-Smith, Judith and Anita Spring (Eds.) 1978 *Women in Ritual and Symbolic Roles.* New York: Plenum Press.

Hogbin, Ian 1970 *The Island of Menstruating Men: Religion in Wogeo, New Guinea.* Scranton: Chandler.

Hrdy, Sarah B. 1999 *The Woman That Never Evolved.* Cambridge, MA: Harvard University Press.

—— 1999 *Mother Nature: Maternal Instincts and How They Shape the Human Species.* New York: Ballantine Books.

Human Rights Watch/Asia 1995 *Rape for Profit: Trafficking of Nepali Girls and Women to India's Brothels.* New York: Human Rights Watch.

Inhorn, Marcia C. 1996 *Fertility and Patriarchy: The Cultural Politics of Gender and Family Life in Egypt.* Philadelphia: University of Pennsylvania Press.

—— 1994 *Quest for Conception: Gender, Infertility, and Egyptian Medical Traditions.* Philadelphia: University of Pennsylvania Press.

Jacobs, Sue-Ellen, Wesley Thomas, and Sabine Lang 1997 *Two-Spirit People: Native American Gender Identity, Sexuality, and Spirituality*. Urbana: University of Illinois Press.

Jankowiak, William (Ed.) 1995 *Romantic Passion: A Universal Experience?* New York: Columbia University Press.

Jenness, Valerie 1993 *Making It Work: The Prostitutes' Rights Movement in Perspective*. New York: Aldine de Gruyter.

Jordon, Brigitte 1993 *Birth in Four Cultures: A Cross-Cultural Investigation of Childbirth in Yucatan, Holland, Sweden, and the United States*. 4th ed. Revised and expanded by Robbie Davis-Floyd. Prospect Heights, IL: Waveland Press.

Jules-Rosette, Bennetta (Ed.) 1979 *The New Religions of Africa*. Norwood, NJ: Ablex.

Katchadourian, Herant A. (Ed.) 1979 *Human Sexuality: A Comparative and Developmental Perspective*. Berkeley: University of California Press.

Keesing, Roger 1982 "Prologue: Toward a Multidimensional Understanding of Male Initiation." In Herdt (Ed.) 1982:1–52.

Kempadoo, Kamala and Jo Doezema 1998 *Global Sex Workers: Rights, Resistance and Redefinition*. New York and London: Routledge.

Kendall, Laura 1985 *Shamans, Housewives, and Other Restless Spirits: Women in Korean Ritual Life*. Honolulu: University of Hawaii Press.

Kerns, Virginia and Judith K. Brown (Eds.) 1992 *In Her Prime: New Views of Middle-Aged Women*. Urbana: University of Illinois Press.

Koblinsky, Marge, Judith Timyan, and Jill Gay 1993 *The Health of Women: A Global Perspective*. Boulder, CO: Westview Press.

Kuipers, Joel 1986 "Talking about troubles: Gender differences in Weyéwa speech use." *American Ethnologist* 13(3):448–462.

Laderman, Carol and Marina Roseman 1996 *The Performance of Healing*. New York: Routledge.

Lakoff, Robin Tolmach 2004 *Language and Woman's Place, Text and Commentaries*. Edited by Mary Bucholtz, Oxford: Oxford University Press.

——— 1975 *Language and Woman's Place*. New York: Harper and Row.

Lamphere, Louise 1972 "Strategies, Cooperation and Conflict among Women in Domestic Groups." In Rosaldo and Lamphere 1972:97–112.

Lamphere, Louise, Helen Ragoné, and Patricia Zavella (Eds.) 1997 *Situated Lives: Gender and Culture in Everyday Life*. New York: Routledge.

Landes, Ruth 1994 *City of Women*. Introduction by Sally Cole. Albuquerque: University of New Mexico Press.

Lang, Sabine 2000 *Men as Women, Women as Men: Changing Gender in Native American Cultures*. Austin: University of Texas Press.

Langness, Lew 1974 "Ritual power and male domination in the New Guinea Highlands." *Ethos* 2(3):189–212.

Leacock, Eleanor 1993 "Being an Anthropologist." In Sutton 1993:1–32.

——— 1981 *Myths of Male Dominance: Collected Articles on Women Cross-Culturally*. New York: Monthly Review Press.

Lepowsky, Maria 1993 *Fruit of the Motherland: Gender in an Equalitarian Society*. New York: Columbia University Press.

Lerner, Gerda 1986 *The Creation of Patriarchy*. Oxford: Oxford University Press.

Levinson, Daniel 1989 *Family Violence in Cross-Cultural Perspectives*. Newbury Park, CA: Sage.

——— 1988 "Family Violence in Cross-Cultural Perspective." In Van Hasselt et al. 1988:435–455.

Levy, Robert 1971 "The community function of Tahitian male transvestism: A hypothesis." *Anthropological Quarterly* 44:12–21.

Lewin, Ellen 1997 "This Permanent Roommate." In Lamphere, Ragoné, and Zavella 1997:192–207.

Lewin, Ellen 1993 *Lesbian Mothers: Accounts of Gender in American Culture*. Ithaca, NY: Cornell University Press.

Lewis, I. M. 1971 *Ecstatic Religion: An Anthropological Study of Spirit Possession and Shamanism*. New York: Penguin.

Lock, Margaret 1993 *Encounters with Aging: Mythologies of Menopause in Japan and North America*. Berkeley: University of California Press.

MacCormack, Carol 1982 *Ethnography of Fertility and Birth*. New York: Academic Press. 1994 2d ed. Waveland Press.

———— 1979 "Sande: The public face of a secret society." In Jules-Rosette 1979:27–38.

MacKenzie, Maureen 1991 *Androgynous Objects: String Bags and Gender in Central New Guinea.* Cooper Station, NY: Harwood Academic.

McClain, Carol (Ed.) 1989a *Women as Healers: Cross-Cultural Perspectives.* New Brunswick, NJ: Rutgers University Press.

———— 1989 "Reinterpreting Women in Healing Roles." In McClain 1989:1–19.

McDowell, Nancy 1991 *The Mundugumor: From the Field Notes of Margaret Mead and Reo Fortune.* Washington DC: Smithsonian Institution Press.

Mageo, Jeannette Marie and Alan Howard (Eds.) 1996 *Spirits in Culture, History, and Mind.* New York: Routledge.

Maggi, Wynne 2001 *Our Women Are Free: Gender and Ethnicity in the Hindukush.* Ann Arbor: The University of Michigan Press.

Makhlouf, Carla 1979 *Changing Veils: Women and Modernization in North Yemen.* Austin: University of Texas Press.

Martin, Emily 1992 *The Woman in the Body: A Cultural Analysis of Reproduction.* Boston: Beacon Press.

Marx, Karl 1948 *The Communist Manifesto.* New York: International.

Mead, Margaret 1975 "Bisexuality: What's it all about?" *Redbook* (January): 29–30.

———— 1974 *Ruth Benedict.* New York: Columbia University Press.

———— 1973 *Coming of Age in Samoa.* New York: William Morrow. First published in 1929.

———— 1972 *Blackberry Winter: My Earlier Years.* New York: William Morrow.

———— 1967 *Male and Female: A Study of the Sexes in a Changing World.* New York: Dell Laurel. First published in 1949.

———— 1963 *Sex and Temperament in Three Primitive Societies.* New York: William Morrow.

———— 1959a *An Anthropologist at Work: The Writings of Ruth Benedict.* Boston: Houghton-Mifflin.

———— 1959b "Preface" to Ruth Benedict, *Patterns of Culture.* New York: Mentor (originally published in 1934).

Medicine, Beatrice 1983 "Warrior Women: Sex Role Alternatives for Plains Indian Women." In Albers and Medicine 1983:267–280.

Meggitt, Mervyn 1964 "Male-female relationships in the highlands of Australian New Guinea." *American Anthropologist* 66(2/4):204–224.

Menchú, Rigoberta 1984 *I, Rigoberta Menchú: An Indian Woman in Guatemala.* Edited and introduced by Elisabeth Burgos-Debray; translated by Ann Wright. London: Verso.

Mernissi, Fatima 2001 *Scheherazade Goes West: Different Cultures, Different Harems.* New York: Pocket Books.

———— 1994 *Dreams of Trespass: Tales of a Harem Girlhood.* Reading, MA: Addison-Wesley.

———— 1975 *Beyond the Veil: Male-Female Dynamics in a Modern Muslim Society.* New York: Schenkman.

Mies, Maria 1986 *Patriarchy and Accumulation on a World Scale.* London: Zed Books.

Mies, Maria, Claudia Von Werlhof, and Veronika Bennholdt-Thomsen 1988 *Women: The Last Colony.* London: Zed Books.

Mikell, Gwendolyn (Ed.) 1997 *African Feminism: The Politics of Survival in Sub-Saharan Africa.* Philadelphia: University of Pennsylvania Press.

Minturn, Leigh 1989 "The Birth Ceremony as a Rite of Passage into Infant Personhood." In Edd Doerr and James Prescott (Eds.). *Abortion Rights and Fetal "Personhood."* Long Beach, CA: Centerline Press.

Mintz, Sidney 1981 "Economic Role and Cultural Tradition." In Steady 1981:515–532.

Modell, Judith S 1983 *Ruth Benedict: Patterns of a Life.* Philadelphia: University of Pennsylvania Press.

Money, John 1994 *Sex Errors of the Body and Related Syndromes: A Guide to Counseling Children, Adolescents and Their Families.* 2d ed. Baltimore, MD: Paul H. Brooks.

Money, John and A. A. Ehrhardt 1972 *Man and Woman/Boy and Girl.* Baltimore, MD: Johns Hopkins University Press.

Momsen, Janet (Ed.) 1993 *Women and Change in the Caribbean.* Bloomington: Indiana University Press.

Montoya, Rosario, Lessie Jo Frazier, and Janise Hurtig (Eds.) 2002 *Gender's Place: Feminist Anthropologies of Latin America.* New York: Palgrave Macmillan.

Morgan, Lewis Henry 1851 *League of the Ho-De-No-Sau-Nee or Iroquois.* 2 Vols. New York: Dodd, Mead and Company.

Morgan, Lynn 1989 "Where Does Life Begin: A Cross-Cultural Perspective on Personhood." In Edd Doerr and James Prescott (Eds.). *Abortion Rights and Fetal "Personhood."* Long Beach, CA: Centerline Press.

Morgan, Lynn and Meredith Michaels (Eds.) 1999 *Fetal Subjects, Feminist Positions.* Philadelphia: University of Pennsylvania Press.

Morgan, Robin 2000 *Sisterhood Is Global: The International Women's Movement Anthology.* New York: Feminist Press.

Moser, Caroline 1993 *Gender Planning and Development: Theory, Practice and Training.* New York: Routledge.

Moses, Yolanda 1981 "Female Status, the Family and Male Dominance in the West Indian Community." In Steady 1981:499–514.

Muecke, Marjorie 1992 "Mother sold food, daughter sells her body: The cultural continuity of prostitution." *Social Science and Medicine* 35(7):891–901.

Murphy, Yolanda and Robert Murphy 1985 *Women of the Forest.* 2d ed. New York: Columbia University Press.

———— 1974 *Women of the Forest.* New York: Columbia University Press.

Nanda, Serena 2000 *Gender Diversity: Crosscultural Variations.* Prospect Heights: Waveland Press.

———— 1990 *Neither Man nor Woman: The Hijras of India.* Belmont, CA: Wadsworth.

———— 1985 "The Hijras of India: Cultural and Individual Dimensions of an Institutionalized Third Gender Role." In Blackwood 1985a:35–54.

Narasimhan, Sakuntala 1990 *Sati: Widow Burning in India.* New York: Anchor Books.

Navarro, Marysa 2002 "Against *Marianismo.*" In Montoya, Frazier, and Hurtig 2002:257–272.

Neft, Naomi and Ann Levine 1997 *Where Women Stand: An International Report on the Status of Women in 140 Countries, 1997–1998.* New York: Random House.

Nelson, Sarah Milledge 1997 *Gender in Archaeology: Analyzing Power and Prestige.* Walnut Creek, CA: AltaMira Press.

Newman, Lucile (Ed.) 1985 *Women's Medicine: A Cross-Cultural Study of Indigenous Fertility Regulation.* New Brunswick, NJ: Rutgers University Press.

Newton, Esther 2000 *Margaret Mead Made Me Gay: Personal Essays, Public Ideas.* With Forewords by Judith Halberstam and William L. Leap. Durham, NC: Duke University Press.

O'Brien, Denise 1977 "Female Husbands in Southern Bantu Societies." In Alice Schegel (Ed.). *Sexual Stratification: A Cross-Cultural View.* New York: Columbia University Press.

Ong, Aihwa 1991 "The gender and labor politics of postmodernity." *Annual Reviews of Anthropology* 20:279–309.

Ortner, Sherry 1993 "The Virgin and the State." In Caroline Brettell and Carolyn Sargent (Eds.). *Gender in Cross-Cultural Perspective.* Englewood Cliffs, NJ: Prentice-Hall. 257–268.

Otnes, Cele C. and Elizabeth H. Pleck 2003 *Cinderella Dreams: The Allure of the Lavish Wedding.* Berkeley: University of California Press.

Pasupathi, Monisha 2002 "Arranged Marriages: What's Love Got to Do with It?" In Yalom and Carstensen 2002: 211–235.

Patai, Daphne 1993 *Brazilian Women Speak: Contemporary Life Stories.* New Brunswick, NJ: Rutgers University Press.

Potash, Betty 1989 "Gender Relations in Sub-Saharan Africa." In Morgan 1989:189–227.

Powdermaker, Hortense 1933 *Life in Lesu: The Study of a Melanesian Society in New Ireland.* New York: W. W. Norton.

Price, Sally 1993 *Co-Wives and Calabashes.* 2d ed. Ann Arbor: University of Michigan Press.

Prior, Marsha 1993 "Matrifocality, Power, and Gender Relations in Jamaica." In Caroline Brettell and Carolyn Sargent (Eds.). *Gender in Cross-Cultural Perspective.* Englewood Cliffs, NJ: Prentice-Hall. 1993:310–317.

Pulsipher, Lydia Mihelic 1993 "Changing Roles in the Life Cycle of Women in Traditional West Indian Houseyards." In Momsen 1993:50–63.

Purkayastha, Bandana and Mangala Subramaniam (Eds.) 2004 *The Power of Women's Informal Networks: Lessons in Social Change from South Asia and West Africa.* Lanham, MD: Lexington Books.

Ragoné, Helena 1994 *Surrogate Motherhood: Conception in the Heart.* Boulder, CO: Westview Press.

Ragoné, Helena and France Winddance Twine (Eds.) 2000 *Ideologies and Technologies of Motherhood, Race, Class, Sexuality, Nationalism.* New York: Routledge.

Rapp, Rayna 1999 *Testing Women, Testing the Fetus: The Social Impact of Amniocentesis in America.* New York and London: Routledge.

—— 1993 "Leacock's Contributions to the Anthropological Study of Gender." In Sutton 1993:87–94.

Reanda, Laura 1991 "Prostitution as a human rights question: Problems and prospects of United Nations action." *Human Rights Quarterly* 13:202–228.

Reiter, Rayna (Ed.) 1975 *Toward an Anthropology of Women.* New York: Monthly Review Press.

Riddle, John M 1997 *Eve's Herbs: A History of Contraception and Abortion in the West.* Cambridge, MA: Harvard University Press.

—— 1992 *Contraception and Abortion from the Ancient World to the Renaissance.* Cambridge, MA: Harvard University Press.

Rodriquez, Jeanette 1994 *Our Lady of Guadalupe: Faith and Empowerment among Mexican-American Women.* Austin: University of Texas Press.

Rogers, Barbara 1986 *The Domestication of Women: Discrimination in Developing Societies.* London: Tavistock.

Rosaldo, Michelle and Louise Lamphere 1974 *Women, Culture and Society.* Stanford CA: Stanford University Press.

Roscoe, Paul B. 1995 " 'Initiation' in Cross-Cultural Perspective." In Lutkehaus and Roscoe 1995:219–238.

Roscoe, Will (Ed.) 2000 *Changing Ones: Third and Fourth Genders in Native North America.* New York: St. Martin's Press.

Roscoe, Will 1991 *The Zuni Man–Woman.* Albuquerque: University of New Mexico Press.

Rose, Kalima 1992 *Where Women are Leaders: The SEWA Movement in India.* London: Zed Books.

Rowell, Thelma 1972 *The Social Behavior of Monkeys.* Baltimore, MD: Penguin Press.

Russell, Diana E. H. and Roberta A. Harmes (Eds.) 2001 *Femicide in Global Perspective.* New York: Columbia University Teachers' College Press.

Rylko-Bauer, Barbara (Ed.) 1996 "Abortion from a cross-cultural perspective: An introduction." *Social Science and Medicine* 42(4):479–524.

Sacks, Karen 1992 "Introduction: New Views of Middle-Aged Women." In Kerns and Brown 1992:1–6.

Safa, Helen 1994 *The Myth of the Male Breadwinner: Women and Industrialization in the Caribbean.* Boulder, CO: Westview Press.

Sanday, Peggy Reeves 2002 *Women at the Center: Life in a Modern Matriarchy.* Ithaca, NY: Cornell University Press.

—— 1996 *A Woman Scorned: Acquaintance Rape on Trial.* New York: Doubleday.

—— 1990 *Fraternity Gang Rape: Sex, Brotherhood and Privilege on Campus.* New York: New York University Press.

Sanjek, Roger and Shellee Cohen (Eds.) 1990 *At Work in Homes: Household Workers in World Perspective.* Washington DC: American Anthropological Association. American Ethnological Society Monograph Series #3.

Sankar, Andrea 1985 "Sisters and Brothers, Lovers and Enemies: Marriage Resistance in Southern Kwangtung." In Blackwood 1985a:69–81.

Schaeffer, Claude 1965 "The Kutenai female berdache: Courier, guide, prophetess, and warrior." *Ethnohistory* 12:195–216.

Scheper-Hughes, Nancy 1992 *Death Without Weeping: The Violence of Everyday Life in Brazil.* Berkeley: University of California Press.

Scheper-Hughes, Nancy and Carolyn Sargent (Eds.) 1998 *Small Wars: The Cultural Politics in Childhood.* Berkeley: University of California Press.

Scrimshaw, Susan 1984 "Infanticide in Human Populations: Societal and Individual Concerns." In Hausfater and Hrdy 1984:463–486.

Seager, Joni 1997 *The State of Women in the World Atlas, New Edition.* London: Penguin Books.

Segun, Mabel 1985 *Sorry, No Vacancy.* Ibadan, Nigeria: Ibadan University Press.

Sered, Susan Starr 1994 *Priestess, Mother, Sacred Sister: Religions Dominated by Women.* New York: Oxford University Press.

Sexton, Lorraine 1986 *Mothers of Money, Daughters of Coffee: The Wok Meri Movement.* Ann Arbor, MI: UMI Research Press.

Shell-Duncan, Bettina and Ylva Hernlund (Eds.) 2000 *Female "Circumcision" in Africa: Culture, Controversy, and Change.* Boulder, CO: Lynne Riener Press.

Sherzer, Joel 1987 "A Diversity of Voices: Men's and Women's Speech in Ethnographic Perspective." In Susan Phillips, Susan Steele, and Christine Tanz (Eds.). *Language, Gender and Sex in Comparative Perspective.* Cambridge: Cambridge University Press, 1987:95–120.

Shostak, Marjorie 1981 *Nisa: The Life and Words of !Kung Woman.* New York: Vintage Books.

Shumway, David R. 2003 *Modern Love: Romance, Intimacy, and the Marriage Crisis.* New York: New York University Press.

Sleightholme, Carolyn and Indrani Sinha 1996 *Guilty without Trial: Women in the Sex Trade in Calcutta.* New Brunswick, NJ: Rutgers University Press.

Small, Meredith F. 2001 *Kids: How Biology and Culture Shape the Way We Raise Our Children.* New York: Doubleday.

——— 1995 *What's Love Got to Do With It? The Evolution of Human Mating.* New York: Anchor Books.

——— 1993 *Female Choices: Sexual Behavior of Female Primates.* Ithaca, NY: Cornell University Press.

Smuts, Barbara 1999 *Sex and Friendship in Baboons.* New York: Aldine.

Soranus 1965 *Gynecology.* Translated by Owsei Temkin. Baltimore, MD: Johns Hopkins University Press.

Spring, Anita 1978 "Epidemiology of Spirit Possession among the Luvale of Zambia." In Hoch-Smith and Spring 1978:165–190.

Sreenivasan, Jyotsna 2000 *Ela Bhatt: Uniting Women in India.* New York: Feminist Press.

Steady, Filomina Chioma (Ed.) 1981 *The Black Woman Cross-Culturally.* Rochester, VT: Schenkman.

Strum, Shirley 1987 *Almost Human: A Journey into the World of Baboons.* New York: Random House.

Strum, Shirley C. and Linda Marie Fedigan (Eds.) 2000 *Primate Encounters: Models of Science, Gender, and Society.* Chicago and London: University of Chicago Press.

Sutton, Constance (Ed.) 1993 *From Labrador to Samoa: The Theory and Practice of Eleanor Burke Leacock.* Washington DC: American Anthropological Association.

Tannen, Deborah 1990 *You Just Don't Understand: Women and Men in Conversation.* New York: Ballantine Books.

——— 1994 *Gender and Discourse.* New York: Oxford University Press.

Toubia, Nahid 1995 *Female Genital Mutilation: A Call for Global Action.* 2nd Ed. New York: Women, Ink.

Toubia, Nahid and Anika Rahman 2000 *Female Genital Mutilation: A Guide to Worldwide Laws and Policies.* London: Zed Press.

Truong, Tranh-Dam 1990 *Sex, Money and Morality: Prostitution and Tourism in Southeast Asia.* London: Zed Books.

Underhill, Ruth 1979 *Papago Woman.* New York: Holt, Rinehart and Winston. Reissued 1985 Waveland Press.

United Nations 2000 *The World's Women 2000: Trends and Statistics.* New York: United Nations Publications.

——— 1998 *Too Young to Die: Genes or Gender?* New York: United Nations Publications.

——— 1995 *The World's Women 1995: Trends and Statistics.* New York: United Nations.

——— 1991 *The World's Women: Trends and Statistics 1970–1990.* New York: United Nations.

United Nations Population Fund 2000 *The State of World Population 2000. Lives Together, Worlds Apart: Men and Women in a Time of Change.* New York: United Nations Publications.

Van Hasselt, Vincent, Randall Morrison, Alan Bellack, and Michel Hersen (Eds.) 1988 *Handbook of Family Violence.* New York: Plenum Press.

Van Willigen, John and V. C. Channa 1991 "Law, custom and crimes against women: The problem of dowry death in India." *Human Organization* 50(4):369–377.

Walker, Alice 1992 *Possessing the Secret of Joy.* New York: Harcourt Brace Jovanovich.

Walker, Alice and Pratibha Parmar 1993 *Warrior Marks: Female Genital Mutilation and the Sexual Blinding of Women.* New York: Harcourt Brace.

Ward, Martha C. 2005 *Nest in the Wind: Adventures in Anthropology on a Tropical Island,* 2nd ed. Prospect Heights, IL: Waveland Press.

Waring, Marilyn 2000 *Counting for Nothing: What Men Value and Women Are Worth*. 2nd Ed. Canada: University of Toronto Press.

Weiner, Annette 1976 *Women of Value, Men of Renown: New Perspectives in Trobriand Exchange*. Austin: University of Texas Press.

Weiner, Annette and Jane Schneider (Eds.) 1989 *Cloth and Human Experience*. Washington, DC: Smithsonian Institution Press.

Weston, Kath 1993 "Lesbian/gay studies in the house of anthropology." *Annual Reviews of Anthropology* 22:339–67. New York: Annual Reviews Inc.

——— 1991 *Families We Choose: Lesbians, Gays, Kinship Between Men, Between Women*. New York: Columbia University Press.

Wheelwright, Julie 1989 *Amazons and Military Maids: Women Who Dressed as Men in Pursuit of Life, Liberty and Happiness*. London: Pandora.

White, Jenny 1994 *Money Makes Us Relatives: Women's Labor in Urban Turkey*. Austin: University of Texas Press.

Whitehead, Harriet 1981 "The Bow and the Burden Strap: A New Look at Institutionalized Homosexuality in Native North America." In Sherry Ortner and Harriet Whitehead (Eds.). *Sexual Meanings. The Cultural Construction of Gender and Sexuality*. Cambridge: Cambridge University Press, 1981:80–115.

Wikan, Unni 1982 *Behind the Veil in Arabia: Women in Oman*. Baltimore, MD: John Hopkins University Press. (1991 ed. University of Chicago Press).

——— 1977 "Man becomes woman: Transsexualism in Oman as a key to gender roles." *Man N.S.* 12:304–319.

Williams, Walter 1986 *The Spirit and the Flesh: Sexual Diversity in American Indian Culture*. Boston: Beacon Press.

Yalom, Marilyn 2001 *A History of the Wife*. New York: HarperCollins.

Yalom, Marilyn and Laura L. Carstensen (Eds.) 2002 *Inside the American Couple: New Thinking, New Challenges*. Berkeley: University of California Press.

Photo Credits